S0-AIS-052

The Red Atlantic

The Red Atlantic

AMERICAN INDIGENES AND THE MAKING OF THE MODERN WORLD, 1000–1927

❦

Jace Weaver

The University of North Carolina Press
Chapel Hill

CABRINI COLLEGE LIBRARY
610 KING OF PRUSSIA ROAD
RADNOR, PA 19087

857743849

This book was published with the assistance of the Anniversary Endowment Fund of the University of North Carolina Press.

© 2014 Jace Weaver
All rights reserved

Manufactured in the United States of America
Designed and set in Calluna with ITC Giovanni Book Italic and
Adobe Caslon Italic Swash by Rebecca Evans

The paper in this book meets the guidelines for permanence and durability of the Committee on Production Guidelines for Book Longevity of the Council on Library Resources. The University of North Carolina Press has been a member of the Green Press Initiative since 2003.

Library of Congress Cataloging-in-Publication Data
Weaver, Jace, 1957–
The Red Atlantic : American indigenes and the making of the modern world, 1000–1927 / Jace Weaver.
    p. cm.
Includes bibliographical references and index.
ISBN 978-1-4696-1438-0 (cloth : alk. paper)—
ISBN 978-1-4696-1439-7 (ebook)
1. Indians of North America—Atlantic States—History. 2. Indians of North America—First contact with Europeans—Atlantic States. 3. Indians of North America—Atlantic States—Social life and customs. 4. American literature—Indian authors. 5. Indians in literature. 6. Atlantic States—Discovery and exploration. I. Title.
E78.A88W43 2014 973.04'97—dc23 2013035600

18 17 16 15 14 5 4 3 2 1

CONTENTS

PREFACE

MY NON-NATIVE FATHER was born in northern Indiana and grew up in Oklahoma. Perhaps because he was the product of two landlocked states, this midwesterner longed for the adventure of the sea. He secured an appointment to the U.S. Merchant Marine Academy in New York, but after the United States was attacked in December 1941, he resigned in order to fight in the war. He received commissions in the U.S. Navy and U.S. Army, in addition to the Merchant Marine. As an officer, he sailed both the Atlantic and Pacific. Mustered out in 1946, he married and went to work to support a family. He never returned to college.

My mother started college at the University of Oklahoma, but the war interrupted her plans, too. Her family moved to California, where most of them, including my mother, went to work in an aircraft factory. She married my father and set about raising two sons with him. She never completed her education, either.

Though neither of my parents were highly educated in a formal sense, they were avid readers. My father, especially, read voraciously—history, philosophy, psychology, religion. Two of his favorite authors were Thomas Paine and Bertrand Russell. My mother and father participated in a strong tradition of autodidacticism in my family. When my mother was growing up, she read from the ten volumes of *Berle's Self Culture* that my grandmother had bought. Published by the Twentieth Century Self Culture Association, it was edited by Adolf Augustus Berle, the father of the New Deal–era lawyer and diplomat of the same name. In the books' introduction, Dr. Berle wrote: "*Self Culture* is a compendium of knowledge, and an arrangement of literature, science and the arts by which any household which makes a careful and faithful study of the same, may obtain the elements of a liberal cultivation. A university is now known merely to be a collection of books. And if these books be wisely chosen, and the materials in them be studiously examined, one has all the opportunities of a liberal education. The aim of this collection is to secure both ends, namely a liberal cultivation and a liberal education."[1] A college education on a shelf. Today, this oddly American artifact is one of my prized possessions.

I grew up in a house filled with books. Long before I could read, I sat for hours looking at the pictures in an ancient set of *The Book of Knowledge*. It had pictures of *everything*—heavy-suited deep sea divers, scenes from the Great War, bird's eggs, telephone operators. I immediately loved and respected books for their ability to take me to times and places to which I had never been and could only dimly imagine. Later, almost as soon as I could read, I picked up one of my father's cherished books, his copy of the 1938 edition of the *American Practical Navigator* that he used aboard ship as a navigator during World War II. The volume was most often simply called the "Bowditch," after its original 1802 author, Nathaniel Bowditch, and the heart of it for me was "Appendix IV: Maritime Positions."[2] These tables had the latitudinal and longitudinal coordinates for every island in the world, in addition to coastal locations. I remember sitting on the floor with his Bowditch and a large National Geographic map spread out, heavy books at each of its corners to keep it from rolling up. Using the book, I located islands in every ocean, the smaller and more obscure the better.[3]

Though I was certainly unaware of it at the time, I believe that in some real fashion, *The Red Atlantic* began to take shape during those hours on our living room floor with books and maps. Synapses formed, and connections were made.

The most obvious precursor to this book is *The Black Atlantic* by Paul Gilroy. Published originally in 1993, it has entered the discourse in history, American studies, and various other fields at a foundational level. I began to rethink Gilroy's text as I read the anonymous 1767 novel *The Female American*, discussed herein. While I read this work about a Native, yet transnational, heroine, a "Red Atlantic" took shape in my mind. In the introduction to this book, I refer to historian David Armitage's review of Peter Linebaugh and Marcus Rediker's *The Many-Headed Hydra* in *Reviews in American History*; his review is titled "The Red Atlantic." I discovered it during my research to make sure that no one had earlier conceived of the "Red Atlantic" as I did. Armitage uses "red" as in the sense of "radical." A few other predecessors need to be mentioned here, though I had read none of them before submitting my original article, "The Red Atlantic: Transoceanic Cultural Exchanges," to *American Indian Quarterly*.

After reading the manuscript of my original piece, Colin Calloway was kind enough to send me his then-unpublished presidential address from the 2008 annual meeting of the American Society for Ethnohistory, "Indian History from the End of the Alphabet."[4] Because, in my original *AIQ* piece, he recognized someone of kindred spirit, he suggested that while we might not be "separated at birth," we must be related distantly through some Scottish trader among the Cherokee as a common ancestor.

In the September 2008 issue of *Ethnic and Racial Studies*, Fred Hoxie published an article titled "Retrieving the Red Continent: Settler Colonialism and the History of American Indians in the US." It was clearly sparked, in part, by Gilroy's book, too. After reading the piece, I told Fred that although what we were doing was different, I thought we were working two sides of the same street—or, more precisely, the same ocean. He agreed that we shared an intellectual agenda.

Tim Fulford uses the term in his 2006 *Romantic Indians: Native Americans, British Literature, and Transatlantic Culture, 1756–1830* to refer to the image of Natives in romanticism. He also edited a 2009 volume with Kevin Hutchings, *Native Americans and Anglo-American Culture, 1750–1850*, the subtitle of which is "The Indian Atlantic." Fulford then is a predecessor in considering the place of the Indian in non-Native literature.

Finally, in *The Transatlantic Indian, 1776–1930*, published in 2009, Kate Flint references Gilroy in her first chapter. In the last sentence of that introduction, in contrast to Gilroy, she refers to a "*Red* Atlantic."[5] She, however, does not pursue it, and the single casual use has not been taken up in the discourse of Native American studies. Further, although congruent, Flint's project is very different from mine herein.

I am happy to share this journey with such *compagnons de voyage*.

Since Gilroy's initial intervention, the black Atlantic has been widely discussed and refined by others. Yet when other scholars—nonspecialists in indigenous studies—seek to expand his vision of the black Atlantic to include other Others, they only end up reinscribing the marginality of the indigenes of the Western Hemisphere. This erasure is indicative of what has occurred for centuries. Three examples will suffice. The subtitle of Thomas Benjamin's book *The Atlantic World* is "Europeans, Africans, Indians and Their Shared History, 1400–1900." Yet Natives, though mentioned periodically, are largely confined to a single chapter titled "Engagement."[6] Africans fare somewhat better, but the overall effect is one of the White Atlantic with a really good tan. Walter Goebel and Saskia Schabio's edited volume, *Beyond the Black Atlantic*, purports to reexamine peripheral modernities in an effort to expand Gilroy's concept. It is, however, simply an exercise in postcolonial studies critique. Though there are essays on South African poetry, Mohandas Gandhi, and Hanif Kureshi, there are none on the Western Hemisphere's indigenous peoples.[7] Another postcolonial turn was taken in the spring of 2012 by Robert Stam and Ella Shohat in their book *Race in Translation: Culture Wars around the Postcolonial Atlantic*. In it they discuss "Black," "White," and "Red" Atlantics. In the first endnote to their preface, they write, "While the term 'Black Atlantic' has been a wide circulation, the terms 'Red Atlantic' and 'White Atlantic' have appeared only sporadically. After writing our section on the 'Red Atlantic,' we discovered that a number of writers have referred in passing to the 'Red Atlantic.' Most of these authors use the expression either in the sense of 'radical left' [as in Armitage] or in a historical-ethnographic sense of movement of peoples. We assume that core sense but overlay it with a more conceptual sense of the movement of *ideas*."[8] Thereafter, they cite my 2011 *AIQ* article. They, however, omit the piece's title, the subtitle of which refers to cultural exchange. They fail to cite Flint at all. Thus, once again, in the postcolonial, not only Natives but Native scholars and scholars of the Native experience are marginalized.

It is not my intent in defining the Red Atlantic to catalog and discuss every known Native from the Americas who traveled to one or another colonial metropole—sometimes multiple metropoles. This work has been done by various other scholars. Probably the earliest attempt was by Carolyn Thomas Foreman in her 1943 book, *Indians Abroad, 1493–1938*. Alden T. Vaughan picked up the theme in his masterful (though limited in geographic scope) *Transatlantic Encounters: American Indians in Britain, 1500–1776*. Kate Flint's book essentially takes up temporally where Vaughan's leaves off.

My purpose is to restore Indians and Inuit to the Atlantic world and demonstrate their centrality to that world, a position equally important to, if not more important than, the Africans of Gilroy's black Atlantic. I examine them as active agents involved in that world in a variety of capacities: diplomats, soldiers and sailors, slaves, tourists, performers, and more. A great many are mentioned in this text only briefly. Others serve as slightly longer case studies in participation in the Red Atlantic. I restore Paul Cuffe to Native American studies, where before he was too often thought of as merely an African American who just happened to have a Native American mother and wife, as one of my correspondents put it. I perform a similar maneuver with the Inca Garcilaso de la Vega, a figure ignored in Native American studies. In this book, I also give fuller treatment to other figures, some well-known, others not, including Ourehouaré, Paul Teenah, Oconostota, Joseph Brant, Samson Occom, E. Pauline Johnson, and Attakullakulla.

The inclusion of Cuffe (and his son) and Garcilaso, as well as figures such as William Apess, Peter Jones, and Knud Rasmussen, is both important and strategic. In this book, I intend to explode broadly held (and tenacious) misconceptions about indigeneity that I have been refuting my entire career. Too many want to see mixed bloods, mestizos, métis, or (to use Gerald Vizenor's useful descriptive term) crossbloods as somehow diminished in Indianness. One must interrogate each case individually and examine the figure's self-identification and commitments. In the case of those I mentioned, Garcilaso, Jones, and Rasmussen were all raised in their formative years by their indigenous mothers within their cultures. Hybridity—whether genetic or cultural—and cosmopolitanism are natural by-products of the Red Atlantic, but they do not necessarily represent a diminution of indigenousness. To be bicultural is to be *bicultural*—not to be somehow non-Native. And as this book demonstrates, all do not share equally in these results.

My original *AIQ* piece covered the period only to 1800. I noted, however, that the division was arbitrary, dictated by the relatively brief space of a journal article. As I make clear in this present book, Natives continued to participate in and define the Red Atlantic for more than a century thereafter. Most periodizations are arbitrary anyway. Kate Flint ends her study with the year 1930, while Carolyn Thomas Foreman halts her earlier work in 1938. In the subtitle to this text, I label the time period of the Red Atlantic as stretching from 1000 C.E. to 1927. Although I look back at tantalizing "prehistoric" clues, our best evidence begins with the Viking sighting and invasion in 1000. Like the black Atlantic, the Red Atlantic is, in part, about contending with modernity. The end date of 1927 represents Charles Lindbergh's solo flight, which changed forever how people interact with the Atlantic Ocean. This brings in World War I, when large numbers of North American indigenes crossed the Atlantic, encountering not only modern warfare but a reception in France far more hospitable than their treatment at home, as Gerald Vizenor's powerful novel *Blue Ravens* skillfully portrays. The last major events of the Red Atlantic depicted herein are Danish-Inuit explorer and trader Knud Rasmussen's ambitious Fifth Thule Expedition (1921–24) and Deskaheh's ultimately futile diplomacy before the League of Nations in Geneva (1923–24).

As Natives have been marginalized in the history of the Atlantic world, in the wider telling of the story of Western civilization, Western Hemispheric indigenes are curiously absent. There is nary a mention in *L'Europe: Histoire de ses Peuples*, Jean-Baptiste Duroselle's "Plato to NATO" study.[9] In Jacques Barzun's almost as sweeping *From Dawn to Decadence: 500 Years of Western Cultural Life, 1500 to the Present*, they merit scarcely more mention.[10] Yet modern Europe and Western civilization, more generally, were forged in the encounter with those indigenes.

This book contains both a historically rooted analysis of the Red Atlantic and literary exegeses of certain key pieces of literature. Although I have done substantial archival research for this book, I am not a historian.[11] While I am thought of perhaps primarily as a literary critic, I am not a professor of English. I have two doctorates, one in law and one in religion, both of which come into play here. Both trained me in careful research and in close reading of texts. Within Native American studies, I have always considered myself principally a theorist and a critic. With the Red Atlantic, I believe I continue in this vein.

I have long been one of the most vocal in arguing for Native American studies as an interdisciplinary field. My own work has been deeply interdisciplinary. This book is no exception. As a result, with its twin foci on historical and literary analyses, this book will strike some scholarly readers as neither fish nor fowl. It is interesting to me that when I sent out some (particularly the original journal article) or all of this manuscript, the literary types tended to be appreciative of the whole. While some historians were, as well, others e-mailed me the equivalent of a professorial "I stopped reading here" when they reached the literary analysis. For me, however, the two foci are important and part of an integrated whole. My purpose is to look not only at how Natives and non-Natives interacted across the Red Atlantic but also at how they thought about it, conceptualized it, and articulated it.

I have worked in a number of archives and museums that have contributed enormously to this project. They have been uniformly helpful, and I would like to acknowledge them: the Archivo General de Indias (Seville, Spain); the Archivo Regional del Cusco, currently housed at the Universidad Nacional de San Antonio Abad (Cuzco, Peru); the Biblioteca Palofoxiana in Puebla, Mexico, where I examined texts by Vasco de Quiroga; Bibliothèque et Archives Nationales du Québec (Québec City, Québec); the Centro de Investigaciones y Documentacion de la Costa Atlantica (Bluefields, Nicaragua); the Museo de Arte Precolombiano (Cuzco, Peru), which also possesses a world-class gourmet restaurant that helps a poor visitor and researcher keep body and soul together; the Museo Inka (Cuzco, Peru); the Nationalmuseet (Copenhagen, Denmark); and the Sequoyah National Research Center at the University of Arkansas at Little Rock.

Although I have done substantial primary research, this book is also a synthetic work. Its value lies in establishing a theoretical framework and drawing all this material together. I also want to introduce, especially, general readers to the rich scholarship on all manner of indigenous experience in the Americas that makes a book like this one possible. I have therefore perhaps quoted more than one might normally. In doing so, it is my intent to let these other scholars speak for themselves.

Since my first book, something I have found essential is to visit the locations where my subjects existed, to see the sights they saw, to walk where they walked. There are far too many subjects this time for me to put my footprints in all of theirs. But to name only a few: I have stood on the parapet of Fort Marion in St. Augustine and looked upon the view that Cheyenne and Apache prisoners saw on the Atlantic littoral; I have walked the streets of Cuzco and been to Garcilaso's house (which in past times housed the regional archive); I have strolled the streets of London and been to the locations seen by so many Indians; I have visited the whaling ports of Connecticut and Massachusetts; I have been to the royal palace where Peter Freuchen's Inuit wife, Navarana, had an audience with King Christian X of Denmark; and I have explored the United Nations buildings in Geneva, once the headquarters of the League of Nations, where Deskaheh unsuccessfully sought admission.

One of the things that has always amazed me about the academy (contrary to its reputation for petty jealousies, insecurities, paranoia, and backbiting) is the incredible generosity, openness, and willingness to share of scholars both junior and senior in our field. I could not have produced the work you hold in your hands without the help and enthusiastic support of numerous colleagues, including those who participated in the conference on the Red Atlantic that the Institute of Native American Studies (INAS) hosted at the University of Georgia in November 2010. Several need to be mentioned by name: Matthew Bahar, Mark Carnes, Ian Chambers, Christine DeLucia, Robbie Ethridge, Fred Hoxie, Daniel Justice, Duane King, Arnold Krupat, Scott Lyons, Deborah Madsen, Jason Mancini, Homer Noley, Simon Ortiz, Brett Riggs, Brett Rushforth, Michelle Shenandoah, Nancy Shoemaker, Edward Slack, and Coll Thrush. I would also like to thank some of my INAS colleagues: Ervan Garrison, John Inscoe, Claudio Saunt, Alfie Vick (who helped me with the maps herein), and, of course, my wife, Laura Adams Weaver. Very special thanks must go to Colin Calloway and Gerald Vizenor, both of whom not only offered thoughts about my original *AIQ* article but read this book in manuscript form for the University of North Carolina Press. Their generosity of spirit and their critical comments were invaluable. Finally, special thanks go to the Cherokee artist America Meredith and Bill Wiggins (the owner) for permission to use the fun and beautiful painting of America's on the cover.

In defining and promoting my conceptualization of the Red Atlantic, it became clear that many of my colleagues in the field of Native American studies were thinking in congruent grooves but lacked a language to articulate and draw together their projects. The Red Atlantic provided that language. As my books go, my journeys around and across the Red Atlantic have been longer than most. But I have thoroughly enjoyed boldly retracing where so many have gone before.

The Red Atlantic

—*◊◊◊*—

Beneath the Fall and Beyond

Navigating the Red Atlantic

ON MARCH 4, 1493, his battered caravel *Niña* in need of repairs, Christopher Columbus put into Lisbon, Portugal. Eleven days later, he arrived back at Palos de la Frontera, the Spanish port from which he had set sail in August of the previous year. His return, while hailed, created a problem for the church.

Columbus brought with him a number of captives who appeared to be human. These beings posed no cognitive dissonance for the mariner himself. He, after all, believed that he had reached the Indies, that is to say, the islands off the coast of Asia. He died in 1506 still firm in that conviction. He was the only one.

How were these human-like beings that Columbus brought back from his voyage to be accounted for? Biblical exegesis of the time was clear that there were only three continents, Europe, Africa, and Asia, each of which had been populated by the progeny of a different son of Noah after the Deluge. What was one to make of the Admiral of the Ocean Sea's peculiar cargo?

On May 4, two months after Columbus's return landfall on the Iberian Peninsula, Pope Alexander VI issued the papal bull *Inter Caetera*. Although the document did nothing to address the humanity of the inhabitants of the Americas (that issue would not be settled for years to come), it did authorize their conquest. It began, "Among other things well pleasing to the Divine Majesty and cherished of our heart, this assuredly ranks highest, that in our times especially the Catholic faith and the Christian religion be exalted and be everywhere increased and spread, that the health of souls be cared for and that the barbarous nations be overthrown and brought to the faith itself."[1]

This series of events—Columbus's return from his first voyage bearing indigenous captives, the debate it engendered over the indigenes' humanity, and the papacy's sanction of their subjugation—inaugurated the Red Atlantic. Or, as we shall see, it is more precise to say that these events "re-inaugurated" it.

Study of the Atlantic World

Some four hundred and fifty years after Columbus's first voyage of discovery, on March 5, 1946, Winston Churchill stood behind a lectern at Westminster College in Fulton, Missouri, and delivered a speech titled "Sinews of Peace." The former British prime minister had been introduced by the current president of the United States, Harry Truman. Today, Churchill's remarks are remembered chiefly for his statement that an "iron curtain" had descended across Europe. In the same address, however, in the presence of the American president, he also stated that neither a secure peace nor the continued rise of international cooperative organizations could occur without "a fraternal association of English-speaking peoples. This means a special relationship between the British Commonwealth and Empire and the United States." The remark is commonly cited as the first usage of the now-hackneyed term ("special relationship") to describe the Anglo-American partnership, though the former prime minister had actually coined the phrase a few months earlier, in November 1945.

Indeed, as World War II drew to a close, policy analysts in both Great Britain and the United States envisioned, if not a postwar *world*, at least an Atlantic basin dominated by an Anglo-American alliance. Churchill's Fulton address was firmly within this nascent tradition of activist internationalism. Three years later, politicians from North America and Europe forged the North Atlantic Treaty Organization to secure Western Europe's safety against potential Soviet aggression from the East.

Academics, too, played their part. In the United States, the Cold War provided the generative impulse for American studies, a new scholarly field whose purpose was to define and promote "American culture" or "American civilization." Historians joined in by creating histories of an "Atlantic civilization." The Atlantic Ocean became the new Mediterranean, a new *mare nostrum*—or, more precisely, a *mare internum*—for a Western civilization that was, if not exclusively Anglo-Saxon, at least prevailingly European in origin. The result was an Atlantic world history or Atlantic world studies that was overwhelmingly a Caucasian history. As Harvard historian David Armitage declared in his 2001 review of Peter Linebaugh and Marcus Rediker's *The Many-Headed Hydra: Sailors, Slaves, Commoners, and the Hidden History of the Revolutionary Atlantic,* "Until quite recently, Atlantic history seemed to be available in any color, so long as it was white. To be sure, this was the history of the North Atlantic rather than the South Atlantic, of Anglo-America rather than Latin America, and of the connections between North America and Europe rather than those between both Americas and Africa."[2]

One of the founding figures of Atlantic history, another Harvard historian, Bernard Bailyn, limned the origins of the field in his 2005 book *Atlantic History: Concept and Contours.* While it is beyond the needs of this particular book to trace in detail the formation of this "white Atlantic" history, a few highlights will help provide a little context for understanding my project.

Bailyn traces the origins of the idea of an Atlantic world to the famed journalist and thinker Walter Lippmann in a February 1917 editorial as he argued for U.S. intervention in the Great War, not only to protect the "Atlantic highway" but also to maintain intact the "profound web of interest which joins together the western world. Britain, France, Italy, even Spain, Belgium, Holland, the Scandinavian nations, and Pan-America are in the main one community in their deepest needs and their deepest purposes. . . . We cannot betray the Atlantic community by submitting. . . . What we must fight for is the common interest of the western world, for the integrity of the Atlantic Powers. We must recognize that we are in fact one great community and act as members of it."[3]

Though the idea fell out of favor in the aftermath of World War I, it gained renewed attention during the Second World War (spurred on by the issuance of the Atlantic Charter in August 1941) and the subsequent Cold War from journalists like Lippmann and Forrest Davis and historians such as Ross Hoffman, Carlton J. H. Hayes, and H. Hale Bellot. A key initiative moment came in 1955 when Jacques Godechot of the University of Toulouse (and author of *Histoire de l'Atlantique*) and R. R. Palmer of Princeton University delivered a paper titled "Le Problème de l'Atlantique" at the Tenth International History Congress in Rome. In

1961, former U.S. secretaries of state Christian Herter and Dean Acheson led the formation of the Atlantic Council of the United States. And in 1963, the council founded a scholarly journal, the *Atlantic Community Quarterly*, "on the premise that something new is being born in the world today." That larger something was the Atlantic Community, "tying together . . . nations on both sides of the Atlantic Ocean."[4]

Armitage's "white Atlantic" gained force through the 1970s and 1980s as it drew more scholars and students into its orbit. Colleges and universities added courses and seminars on Atlantic history, perhaps the most famous of which was Bernard Bailyn's own seminar at Harvard. And while all of this would be upended, as we shall see in a moment, in 1993, it nonetheless remains an important impulse, maintaining its grip on imaginations and generating new scholarship.

In 1995, Bailyn established the International Seminar on the History of the Atlantic World at Harvard. For the next fifteen years, the program hosted an annual conference for graduate students and junior scholars engaged in creative research in Atlantic world history. Although the annual meetings ceased in 2010, the seminar still sponsors a grants program and occasional events. Its most recent conference was held in August 2012 on the topic "The Caribbean, the Atlantic, and the Significance of Regional History." According to the seminar's website, 366 scholars have participated in its programs, 202 from the United States and 164 from abroad.[5]

In 2010, the same year that Bailyn's seminar stopped holding its regular annual conferences, popular British writer Simon Winchester, as had Godechot before him, published a history of the Atlantic Ocean. In *Atlantic: Great Sea Battles, Heroic Discoveries, Titanic Storms, and a Vast Ocean of a Million Stories*, the journalist and author easily succumbs to what might be called the old-style "Atlantic exceptionalism" of a predominantly white history with the Atlantic itself as the *mare internum* surrounded by Europe and the Americas. He rhapsodizes:

> The ocean became, in a sense, the cradle of modern Western civilization—the inland sea of the civilized Western world, the home of a new pan-Atlantic civilization itself. All manner of discoveries, inventions, realizations, ideas, the mosaic of morsels by which humankind advanced, were made in and around or by way of some indirect connection with the sea. Parliamentary democracy. A homeland for world Jewry. Long-distance radio communication. The Vinland Map. The suppression of slavery. The realization of continental drift and

plate tectonics. The Atlantic Charter. The British Empire. The knar, the curragh, the galleon, the ironclad, and the battleship. The discovery of longitude. Codfish. Erskine Childers. Winslow Homer. The convoy system. St. Helena. Puerto Madryn. Debussy. Monet. Rachel Carson. Eriksson, Columbus, Vespucci. The Hanseatic League. Ernest Shackleton. The Black Ball Line. The submarine telegraph cable. The Wright Brothers, Alcock and Brown, Lindbergh. Beryl Markham. The submarine. Ellis Island. Hurricanes. Atlantic Creek. Icebergs. *Titanic*. *Lusitania*. *Torrey Canyon*. The Eddystone Light. *Bathybius*. *Prochlorococcus*. Shipping containers. NATO. The polders. The Greenland ice cap. The United Kingdom. Brazil, Argentina, Canada. The United States of America.[6]

He goes on to say that the Atlantic "has been central and pivotal to the human story." He holds up Atlantic world history as proof of how "critical has the idea of an Atlantic identity become to both the contemporary and the future world."[7]

Winchester's lyrical litany of the Atlantic stands as powerful testimony to the grip that a certain telling of Atlantic history maintains on imaginations, both scholarly and popular. Although you would not know it from the immediately preceding discussion, all of this had changed—and changed radically—in 1993 with the publication of *The Black Atlantic: Modernity and Double Consciousness*. Written by Afro-British sociologist Paul Gilroy fifty years after the first stirrings of Atlantic world history, the book was a necessary corrective to the white Atlantic. Gilroy outlines the diasporic peregrinations of Africans and persons of African descent around the Atlantic basin.

In the process, as his subtitle implies, Gilroy also examines W. E. B. Du Bois's concept of "double consciousness," whereby blacks possess twin consciousnesses, a national identity and a recognition that one is African, who will always in some sense be seen as Other by some of the same nationality (if one is in diaspora). As Du Bois writes in *The Souls of Black Folk*, "One ever feels his twoness,—an American, a Negro; two souls, two thoughts, two unrecognized strivings; two warring ideals in one dark body whose dogged strength alone keeps it from being torn asunder."[8] Gilroy looks at the movement not only of black bodies but also of Africalogical ideas such as those of Du Bois. He writes, "The duality which Du Bois placed at its intellectual and poetic core was particularly significant in widening the impact of *The Souls*. Its influence spread out across the black Atlantic to directly inspire figures as diverse as Jean Price

Mars, Samuel Coleridge Taylor, and Léopold Sédar Senghor and to indirectly influence many more."[9]

Price-Mars, Coleridge-Taylor, Senghor—a Haitian nationalist scholar and writer, a British composer who won such acclaim that he was called the "African Mahler," and a poet who became president of Senegal and the first African member of the Académie française. Gilroy acknowledges the relationship of his conceptualization of the black Atlantic to the Negritude movement espoused by, among others, Price-Mars and Senghor. Senghor wrote, "There is no denying negritude is a fact, a culture; it is the whole of economic and political, intellectual and moral, artistic and social values of not only the peoples of Africa but also of the black minorities of Asia and Oceania."[10]

In *The Black Atlantic*, Gilroy places Africans at the center of Atlantic world history. Besides looking at the physical movement of African persons and their ideas, he looks at the cultural imbrications between Europe and its peoples, on the one hand, and on the other, the peoples they encountered as they sallied forth. He writes, "If this appears to be little more than a roundabout way of saying that the reflexive cultures and consciousness of European settlers and those of the Africans they enslaved, the 'Indians' they slaughtered, and the Asians they indentured were not, even in situations of the most extreme brutality, sealed off hermetically from each other, then so be it. This seems as though it ought to be an obvious and self-evident observation, but its stark character has been systematically obscured by commentators from all sides of political opinion."[11]

It is certainly true, as I have written before, that all of us, as scholars and as human beings, have our own particular blinders. It begs saying, however, that in the processes of colonization and empire, it was not only "Indians" who were slaughtered, Asians who were indentured, and Africans who were enslaved.

In looking at transcultural exchanges among Europeans and Africans and the movement of ideas and writings like those of Du Bois, Gilroy deals with what, in the Native American context, Robert Warrior calls "intellectual trade routes." In his book *The People and the Word: Reading Native Nonfiction*, Warrior draws upon the work of Palestinian critic Edward Said, who in his *The World, the Text, and the Critic*, according to Warrior,

famously took up the question of what happens when ideas, specifically theories, travel "from person to person, from situation to situation, from one period to another. Cultural life and intellectual life are usually nourished and often sustained by this circulation of ideas." While it is hard to argue against the concept of ideas traveling—one can argue, for instance, that ideas travel when one person speaks to another or even as they undergo the neurological processes that give them life in one person's mind—Said takes great pains to point out that no idea travels without being transformed by the process.

Ideas that travel not just across a synapse or a room, but across great geographical or cultural divides, he says, can have the good effect of providing alternatives to moribund theoretical positions or dogmas.[12]

Gilroy's "black Atlantic" was a necessary corrective to the way Atlantic history had been done previously. As Armitage points out, the racial, if not ethnic, homogeneity of Atlantic world studies before Gilroy's intervention "was the product of selectivity. Like many genealogists, these early proponents of Atlantic history overlooked inconvenient or uncongenial ancestors. Students of the black Atlantic, from W. E. B. Du Bois to C. L. R. James and Eric Williams were not recognized as practitioners of the history of the Atlantic world, just as Toussaint L'Ouverture's rebellion was not an event in R. R. Palmer's *Age of Democratic Revolution*."[13]

While, however, Gilroy successfully secured for Africans a place of inclusion in the study of the Atlantic world, he did little regarding other potential groups, in particular Western Hemisphere indigenes. Other than his reference to the "Indians" they slaughtered, Native Americans make no further guest appearances in the pages of *The Black Atlantic*. Gilroy does reference Crispus Attucks "at the head of his 'motley rabble of saucy boys, negroes, mulattoes, Irish teagues and outlandish jack tars' at the Boston Massacre."[14] Yet he fails to note that Attucks was Native, his mother a Massachuset.

Since Gilroy's initial deployment, the black Atlantic has been widely discussed and refined by others. Yet when other scholars—nonspecialists in indigenous studies—seek to expand his vision of the black Atlantic to include other Others, they too often end up only reinscribing the marginality of the indigenes of the Western Hemisphere by inadvertence. One such example is historian Paul Cohen in his 2008 essay "Was There an Amerindian Atlantic? Reflections on the Limits of a Historiographical Concept" in the journal *History of European Ideas*. In that piece, Cohen points out and decries the absence of indigenes in studies of Atlantic history. Nevertheless, in that relatively short essay, he offers multiple variations on the following theme: "Relatively few Amerindians ever crossed the Atlantic; few Amerindians took direct part in transatlantic commerce; and no Amerindian diasporas came into being."[15] Although he acknowledges that some Indians did go to Europe, he overlooks those who sailed upon the Atlantic to locales other than Europe voluntarily and ignores those sent into slavery on Bermuda or in the Caribbean after the Pequot War and King Philip's War, as well as the more than 5,000 Garifunas or Black Caribs sent into exile by the British on the islands of Balliceaux and Roatan. He fails to discuss the deep involvement of Natives in the Atlantic economies in manifold ways. Despite the importance of his article and his plea, Cohen ignores the radical mobility of American indigenes. Ultimately, he seems caught in the old tension between presumably local (primitive) Indians and cosmopolitan/international (modern) Europeans (or Euro-Americans or Euro-Canadians).

Today, Atlantic world studies, which Gilroy so skillfully opened up, remains, more than twenty years later, largely a conversation about blacks and whites. It also remains largely an analysis of the Anglo-colonial world. Ibero-America is increasingly discussed; yet too often such discussion is focused primarily on the demographic crash of the indigenous population there. Another corrective is therefore necessary.

One interesting attempt at such a corrective at the turn of the twenty-first century was the call for a "New World studies." Driven primarily by Chicano and Chicana scholars, writing out of their mestizo positionality, it proposed the examination of the hybridities of cultures *and* peoples resulting from the Spanish conquest in the Western Hemisphere as a separate field of study. Work like Virgil Elizondo's "The New Humanity of the Americas," in *1492–1992: The Voice of the Victims*, fed the impulse. In that essay (published before Gilroy's book), Elizondo writes:

> The only way to go beyond simplistic condemnation or arrogant triumphalism is to transcend categories of defeat or victory and see the beginning of the Americas for what it truly was: the long and painful birth of the new human person—a new human individual, community, civilization, religion, and race. Anthropologically speaking, five hundred years is a very brief period in the birth of a race, and that is precisely what we are witnessing in the Americas.
>
> Nothing as painful, as far-reaching and as fascinating has happened in the history of humanity since the birth of the European some 35,000 years ago, when the Cro-magnons migrated, conquered, massacred the native Neanderthals and mated with them to produce

the basis of today's European peoples. The only similar event in world history is the arrival of the Iberians in the Americas which marked the beginning of the new American race—the Mestizo! A new genetic and cultural group was born. It would take centuries to develop. But a new race had been born.[16]

I grant that all of that may be true, but I can't help wondering how the Neanderthals felt about the process. As Elizondo describes it, it seems like merely a benign illustration of one of Charles Beard's lessons of history: the bee fertilizes the flower it robs.

The Atlantic: Does the Thing Really Speak for Itself?

Some critics have averred that Atlantic history is simply a mask for the old, now largely discarded, "imperial" history. Bailyn calls that tradition "venerable" but says that its practitioners "were describing the formal structures of imperial governments, not the lives of the people who lived within these governments, and they concentrated on the affairs of a single nation [Britain, France, Spain, Portugal, the Netherlands]."[17] Gilroy's injection of Africans and diasporic blacks into the Atlantic story began decisively to distance the field from any possible imperial roots.

Still other scholars have objected that there is no Atlantic history, that it is impossible, that the region does not make up a coherent unit—in short, that there is no singular "there" there. Despite my criticisms of Atlantic world history (and its blind spots and lacunae), both in its original form and in Paul Gilroy's revision, I do believe that it points at something real. Unlike Simon Winchester or historian Ross Hoffman, whom he was evoking, I do not believe in the Atlantic as "the inland sea of Western civilization."[18] I have, however, come to believe in what I earlier termed Atlantic exceptionalism.

The Atlantic Ocean is the second largest body of water on earth. It is bounded in the north by the Arctic Ocean and stretches from the coast of North America at 60° north latitude to 60° south latitude and the Southern Ocean. Its eastern boundaries are Europe and Africa, its western North and South America. With its major adjacent bodies of water—the Caribbean, the Gulf of Mexico, Hudson's Bay, the Celtic Sea, the North Sea, the Baltic Sea—it covers nearly 40 million square miles, or 20 percent of the earth's surface and almost 30 percent of its water surface.

Bernard Bailyn is hardly alone in pointing out the perfect natural ordering of the Atlantic to foster connection. He writes, "The integration of the once-disordered American marchlands into the emerging Atlantic system was profoundly favored by the ocean's physiography. The clockwise circulation of winds and ocean currents, sweeping westward in the south and eastward in the north and linked by deep riverine routes—the Elbe and Rhine, the Amazon and Orinoco, the Niger and the Congo, the Mississippi and St. Lawrence—to immense continental hinterlands, drew the Atlantic into a cohesive communication system."[19] In the north, the Canary Current sweeps southward along the northwest African coast. The Gulf Stream runs north along the coast of North America to join up with the Labrador Current and the North Atlantic Drift, the latter meeting the Norwegian Current. In the south, the Benguela Current flows north along southwest Africa, and the Brazil Current flows southward along South America. The Equatorial Currents and countercurrents run east and west across the ocean. A clockwise flow in the north, as Bailyn says, and a counterclockwise flow in the south are as if designed by some unseen hand to facilitate travel between the Old World and the New.

The Atlantic was not an "inland sea" surrounded by the Americas and Europe. Regular trade routes, however, were established. Far from being an impassable barrier, the Atlantic became the highway, the bridge, the connective tissue knitting together the Americas, on one hand, with Europe and with Africa, on the other. And the shores in *both* east and west became the contact zones of the Red Atlantic. The ocean *itself* became a contact zone as American indigenes engaged in trade and supplied maritime labor, working alongside non-Natives in legitimate enterprise and in piracy. As Godechot and Palmer pointed out in their 1955 presentation, the ocean was "more easily traversed in stable routes than many European land areas."[20] A regular Euro-Afro-American economy—or, more precisely, economies—evolved and became routinized.[21]

The Red Atlantic

Many Native peoples have long held a special relationship with the Atlantic (to parody Churchill's description of the Anglo-American alliance destined to dominate that body of water). That relationship has not been limited to those nations that occupied its coasts.

Peter Pitchlynn was born on January 30, 1806, in Noxubee County, Mississippi Territory, more than 200 miles from the Gulf of Mexico. His

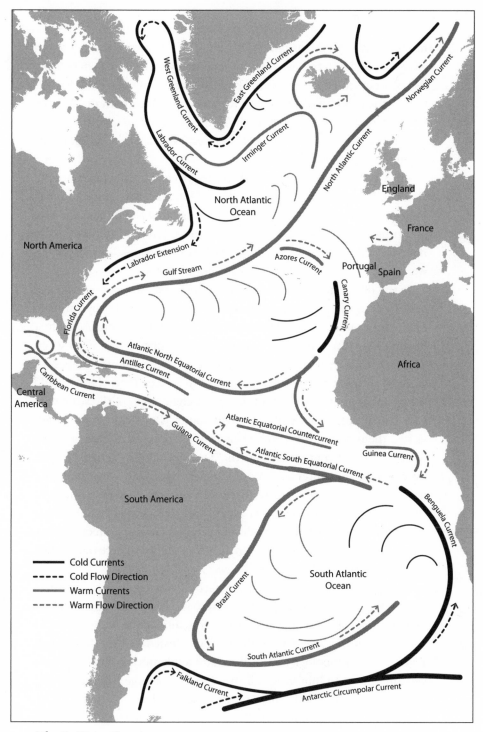

Atlantic Ocean Currents

mother was Sophia Folsom, the daughter of a Choctaw mother and a white trader. His father was Major John Pitchlynn, a white man of Scottish descent who had been raised by the Choctaw from an early age following the death of his own father. He was educated both in Choctaw tradition and at boarding schools in Tennessee. He later graduated from the University of Nashville, one of the finest institutions of higher learning in the region, founded in 1826.

In 1830, Pitchlynn was elected to the governing Choctaw National Council. Because of his background, he often was called upon to act as interpreter in negotiations between the Choctaw Nation and the U.S. government. When the Choctaw were removed from Mississippi to the newly organized Indian Territory west of the Mississippi River, Pitchlynn went, too, and continued his work from the West.

In the 1850s, Pitchlynn told a story of the Choctaw people's origins to an American traveler named Charles Lanman. As recorded by Lanman, Pitchlynn related, "According to the traditions of the Choctaws, the first of their race came from the bottom of a magnificent sea. Even when they first made their appearance upon the earth they were so numerous as to cover the sloping and sandy shore of the ocean, far as the eye could reach, and for a long time did they follow the margin of the sea before they could find a place suited to their wants." But sickness and death visited them on the coast, and their chief, "a prophet of great age and wisdom," told them to march north. "Their journey lay across streams, over hills and mountains, through tangled forests, and over immense prairies. They were now in an entirely strange country." They continued their migration away from the coast until they reached a "great highway of water." They crossed the river and found a land of perfect climate, "surpassing loveliness," and "the greatest abundance." There they settled and remained.[22]

Lanman's retelling of Pitchlynn's account was included by anthropologist John Swanton in his 1931 report to the Bureau of American Ethnology. Swanton states that, according to Lanman, the bodies of water alluded to in the "legend" are the Gulf of Mexico and the Mississippi River. The anthropologist also notes that Pitchlynn's account is the only version known to him in which the Choctaw emerge from under the ocean.[23] Like many Native nations, the Choctaw have multiple origination stories—or creation myths[24]—which may not always be easily reconcilable with each other. Another such tribe is the Cherokee, also from what is today the American Southeast.

The most commonly recited Cherokee creation myth is what is known as an earthdiver myth. Such stories, among the most prevalent protology stories for American Indians, follow a common pattern, which again involves a sea.

In the time before time, the entire world was covered by water. The human beings and the animals—the other-than-human persons—all lived above the vault of the sky. That realm became crowded, and the creatures looked for a place to go. Someone asked about the watery realm below. Someone else offered that was fine for the finned people, but others needed something solid upon which to stand. Finally, according to the Cherokee telling, the most insignificant among them, *dayun'si*, Beaver's Grandchild, the water beetle, stepped forward and offered to investigate. Descending to the earth's watery surface, the water beetle dived down into the primordial sea. Deeper and deeper he went. At last, he could hold his breath no more. He passed out and floated back to the surface, but he had reached the ocean floor and a little bit of mud clung to his leg. When he reached the surface, the mud on his leg spread out and formed all the lands of the world.

This "earthdiver" myth is the most commonly told and discussed Cherokee origin story. Yet the Cherokee also preserve a migration story, relating that the people came to their historical home after a journey across the "great water." Some interpret this myth as about migration across the Bering Strait land bridge that at the time of the last ice age spanned Siberia and Alaska. Others see it as a distant memory of a time when the Cherokee lived in the lake-filled north, much closer to their cousins the Iroquois. It is said that in the migration, five of the twelve clans of the Cherokee were lost (the Cherokee today being seven clans), and the great quest of the tribe is to find their missing brethren and reunite all the People. There is, however, a different Cherokee migration myth and an interpretation that more directly involves the Atlantic.

Some hundred and fifty years after Peter Pitchlynn discussed Choctaw origins with Charles Lanman, Hastings Shade, a former deputy principal chief of the Cherokee Nation, told Cherokee scholar Christopher Teuton the story of "The Journey of the Four Directions," a story preserved, particularly, by the traditionalist Keetoowah Society.

In that time before time, all the Cherokees lived on an island "surrounded by water that was undrinkable." One day, the island began to shake. The mountains opened up with fire. Then the island started to sink beneath the water. They sent out seven detachments, corresponding to the seven clans of the Cherokee, to migrate to *eloh' egwa*, the "main island." It took a long time, but on the fourth day, they reached the top of a tall mountain. They looked back and saw their island sink beneath the waves.

Shade's account continues, "And that's when the journey to the cold started. They didn't say 'north,' they says [*sic*] 'cold.' And they say they journeyed north, you know, this group. Some of them stayed, some came on, and they found a place, you know, of barren lands and fertile lands. Some stayed, some came on. That's the way this migration happened as they headed toward the cold."[25]

Here is a story not of nomadic big game hunters following prey across the Bering Strait land bridge, nor of Natives moving either purposefully or in inadvertent drift away from a northern core population. Shade's origin story tells of the necessity of abandoning an island home in the Caribbean or Gulf of Mexico in the face of volcanic eruption to seek safety in what became known as traditional Cherokee country. Pitchlynn's and Shade's stories thus parallel each other, separated by a century and a half: one for the Choctaw and the other for the Cherokee. Both speak of origins in the Atlantic, though historically neither tribe was associated with that watery body.

In this book, I want to posit a historical reality that I have already invoked several times in prior pages related to this great body of water. I want to discuss the "Red Atlantic."

Gilroy subtitles his monograph *Modernity and Double Consciousness*. It has long ago become a commonplace, though a much contested one, that the year 1492—with the Catholic Monarchs' expulsion of the Moors (and subsequently Jews) from the Iberian Peninsula, the resultant rise of the nation-state, and Columbus's first voyage—marks the beginning point of modernity.[26] There is a reason, as much as some passionately argue to reject the term, that the Americas were called the "New World." For those who came to the Western Hemisphere from Europe, it was, to borrow a Disney musical expression, "a whole new world."

Today, almost half of the world's table vegetables originated in this hemisphere and were cultivated and eaten by the indigenes of the Americas. Algonkian Indians had to show English colonists how to cultivate corn (one of those vegetables). Inca had to perform the same service with potatoes for Spanish conquistadores. And there were twenty-pound lobsters washing up on New England beaches as the Pilgrims starved until Indians showed them how to eat the crustaceans. (But as I always tell my students, the Europeans contributed melted butter, so it was a fair cultural exchange.)[27]

Beyond fruits and vegetables, or foodstuffs more generally, America's peoples provided chocolate and tobacco, to which Europeans adapted themselves in great numbers. Looted American wealth fueled the development of a resource-depleted Europe. Not only the colonists who came but also those who remained in the newly minted "Old World" came to define themselves by comparison with, or in opposition to, the indigenous Other. While Natives were not part of a Triangle Trade, as were black Africans, and while they experienced nothing in transoceanic shipment as horrific as the Middle Passage, they were nonetheless enslaved and shipped abroad in numbers that are startling to most. Many died in the process. And the Atlantic became that multilane highway that American indigenes traveled back and forth in surprising numbers.

Geographically, the Red Atlantic encompasses the Atlantic and its major adjacent bodies of water. Some Atlanticists argue that the Atlantic world stretches far into the interior of the Americas. The effects of Atlantic contact, commerce, and travel were unquestionably felt far from the Atlantic basin. For instance, diplomats from Plains tribes (the Osage and Otoe and Missouria) undertook missions to France. The Red Atlantic, however, in what is today the United States, at least initially, should be thought of as existing "beneath the Fall," on the Atlantic coast below the Atlantic Seaboard Fall Line. The fall line is the escarpment where the Piedmont drops down to meet the Atlantic coastal plain. It runs some 900 miles from the mid-Atlantic to Georgia, separating coast from the interior. The fall line represents the barrier at which riverine navigation would not be possible without portage due to falls and rapids.

Temporally, too, the Red Atlantic is different from the Atlantic world commonly discussed. Atlantic history typically stretches from the Columbus event (or shortly thereafter) through the age of revolution in the early nineteenth century and focuses on the colonial period and early modernity. Some Atlanticists, however, would stretch this time bound-ary. Thomas Benjamin, for instance, in his book *The Atlantic World*, ex-amines the period from 1400 to the turn of the twentieth century.[28]

At the beginning of this introduction, I stated that Columbus's first voyage and events surrounding it constituted a "re-inauguration." Tan-talizing speculations of and fond longings for pre-Columbian contacts by Irish monks, Chinese mariners, African warriors, and even Welsh prince Madoc aside, the first outlanders whom we can firmly document reach-ing the Americas were the Norse. The Red Atlantic commences in the year 1000 C.E. when Indians first encountered Europeans in the person of the Vikings. It runs in time from the start of the second millennium of the Common Era through Eric Hobsbawm's long nineteenth century and World War I, when Natives traveled to the European warfront in notable numbers. It concludes in 1927, when Charles Lindbergh's solo flight signaled forever a change in how people interacted with the Atlan-tic (although regular transatlantic plane service would not begin until 1939).

During that nearly thousand-year period, Western Hemisphere in-digenes sailed forth on the waters of the Atlantic basin both voluntarily and involuntarily. They traveled as spectacles and entertainers, soldiers and sailors, tourists and explorers, captives and slaves, patronage seek-ers and diplomats. The reason that the Red Atlantic period is as long as it is is that Natives continuously traveled the Atlantic in all these capacities throughout the period. Though obviously their options and roles narrowed over time, Indians were nevertheless engaged in colo-nial campaigns in the 1880s through the Spanish-American War and, as mentioned above, fought in the First World War. They were held pris-oner on the verge of the Atlantic at Fort Marion in the 1870s and 1880s. They traveled to Europe with Buffalo Bill's Wild West show as late as 1906. Cayuga chief Levi General, better known as Deskaheh, undertook a diplomatic mission to the League of Nations in Geneva in 1923. Danish-Inuit explorer Knud Rasmussen routinely traveled between Greenland and Denmark and, from 1921 until 1924, led his Fifth Thule Expedition to Canada and across the entire length of Arctic America and down the western coast of Alaska. Throughout the period, Natives continued to engage, contend with, and adapt to a modernity defined by (and some-times prescribed by) their involvement with whites.

In his book *Indians in Unexpected Places*, Philip J. Deloria discusses "expectations" and "anomalies." Focusing on the expectations of non-Natives at the turn of the twentieth century, he asks "how we might revisit the actions of Indian people that have been all too easily branded as anomalous. . . . I want to make a hard turn from anomaly to frequency and unexpectedness."[29] While this interpretive maneuver is important, scholars of the Red Atlantic like Coll Thrush, Jenny Pulsipher, Daniel Justice, and myself want to go further and push beyond Deloria to suggest that from the earliest moments of European/Native contact in the Americas until the first quarter of the twentieth century, Indians, far from being marginal to the Atlantic experience, were, in fact, as central as Africans. Native resources, ideas, and peoples themselves traveled the Atlantic with regularity and became among the most basic defining components of Atlantic cultural exchange.

Of course, it is commonly thought that the number of Natives who journeyed physically across or circulated around the Atlantic basin is dwarfed by the masses of whites and blacks who did so. Among academics, a kind of patronizing paternalism settled in concerning indigenes who made such trips. Since the early 1940s, a number of books have come out that catalog Native journeys beyond the confines of, principally, what are today the United States and Canada: the early *Indians Abroad, 1493–1938* by Carolyn Thomas Foreman; the important *Transatlantic Encounters: American Indians in Britain, 1500–1776* by Alden T. Vaughan; and *The Transatlantic Indian, 1776–1930* by Kate Flint. Even if not articulated, the attitude toward these works and others like them was often a feeling of preciousness. It was as if scholars thought, "Isn't that cute? A few Indians *did* go to Europe."[30]

Without question, if one talks only about the sheer number of Indians transported into slavery versus the number of black Africans, then the Native numbers look very small. Scholars estimate that 12 million (some estimates range as high as 20 million) enslaved Africans were shipped to the Americas. An estimated 12 percent died during the Middle Passage. An approximate estimate for Native slaves traveling in a more or less opposite direction (including to the Caribbean) is 600,000, representing perhaps 5 percent of the African total.[31] (Chapter 1 deals with those Natives who traveled involuntarily, and I return to the discussion of slavery in the conclusion.) Like Africans, many of these indigenes perished in the process. But this relatively small figure does not include those who were enslaved in situ and were never transported over open water but were worked to death in the mines or on the Spaniard plantations known as encomiendas. It also excludes the modest, by comparison, number of Natives who traversed the ocean for other reasons during the period of the Red Atlantic. To put the 600,000 figure in broader perspective compared with white crossings, let us consider the figures for persons migrating from European metropoles during the period of the Atlantic world. Approximately 688,000 immigrants were drawn to Spain's Atlantic colonies. Perhaps 700,000 persons from England, Scotland, and Ireland immigrated. New France and the French islands of the Caribbean together attracted perhaps 345,000 settlers before 1760.[32] Viewed in this light, the movement of indigenes around the Red Atlantic seems more consistent with the movement of other groups in the Atlantic world.

Like Gilroy's black Atlantic, there are several aspects or facets to the Red Atlantic. As with the black Atlantic, it deals in the first instance with the movement around the Atlantic basin of indigenous persons in a variety of capacities. In this, as we will see, the black and Red Atlantics are often braided together—as Gilroy's example of Crispus Attucks attests. "Indigenous" means originating, occurring, or living in a particular place. The indigenes of the Americas are just that—indigenous to their lands in the Western Hemisphere. Africans are indigenous to Africa. Yet in the Red Atlantic, as for Africans in Gilroy's black Atlantic, we see examples of radical mobility while still being tied to or rooted in place. Two examples from what is today the state of Georgia, where I have worked for over a decade, will illustrate this—related examples from the black and Red Atlantics.

The roots of Georgia were planted long ago and far away across the Atlantic. This is hardly surprising. James Oglethorpe, its founder, was born in London and reared in Surrey. The deepest roots of Georgia, however, run not back to England but to Africa.

In 1730, a merchant named Ayuba Suleiman Diallo, the son of a Muslim imam, was captured on the Gambia River by Mandinkas (those formerly called Mandingos) and sold to English slavers (an irony since he himself was a dealer in slaves), who in turn sold him to the owner of a Maryland tobacco plantation. Diallo was himself a devout Muslim. He was initially put to work in the tobacco fields, but when he proved unsuitable for such labor, he was put to work tending cattle.

In Maryland, Diallo was befriended by Reverend Thomas Bluett of the Anglican Society for the Propagation of the Gospel in Foreign Parts.

Bluett convinced the enslaved African's owner to allow his slave to write a letter to his father, explaining what had happened to him. Written in Arabic, the letter found its way into the hands of Oglethorpe during the summer of 1732, a few months prior to the founding of the Georgia colony. Oglethorpe had served briefly as deputy governor of the Royal African Company, a corporation set up to exploit the West African slave trade. He sent the letter to Oxford to be translated. When he read the translation, Oglethorpe was greatly moved by the African's story. He arranged to purchase Diallo and have him sent to England, where he was eventually manumitted.

Although he never met Diallo, the incident deeply affected Oglethorpe. He sold his stock in the Royal African Company and severed all ties with it. He established Georgia as an antislavery colony. Only after his governorship, in 1750, did Georgia reverse itself and legalize the peculiar institution.

During his twelve-month sojourn in England, Job ben Jalla (as Diallo was known there) became what one document refers to as "a roaring lion" of English society. He helped Sir Hans Sloane, founder of the British Museum, organize its large collection of Arabic manuscripts. He was sponsored into membership in the Gentlemen's Society of Spalding, a club whose members included some of the country's most distinguished scholars. (Sir Isaac Newton had been a member until his death five years earlier.) William Hoare painted his portrait. The society tried to expose the Muslim to Christianity by giving him a copy of the New Testament. According to Michael Thurmond in his book *Freedom: Georgia's Antislavery Heritage, 1733–1865*, "The Society's minute book contained a notation dated June 26, 1733, that a Bible was presented to the 'Poor Mahometan Black redeemed by order of Mr. Oglethorpe.'"[33] After Bluett secured contributions from several donors, Diallo was presented a "handsomely engrossed" manumission certificate on December 27, 1733. He returned to Africa in July 1734.[34] Bluett told his story in *Some Memories of the Life of Job, the Son of Solomon High Priest of Boonda in Africa*.[35]

Ayuba Suleiman Diallo, who twice traversed the ocean as a slave to become a metropolitan cosmopolitan in England before sailing once more to Africa, would seem to be a paradigmatic case study in the black Atlantic. Yet Gilroy does not mention him. The African is linked to the Red Atlantic through the person of James Oglethorpe.

In addition to his antislavery views, Oglethorpe, unlike most colonialists, had a reputation for fair dealing with the Indians. Because of a treaty between Carolina and the Muscogee providing that no white settlements would be made south of the Savannah River without the Natives' permission, Oglethorpe knew he needed to secure Indian consent. In early 1733, after selecting a site for his new colony, he traveled to meet the Yamacraw mico, or chief, Tomochichi. Presumably a veteran of the 1715 Yamasee War, the chief was less than ecstatic to see new Englishmen arriving but ultimately agreed to let them settle on Yamacraw Bluff, which led to the founding of Savannah.

Early the following year, circumstances forced Oglethorpe to return to England. The Board of Trustees of Georgia invited Tomochichi to accompany him for the formal ratification of the Articles of Friendship and Commerce, the treaty Oglethorpe had negotiated with the mico that provided for the establishment of the Georgia colony. Bundles of eagle feathers representing all the Lower Creek towns were prepared for Tomochichi to present to the English king. The Indian delegation was composed of Tomochichi; his wife, Senauki; his nephew, Toonahowi; Hillispilli, Tomochichi's brother and war chief of the Lower Creeks; Umpichi, Tomochichi's brother-in-law and a Yuchi chief; and three attendants: Apokutchi, Santachi, and Stimaletchi. The mixed-blood trader John Musgrove served as their interpreter. Oglethorpe and the party of nine Natives set sail on the man-of-war H.M.S. *Aldborough* on April 7.[36] It was the largest Indian delegation to travel to England since that of Pocahontas in 1616.

The group arrived in England on June 16, 1734, visited Oglethorpe's home in Surrey, and then proceeded to the royal capital, where they were ensconced in well-appointed accommodations at the trustees' offices. According to one of Tomochichi's biographers, "When the party arrived in London the city provided a festive welcome. Bells rang in honor of the colorful visitors; there was a tremendous bonfire; and many demonstrations of welcome. Their every move was reported by the newspapers. They received gifts, invitations and even salutations in poetry."[37]

The delegation met with the trustees on July 3. Formalities were exchanged, and the meeting ended with the sharing of tobacco and wine. Tomochichi presented the trustees with twenty-five deerskins, "one Tyger Skin and Six Boufler Skins" (probably the hides of a panther and buffaloes).[38] In return, Sir John Perceval, the Earl of Egmont, the president of the Georgia trustees, gave the mico a silver snuff box, "which the Indian said he would wear around his neck close to his heart."[39] More meetings followed.

The trustees contacted the prime minister Sir Robert Walpole, requesting that he arrange an audience with King George II and asking that the king provide the Indians with coaches and "a Centry to preserve them from the Insults of the Mob."[40] On August 1, they were presented to King George and Queen Caroline at Kensington Palace. The Indians had wanted to wear their own clothes, but Oglethorpe insisted on re-outfitting them in fine robes, trimmed in fur, that seemed to observers to be "of the Moorish Fashion."[41] Tomochichi demonstrated both wit and intelligence. When he was asked later what he had seen at court, "[h]e replied that his hosts had taken him through many houses (rooms) to make him believe that the King's Palace consisted of several establishments. When he noted with surprise, however, that he returned by the same stairs he had already used, the Mico realized that it was all one house. He said that although the English knew many things his people did not know, he doubted that they were happier."[42]

The delegation also visited William Wake, the archbishop of Canterbury, who sent a barge down the Thames for them. Tomochichi and Toonahowi, his nephew and adopted son, were painted by William Verelst, and the portrait hung for many years in the offices of the trustees. Verelst also painted a group portrait of the delegation. Prince William, the Duke of Cumberland, gave Toonahowi a gold watch. And, of course, the group was treated to the sights of London, including the Royal Garden, Greenwich, Eton, and the Tower. According to Carolyn Thomas Foreman, in her 1943 book, *Indians Abroad*, "Nothing was spared by the British government to impress the Indians with the strength of England."[43] In all, more than £1,000 was spent on gifts and support for the Natives during their stay.

Throughout the visit, Tomochichi impressed his hosts by following English protocol. He also proved himself a serious negotiator with a developed and sophisticated understanding of the diplomacy of the Red Atlantic. According to Helen Todd:

> The Trustees appointed a committee to confer with Tomochichi to determine what he would like done for his people. He requested that

rules and regulations be set up for weights and measures in trading Indian goods, deerskins, and other pelts. In justification of this application he stated that he had paid ten pounds of leather for a blanket at Yamacraw. He asked that traders be licensed; that store houses be established in every principal village where the natives could be supplied at a fair price for such articles as they wished to purchase; that if Indians were cheated they might have means of restitution; that rum not be sold to the red men; that his nephew Toonahowi and other children be given teachers to instruct them in religion and the English language; and that they be given the picture of the "Great Lyon they saw at the Tower" to be placed in a great hall they intended to build.[44]

Education was always at the forefront of any conversations the mico had with Englishmen.

The Indian diplomats, minus one of their number who had expired of smallpox, weighed anchor in England on October 31, 1734. Todd writes, "Londoners, much impressed with the dignity, conduct, and intelligence of the Indians, no longer considered them savages."[45] Tomochichi himself was hailed for his sagacity, integrity, and statesmanship. Yet by the time Tomochichi and his compatriots made their round-trip Atlantic voyage, Indians were already old hands at oceanic travel, having been sailing to Europe for more than 700 years, many voluntarily but many more less so.

The party arrived back in Georgia on December 28, 1734. The Creek delegation's mission to England had created a swell of enthusiasm for Oglethorpe's colony. The Reverend John Wesley and his brother Charles agreed to accompany their friend Reverend Benjamin Ingham as missionaries to America. They sailed with more than 200 other colonists aboard the brigs *Simonds* and *London Merchant* on October 18, 1735, landing on Cockspur Island in early February 1736.

When Tomochichi heard of the missionaries' arrival, he sent a side of venison along with word that he and his entourage would arrive to greet them directly. When the Indians did come (all but Tomochichi dressed in Western garb), the Wesleys donned their surplices, and John grabbed his Greek scriptures and went to meet them. "I am greatly pleased," the chief said in English as he shook hands with the Anglican priest. Then, through Mary Musgrove acting as interpreter, he again pressed the issue of education:

I am glad to see you here. When I was in England I desired that Some might Speak the Great Word to me, and my Nation then desired to hear it; but Since that time We have all been put into Confusion. The French built a Fort with 100 Men in one place, and a Fort with 100 Men in another place, and the Spaniards are preparing for War. The English Traders too, put us into confusion, and have Set our people against hearing the great word for they speak with a double tongue. Some Say one thing of it, and Some another. This does not commend the Christian religion to my Tribe. But we would not be made Christians after the Spanish way to make Christians. We would be taught first, and then baptized. But I am glad you are come. I will go up and Speak to the wise men of our Nation, and I hope they will hear.[46]

The obtuse and theological reply of the prim and priggish John Wesley left Tomochichi unimpressed. The priest responded through Mary Musgrove, "Though we are come so far, we do not know whether He will please to teach you by us or no. If He teaches you, you will learn wisdom, but we can do nothing."[47]

Benjamin Ingham, however, understood the mico's request and responded to it positively. By the end of February, land had been given for a school at an abandoned Mississippian mound site on the Savannah River, a few miles from both the colonists' settlement and Tomochichi's village of New Yamacraw. To be called Irene, after the Greek goddess of peace, construction began on the school in August and was completed in September. The enterprise pleased Tomochichi greatly, and he and Senauki agreed to send Toonahowi there for instruction.

Though they saw each other with some frequency, John Wesley never understood Tomochichi and worried that the mico disliked him. For his part, Tomochichi always wished Wesley well in his endeavors, though he doubted their efficacy, and he himself rejected the new religion because of the discrepancies he witnessed between what the Christians preached and what they practiced.

In his last years, Tomochichi continued to try to maintain peace with the English. He acted as an advisor to Oglethorpe and as his intermediary with other Indians. In the fall of 1739, he fell gravely ill. John Wesley and George Whitefield, who had joined Wesley in ministry in Georgia, each visited the mico on his deathbed. Unfortunately, Oglethorpe could not. As the Georgia founder neared New Yamacraw on October 5, 1739,

Tomochichi urged his people to maintain their friendship with the English and then died. His body was conveyed by water to Savannah, where he was buried, Oglethorpe acting as a pallbearer.

Tomochichi had traveled to Britain and returned to North America, but he continued to negotiate the Red Atlantic even when back in his homeland. In point of fact, however, such were the dynamics of the Red Atlantic and, after a certain point in history, so pervasive were its effects that Native Americans did not have to journey abroad to participate in it.

In 1842, Charles Dickens traveled to the United States. On a riverboat from Cincinnati to Louisville, Kentucky, the English writer happened to meet future Choctaw chief Peter Pitchlynn returning home after nearly a year and a half in Washington City negotiating with the general government. The Englishman was impressed from the start, when Pitchlynn "*sent in his card* to me." The Indian knowledgeably discussed George Catlin's traveling exhibition of art, artifacts, and actual Indians in Britain (for which his portrait had been painted) and the works of Sir Walter Scott. He also expressed his long-held desire to visit the British Isles. When Dickens assured him that were he to travel to Britain he would be well-received (unaware that Pitchlynn was a major slaveholder—something of which Dickens would have disapproved), the American aborigine replied tartly "that the English used to be very fond of the Red Men when they wanted their help, but had not cared much for them since." Though Pitchlynn never achieved his wish to cross the ocean, this erudite "stately and complete gentleman" who read Scott's poetry and understood British colonial affairs quite well participated in the Red Atlantic, even as he cheekily rejected it.[48]

The Red Atlantic, however, encompasses more than the transportation, physical or merely intellectual (like Pitchlynn's), of Natives around the Atlantic basin. A second aspect is material.

From the earliest days of their exploration, Europeans exploited the resources of the New World. Vikings took cargoes of grapes and vines back with them from Vinland (modern-day Newfoundland). They traded for furs and pelts with the Natives. The real prize, however, was timber from Markland, the wooded coast of Labrador. "Markland" means "forest-land." In the *Greenlanders' Saga*, Leif Erikson declares, "This country shall be named after its natural resources: it shall be called *Markland*."[49] Lumber was badly needed by Norse settlers in relatively tree-barren Greenland. Erikson took a "full cargo of timber" with him upon his return.[50] The Vikings continued to harvest timber from Labrador, long after abandoning settlement of Vinland during the first decade of the second millennium. According to the *Icelandic Annals*, as late as 1347, a Greenlander ship carrying timber was driven by storm to Iceland.[51]

Recent discoveries by archaeologist Patricia Sutherland have produced evidence of a second Viking settlement (beyond the previously known settlement in Newfoundland)—probably a seasonal camp—in the Tanfield Valley of Baffin Island, an area the Norse called Helluland, meaning "Stone-slab land." A report on the finds, published in *National Geographic*, also suggests indications of a developed trade with the Dorset people (commonly referred to as a "paleo-Eskimo" culture) in the area. The Dorset could have supplied the Vikings with prized luxuries like walrus ivory, narwhal tusks, and soft Arctic furs, and in return they would have received metal and wood. Radiocarbon dating of some material at the Tanfield Valley site produced a date in the fourteenth century, matching Norse occupation of Greenland.[52]

Centuries later, of course, Spaniards would plunder silver and gold from the Western Hemisphere indigenes. So consistent and persistent were Spanish demands for gold that Bartolomé de Las Casas would note that the Indians thought gold must be the Spaniards' god because that was all they seemed to care about. Though this vast wealth was taken to Spain, because of that country's failure to develop its own manufacturing and industrial base, much of it drained directly to other European powers. According to Stanley Stein and Barbara Stein, by 1700, the Spaniards were "mere fronts for Genoese, French, Dutch, and English . . . merchants." Spain became, in many ways, simply a pass-through, as American wealth became "a major (perhaps even the determining) factor in the development of commercial capitalism in western Europe." According to Bailyn, "It seems perverse . . . that the more passive Lower Andalusia's role in Atlantic commerce became, the more it stimulated Europe's economy."[53] The situation led German philosopher Samuel von Pufendorf to observe sardonically, "Spain kept the cow and the rest of Europe drank the milk."[54]

I have already mentioned that nearly half of the contemporary world's table vegetables, 46 percent, originated with Western Hemisphere indigenes. Another important foodstuff often overlooked is the turkey. The Aztec raised—and ate—turkeys in remarkable numbers. According to food anthropologist Sophie Coe, "Motolinia says that the market of

Tepeyacac, just one of several suburban markets around Tenochtitlan, sold eight thousand birds every five days, and this all this year round. Matlalaca, the majordomo of the poet-king of Texcoco, Nezahualcoyotl, sent one hundred turkeys to court daily, as well as great quantities of other edibles." In addition to serving as human food, the birds were also fed to the animals in the Aztec emperor Moctezuma's zoo. According to Spanish colonial historian Juan de Torquemada in his *Monarchia Indiana*, published in 1615, five hundred birds a day went to feed the zoo animals.[55] Turkeys were one of only two domesticated animals north of Mexico (the other being the dog). When Europeans first saw them, they mistook them for a species of guinea fowl.

Spaniards imported the turkey in 1519. They quickly became prized for their flavor, and they were domesticated in Europe, as well. When the Pilgrims came to North America in 1620, they brought domesticated turkeys with them. These, in turn, interbred with their wild cousins. The birds became an important protein source for colonists.

The previously referenced table vegetables and fruits included maize, beans, squash, tomatoes, potatoes, avocados, pumpkins, sweet potatoes, pineapples, peanuts, cranberries, papayas, and chilies—not to mention food commodities like vanilla and sassafras, the raw material modernly of root beer and its frontier predecessor, sarsaparilla. Imagine the world's cuisines today absent corn, beans, squash, and quinoa.[56] What would southern Italian food look like without the tomato? Think of what the diet of India or parts of East and Southeast Asia would be without chilies. If one lets this mind exercise wander further, suppose the potato had never been taken to Europe. There would have been no potato famine in Ireland and possibly no Irish Diaspora. The world might be manifestly different in ways both major and minor were it not for the riches of the Western Hemisphere and the Red Atlantic. In fact, during the very real, historical potato famine, Peter Pitchlynn's Choctaw sent relief to the Irish, despite the fact that they had experienced their forced relocation only relatively recently. In spite of their own meager resources, the tribe sent $170, plus corn and blankets, a transatlantic gesture still remembered in Ireland today.

I also already have mentioned tobacco and chocolate. In her fine book *Sacred Gifts, Profane Pleasures: A History of Tobacco and Chocolate in the Atlantic World*, Marcy Norton writes, "Given the importance of tobacco and chocolate to both pre-Columbian Amerindian societies and 'post-

Columbian' European societies, it is somewhat surprising that they have not occupied more prominent positions in general histories of the Atlantic world. Part of the reason, I suspect, is the tendency, one initiated in the sixteenth century . . . to view both goods as neutral resources, products of the natural world, devoid of cultural content." Nothing could be further from the truth, of course. Norton concludes, "[T]hey are no less *cultural* artifacts than, say, guns or writing. Tobacco and chocolate—as they are used today and as they were used when Europeans arrived in the fifteenth and sixteenth centuries—would not exist without knowledge and techniques developed over millennia in the western hemisphere."[57]

In the pre-Columbian Western Hemisphere, tobacco was found from the sub-Arctic region to southern South America. It was used in a variety of ways and consumed in a number of different forms. It was smoked in pipes and as cigars, sucked like modern chewing tobacco, and inhaled like snuff. It was employed as poultices on wounds and infections, and decoctions of the leaves were drunk to fight parasites.[58] Tobacco smoke was blown into ears to treat earaches.

The first documented European initiation to tobacco use was in 1518 when it was shared ceremonially by the Maya with the expedition of Juan de Grijalva in Mexico. Tobacco use and chocolate consumption often went together. According to the conquistador Bernal Diaz del Castillo in his memoir, *The Conquest of New Spain*, both were offered to Hernán Cortés at a banquet with Moctezuma.

The residents of Teotihuacan traded with the Maya, on the Pacific coast of what is today Guatemala, for cacao. After entering the Valley of Mexico in the late thirteenth century, the Aztec adapted to chocolate, as well. When Spaniards began its widespread use in the late sixteenth century, Pope Gregory XIII was twice consulted by the colonists in Chiapas as to whether chocolate should be considered a food or a drink, since when Christians fasted, they were allowed only one solid meal a day. The pope replied that chocolate was a drink and therefore did not break the fast.[59]

In 1627, Norton notes, the great Spanish poet and satirist Francisco de Quevedo cataloged the ravages of tobacco and chocolate (both substances of which he himself partook) on the body. Tobacco abusers went about "snuffling and sneezing." Chocoholics were afflicted with dizziness and flatulence. Moreover, both indulgences ensorcelled their users, turning them from Christ. Tobacco users "apprenticed for hell" by smoking, while chocolate fanciers "venerated" their vice. Quevedo saw the twin luxuries as the New World's revenge, writing, "The devil of tobacco and the devil of chocolate told me that they had avenged the Indies against Spain," since they had done more damage in the Old World than the conquistadores had managed in the Americas.[60] Contemporary Native Americans today are fond of saying that tobacco was never carcinogenic until Europeans began using it in a nonsacred way, and given the manner and patterns of use by indigenes, the observation probably contains an element of truth.

While one should take issue with the Spaniard Quevedo's assessment of the relative devastation caused by Spanish conquistadores and the New World exports of tobacco and chocolate, there is a vestige of the revenge theme surrounding tobacco that survives in the Western Hemisphere.

The Maya in the Guatemalan highlands and parts of Mexico venerate a syncretic folk saint or minor deity named Maximón. His name is a blend of *max*, the word for tobacco in the Mam Mayan language, and Simón, for San Simón. St. Simon is the apostle known as Simon the Zealot. He is severe in his indignation at those who profess Christianity with their lips but defile it by their actions, a common observation by Natives about Europeans and Euro-Americans. Maximón is depicted in statue form as dressed in clothes from any period from the seventeenth through the twentieth centuries. A lit cigarette or cigar is placed in his mouth as an offering. Often he sports dark glasses to hide his eyes, the mirrors of his soul. He is identified as the god of revenge, who grants prayers for vengeance or success at another's expense.

A few moments ago, I asked you as readers to engage in a thought experiment and imagine how world history might have been different without the importation to Europe of the potato. I want you to open your mind again, not for another counterfactual but to see something entirely plausible. Imagine a prosperous Dutch shipping merchant sitting in a coffee house in Amsterdam. He is smoking tobacco from a long-stemmed clay churchwarden pipe and sipping chocolate. His wealth has been fueled by the Indian and African slaves shipped to Willemstad and working plantations in the Antilles. This cosmopolitan is but a single, obvious beneficiary of both Red and black Atlantics.[61]

A third facet of the Red Atlantic, closely related to the material, is what might be called technological. The indigenous peoples of the Americas provided Europeans with innovations as major as rubber processing, terrace farming, and the suspension bridge. Indigenes showed them the canoe, the kayak, snowshoes, and barbecue. And words from autochthonous Western Hemisphere languages colonized European tongues for these things and more. These, too, are legacies of the Red Atlantic.

This "technology transfer" did not always function seamlessly. According to local legend, for instance, early settlers noticed that the Natives of the Sea Islands, which stretch from South Carolina to Florida, used Spanish moss to produce both clothing and bedding. The colonists stuffed pillows and mattresses with the plentiful material, believing that they had found in the plant the makings of a New World export. Unfortunately, they apparently did not learn the indigenes' technique of smoking Spanish moss over a fire to remove the red bugs—colloquially known as "chiggers"—that often reside in it. The nascent industry failed to materialize.

Of course, the circulation of information, material culture, and technology did not flow unidirectionally. Europeans brought horses, cloth, tools, metal pots, pans, other material goods, and those most Old World of imports: alcohol and Christianity. In the process, Natives were drawn increasingly into multiple complex economies with whites. With a Eurocentric and patronizing tone, Alexis de Tocqueville wrote in his 1835 *Democracy in America*:

> The Europeans introduced amongst the savages of North America fire-arms, ardent spirits, and iron: they taught them to exchange for manufactured stuffs, the rough garments which had previously satisfied their untutored simplicity. Having acquired new tastes, without the arts by which they could be gratified, the Indians were obliged to have recourse to the workmanship of whites; but in return for their productions the savage had nothing to offer except the rich furs which still abounded in his woods. Hence the chase became necessary, not merely to provide for his subsistence, but in order to procure the only objects of barter which he could furnish to Europe. Whilst the wants of the natives were thus increasing, their resources continued to diminish.[62]

Though a fair thumbnail summary of the fur trade and the factory system in, variously, deerskins, beaver pelts, and later buffalo hides, it nonetheless sells short Natives as actors in the Atlantic economy. Natives became integrated into Western economic systems. This occurred in a variety of ways, including participation in the wage economy through, for instance, maritime labor (a subject I treat in chapter 2). By far, however, the major imbrication came through trade. In North America, this primarily meant the fur trade. As de Tocqueville hints, to satisfy their desires for European and American manufactures, Indian hunters decimated the deer populations and drove the beaver to near-extinction. When they lacked sufficient pelts to procure what they needed, American factors encouraged Indians to incur debts; when the debts grew high enough, they could be satisfied only through land cessions. I discuss these complex dynamics again in my conclusion.

The Atlantic formed a multilane, two-way bridge across which traveled ideas and things that changed both Europeans and American indigenes. Some scholars see in the cosmopolitanism and hybridity of Indians and their cultures a loss of indigenous authenticity, a diminution of Indianness. Such a position fails to account for the fact that Natives and their cultures had always been highly adaptive, appropriating and absorbing anything that seemed useful or powerful. They put these things to their own use without challenging the integrity of their cultures. When Cherokee chief Oconostota put on a pair of spectacles (material goods) to see clearly during prisoner exchange negotiations with Continental army colonel John Sevier during the Revolutionary War, when Pequot Methodist clergyman and writer William Apess turned the rhetoric of evangelical Christianity (idea) on its head in an attempt to shame whites into equal treatment of Indians, and when the Master of Life told Shawnee prophet Tenskwatawa that the People must give up everything they had gotten from whites *except* guns and horses (technology), all of them were engaged in deeply indigenous acts, putting these things to use in the service of their peoples.

Yet another aspect of the Red Atlantic involves literature. From the very beginning of European/Native contact and interaction, both colonists in the New World and their counterparts who remained behind in Europe began to define themselves by comparison with, and in opposition to, the indigenous Other. A key situs for working out this self-invention was in literature. In Spain, pro-Indian members of the *indigenista* movement like Las Casas, Alonso de la Vera Cruz, Vasco de Quiroga, and Michael de Carvajal contributed to the literature of the Red Atlantic. So did their opponents like Juan Ginés de Sepúlveda. In

England, Shakespeare famously did so in *The Tempest*. From France, Voltaire contributed *Candide* and *L'Ingenu*. Later, popular German novelist Karl May participated through his frontier romances of the Übermensch "Old Shatterhand" and his noble Apache friend Winnetou. Edgar Allan Poe's only completed novel, *The Narrative of Arthur Gordon Pym of Nantucket*, represents just one American entry.

It is not, however, only non-Natives who contributed to the Red Atlantic through literature. As soon as they learned to write, indigenes did so, too.[63] Garcilaso de la Vega, known as El Inca, produced important literature in the early seventeenth century. In the subsequent centuries, other contributors included Samson Occom, George Henry, Peter Jones, George Copway, and E. Pauline Johnson, among others. Following the closing of the Red Atlantic, especially since the inauguration of the so-called American Indian Literary Renaissance in 1968, many contemporary Native authors have traveled the Red Atlantic imaginatively in their writings. These include—but are by no means limited to—John Joseph Mathews, Michael Dorris and Louise Erdrich, Gerald Vizenor, Thomas King, Leslie Silko, James Welch, Joseph Boyden, and Mat Johnson.

This Study

As I mentioned in the preface, I first outlined the Red Atlantic in an article titled "The Red Atlantic: Transoceanic Cultural Exchanges" in the Summer 2011 issue of *American Indian Quarterly*. This book, which grows out of that piece, examines all the aspects of the Red Atlantic outlined above, but it explores some more than others. Like that original article, however, it focuses foremost on the physical movement of indigenes themselves across and around the Atlantic basin.

Chapter 1 begins with those persons who participated in the Red Atlantic involuntarily, traveling to it or around it as slaves, captives, and exiles. Chapter 2 examines soldiers and sailors. Chapter 3 looks at the long history of red diplomats, like Tomochichi. Chapter 4 takes up so-called celebrity Indians, those who traveled as performers and as part of entertainment spectaculars or became celebrities by their mere presence (like that representative of the black Atlantic Ayuba Suleiman Diallo, discussed above). Finally, chapter 5 discusses the literature of the Red Atlantic. I then consider the closing of the Red Atlantic and offer my conclusions. Discussion in each chapter is meant to be illustrative rather than catalogic. As with any piece of scholarship, it is my hope that this examination of the Red Atlantic will spark further study on the subject by others. I hope to provoke a conversation.

A couple of final observations must be made. Because of this structure, this book does not have a straight-line chronological narrative. Instead, it moves back and forth in time from chapter to chapter as each category of participant is considered. Further, there are no hard-and-fast delineations between the above-listed categories—slaves, soldiers, diplomats, performers, and so on. Some persons begin in one category and move into another. For instance, Samson Occom, an educated Mohegan Indian, traveled to England to raise money for what would become Dartmouth College and went on to become a man of letters. Other figures inhabited several of these worlds more or less simultaneously. Garcilaso was a patronage seeker, an immigrant, a soldier, and a writer. And it is difficult to separate out these disparate roles. All of this is to say that many people could appear in several different places in this story. For the sake of convenience and coherence, however, though a given individual may be referred to in several places, I have tried to limit primary discussion of him or her to a single chapter.

The Red Atlantic is part of a larger story of globalization and the worldwide movement of Western Hemisphere indigenes and their technologies, ideas, and material goods. It therefore bulges occasionally into the Pacific as part of this wider story.

In his *Royal Commentaries*, Garcilaso discusses the exploits of his great-grandfather Túpac Inca Yupanqui. According to Inca legend, Yupanqui led a voyage of exploration into the Pacific around 1490. Pedro Sarmiento de Gamboa, in his 1572 *History of the Incas*, writes:

> There arrived at Tumbez some merchants who had come by sea from the west, navigating in balsas with sails. They gave information of the land whence they came, which consisted of some islands called Avachumbi [Outer Island] and Ninachumbi [Island of Fire], where there were many people and much gold. Tupac Inca was a man of lofty and ambitious ideas, and was not satisfied with the regions he had already conquered. So he determined to challenge a happy fortune, and see if it would favor him by sea. . . .
>
> The Inca, having this certainty, determined to go there. He caused an immense number of balsas to be constructed, in which he embarked with more than 20,000 chosen men. . . .

Tupac Inca navigated and sailed on until he discovered the [afore-mentioned] islands, and returned, bringing back with him black people, gold, a chair of brass, and a skin and jawbone of a horse. These trophies were preserved in the fortress of Cuzco until the Spaniards came. The duration of this expedition undertaken by Tupac Inca was nine months, others say a year, and, as he was so long absent, everyone believed he was dead.[64]

The referenced islands are often identified as the Galapagos, though other locations have also been suggested.

Some have questioned whether any work on the Red Atlantic should even reference Peru. Peru is mentioned, however, neither because of its geographic location (on the Pacific, not the Atlantic) nor for the legendary travels of Yupanqui. Peru enters the Red Atlantic story because it sent both matériel (gold, silver, mercury, potatoes) and people (Garcilaso himself, but also others like Inca caciques Antonio Collatopa and Vicente Mora Chimo Capac) across the Atlantic.[65] Peru became Spain's "treasure house," and the saying "Vale un Peru [It's worth a Peru]" entered the Spanish language as an expression of opulence.

Beyond Peru, Spain was an important naval presence in the Pacific as it sought to project its power as far north as what is today British Columbia, and some Northwest Coast tribes' first encounter with Europeans was with Spaniards. Juan Francisco de la Bodega y Quadra, a white creole born in Lima, became the most important Spanish naval officer on that coast. In 1775, Bodega participated in a clash that resulted from first contact with the Quinault that led to the death of six sailors. He later engaged in diplomacy with the Nuu-chah-nulth (the people formerly called Nootka).[66]

North American Natives, as well, found their way from the Atlantic to the Pacific. This was particularly true of those who went in search of whales as crewmembers aboard the ships that sailed out of New England. Some of these inevitably stayed to lead an expatriate existence. For instance, Barry O'Connell found out that in 1838, William Elisha Apess, the son of William Apess and a crewmember on the *Ajax*, mutinied with one other seaman, taking control of the vessel and forcing it to put into Port Otago, New Zealand. He subsequently married a Maori woman and had seven children. Today there are Pequot/Maori descendants of William Apess still living in New Zealand.[67]

O'Connell writes that for William Elisha Apess and the lives of other nineteenth-century Natives, "there exists so far only a tantalizing out-line."[68] Yet O'Connell's observation is true for far more than just the Indians of the northeastern United States. These contacts and leads in the Pacific are beginning to be taken seriously. Whether there is a Pacific equivalent to complement the Red Atlantic must be a subject left for further investigation.

Now we must turn our attention squarely back to the Red Atlantic. In chapter 1, we begin by examining the stories of those who traveled to it and around it unwillingly.

1

⁓

For He Looks upon You as Foolish Children

Captives, Slaves, and Prisoners of the Red Atlantic

THE LATE JACK FORBES, in his provocative book *Africans and Native Americans*, notes a curious incident reported by Pliny the Elder in his *Naturalis Historiae* on the authority of Cornelius Nepo. Pliny states that Quintus Metellus Celer, who was a colleague of Lucius Africanius in the consulship of Rome, while in Gaul received the gift of "*Indos,*" "who on a trade voyage had been carried off course [from India] by storms to Germany," from a Germanic chieftain.[1] Forbes says that the event, which would have taken place around 60 B.C.E., and the presence of Indians in Germany would have been explicable to Pliny because he believed a sea connected the Indian Ocean with the Baltic. Such a waterway is, of course, fictitious. Forbes writes, "We know, however, that the only way people looking like 'Indians' could have been driven by a storm to northern Europe would have been across the Atlantic from America."[2] He speculates that these might have been Olmecs or "the builders of Teotihuacan."[3]

There is much reason to doubt Pliny's account. His ethnographic materials are largely fantasy. And Forbes overlooks that it was Columbus, more than fourteen centuries later, who labeled Western Hemisphere indigenes "Indians" because he thought he had reached the Indies. If we discount wish fulfillment or fanciful speculation, the first indigenous North Americans to reach Europe were almost certainly Beothuks (or members of an ancestral population thereof), and like Pliny's and Forbes's "*Indos,*" they were captives.[4]

They were merely the first of over thousands upon thousands of Western Hemisphere indigenes to become captives and slaves. These

Natives would find their way to Iceland and Norway, England, France, Portugal, Germany, Bermuda, the Caribbean and other islands off the Americas, and even North Africa, among other far-flung destinations.

Two Beothuk Boys

Leif Erikson sighted the northern coast of North America in approximately 1000 C.E., calling it Vinland. Shortly thereafter, around 1003, the Vikings founded a settlement in present-day L'Anse aux Meadows, Newfoundland. They encountered "Red Indians" (as distinguished from the Inuit), whom they called *skrælings*, an archaic word of uncertain meaning but commonly assumed to mean something like "wretches." These meetings are recorded in the Icelandic sagas.

According to the *Grænlendinga Saga*, encounters with the Natives were initially friendly. Despite the language barrier, trade was opened, but the relationship soon turned hostile.[5] In *Eirik's Saga*, we learn that Leif's brother Thorvald was struck in the groin by an arrow in one skirmish with *skrælings*. As he pulls the arrow out, he poetically and tragically says, "This is a rich country we have found; there is plenty of fat around my entrails." Then he expires—nobly.[6]

Controversial historian Jayme Sokolow summarizes: "The Vikings treated the *Skraelings* as they would any other outsiders. When the opportunity arose, they killed the adults and enslaved their children. On other occasions, they traded bolts of red cloth for furs."[7] After Thorvald Erikson's death, the Vikings fled. They spotted five Natives, "a bearded man, two women, and two children."[8] Though the adults manage to escape, Thorfinn Karlsefni and his men captured the boys, whom they took with them. The boys were taught Norse and baptized.[9] Thus in 1009, Indian captives were taken to Norway (and perhaps Iceland).[10]

The names of these boys forcibly orphaned are not recorded, but those of their mother and father are: according to the sagas, the children identified them as Vætild and Ovægir, respectively. Jennings Wise and Vine Deloria Jr. say that the boys were christened Valthof and Vimar.[11]

Continuing conflict with the *skrælings* convinced Karlsefni of the futility of attempting a permanent settlement in North America. According to Gwyn Jones, "His numbers were small, and their weapons inadequate. They were unwilling to woo and unable to conquer."[12] The fact that they took the boys and taught them their language is strong evidence that they intended to continue trading with the region's indigenous people. Valthof and Vimar would be able to serve as interpreters. Such abductions became an established strategy in this regard.

The penultimate chapter of the *Grænlendinga Saga* begins, "Now there was renewed talk of voyaging to Vinland, for these expeditions were considered a good source of fame and fortune."[13] Annette Kolodny writes, "Obviously, the potential threat posed by the Native population has not dissuaded some individuals from further expeditions, although there is no longer any suggestion at attempting a permanent colony."[14] The Vikings "continued visiting the North American coast in search of timber and furs, but after 1300 the climate grew colder and travel became more difficult."[15] Eventually they ceased entirely. Around 1350, the Vikings abandoned the Western Settlement in Greenland, and by 1500, settlement on that island ceased entirely. By then, however, Greenland's days as a jumping-off point for North American exploration were long in the past. The last record of a specific voyage to Vinland was that of Bishop Eirik (probably Eirik Gnupsson) in 1121, and we do not even know if he reached it successfully.[16] According to Dutch anthropologist Harald Prins, however, there is "an intriguing historical snippet" about a large canoe that Newfoundlander Natives were putting into port at Lubec in 1153. Prins concludes that, if the incident happened at all, both Natives and canoe most probably came on a Viking *knarr*.

Years later, circa 1420, Inuit captives were taken to Scandinavia. Their kayaks were displayed in the cathedral at Tromsø, Norway. In 2010, DNA analysis of contemporary Icelanders revealed a strain of mitochrondrial DNA most closely associated with Amerindian populations. This so-called C1 lineage is carried by more than eighty Icelanders, and church records have permitted researchers to trace the specific substrain (or subclade), known as C1e, to four women from shortly before 1700, though they believe it arrived much earlier. C1e has been found only in Iceland and does not match Greenlander or any other Inuit population. Nor does it precisely match any modern Native population. Since mitochondrial DNA is passed down only through the female line, the logical conclusion is that it entered via a woman from some now extinct Amerindian lineage. The Beothuk, the last of whom died in 1829, would seem the likely candidate. Razib Khan, a science writer for *Discover*, writes, "Perhaps the Europeans had enslaved a native woman, and taken her back to their homeland when they decamped? But more likely to me is the probability that the Norse brought back more than lumber from Markland, since their voyages spanned centuries."[17] It is certainly possible; grabbing a few North American indigenes quickly became a standard operating procedure of European sailors, and the Vikings certainly had a reputation for being rapacious.

Though Valthof and Vimar may have become the first Amerindian cosmopolitans, the Vikings departed for their homelands and left no continued colonial presence in North America. Their clashes with the Natives and their capture and kidnapping of the two Beothuk boys, however, established the pattern of European interaction with the continent's indigenes that would be replicated many times over. That information undoubtedly traveled from tribe to tribe beneath the Fall and beyond through trading networks. The seeds of distrust and knowledge of settler violence and indigenous captivity were sown from Newfoundland to Florida. Unfortunately for the next people to be "discovered" by explorers from Europe, they were not part of the trade routes that would have carried word of the *"skrœlings'"* difficulties with such people.

A Man Obsessed I

Christopher Columbus was a man of consuming personal ambition. He was also a man of many obsessions. These two aspects of his personality were symbiotic. His ambition drove him to multiple obsessions. And, in turn, the objects of his obsessions became, he believed, the means to fulfill his ambitions.

Born Cristoforo Columbo in or near Genoa on the Italian coast, he was the son of a weaver. Little reliable is known about his childhood, but it seems he went to sea at a fairly early age, alternating between voyages on the Mediterranean and periods onshore, working for his father. Without formal education, he became an autodidact, reading and internalizing the travel accounts that were popular at the time. Seven of the books he owned survive. These include Pliny the Elder's *Naturalis Historiae* with its travelers' tales and fantastic ethnographies, Marco Polo's exaggerated report of his journey to China, and Pierre d'Ailly's *Imago Mundi*. Published in 1410, the last of these, written by a French cleric, was an imaginative, pseudo-scientific cosmography.[18] Such works fueled Columbus's imagination and his desire to travel to exotic locales. D'Ailly's book in particular influenced him. D'Ailly suggested the possibility of reaching Asia by sailing west from Europe. Columbus's copy is filled with the sailor's marginalia.

The myth that surrounds Columbus claims that he was among the first to believe that the world was round. Others feared sailing west for fear of falling off the edge of a flat earth. Such tales are the product of modern childhood stories and grade school textbooks. In truth, most educated people at the time knew the earth was round. Sailors were merely reluctant to sail west into a vast, open Atlantic. Yet writers like d'Ailly fixed Columbus's obsession to reach the Indies, Japan, and China by sailing west. His fixation led to his "discovery" of the Americas and the re-inauguration of the Red Atlantic.

Columbus's second obsession, less peculiar to himself, was gold. In a letter to Father Martinez, Paolo Toscanelli urged the priest to let the Portuguese king know how profitable an undertaking a voyage to Asia would be: Japan, he said, was rich in gold. As noted in the introduction, one need only read Bartolomé de Las Casas's *Brief Account of the Destruction of the Indies* to get a sense of the place indigenes' gold held in the minds of later Spanish explorers and conquistadores. All came in search of the wealth of the Americas. For Columbus, there was a special urgency. In exchange for the Catholic Monarchs' investment in his enterprise, the mariner had promised them riches beyond measure. In return, they had promised him 10 percent of the wealth brought from Asia along his new route, not only by himself but by anyone and not only in his lifetime but to his heirs for all future time. Some obsession is understandable.

On October 12, 1492, Columbus set his first dry foot on Western Hemisphere land on what is today commonly assumed to be Watlings Island in the Bahamas. Columbus's original log of that first voyage was lost. What we have is an abstract of it produced by Las Casas some forty years after the Admiral's death. In that document, commonly called the *Journal of the First Voyage to America*, the narrator is sometimes Las Casas and sometimes Columbus himself, whom Las Casas quotes. We also have a letter that Columbus wrote, reporting on his journey, after his arrival at Lisbon in March 1493.

Stepping ashore, Columbus called the men in his landing party together "to bear witness that he before all others took possession (as in fact he did) of that island for the King and Queen his sovereigns, making the requisite declarations."[19] In his letter addressed to the royal treasurer Luis de Santángel, Columbus himself describes the incident and

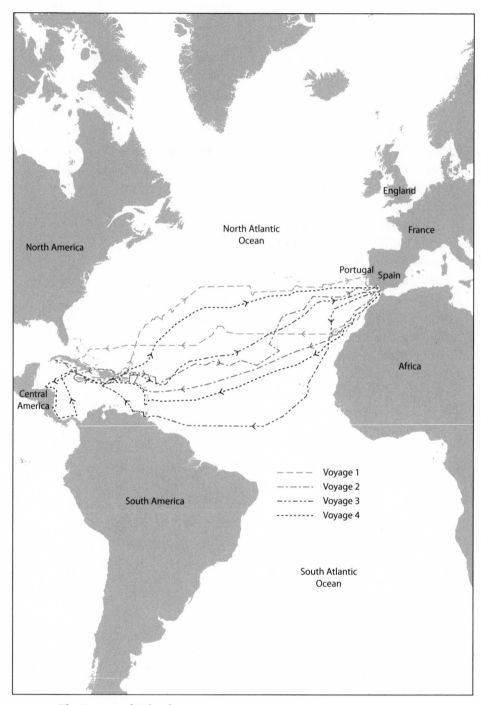

The Voyages of Columbus

others like it: "I came to the Indian sea, where I found many islands in-habited by men without number, of all which I took possession for our most fortunate king, with proclaiming heralds and flying standards, no one objecting."[20] He named the place San Salvador for the Holy Savior. Seemingly conveniently for Columbus, as he was completing his legalis-tic rituals of discovery, according to Las Casas, "Numbers of the people of the island straightway collected together."[21] Of the encounter, the Admiral declared, "As I saw that they were very friendly to us, and per-ceived that they could be much more easily converted to our holy faith by gentle means than by force, I presented them with some red caps, and strings of beads to wear upon the neck, and many other trifles of small value, wherewith they were much delighted, and became wonderfully attached to us."[22]

The people who gathered around Columbus on the beach as he claimed their land for the Spanish crown were the Taino, who called the island Guanahani. By the time they set eyes on the Spanish seamen, they were themselves old hands at plying the Atlantic. The Taino are also called the Island Arawak to both relate them to, and distinguish them from, the Arawak who reside in northeastern South America. Sometime around 500 B.C.E., Archaic Taino—the ancestors of those whom Colum-bus would meet—split off from their non-seafaring Arawak relatives and set forth on the Caribbean. By 900 C.E., they occupied the Greater Antil-les islands of Cuba, Hispaniola (present-day Haiti and the Dominican Republic), Jamaica, and Puerto Rico and the southern part of the Baha-mas. They routinely used their large dugout canoes to travel between islands.[23]

There is no record of what Columbus said to the curious Indians who crowded around him on that beach on Guanahani. An educated guess, however, is that the first confusing words the indigene heard this white man utter were "Salaam aleichem," the standard Muslim greeting, trans-lated as "Peace be upon you." Arabic, the language of that salutation, was the lingua franca of commerce at the time, and almost anyone engaged in trade and commerce would speak at least some of it. The Admiral's interpreter was fluent, and Columbus himself assumed he had reached Asia where he would be addressing merchants: "Salaam aleichem [Peace be upon you]."

Whatever the form and substance of Columbus's address to what must have been confused indigenes, at that moment of first contact, he reestablished the Red Atlantic, first commenced far to the north by the Vikings' arrival. He also initiated a delicate minuet, a dance in which European and indigenous partners came together and then moved apart amid demand and coercion on one hand and resistance on the other. It was a dance in which the participants put distance between themselves but never entirely detached and separated, as much as the indigenes might have wished to do so.

Columbus wrote, "I was very attentive to them, and strove to learn if they had any gold. Seeing some of them with little bits of this metal hanging at their noses, I gathered from them by signs that by going southward or steering round the island in that direction, there would be found a king who possessed large vessels of gold, and in great quantities. I endeavoured to procure them to lead the way thither, but found they were unacquainted with the route."[24] Here, without ever having seen another European and with communication with the ones before them limited to gestures, the Taino developed what would become a routine stratagem. In the face of avaricious demands by Spaniards for gold, Natives simply pointed them farther down the line: "Oh, you want gold? You know who has gobs of gold? That king over there. Just keep moving. This way to the gold." Columbus, for his part, was quicker than most to catch on to the ruse. On October 15, he wrote in his journal, "About sunset we anchored near the cape which terminates the island towards the [West] to enquire for gold, for the natives we had taken from San Salvador told me that the people here wore golden bracelets upon their arms and legs. I believed pretty confidently that they had invented this story in order to escape from us, still I determined to pass none of these islands without taking possession, because being once taken, it would answer for all times."[25]

Although Columbus's obsession with gold remained largely unsated, it would endure as a major theme throughout the first voyage. In the portion of the journal entry from October 15 quoted above, however ("the natives we had taken from San Salvador," "I believed pretty confidently that they had invented this story in order to escape from us"), yet another of his obsessions is revealed: slavery.

Biographer Kirkpatrick Sale, in his *The Conquest of Paradise: Christopher Columbus and the Columbian Legacy*, notes that it is unknown whether slavery was in Columbus's mind from the start of his enterprise (as his other two obsessions unquestionably were). Yet once in the Indies, he seized upon the notion immediately. In his journal entry for October 12—the very day he first met the Taino—he offered the following assessment: "I appears to me, that the people are ingenious, and would be good servants; and I am of the opinion that they would very readily become Christians, as they appear to have no religion. They very quickly learn such words as are spoken to them. If it please our Lord, I intend at my return to carry home six of them to your Highnesses, that they may learn our language." Sale states, "It may fairly be called the birth of American slavery."[26] Columbus said that, should the monarchs wish it, the entire populace could be shipped to Castile or enslaved in situ to work on the island. He wrote, "I could conquer the whole of them with fifty men, and govern them as I pleased."[27]

As the Vikings had done in kidnapping Valthof and Vimar, Columbus immediately began nabbing Tainos and detaining them aboard his ships. Columbus used them, in the first instance, as guides to sources of the gold he so fervently sought. Also like the Norse, though, he desired to bring his captives back to the homeland for language instruction. In the report made upon his return, he wrote, "As soon as I reached that sea [the Caribbean], I seized by force several Indians on the first island, in order that they might learn from us, and in like manner tell us about those things in these lands of which they themselves had knowledge; and the plan succeeded, for in a short time we understood them and they us, sometimes by gestures and signs, sometimes by words; and it was a great advantage to us. They are coming with me now."[28]

In his journal, Columbus refers to six such captives accompanying him. Elsewhere in the same document, he refers to seven. Both numbers are post-diction—as opposed to pre-diction—calculated and written after the fact. Columbus did take six Indian captives with him when he met with Ferdinand and Isabella. These, however, were only the survivors.

Columbus and his captains seized many more captives. Perhaps the most callous incident of kidnapping is described by Columbus in his journal entry for November 12:

Yesterday a canoe came to the ship with six young men; five of them came on board, whom I ordered detained, and have them with me; I then sent ashore to one of the houses, and took seven women and three children: this I did that the Indians might tolerate their captivity better with their company. . . . Besides, these women will be a great help to us in acquiring their language, which is the same throughout all these countries, the inhabitants keeping up a communication among the islands by means of their canoes. . . . This evening came on board the husband of one of the women and father of the three children, which were a boy and two girls; he intreated me to let him accompany them, which I very willingly granted; the natives whom I had taken from here were all so delighted at this as to induce me to think them his relations.[29]

Columbus evokes the experience of the Portuguese with slaves they had taken from Guinea in Africa.

Columbus arrived in Portugal on March 4, 1493, with ten captive indigenes. The following day, an official arrived under armed escort and instructed him that he must accompany them to give an accounting to the stewards of King João. Columbus replied that he would comply only under force. He served the king and queen of Castile, "and it was the custom of Castilian Admirals rather to die than deliver up either themselves or their men."[30] The Portuguese relented and, after examining Columbus's letters from the Catholic Monarchs, withdrew.

By March 6, news of Columbus and his curious cargo's arrival had spread, and "there came a vast multitude from the city to visit him, and see the Indians."[31] The throng of gawkers continued unabated the following day. Among the crowd were two royal stewards. On March 8, Columbus received a letter from King João, asking that the Admiral visit him at Val do Paraiso, a monastery about twenty-five miles northeast of Lisbon.

Columbus arrived at the royal court on March 9, bringing with him several of the Indians. These captives thus became the first Western Hemisphere indigenes ever presented to a European ruler. According to accounts, King João was "startled by their nakedness yet impressed by their intelligence."[32] The king's purpose in requesting the audience was not, however, to inspect Columbus's exotic specimens. It was rather to inform the mariner that, pursuant to the Treaty of Alcaçovas, which João had signed with Ferdinand and Isabella in 1479, all the lands Columbus had claimed belonged to Portugal. For his part, Columbus responded that he knew nothing of the treaty, but in any event he had not visited Africa but the Indies. On March 11, as Columbus took his leave, the king gave him a letter for the Catholic Monarchs. On the way back to his ship, the Admiral stopped at the monastery of St. Anthony to pay his respects to the Portuguese queen, at her request. He raised anchor on March 13.[33]

Two days later, Columbus arrived back in Palos de la Frontera, the port from whence he had set sail for the Indies. He then proceeded to Seville. There he received a letter from the king and queen addressed to "Don Cristóbal Colón, Admiral of the Ocean Sea, Viceroy and Governor of the islands he has discovered in the Indies."

Among those who were there to see Columbus was Bartolomé de Las Casas. In time, he would play a major role in the Red Atlantic as a leader of the so-called *indigenista* movement of Spaniards who sought fairer treatment of the indigenous peoples of the Americas, but that day in Seville, he was a mere child, a boy of nine. On that day, young Bartolomé glimpsed his first Indians. He later recalled seeing seven of them: "They had been put alongside the Arch of the Images, at San Nicolás." Las Casas biographer Gustavo Gutiérrez writes of the scene and the thoughts it must have conjured in the boy's mind:

> At that tender age, then, he saw for the first time, with innocent cu-
> riosity and astonishment, those to whom—and this time it was they
> who would be astonished—he would later devote his life. There would
> be no point in our trying to penetrate what went through this child's
> head at the sight he beheld at the arch of the Images. But we may
> surely think that the grown man recounting this scene is rereading
> that first experience, and, in retrospect, feels that it was by God's will
> that it occurred symbolically in his native city, with which he would
> always feel such close ties. . . . The friar from Seville is fully aware of
> the crucial role of personal experience and will refer to it a thousand
> ways all his life long.[34]

Later, in November 1493, the boy's father, Pedro de Las Casas, and three of his uncles would ship out with Columbus on his second voyage to the Indies. The results of that second voyage would make an even more lasting impression on the boy. But at this moment, he was merely another gawker, but an extra in the unfolding drama.

Columbus left four of the Indians in Seville, almost certainly due to critically ill health (had they been able to travel, Columbus would have been deeply desirous that they accompany him to court). Nothing more is reported of them, and they no doubt expired from some European disease to which they had no immunity, as would so many other indigenes who would travel the Red Atlantic. The Admiral took the surviving six with him on the 800-mile journey to Barcelona, where the Spanish court was sitting at the time.

Columbus was eager to give the king and queen an account of his voyage and justify himself in the face of "the opposition of so many of the principal persons of your [the monarchs'] household, who were all against me, and ridiculed my project."[35] According to Columbus's illegitimate son Fernando, in his 1538 work *The Life of Admiral Christopher Columbus* (also written partly by Las Casas), "Everyone came from everywhere . . . to gaze at him and at the Indians and other strange objects that he brought with him."[36] One cannot help but notice the casual colonialist equation of the indigenes with "other strange objects"—parrots, exotic species of flora, and so forth. Unfortunately, similar comparisons became all too common in the process of conquest and colonization. Europeans often saw and depicted Western Hemispheric indigenes as merely part of the natural environment—like plants and animals—and thus less than human.

Once the group reached the royal court, the Catholic Monarchs arranged and witnessed the first ritual event of its kind—the religious conversion of Indians to the Christian faith. According to Vaughan, "In an elegant and poignant ceremony, six Indians received baptism and prestigious new names, among them 'Fernando de Aragon,' 'Don Juan de Castilla,' and 'Don Diego Colon'; the Spanish king, queen, and young prince served as godparents. Newly named Don Juan de Castilla would attend the royal family for the remaining two years of his life as evidence of Columbus' navigational achievement and the natives' adaptability to Spanish customs."[37] As the Vikings undoubtedly intended for the Beothuk boys Valthof and Vimar, and as the Admiral explicitly stated in his journal of his first voyage, language instruction was a principal reason for bringing Natives to Spain, so that they might serve as interpreters on future expeditions. That first Native sacrament of baptism that the royals observed in 1493 would be replicated many times over in the years to come. To again quote Vaughan, "Many subsequent Indian captives who survived the Atlantic crossing and the onslaught of European pathogens learned the Castilian language, converted to Catholicism, imparted information about their homelands, and returned to America as quasi-

Spaniards."[38] A new class, indeed a new caste, was born. It is important to note that not all transatlantic Natives came as captives. Some came willingly. In 1502, Ferdinand and Isabella issued a decree that any who wanted to come, learn Spanish, and return home should be brought over. Two of the original surviving six Columbian captives would return with the Admiral on his second voyage in September 1493, serving as interpreters.

This second voyage was very different in a number of ways from the first just one year earlier. Instead of two small caravels and a *náo*, the Admiral of the Ocean Sea now led a veritable fleet of no less than seventeen ships, carrying 1,200 to 1,500 men. The second major difference was the relative ease of the passage. The ships got underway on September 24 and sailed first to the Canary Islands off the coast of Africa. They weighed anchor there on October 13 and arrived at the island of Dominica in the Lesser Antilles on November 3. As Hans Koning states, the easy voyage makes one wonder "why it had not been done long before." The answer is obvious, of course, and Koning himself provides it, writing, "Geographically no other crossing . . . matched the first one. The mystery barrier had been broken."[39] The Red Atlantic had been opened up.

A third crucial difference was the reception and reaction of the indigenous peoples. Their main acts of resistance during the first voyage were what might be considered passive, attempting to meet Spanish demands for gold by simply pointing them down the line to other islands. By now, news of the Spaniards' activities had spread throughout the islands, and their inhabitants employed strategies that they had begun to use increasingly by the end of Columbus's first voyage. Repeatedly, Columbus found abandoned villages upon his arrival. The indigenes fled at his approach.

But physical violence was yet another response. When Columbus had departed for Spain on the first voyage, he left behind thirty-nine men to garrison a fort, which he named La Navidad, on Hispaniola. He returned on November 27, 1493, expecting to see a thriving settlement. He found instead corpses littering the beach and the colony destroyed. Through his captive Taino interpreters, local Indians told Columbus that after his departure, the men of La Navidad had rampaged over the island, searching for gold, taking captives, raping women and boys. Finally, the people whom the Admiral had viewed as innocent, peaceful, and "inoffensive," long ago relieved of their innocence, retaliated. No member of the garrison survived. Other violent clashes were to follow.[40]

A final, related critical difference between Columbus's first and second voyages was the actions of the Spaniards themselves. This last is a difference not so much in fundamental character as in what might be called volume.

Columbus was under pressure to show some tangible return on the investment of his royal patrons. Since gold had not materialized in promised quantities, another commodity had to be found. On his second voyage, Columbus became a serious slaver. In massive slave raids, Spaniards rounded up 1,600 men, women, and children to fill the holds of supply ships returning to Spain and placed them in open pens at the new Spaniard settlement of Isabela, named for the Spanish queen. Because the returning vessels could hold only around 500 slaves as cargo, only the best were selected for transport. Spaniards in Hispaniola were permitted to select from the remainder. Those not chosen, numbering about 400, were simply considered something like "army surplus" and summarily released. According to Michele de Cuneo, an Italian nobleman on the voyage who described the pitiable scene, "They rushed in all directions like lunatics, women dropping and abandoning infants in the rush, running for miles without stopping, fleeing across mountains and rivers."[41] These terrified indigenes were the lucky ones.

The 550 Indians selected for shipment were loaded into the departing ships. By the time the ships dropped anchor in Cadiz, 200 had died, their bodies simply thrown overboard. Half of the remainder were sick. Cuneo attributed it to "unaccustomed air, colder than theirs." Cuneo concluded that "they are not working people and they very much fear cold, nor have they long life."[42] Most of the survivors, including the seriously ill, were put up for sale in Seville. Only a handful survived.

One of those who did survive was a Taino boy whom they called Juanico ("little Juan"). Pedro de Las Casas gave him as a present to his son Bartolomé. The gift has been described variously as one of a "companion," a "servant," even a "pet." Regardless of how he has been characterized, he was by any definition a captive and a slave.

Queen Isabella was reportedly enraged that her Indian subjects were being enslaved. After judicial proceedings, by royal decree, the surviving Natives were ordered released and returned to their homeland. Among those who set sail in June 1500 was Juanico.

The high mortality rates rendered the slave trade unprofitable, and Columbus focused again on gold. Nevertheless, he wrote, "Let us in the name of the Holy Trinity go on sending all the slaves that can be sold."[43] Slavery and lust for gold would shortly come together in a very important way with major repercussions for the Red Atlantic.

Isabella's horror at having her Native subjects enslaved led the Catholic Monarchs to order a halt to the importation of indigenes purely for the purposes of slavery; the church also worried about the effect of the practice on potential converts. Yet, as Vaughan notes, the monarchs' rules were sometimes laxly enforced, and there were major exceptions: "Slavery was permissible as a punishment for resisting Spanish occupation, for rebellion against Spanish authority, and for actions deemed criminal in Spanish law."[44] Columbus and others on his second voyage became convinced (or rather convinced themselves despite a total lack of evidence) that the Carib of the eastern Caribbean were cannibals, and in 1494 the Admiral asked the crown for permission to capture Caribs for shipment to Spain, describing them as "a people so fierce, healthy, well-proportioned, and intelligent that, once rid of that inhumanity, they would make better slaves than any others."[45] The monarchs decided, however, that was an insufficient reason to enslave the Carib, a position that Isabella would rescind in 1503.[46]

Ferdinand and Isabella's abjuration of slavery applied only to shipments of slaves to Spain. In the New World, Columbus required Indians—men and women—to produce a fixed amount of gold every three months. The results were meager. When this system of forced labor proved unworkable, in 1496, Columbus instituted on Hispaniola a prototype for the encomienda system. An encomienda was the grant of a specific tract of land to a Spaniard (the encomendero) as an estate or plantation. The encomendero was entitled to collect tribute or require labor from the Natives within his entrusted territory. Though there were supposed formal safeguards, in practice it differed little from outright slavery. The system was eventually introduced throughout Ibero-America.

In March 1496, Columbus set sail for Spain. With him, he took thirty-six more slaves. Spain would outlaw Indian slavery in the middle of the next century, but before that happened, Spaniards enslaved tens of thousands of Natives. Most of these were kept in situ, where they were worked to death. In Guatemala, for instance, the Spanish had a saying, "Who needs horses, when you have Indians?" Even so, thousands of Western Hemisphere indigenes would see slavery in Spain. Many more died in transit.

Christopher Columbus would make two more voyages to the New World, gold and slaves being prominent motifs in both. But it was the first two trips that established the critical patterns for all that subsequently transpired. According to historian Felipe Fernández-Armesto, "Between them, Columbus's ocean crossings of 1492–93 established the most practical and exploitable routes back and forth across the Atlantic, linking the densely populated belt of the Old World, which stretched from China across southern and southwestern Asia to span the Mediterranean, with the threshold of the richest and most populous regions of the New World."[47] By the close of the fifteenth century, less than eight years after Columbus set foot on Guanahani, Europeans had made landfalls from Newfoundland to Brazil. The actions of the Admiral also, most crucially, created the woeful template for European interaction with the indigenous peoples of the Americas. Subsequent explorers and other sailors routinely followed his practice of kidnapping and enslaving Natives. Despite the "Black Legend" of Spanish cruelty (which, as we will see in chapter 5, Las Casas inadvertently did much to create), no country's adventurers were immune. Among the notable explorers who captured Natives in the late fifteenth and early sixteenth centuries were the Portuguese Gaspar Corte Real; Sebastian Cabot, sailing for England; and Giovanni da Verrazzano and Jacques Cartier, both in the service of Francis I of France.[48] And while Sir Walter Raleigh was imprisoned in the Tower of London by King James I from 1603 until 1616, he was sometimes served by Natives from Trinidad or Guiana.[49]

Regarding Spain, in her book *Indians Abroad, 1493–1938*, Carolyn Thomas Foreman says that Amerigo Vespucci (the man from whom the Americas take their name), on his first voyage in 1501 brought back 222 Indians to Cadiz, which he sold as slaves. According to her, when Vespucci found friendly indigenes "better conditioned" than those he had encountered previously, "He determined to take a pair of men from this place, that they might teach [them] their language, and three of them volunteered to go to Portugal."[50] Foreman's statement is based on questionable evidence. If the incident did occur, it would not have taken place in 1501 but as a result of the voyage of Alonso de Hojeda, whom Vespucci accompanied, in 1499. That the account was at all credible speaks to the prevalence of such activities. Hojeda had sailed with Columbus on his second and third voyages and had participated with the Admiral in slave raiding.

The Destruction of a People

In Vine Deloria's 1971 revised edition of Jennings Wise's 1931 *The Red Man in the New World Drama*, there is a fable. The authors state that at one time there was an annual gathering of men of letters at the Inn of William the Conqueror at Dives-sur-Mer in Normandy. In that seaside setting, each participant took a turn telling his fellows "an informing story." One of these ran as follows:

> A whaling vessel came upon an undiscovered arctic island. About the crew the unaffrighted penguins crowded with a show of confidence that appealed to the sympathies even of the rough seamen. The men conceived a great fondness for the dumb creatures who seemed almost human in their affections. Unfortunately the ship's dog got loose in the night before the ship sailed and killed an entire brood of helpless young penguins. The next year the sailors longing to see their bird friends again returned to the island. Not a penguin was seen until they were discovered in their distant hiding place. The dog had destroyed their trust. Fear had been born among them. Now they only desired to be let alone in their solitude. Man had nothing to offer them which they prized as much as security.[51]

I am well aware, of course, that there are no penguins in the Arctic. So were Deloria and Wise. The term "penguin" was often used, however, to refer to the great auk (now extinct) well before the discovery of the Antarctic species. The story is completely in keeping with how the bird was described in other accounts.[52] As I said, what is offered is a fable, an apologue illustrating a simple moral point. The penguins are transparent stand-ins for Natives. After initially approaching the strange newcomers in a spirit of welcome and hospitality, they were victimized by the Europeans: fear supplanted trust.

The Beothuk were the first indigenous people in North America to encounter Europeans in the form of the Vikings. Some of them died. Others, like Valthof, Vimar, and perhaps others unknown to us, were captured and carried away to Iceland and Norway. And because the lords of history seem to have, by turns, first an ironic and then a tragic sense of humor, the Beothuk would get to repeat the process. Nearly 500 years after meeting the Norse, they would have the chance to be first a second time.

The Beothuk occupied the island we know today as Newfoundland. Much of the year they lived on the shore. They gathered shellfish along the beach; they fished and hunted sea mammals from their canoes. Those canoes were sturdy, and the Beothuk were highly skilled at handling them. According to anthropologist Alan McMillan, "Collecting birds' eggs was an important activity, for which expeditions were made as far away as Funk Island, a trip of about 65 kilometres across the rough North Atlantic."[53] During the winter, they migrated inland, where they lived off caribou.

Much of what we know about the Beothuk comes from accounts from the eighteenth and early nineteenth centuries. They traditionally may, in fact, have lived on the coastline year-round. Archaeological evidence suggests that moving to the interior of the island was a late pre-Contact adaptation. It is even possible that such migrations may have been a response to European incursions. Given Beothuk behavior after renewed European contact, this seems probable. After the Columbus event, such contacts came early and often.

Christopher Columbus was known by many names. The sailor from Genoa would have been known in his hometown as Christoffa Corombo. Elsewhere in Italy he was known as Cristoforo Columbo. In Portugal, where he lived and worked for several years, he was Cristofõm Colon. In Queen Isabella's Castile, he was called Cristóbal Colón. In Catalan-speaking Barcelona, he was Christobal Colom. Christopher Columbus is an Anglicization of his name in Latin: Christophorus Columbus.

John Cabot, the mariner who now enters our story of the Red Atlantic, shared much in common with the Admiral of the Ocean Sea. Like Columbus, he was Italian, and he, too, was a man of many identities. As a citizen of Venice, he signed himself Zuan Chabotto. In Italian, he was called Giovanni Caboto. In Spain, where he appears to have fled to avoid his creditors, he was known as Juan Caboto and Johan Caboto Montecalunya (in Catalan-speaking Valencia, where he lived after fleeing Venice). Sometime, probably in his forties, he moved to Bristol, England, and became John Cabotto, or simply John Cabot. And, finally, like his contemporary, a fellow-Italian sailor, he was a man of consummate ambition who found his greatest success sailing for a country other than his own.[54]

After news of Columbus's voyage reached England, Cabot petitioned King Henry VII for permission to undertake a western voyage. In March 1496, the king responded by granting a patent "to sail to all parts, regions and coasts of the eastern, western and northern sea, under our banners, flags and ensigns, with five ships or vessels of whatsoever burden and quality they may be, and with so many and with such mariners and men as they may wish to take with them in the said ships, at their own proper costs and charges, to find, discover and investigate whatsoever islands, countries, regions or provinces of heathens and infidels, in whatsoever part of the world placed, which before this time were unknown to all Christians."[55]

Cabot launched his first voyage of exploration from Bristol, apparently during the summer of 1496, with a single ship. According to a contemporary letter written by John Day, a London merchant living at the time in Bristol, to the "Great Admiral" of Spain (presumably Columbus), this expedition was cut short: "his crew confused him, he was short of supplies and ran into bad weather, and he decided to turn back."[56] Undeterred and better equipped and provisioned (and presumably with a less "confusing" crew), Cabot set sail from Bristol sometime in May 1497. Thirty-five to fifty days later, on June 24, Cabot and his crew made landfall in North America, almost certainly in Newfoundland. That day, John Cabot became the first documented European since the Norse to set foot in North America.

The scant documentary evidence and modern scholars generally agree that Cabot made no direct contact with indigenes on that second voyage. He did discover what appeared to be a deserted Beothuk camp on the beach. There was a dead fire, a net, a needle for making nets, a carved wooden tool painted with red ochre, and snares (presumably for birds or small game). A trail led from the campsite inland.

It had been at least 150 years since the Vikings last sailed to Vinland. Did the Beothuk remember? Did they carry stories of those contacts in their oral tradition? Did they resort to the same tactic that Columbus encountered among the Taino (especially on his second voyage) and flee? Certainly they would employ this stratagem later on. Perhaps they had seen Portuguese or other sailors who are rumored to have preceded Cabot.

This represented Cabot's only landfall on that voyage. He and his men stayed just long enough to inspect the site, take on fresh water, and claim the land for Henry VII. They penetrated the land no farther than the distance a crossbow could shoot a bolt. Anthropologist and historian Peter Pope, in his book *The Many Landfalls of John Cabot*, writes that "he feared contact, given his small crew. . . . The fact that he landed only once speaks volumes."[57] After leaving this single landing, Cabot's ship did skirt the coast, taking in the landscape.

It is possible that Cabot saw Beothuks at a distance through the trees. They would likely have wanted to monitor this visitor. At any rate, whether through Cabot or via those who would shortly come after him, the Beothuk became the original "Red Indians." The designation had nothing to do with skin color. Rather, the Beothuk, along with their neighbors the Mi'kmaq and Innu, decorated their faces and bodies with red ochre paint.

The Beothuk survived the incursions of the Vikings relatively unscathed. To be sure, there were armed clashes. And some, like Valthof and Vimar (and at least a few others), were carried away. There is no indication in the archaeological record, however, of a demographic collapse due to virgin soil plagues—those European diseases against which Western Hemisphere indigenes were defenseless—or any other reason, such as occurred in the Caribbean in the wake of Columbus's coming (and as would occur in many other places in the wake of Contact and colonization). Their population seems to have come through relatively stable. Estimates for the number of Beothuks at the time of Cabot's voyage range from a few hundred to several thousand.[58]

This time, however, the Beothuk were not to be so fortunate. Cabot's arrival set in motion a chain of events that would devastate them.

A moment ago, I said that the limited documentary testimony about Cabot's voyage supported the view that the explorer did not make direct contact with Indians on his expedition. There is, however, an exception. In his 1582 *Divers Voyages Touching the Discoverie of America*, the English writer Richard Hakluyt, a major early advocate of colonization of North America, quotes an unpublished and otherwise unknown section of the *Chronicle* of Robert Fabyan, a history of England until Henry VII published in 1515 (Fabyan died in 1513). The quoted passage details three Newfoundlanders brought to Henry's court by John Cabot: "three savage men . . . clothed in beasts skinnes" ate raw meat and "spake such speech that not a man coulde understand them." Fabyan, according to Hakluyt, then recounted that "two yeeres after, I saw two [of the three] apparelled after the manner of Englishmen in Westminster pallace, which that time I could not discerne from Englishmen." Although Hakluyt's placement of this story of the acculturating powers of English civilization seems to indicate that Cabot was responsible, the incident referred to the seventeenth year of Henry's reign, making it 1502, at least three years after the mariner disappeared during his third expedition to the New World.[59]

Yet what fired European imaginations about Cabot's discovery was neither a few pieces of Atlantic coastal material culture—a net, a needle, a wooden tool of unknown usage—nor three indigene captives purportedly brought back to England. It was rather something else the adventurer saw on his voyage: fish. John Day told the Spanish "Admiral," "All along this coast, they found many fish like those which in Iceland are dried in the open and sold in England and other countries, and called in English 'stockfish,'" that is to say, cod. Cabot himself reported that the Atlantic was "swarming with fish, which can be taken not only with the net, but in baskets let down with a stone."[60] Such an overly abundant resource could not go unexploited and would inevitably attract an avaricious element eager to profit, just as Ibero-America drew not the flower of Spanish society but those so greedy for yellow wealth that Indians would think gold their god. Indigenes, especially the Beothuk, would bear the brunt of the assault.

As I alluded above, there are unsubstantiated and discredited rumors of English or Portuguese sailors or fishermen reaching what is today the north Canadian coast prior to Cabot, dating back to perhaps 1494 (and, of course, there are wildly speculative stories of others earlier still). It seems incredible that if such a rich resource had been discovered, it would or could have been kept secret. Almost immediately in Cabot's wake, fishermen from Portugal, Spain, and France, as well as England, moved to exploit the Newfoundland cod fishery. If gold brought Spaniards to the Caribbean and what became known as Latin America, fish lured Europeans to North America. Though Cabot claimed this "new found land" for Henry VII of England, the fishery was utilized in the early years more by Bretons, Normans, Basques, and Portuguese than by Englishmen until the 1560s.[61] By 1504, seasonal fishing stations were likely being established onshore; some of these may have been inhabited year-round. Thus, fish also dictated the earliest European building and settlement patterns. In each instance, the reaction of the Beothuk was to try to avoid the newcomers and withdraw into the interior.

In 1500, Gaspar Corte Real received a commission from King Manuel I of Portugal to find the Northwest Passage to Asia. On his first voyage in that year, Corte Real reached Greenland but did not land, and he was forced to turn back, probably by ice. The following year, he embarked with three caravels on a second voyage. This time he reached Newfoundland, where he found a broken Italian sword and a pair of Venetian earrings, apparently evidence of John Cabot's lost third voyage.[62] He also seized fifty-seven Beothuk captives.

Corte Real sent the captives and two of his ships back to Portugal under the command of his brother Miguel. He was last seen sailing south. His exact fate is unknown. The fate of the Indians, however, is more certain. They were sold as slaves to defray the cost of the expedition.

As fishing became increasingly common along the Newfoundland shore, although the Beothuk attempted to remain reclusive, both contact and conflict escalated between them and the Europeans. By 1506, only nine years after Cabot's first landfall, the fishery had enlarged to the point where the Portuguese crown was taxing it. And Beothuk slaves were showing up in European markets with increasing frequency. As seasonal fish-drying stations continued to spring up onshore, Beothuks raided them when the fishermen were away and during the winter to get European iron, stealing nails, tools, and metal scraps.[63] These were in turn moved down the line to other tribes through established trade routes.

In 2011, archaeologists excavated the so-called Mantle site at Whitchurch-Stouffville in Ontario, near Toronto. This Wendat (the people previously known as Huron) village proved to be the largest Iroquoian site ever found. Radio carbon evidence showed it to date from 1500 to 1530 C.E. Buried in the 500-year-old village was a piece of a Portuguese ax.[64] This find shows up in the archaeological record a full hundred years before the Wendat encountered actual Europeans. Such was the reach of the Red Atlantic that modern archaeologists found this fragment a thousand miles from the coast from which it was originally taken.

As the coast became increasingly occupied, the Beothuk continued to huddle in the interior. Eventually, they were cut off from their traditional coastal resources and economy. Isolated, their numbers dwindled. Their world closed in around them. The last known surviving member of the tribe, Shanawdithit, was captured in 1823 and died in captivity in 1829. The Beothuk were extinct.

Yet even in death, some of the Beothuk made a last macabre voyage on the Atlantic. The macerated skulls of some of the last were sent to Britain for study. Some of these wound up in the National Museum of Scotland in Edinburgh, where they rest uneasily to this day. That of Shanawdithit—the last of the last—was taken to London. It was destroyed during the blitz in World War II.

The slow withering of the Beothuk has been well documented. Their elegy has been sung in poetry and prose. Less than 350 years after John Cabot first stepped on their home island of Newfoundland, they had vanished completely. Our next account of slavery and the Red Atlantic is a story of a much more rapid extinguishment, but both are equally total.

A Deafening Silence

The first successful permanent English settlement in North America was Jamestown, founded in 1607. Plimoth Plantation was established in "North Virginia" in 1621. Prior to that time, however, English explorers regularly visited the Grand Banks and the New England coast. Martin Pring visited the area in 1603. George Weymouth came in 1605, John Smith in 1614. As it did in what would become Newfoundland and Canada, fishing played a major part. Smith established a fishing camp on Monhegan Island off the coast of Maine. It was fishermen at Monhegan who taught the Abenaki sachem Samoset enough English that he was able, according to William Bradford, to address the startled Pilgrims he met with the hearty greeting, "Hello, Englishmen."

Weymouth anchored off Monhegan on May 17, 1605. Welcomed by local Indians, he lured five aboard his vessel and seized them. Tisquantum (better known to history as Squanto), Manida, Dehamda, Skettawarroes, and Assacumet were taken to England aboard the *Archangel*. On July 18, the ship arrived in Plymouth. It was here that an important figure entered their lives. Sir Ferdinando Gorges commanded the harbor in Plymouth. According to him, "[I]t so pleased our great God" that Weymouth came to his anchorage. He immediately took charge of the captives, sending Dehamda and Assacumet to Sir John Popham, the lord chief justice, and keeping the other three.[65]

Though for the most part forgotten today, Sir Ferdinando looms large in the story of the Red Atlantic, both historically and, as we shall see, literarily. He was deeply interested in settlement in the New World and (among those who do remember him) is sometimes referred to as the father of English colonization in North America. According to Foreman, the New England Natives had a profound effect on him: "Gorges, who devoted himself to learning all he could from the Indians, came to the conclusion their country was well worth developing. He found that the Indians in his care were inclined to follow the manners of the better sort of people and they displayed more civility than common English people. He kept them three years and had them describe the rivers in their land and men of note who lived on them; how powerful they were, how allied, and what enemies they had."[66] Note the colonialist mind at work: Gorges "kept" the Indians "in his care" three years to gain intelligence about their homeland.

As noted in the introduction concerning the later visit of Tomochichi, the English were fascinated by these exotic creatures, all the more so because at this early date, they were such a rarity. Crowds followed them to gawk as they moved through the streets. In *The Tempest*, William Shakespeare has the jester Trinculo marvel, "When they will not give a doit to relieve a lame beggar, they will lay out ten to see a dead Indian."[67]

The stories of these involuntary indigenous guests so inflamed the imaginations of their captors that Gorges and Popham joined with others to form the Plymouth Company in 1606. They financed and outfitted an expedition to further explore the region, which departed in August of that year. Manida and Assacumet accompanied them. Unfortunately, the ship was intercepted by the Spanish and never reached its destination. A second vessel, captained by Pring, was sent out two months later with Dehamda and Skettawarroes as guides.[68]

Based on this reconnaissance, the company founded the so-called Popham Colony at the mouth of the Kennebec River in Maine in June 1607, only a few months after the settlement at Jamestown in the south. The colony lasted only a year, abandoned in 1608. Ironically, it failed because the colonists were unable to secure the help of the local indigenes. The Indians were unwilling because they remembered the captives taken by Weymouth in 1605.

Much about Tisquantum's life is uncertain and conjectural. It is surmised that he returned to North America in 1614 with John Smith. Apparently freed by Smith, his attempt to return to his Patuxet people was cut short when he was intercepted and recaptured by an associate of Smith's, Thomas Hunt. Hunt took twenty-four Nauset and Patuxet captive, sailing to Málaga in Spain to sell them into slavery. Smith and Gorges had hoped to establish a lucrative fur trade with the Indians, but Hunt's slaving spoiled those desires. Sir Ferdinando wrote: "One Hunt (a worthless fellow of our nation) set out by certain merchants for love of gain; who (not content with the commodity he had by the fish, and peaceable trade he found among the savages) after he had made his dispatch, and was ready to set sail, (more savage-like than they) seized upon the poor innocent creatures, that in confidence of his honesty had put themselves into his hands."[69] With the help of some friars, Tisquantum apparently made it back to England, where it is believed he was indentured to John Slaney, the treasurer of the Newfoundland Company.

The kidnappings of captives by Weymouth, Hunt, and others enraged Natives up and down North America's northern Atlantic coast. Europeans were "no longer welcomed with profitable beaver trade, as an unwitting French captain and crew would discover in 1617, when their ship was burned and almost everyone killed (a few were enslaved) by the Nauset."[70]

In 1610, the Newfoundland Company established a colony at Cupers Cove. According to Caleb Johnson, Squanto, already the premier Red Atlantic cosmopolitan, was sent by Slaney to Newfoundland in 1618

> and worked with Captain John Mason, governor of the Newfoundland Colony. While in Newfoundland, Tisquantum encountered a ship's captain by the name of Thomas Dermer, who had worked with Captain John Smith. . . . Dermer was employed by the New England Company, headed by Sir Ferdinando Gorges; they still had hopes to profit from beaver trade with the Indians of Massachusetts: but this would not be possible as long as hostilities remained. Thomas Dermer recognized that Tisquantum, who had now been living with Englishmen for a number of years, could act as an interpreter and peacemaker between the English and the still-enraged Indians of Patuxet and Nauset. He sent a letter off to Sir Ferdinando Gorges expressing the good use Tisquantum could be put to, and Gorges had them come back to England to discuss their plans.[71]

In 1619, in the company of Dermer, Squanto embarked on what was presumably his sixth transatlantic voyage in an attempt to reestablish peaceable relations and the fur trade with coastal tribes. Tragically, on his return to Patuxet, he was met with only a deafening silence. He discovered that the most numerous and European colonizers—germs—had exterminated his people. His tribesmen were dead, and his village was deserted. The common culprit is assumed to be smallpox. Another candidate is tuberculosis. Most recently, it has been speculated that it was leptospirosis.

Squanto's experience on his return home was all too common. Virgin soil plagues ravaged Native nations and depopulated the landscape. Historian Francis Jennings, in his influential study *The Invasion of America: Indians, Colonialism, and the Cant of Conquest*, writes, "The American land was more like a widow than a virgin. Europeans did not find a wilderness here; rather, however involuntarily, they made one. . . . The so-called settlement of America was a *resettlement*, a reoccupation of a land made waste by diseases and demoralization introduced by the newcomers."[72] Embracing the providential theory of empire, the English saw in this inadvertent biological warfare the hand of the Christian God, clearing the new "Promised Land." In this unfolding drama, they cast themselves as the new Israelites, the Chosen People given the land, and the Indians as the Canaanites, impeding possession of that which was rightfully theirs.[73]

A week after Samoset greeted the suffering Pilgrims in their own language, he returned with Tisquantum, who spoke it fluently. The peripatetic Squanto settled with the colonizers on the site of his former village.

While Tisquantum was undertaking his numerous voyages, Sir Ferdinando became involved with another captive. This encounter did not turn out so well for the colonial strategist.

In 1611, six years after George Weymouth grabbed Tisquantum and his companions, Captain Edward Harlow seized five other Algonkian-speaking coastal Natives. One of these was Epenow from the island of Capawack (Martha's Vineyard). Gorges acquired him from Harlow. The Indian proved a sensation in England. John Smith considered him a man of bravery, intelligence, and strength who "was shewed up and downe *London* for money as a wonder." Sir Ferdinando took a dimmer view of his charge, claiming he learned enough English only "to bid those who wondered at him, welcome, welcome." His celebrity, according to Alden Vaughan, makes Epenow "a likely model" for the "strange Indian" in William Shakespeare and John Fletcher's 1613 play *Henry VIII*, who so impressed women with his "great tool."[74]

Epenow indeed proved himself clever, living up to Smith's assessment rather than down to Gorges's. Playing upon the Europeans' greed for indigenous American wealth, the Indian told them of a rich mine on his home island and offered to be their guide. Gorges, along with the Earl of Southampton Henry Wriothesley and sea captain Nicholas Hobson, eagerly agreed to finance an expedition, which set sail in June 1614. The day the ship dropped anchor off Capawack, Epenow's fellow tribesmen came on board to welcome him back. On Gorges's orders, however, the Native was closely guarded to prevent escape. The following day, the Indians came back in force. As they distracted the Englishmen, Epenow dove off the ship and swam to the shore while the Indians provided a covering fire of arrows. Years later, in 1619, when Thomas Dermer visited Capawack, he met Epenow, who laughed heartily and regaled the ship's captain with the tale of his escape.[75]

As the skirmish surrounding Epenow's flight shows, tensions between the English and indigenous peoples sometimes flared. Once they were permanently established in their "New England," however, through aid provided by Tisquantum and Massasoit, the great sachem of the Wampanoag Confederacy, the colonizers enjoyed more than a decade of peace with the Native nations. Settlers and settlements proliferated. By the mid-1630s, Indians occupied the shaky middle ground between the English in Connecticut and the Dutch in New Amsterdam. Efforts by the English to control the fur trade and break the Pequot monopoly in wampum escalated tensions until war broke out in 1636. The massacre of 600 or more Pequots at Mystic Fort by settlers and their Mohegan and Narragansett allies on May 26, 1637, effectively ended Pequot resistance, though the war dragged on until autumn of the following year. A remnant of approximately 200 Pequot survivors was given into slavery. Most were dispersed among the Mohegan and Narragansett. Some were forced into servitude in colonial households. A small group were transported as slaves to Bermuda and the West Indies. John Mason, the commander of the Connecticut militia at Mystic, once again recognized divine intervention, writing, "Let the whole Earth be filled with his Glory! Thus the LORD was pleased to smite our Enemies in the hinder Parts, and to give us their Land for an Inheritance."[76]

Native survivors of King Philip's War in 1676 endured similar fates. Hundreds were carried away into bondage, 178 to Spain and even a few to Morocco. Most, like Metacomet's wife and son, were dispatched to the Caribbean, where they were sold. Reverend John Cotton cried out: "What was the fate of Philip's wife and child? They surely did not hang them? No. That would have been mercy. They were sold into West-Indian slavery! An Indian princess and her child sold from the breezes of Mount Hope, from the wild freedom of a New England forest, to gasp under the lash beneath the blazing sun of the tropics! Bitter as death! Ay, bitter as Hell!"[77]

No Ordinary Galley Slave

Throughout the seventeenth century, war captives, like those of the Pequot War and King Philip's War, supplanted the randomly snatched Natives of the "Age of Discovery" as transportees into slavery. They served in the galleys of France and were shipped to Europe, Barbados, Bermuda, Curaçao, and Trinidad. Refugees from the Yamasee War in Georgia in 1715 fled south into Spanish-held Florida. Some eventually wound up in Cuba. Some of these would be lucky enough—like Tisquantum—to find their back across the ocean. Most would not. Like the progeny of the H.M.S. *Bounty* mutineers on Pitcairn Island, descendants of these wayward Indians can be found living in these places to this day.

One who did make it back was Ourehouaré, or Tawerahet, a Cayuga chief. On June 17, 1687, Jean Bochart de Champigny, the intendant of Nouvelle France, captured a group of Cayuga warriors near Fort Frontenac at the mouth of the Cataraqui River. He reportedly lured others into the fort, promising a feast but imprisoning them instead. Separately, Jean Peré, another member of expedition, captured Ourehouaré and several others near Montreal, transporting them to the fort. According to the *Dictionary of Canadian Biography*, "The tribesmen, numbering 51 braves, were stripped, and tied to stakes in the compound of the fort, where they underwent torture at the hands of the French and their Indian allies. On the return of the invading French army [from Iroquoia], the captives were transported down the St. Lawrence River to Québec City, leaving behind them 150 helpless women and children."[78]

Pierre François Xavier Charlevoix, in his 1744 *Histoire de la Nouvelle France*, reports that King Louis XIV instructed Joseph-Antoine Le Febvre de la Barre, the governor-general of New France, to reduce the number of warriors of the Haudenosaunee (Iroquois) Confederacy by sending captives to France as galley slaves. De la Barre's successor, Jacques-René de Brisay de Denonville, ordered the Haudenosaunees from Fort Frontenac transported to France for the king's galleys, Ourehouaré among them. The action made the French hated among the Iroquois.

Shipped to Marseilles, Ourehouaré spent two years at the oars on the

Mediterranean. The savage warfare that resulted from the Fort Frontenac incident terrified the French. In August 1689, Haudenosaunee warriors attacked at Lachine, cutting off the fort. Brisay abandoned the fort
and ordered it torched. Louis recalled Brisay, replacing him with Louis
de Baude de Frontenac, governor-general previously from 1672 to 1682.
Comte Frontenac arrived in Québec City on October 15. With him, on
orders from King Louis, were the thirteen surviving Cayugas, including
Ourehouaré, "gorgeously clad in French attire."[79]

In Ourehouaré, we see the dark side of cosmopolitanism and the Red
Atlantic. According to Francis Parkman, Frontenac, hoping that the respected chief could be useful in reaching an accommodation with the
Haudenosaunees, worked on him during the voyage, gaining his confidence and goodwill. Arriving in Québec, Ourehouaré, the former galley
slave, disembarked in his French frippery, a victim of what modernly we
would call Stockholm syndrome. Frontenac lodged him in a fine apart-
ment in the Chateau Saint-Louis and generally "treated him with such
kindness that the chief became his devoted admirer and friend."[80] Parkman writes:

> [Frontenac] placed three of the captives at the disposal of the Cayuga,
> who forthwith sent them to the Onondaga [the central fire of the
> Haudenosaunee Confederacy] with a message which the governor
> dictated, and which was to the following effect: "The great Onontio
> [Frontenac], whom you all know, has come back again. He does not
> blame you for what you have done, for he looks upon you as foolish
> children and blames only the English, who are the cause of your folly
> and have made you forget your obedience to a father who has always
> loved and never deceived you. He will permit me, Ourehouaré, to re-
> turn to you as soon as you will come to ask for me—not as you have
> spoken of late, but like children speaking to a father.[81]

Frontenac also dispatched an Iroquois Christian convert named Cut
Nose, carrying enough wampum to express the seriousness of Onontio's
intent. This messenger took an even tougher line. Proffering the wampum, he declared, "Ourehouaré sends you this. By it he advises you to
listen to Onontio, if you wish to live."[82]

Frontenac overestimated his own popularity among the Haudenosaunee. He and Ourehouaré both misjudged the chief's influence
with his people after a two-year absence. Everyone underestimated the

sophistication of the Indians. The Iroquois Grand Council formally responded to them:

> Ourehouaré, the whole council is glad to hear that you have come back. Onontio, you have told us that you have come back again, and brought with you thirteen of our people who were carried prisoners to France. We are glad of it. You wish to speak to us at Cataraqui [Fort Frontenac]. Don't you know that your council fire there is put out? It is quenched in blood. When our brother Ourehouaré is returned to us, then we will talk with you of peace. You must send him and the others home this very winter. . . . You are not to think, because we return you an answer, that we have laid down the tomahawk. Our warriors will continue the war till you send our country men back to us.[83]

Not comprehending the clear message of the Grand Council, Comte Frontenac asked Ourehouaré, whose devotion to his patron-savior "never wavered," to send another message. The chief sent four representatives "with a load of wampum belts, expressing his astonishment that his countrymen had not seen fit to send a deputation of chiefs to receive him from the hands of Onontio, and calling upon them to do so without delay, lest he should think that they had forgotten him."[84] Parkman continues the story: "Along with the messengers, Frontenac ventured to send the Chevalier d'Aux . . . with orders to observe the disposition of the Iroquois, and impress them in private talk with a sense of the count's power, of his goodwill to them, and the wisdom of coming to terms with him, lest, like an angry father, he should be forced at last to use the rod. The chevalier's reception was a warm one. They burned two of his attendants, forced him to run the gauntlet, and, after a vigorous thrashing, sent him prisoner to [the English]."[85]

Ourehouaré, undoubtedly enjoying his ambassadorial status and his vastly increased lifestyle from the bilge to comfortable boudoir, angered by the failure of the Iroquois to ransom him upon demand, and loyal to Frontenac and the French, who made all these things possible, "took up the hatchet" against his own people, participating in a series of retaliatory raids. Though he recrossed the Atlantic to come back to North America, he never returned home. He was pensioned by the Sun King, died at Québec City, and was "mourned by Frontenac and eulogized by the church"—much as Oglethorpe acted as a pallbearer for Tomochichi, who was celebrated in death by his white friends.[86]

While Ourehouaré and his fellow Cayugas were captured by Frenchmen and shipped across the Atlantic, one should not think that Natives were totally without agency in the Indian slave trade as it helped create the Red Atlantic. In his article "'A Little Flesh We Offer You': The Origins of Indian Slavery in New France," Brett Rushforth writes: "Between 1660 and 1760, the colonists of New France pursued two seemingly contradictory policies toward their Indian neighbors. Through compromise, gift giving, and native-style diplomacy they negotiated the most far-reaching system of Indian alliances in colonial North America. At the same time, they also developed an extensive system of Indian slavery that transformed thousands of Indian men, women, and children into commodities of colonial commerce in French settlements."[87] The key word in this quote, as Rushforth himself makes clear, is, of course, "seemingly." French policy was not schizophrenic. The two systems were not divorced one from another but were rather integrally related to each other.

As part of diplomacy with Native nations, the French learned early on to accept gifts of Indian captives from their Indian allies as a way of cementing alliances and as retribution for depredations by tribes against the French. Over time, this evolved into a system of Indian slavery. According to Rushforth, "Although these slaves never constituted more than 5 percent of the colony's total population, they performed essential labors in the colonial economy as domestics, farmers, dock loaders, millers, and semi-skilled hands in urban trades."[88] These workers became so essential that Louis XIV was compelled to legalize Indian slavery in New France when it was illegal in Louisiana and the French Caribbean.

Most of these Native slaves found their way to Québec and Montreal. Yet Rushforth writes, "Indian slaves did not always travel to the St. Lawrence [Valley]," noting that "French and Indian traders . . . often sold slaves to the much more developed markets of English Carolina, where thousands of Indian slaves either labored on plantations or embarked for the Caribbean."[89]

The colonists of New France and their system of Indian allies were not the only sources for these thousands of slaves. In New England, however, as in New France, the Haudenosaunee played a central role. Historian Robbie Ethridge states: "The trade in Native American slaves first began in the Northeast. The Iroquois, seeking access to European goods and war captives whom they adopted into their kin groups to replace their dead, began doing business with English, French, and Dutch traders in the first few decades of the seventeenth century. Almost immediately this trade created a shatter zone of regional instability from which shockwaves radiated out for hundreds of miles."[90] From New England, the trade moved south. In the Southeast, in particular, opportunistic "coalescent societies" or recombinant neotribes like the Westos became slavers, raiding neighboring groups to secure their "merchandise."[91] Alan Gallay estimates that more than 50,000 Native slaves passed through South Carolina between 1670 and 1715.[92]

A Man Obsessed II

Perhaps one has to be a little bit crazy to go to sea as a profession, to choose the relatively solitary and peripatetic life of a sailor instead of the more sedentary and stable existence of a landlubber. Or perhaps that life may drive someone to a little madness. Or it may be that such was the case only during the era of wooden ships and iron men, when voyages might take seamen away from home port for years. Regardless of causation, Robert FitzRoy, like Christopher Columbus, was a man obsessed. Whereas, however, the Admiral of the Ocean Sea's manifold obsessions lay close to the surface, easily observable, nothing in FitzRoy's personality or actions gave an early indication of any compulsions. As Nick Hazlewood puts it succinctly, "It was a whale-boat that caused FitzRoy to snap."[93]

Pringle Stokes, the first captain of the H.M.S. *Beagle*, quietly slipped into depression and madness and took his own life two years into the expedition's four-year surveying mission. Rear Admiral Sir Robert Otway put his aide, the twenty-three-year-old flag lieutenant Fitzroy, in command. The *Beagle* was accompanying the larger H.M.S. *Adventure* in an effort to map the coast of Patagonia and Tierra del Fuego at the extreme southern tip of South America.

Despite his youth, FitzRoy seemed a reasonable and experienced choice for the promotion. He had entered the Royal Naval College at age twelve and had voluntarily shipped out to South America at fourteen. Aboard the *Beagle*, he at first appeared to be a fit and capable commander. Then what can only be considered "the incident" occurred.

On January 29, 1830, FitzRoy anchored the *Beagle* and dispatched a party in one of its whaleboats under the ship's master to chart the western edge of Tierra del Fuego. The next day, while the away party was camped onshore, the whaleboat was stolen by Yamana Indians who lived in the area. When he was informed, an enraged FitzRoy set off with a detachment of armed men to retrieve it. As Richard Lee Marks describes it in his book *Three Men of the Beagle*, "He found pieces of the missing whaleboat in almost every canoe and wigwam he came upon—the lead line in one canoe, the broken mast in an abandoned wigwam, canvas from the whaleboat in another canoe. With each finding he would try to lay hands on the nearest Indians to force them to tell him where those with the stolen whaleboat had gone."[94] Those he grabbed, however, escaped. Like some of the Tainos taken by Columbus and freed as "surplus," women even abandoned their children in their flight.

It was not the *Beagle* crew's first run-in with the indigenes. A month previous, a band of Yamanas had robbed and beaten two of the ship's seamen. FitzRoy had then gone ashore with some of his men to punish the offenders, but when confronted by armed Indians, he backed off.

Now, frustrated and furious, FitzRoy determined to take hostages and hold them until his whaleboat was returned. According to FitzRoy's biographer Peter Nichols, "For him it was an act that required no justification. It was a quick, practical decision, born of the necessity of the situation, but was a signal moment of change in FitzRoy's relationship with the Fuegians [as the British called all the Indians of the area]."[95] When the British rushed one Native encampment—that of the "boat stealers' family"—a skirmish erupted. One seaman was attacked and beaten, losing an eye. The ship's master, Mr. Murray, who was responsible for the boat's loss, fired upon and killed one of the attackers.[96]

Days dragged into weeks in the fruitless search for the missing whaleboat. Eventually, FitzRoy had three Indian hostages aboard the *Beagle*, two men and a girl. He called the males York Minster and Boat Memory. The girl, who was known as Yokcushlu in her native tongue, he named Fuegia Basket. The naval officer decided "kindness towards these beings [the Fuegians], and good treatment of them, is as yet useless. . . . Until a mutual understanding can be established, moral fear is the only means by which they can be kept peaceable." As Hazlewood summarizes, "There was no hope for them, and no hope for relations with them, he concluded, while they could not understand European languages, European ways and European power."[97] A plan began to take form in FitzRoy's mind. Just as the Vikings—and other Europeans after them—had, he would take these "Fuegians" and train them to serve as intermediaries between their own people and the superior white men. "Three natives of Tierra del Fuego, better suited for the purpose of instruction, and for giving, as well as receiving information, could not, I think, have been found," he wrote.[98]

The *Beagle*'s voyage continued. In eastern Tierra del Fuego on May 11, FitzRoy was in a small boat when he was approached by three canoes of Natives of a band different from his first hostages, wanting to trade. The captain motioned to a boy in one of the craft to come into his boat. The youth willingly complied. When one of his sailors suggested that the other Indians might think he was stealing the boy, "FitzRoy, still fuming, tore a large mother-of-pearl button from his coat and flipped it into the Fuegian bark-boat as payment."[99] The boy's name was Orundellico, but sailors dubbed him Jemmy Button after his purchase price. FitzRoy now had four indigenous prisoners.

The French would come to think of their colonialism as a *mission civilisatrice*, a civilizing mission. The Portuguese employed an equivalent term (*missão civilizadora*) for their own. Late in the nineteenth century, Rudyard Kipling would coin the term "white man's burden," first for British and then for American imperialism, symbolizing the necessity of colonizing and ruling other lesser-developed peoples for those peoples' benefit. Though none of these terms had yet been coined when Robert FitzRoy surveyed his Native charges in that pre-Victorian time, something like their intellectual underpinnings were nonetheless working on his mind. He wrote:

> I had . . . made up my mind to carry the Fuegians . . . to England; trusting that the ultimate benefits arising from their acquaintance with our habits and language, would make up for the temporary separation from their own country. But this decision was not contemplated when I first took them on board; I then only thought of detaining them while we were on their coasts; yet afterwards finding that they were happy and in good health, I began to think of the various advantages which might result to them and their countrymen, as well as to us, by taking them to England, educating them there as far as might be practicable, and then bringing them back to Tierra del Fuego. . . . In adopting the latter course I incurred a deep responsibility, but was fully aware of what I was undertaking.[100]

He further stated that the Natives "understood clearly when we left the coast that they would return to their country at a future time, with iron, tools, clothes, and knowledge which they might spread among their countrymen."[101]

Anyone who has objectively examined the story of FitzRoy and his "Fuegians" has concluded that the above self-justifying remembrances of FitzRoy about the mental grasp the Natives had of their situation were in error. At that early stage of the voyage, communication among the parties involved was labored and rudimentary. The Natives were on board a ship, surrounded by strange people who dressed them in strange clothes and fed them strange foods. York Minster had seemed pleased when introduced to the girl, Fuegia Basket. He was much less cordial, at least at first, to Boat Memory. The three initial hostages made fun of Orundellico. Discussing the difficulty experienced by the newly christened Jemmy Button, Hazlewood notes that he had to endure all the novelty outlined above, but aboard the ship he was also "expected to live in close quarters not only with the foreigners but also with three mocking members of an enemy tribe."[102] The Indians clearly did not comprehend FitzRoy's vision of their ultimate destiny. They had no way of knowing that the intention was to turn them into simulacra of Englishmen; these shadowy resemblances would then be returned to their homes as missionaries of British culture. They were to be a virus to infect autochthonous cultures with European civilization.

On the night of October 13, 1830, as the *Beagle* entered Falmouth harbor on a mail call, the Natives' eyes were almost closed. Then a steamship passed close by. To them the thing belching smoke seemed like a monster. It was their first reaction to England. As for what Britons made of them, they received a more subdued reception than those who came in earlier eras. From Falmouth, the ship proceeded to Plymouth. Indians were becoming old hat.

FitzRoy had taken care to get the quartet vaccinated for smallpox at a stopover in Uruguay, but he did not trust the quality of the foreign vaccine. He was right to be skeptical. Records indicate that when he took them to be revaccinated at the Royal Naval Hospital at Plymouth in November, Boat Memory had the disease. He died on November 11. By then, FitzRoy had had the Natives vaccinated four times.[103]

FitzRoy's grand plan was that the Indians would remain in Britain about three years. Through his connections, he made arrangements for them with Walthamstow Infants School, a boarding school outside of London. He asked that those in charge educate the Indians in "English, and the plainer truths of Christianity, as the first objective; and the use of common tools, a slight acquaintance with husbandry, gardening and mechanism, as the second."[104]

The two youngsters, Basket and Jemmy Button, were malleable and made good progress in their studies. The boy liked his English clothes and enjoyed looking at himself in the mirror. His vocabulary picked up some of the "quainter expressions of the day." When asked about his health, he would respond, "Hearty, sir, never better."[105] From the beginning, however, York Minster was a problem. He did not like the foreign land to which he had been taken, and he especially bridled at being in the classroom with children. He was in his mid-twenties. Basket and Jemmy Button were about ten and fourteen, respectively. Many English children in the classes were even younger—three, four, five years old. York became glum and quarrelsome.

York Minster's attitude probably resulted in FitzRoy's sometimes leaving him behind when he took the other two surviving indigenes on social outings. According to Nichols, "As an accomplished amateur scientist and already a renowned explorer, FitzRoy was exhibiting 'his' Fuegians as performing curiosities."[106] York was included in the most significant of the Natives' "showings," a royal audience with King William IV and Queen Adelaide.

An engraved summons arrived from the British monarch and his queen. Marks notes that there was no word for "king" in either of the Fuegian languages spoken by the three (Alakaluf and Yamana). FitzRoy's charges could not understand what was really about to happen, though it was impressed upon them that it was of great significance. Jemmy spit-polished his best boots and chose "a pair of yellow chamois gloves that fit him tightly and well."[107] Basket was given a new dress and bonnet, while York Minster rather inexplicably was put in clerical garb, oddly enough perhaps solely for the reason that he had been dubbed "York Minster."

FitzRoy described the meeting and how it came about as follows: "During the summer of 1831, His late Majesty expressed a wish to see the Fuegians, and they were taken to St. James's. His Majesty asked a great deal about their country, as well as themselves; and I hope I may be permitted to remark that, during an equal space of time, no person ever asked me so many sensible and thoroughly pertinent questions re-specting the Fuegians and their country also relating to the survey in which I had myself been engaged, as did his Majesty. Her Majesty Queen Adelaide also honoured the Fuegians by her presence, and by acts of genuine kindness which they could appreciate, and never forgot."[108] In particular, it seems that Fuegia Basket charmed the royal couple. Ac-cording to FitzRoy, "She [the queen] left the room, in which they were, for a minute, and returned with one of her own bonnets, which she put upon the girl's head. Her Majesty then put one of her rings upon the girl's finger."[109] The queen also gave her a small embroidered purse. A merry King William filled the bag with coins, telling the child to use it to buy her "trousseau."[110]

Charles Darwin will enter our story of the Red Atlantic momentarily, but FitzRoy in his narrative of the voyages of the *Beagle* expressed what might be called a proto–social Darwinism. In his account of his Native wards, education and exposure to British culture and Christianity not only refined their demeanor but also gave them, to his English colonialist eye, finer physical features. Describing their appearance, he wrote, "The nose is always narrow between the eyes and, except in a few curious in-stances, is hollow in profile outline, or almost flat. The mouth is coarsely formed (I speak of them in their savage state, and not of those who were in England, whose features were much improved by altered habits and by education)."[111] His view is reflected in sketches he made of the indi-genes: in their "savage state," they are drawn as he describes, while when depicted in Western clothes, they resemble muddy-complected English-men, their features, if not their color, much refined.

FitzRoy's original scheme was that the Indians would remain in Brit-ain for three years. Yet after less than a year, hasty plans were made for a second voyage of the *Beagle*, upon which the captain would return the indigenes to their Tierra del Fuego homelands. There were probably multiple reasons for this, but the precipitating factor appears to have been that York Minster developed an excessive—and presumably sex-ual—attachment to the pubescent Fuegia Basket. FitzRoy was not the only man in this story with an obsession. The entire experiment in social and moral uplift teetered on the verge of collapse.

The second voyage of the *Beagle* began, after several frustrating de-lays, on December 27, 1831. On board the ship, in addition to the three South Americans, was a budding young naturalist named Charles

Darwin. His observations from the trip would lead to his books *Voyage of the Beagle* and *On the Origin of Species*, establishing the foundations of our modern theory of evolution, hence the title of Peter Nichols's biography of FitzRoy, *Evolution's Captain*. Yet in that book, Nichols notes, "Although thrown into intimate contact with them for more than a year, Darwin's impressions of the Fuegians were less savvy than his observations of the natural landscapes he glimpsed at the *Beagle*'s ports of call. He agreed largely with FitzRoy's opinions of their innate personalities and characteristics, which the captain had derived from his ideas about facial features and the mumbo jumbo of phrenology."[112] For their part, the returnees strolled the deck of the vessel in their English finery, looking like oddly displaced tourists. Finally, the last passenger on board was a young and eager missionary named Richard Matthews. The objective was to establish a Christian mission station in Tierra del Fuego with the participation of the returnees, whom he would continue to tutor.

The *Beagle* reached the southern extreme of South America in December 1832. In his first encounter with Natives in their natural environment, Darwin was impressed, of course, mainly with their primitiveness. In his diary, he declared, "I would not have believed how entire the difference between savage and civilized man is." And again: "If their dress and appearance is miserable, their manner of living is still more so.—Their food chiefly consists of limpets & mussels, together with seals & a few birds; they must also catch occasionally a Guanaco [a llama-like animal]. They seem to have no property excepting bows & arrows & spears: their present residence is under a few bushes by a ledge or rock: it is no ways sufficient to keep out rain or wind. . . . I believed if the world was searched, no lower grade of man could be found.—The Southsea Islanders are civilized compared to them, & the Esquimaux, in subterranean huts may enjoy some of the comforts of life."[113] York Minster and Jemmy Button were embarrassed by these indigenes. Dressed in their gentlemen's finery, they both mocked them. Jemmy in actuality couldn't even understand them—though York could but pretended not to.

The following month, having sailed on, the *Beagle* reached the territory of Jemmy Button's people, "Buttonsland," as the Englishmen of the sloop called it. The original idea had been to deposit York Minster and Fuegia Basket—who were now, for all intents and purposes, husband and wife—in York's land and Jemmy and the missionary Matthews in Buttonsland. But York declared that he thought it best that the three indigenes and Matthews all remain together.

Going ashore, crewmen of the *Beagle* hastily established a perimeter line for a makeshift village and began to construct three huts—one for Matthews, one for Jemmy, and one for York and Basket—and to plant two gardens. Natives showed up in force. There were thirty sailors and more than 300 Indians. The Englishmen enforced the perimeter, but only with difficulty. Jemmy's family—mother, sisters, brothers—arrived. The women kept their distance. His brothers approached him and gathered round but simply stared at him. Describing the scene, FitzRoy said, "Strange dogs meeting in a street shew more anxiety and more animation than was manifested at this inhuman meeting of a lost child and his afflicted mother and relatives."[114] Jemmy attempted to speak to his oldest brother in his mix of native language and English but was frustrated that he could not make himself understood. He resorted to the Spanish jargon of sailors, repeatedly inquiring, "No sabe? No sabe?" Darwin wrote in his diary, "It was pitiable, but laughable, to hear him talk to his brother in English & ask him in Spanish if he understood it. I do not suppose, any person exists with such a small stock of language as poor Jemmy, his own language forgotten, & his English ornamented with a few Spanish words, almost unintelligible."[115] During his time in France, Ourehouaré may have been no longer capable of understanding the subtleties of Iroquois diplomacy, but "poor Jemmy," after his sojourn in Britain, was unable to communicate at all.

After several days, with genuine apprehension, FitzRoy ordered the crew to lift anchor, and the *Beagle* slipped out of sight. Nine days later, however, they returned to check on those he had left behind, his former captives and the missionary. Matthews and York and Jemmy, still in their English clothes, came down to the beach. Although initially everything seemed in order, Matthews privately informed FitzRoy that all was not well: after the *Beagle*'s departure, there had been thievery, aggressive panhandling, even overt threats, and minor assaults on his person. The gardens had been deliberately trampled. The missionary said that he feared for his safety if he remained. Promising York and Jemmy to again return in a few days to see how things were going, FitzRoy took Matthews away.

On February 14, eight days later, FitzRoy returned with a small party in a single whaleboat. Things seemed much improved. All three of his former charges met the captain on the beach, York and Jemmy dressed as usual. Basket, who had not left her hut a week earlier, wore a clean dress. And Jemmy's mother appeared, wearing a dress her son had given her. The huts were undisturbed. Even the garden showed signs of recovery. Relieved, FitzRoy departed.

In March 1834, FitzRoy and the *Beagle* returned one last time. When Jemmy canoed out to the ship, he was no longer in his fine clothes. He looked like any other Native. FitzRoy observed that his fine features had reverted to their original appearance. Jemmy seemed so embarrassed by his appearance that he turned his back. Once on board, however, he seemed happy. He was bathed and clothed. His English was as good as it had ever been, and he proclaimed, "I am hearty, sir, never better." He dined at the captain's table, and acted as if nothing had happened.[116]

Yet the young man could not remain on the ship. He canoed back to the beach. Nick Hazlewood describes the pitiable scene in his biography, *Savage: The Life and Times of Jemmy Button*: "As York stripped him of his clothes—the crisp white shirt and the stiff breeches, the kid gloves and the button boots—he took from him the last vestiges of Englishness. Frightened, cold and lost, this was when Jemmy realized his isolation. He could choose to maintain the charade that he was something else, that he had a mission to achieve, a new way of life to pass on, or he could accept that he had been cast aside by all but those closest to him. Now, a Yamana Indian, he chose the only path that was open to him. He returned to his people."[117] FitzRoy's dream dried to dust in front of his eyes. There was no more Jemmy Button. There was only Orundellico.

The Atlantic Littoral

At St. Augustine, Florida, on America's Atlantic littoral, stands the Castillo de San Marcos National Monument. Originally built by the Spanish between the years 1672 and 1695, it is a star-shaped fort, constructed of coquina, a limestone-like sedimentary rock composed of shells. The fort was literally built out of the Atlantic.

When Spain ceded Florida in 1821 following an American invasion known as the First Seminole War, Castillo de San Marcos became an American military post, rechristened Fort Marion after Revolutionary War hero Francis Marion. It was here in 1837 that Osceola, a leader in

the revolt the United States called the Second Seminole War, was imprisoned. He had been lured into an American trap on the promise of
truce negotiations. He died of malaria at another Atlantic outpost, Fort
Moultrie on Sullivan's Island at Charleston, South Carolina.

Osceola was a Seminole from Florida. Yet Fort Marion on the Atlantic
littoral became the place of confinement for Indian prisoners from hundreds of miles deep in the interior of the continent. It is through their
lives that Fort Marion became a station on the Red Atlantic.

Following the American Civil War, westward expansion began again
in earnest, and the United States sought to confine the Indians of the
horse cultures of the Great Plains to reservations in order to get them
out of the way of settlement and, in theory, to protect their Indian wards
from white depredations. Beginning about 1870, white hunters began
the indiscriminate slaughter of the great buffalo herds of the plains. This
was in part to satisfy the market demand for buffalo robes (hides). It was
also, however, part of the federal policy of reservation containment. It
was a form of economic warfare against the tribes. The bison provided
them with everything—food, clothing, shelter, tools. By depriving the
Plains Indians of their traditional source of economy, the United States
could more easily drive them to reservations and create a dependency
on the government in them. U.S. Army general Nelson Miles, himself
a veteran Indian fighter, captured the dual purpose behind the bison
extermination in his memoirs, noting that within a few years, millions
had been killed for their hides, and then writing, "The buffalo, like the
Indian, stood in the way of civilization and in the path of progress, and
the decree had gone forth that they must both give way."[118] Miles pointed
out that the domestic livestock that fed the nation took the place of the
bison on the Great Plains. The unspoken irony is that Native hunters also
participated in the slaughter and did so for reasons similar to some white
hunters—to gain the money paid for buffalo robes.

The Plains tribes, however, did not consent or easily capitulate to this
economic targeting by whites. On December 12, 1874, *Harper's Weekly*
reported, "The indiscriminate slaughter of the buffalo has brought many
evils in its train. Among other bad consequences it has been the direct
occasion of many Indian wars. Deprived of one of their chief means of
subsistence through the agency of white men, the tribes naturally take
revenge by making raids on white settlements and carrying off stock, if
they do not murder the settlers."[119] Though the periodical referred to

multiple wars, the most immediate event that precipitated the remark was the conflict that came to be called the Red River War, which was winding down at the time.

By the spring of 1874, Native anger toward the buffalo hunters on the southern plains had reached a breaking point. The bison herds were being systematically extirpated. At the same time, there were ever-increasing numbers of white settlers moving into the area from which the Indians were being displaced.

In the winter of 1873–74, a Comanche medicine man and prophet named Isatai rose up with a vision that he had received directly from the Creator while in the spirit world, claiming that he possessed control over the elements of nature—the wind, rain, lightning, thunder, hail—and had the power to render himself and his followers impervious to bullets. He could even raise the dead. There were about 2,000 Comanches at large, and Isatai began to unify them all. In May 1874, he summoned them to a meeting where Elk Creek joins the Red River. For the first time in old men's memories, all the Comanche bands attended and met in council. Moreover, such was the power and appeal of Isatai's message that most of the at-large Cheyennes and Kiowas showed up, as well.[120]

In the early summer, violence broke out. On June 27, 1874, Isatai and the great Comanche war chief Quanah Parker led a force of up to 700 warriors against Adobe Walls, a small buffalo hunters' station in the Texas panhandle. Among the handful of defenders was William Barclay Masterson, a buffalo hunter who would later become famous as a lawman better known as "Bat" Masterson. A few whites were killed at the beginning of the engagement, but fewer than thirty defenders held the attackers at bay. After a short siege, the attackers gave up. Isatai had stayed aloof from the battle, and despite a coating of bulletproof paint, his horse was shot out from beneath him. His followers deemed his prophecy false.[121] In the wake of their failure at the Battle of Adobe Walls, the Indians began raiding all along the frontier.

The uprising stunned the U.S. government and embarrassed the army. Both had assumed that the Indians of the southern plains had already been pacified. In hindsight, there may have been warning signs. On February 4, there had been a battle at the Double Mountain Fork of the Brazos River. Soldiers had killed ten Comanches in a running fight, but that had been the culmination of a punitive operation after the Indians stole livestock from local ranchers, more of a criminal action than warfare. And just a few days before Adobe Walls, thirty or so Cheyennes twice attacked troops escorting mail in northern Indian Territory and southern Kansas. These, however, were nothing like the massed attack on the buffalo hunters' station.[122]

The government gave the army a free hand, ordering it to subdue all the southern plains "hostiles" by whatever means necessary. Three thousand troops were dispatched in five columns from Texas, New Mexico, Colorado, and Indian Territory (one of the columns commanded by Nelson Miles) to converge on the Texas panhandle. The Indians mainly tried to avoid fights, but they occurred nonetheless. Though the Red River War dragged on into 1875, as the winter of 1874–75 settled in, resistance faded.

In order to ensure the pacification of the Indians of the southern plains—to make sure that the hostiles remained on the reservation—some, like Quanah Parker, were selected to remain on the reservation as chiefs. Others, warriors and chiefs deemed most responsible for the fighting or for committing crimes during the outbreak—the worst of the worst—were to be shipped to Fort Marion for incarceration without benefit of a hearing. The selection process did not go smoothly. Chiefs were exempted if they assisted with the selection or if they identified those "guilty" of crimes such as rape, murder of civilians, or horse theft. In other instances, the choice was simply arbitrary.

During the spring of 1875, as the resistance of the Red River War collapsed, Indians surrendered in large numbers. The bands of the Cheyenne chiefs Grey Beard and Stone Calf were instructed to camp near the Darlington Agency (the Cheyenne agency in Indian Territory) and Fort Reno. Thirty-three of the most incorrigible were selected for imprisonment in Florida.

A Cheyenne woman teased a prisoner named Black Horse as he was being shackled by an army blacksmith. Black Horse knocked the smithy to the ground and ran. As he fled, he was shot. A melee resulted, and about 150 Indians broke out. On April 6, soldiers caught up with the runaways at the Sand Hills nearby, and a battle ensued. Indian survivors fled to the camp of the holdout chief Little Bull at Sappa Creek, twenty-five miles north of the Darlington Agency. On April 23, 1875, U.S. troops attacked the sleeping camp. The event became known as the Sappa Creek massacre.[123]

Regarding the capriciousness referred to above, historian Herman

Viola writes, "On the Cheyenne Reservation . . . a drunken Army officer lined up recently surrendered Indians, and to expedite matters 'cut off eighteen from the right of the line,' promising to review his selections at a later time." The promised reassessment never took place. All eighteen were sent to Fort Marion.[124]

In the end, seventy-two were selected for transport to Florida. The contingent comprised thirty-three Cheyennes, twenty-seven Kiowas, nine Comanches, two Arapahos, and a single Caddo. Some, like Black Horse, Grey Beard, Lone Wolf, Yellow Bear, and Many Magpies, were well-known leaders. Many Magpies suffered an indignity akin to 'that experienced by European immigrants at Ellis Island: somewhere along the way, he was registered in English as "Heap of Birds," and Heap of Birds he and his descendants would remain.[125]

The prisoners were taken to Fort Sill, about seventy-five miles south of Fort Reno and the Darlington Agency. There they were put in the charge of Lieutenant Richard Henry Pratt.

When the American Civil War broke out, Pratt enlisted in the Ninth Indiana Volunteer Infantry, moving later to the cavalry. Entering as a private, he distinguished himself. By the war's end, he had been breveted to the rank of major. He was mustered out in May 1865. He reentered the army in March 1867, commissioned as a second lieutenant with the Tenth U.S. Cavalry, a white officer commanding a company of a black regiment—freedmen commonly referred to as "buffalo soldiers"—at Fort Sill, Indian Territory.

Though the image bequeathed to us by years of western movies is of a blindingly white, Anglo-Saxon frontier cavalry, the reality was starkly different. The army that fought the Indian Wars was composed largely of German and Irish immigrants and African Americans. Pratt and his buffalo soldiers fought at the Battle of Double Mountain Fork during the Red River War.[126] Now Pratt found himself the jailer of the hostiles, responsible for overseeing their transportation to Fort Marion.

Cheyenne scholar and educator Henrietta Mann writes: "Viewed from the Cheyenne perspective, this exile was a disaster; banishment or isolation was the sentence for intratribal murder, the most extreme of behavior in their social fabric. The men and the [one] woman had committed no crime in their cultural context to warrant such harsh punishment. As their prophets had predicted, the strange white man had even stranger concepts that were anathema to The People's way of life. The anguished wailing of the women massed along the hillside as their people were taken from them could not convey the heartbreak and wrong associated with exile."[127] What Mann so movingly describes was true no less for the other tribal nations facing the deportation of their citizens than it was for the Cheyenne.

Pratt loaded his prisoners onto wagons to carry them to the closest rail depot—165 miles away. Once they arrived at the railhead, they were taken by train to Fort Leavenworth in Kansas. There they languished, while the government invited bids from carriers for their transport. Eventually, they were put aboard a train once more, passing through St. Louis and Indianapolis (a diversion so that Pratt's family could join him) and then on to Nashville, Atlanta, Macon, and Jacksonville, Florida.[128] White citizens flocked to train stations to catch a glimpse of the red warriors, just as people in Spain and England gaped at Indians in an earlier era. The difference was that in this modern era, with the Indian Wars still being waged in the West, some of the Americans came to taunt and jeer a much-feared enemy now subdued and from a safe distance. They were not above throwing the occasional vegetable or more solid object. Most of these people had not seen an Indian in years. But during the Indian Wars, "waiting for the word from the West" became a pastime for a worried nation.

Somewhere between Red Oak and Lake City, Florida, near Baldwin, Grey Beard jumped from the moving train. The locomotive was halted and the Indian hunted down. He was shot in the back as he tried to flee.[129] One of the Kiowa prisoners, Zotom (or, in English, Biter), created a visual diary of the journey and life in Florida. He drew depictions of the death of Grey Beard and "Leaving 'Lean Bear' at Nashville."[130]

As Viola puts it, "another casualty of the trip was Lean Bear, a Cheyenne chief accused of being a ringleader." Outside of Nashville, the warrior cut his throat with a penknife and repeatedly stabbed himself. He also stabbed two military guards who tried to interfere. He was left for dead in Nashville, but, against all expectations, he lived. He was sent on after his compatriots to Fort Marion. Upon arrival, he refused to speak and went on a hunger strike. According to Mann, he was "homesick and heartbroken." Adjudged "demented," he was transferred to St. Francis Barracks, outside the fort walls. He died shortly after.[131]

Arriving in Jacksonville, the original party—minus Grey Beard and Lean Bear—was put aboard a steamship, which took the Indians not

onto the Red Atlantic but on the St. John's River to Tocoi, Florida. There
they got on a train once more for St. Augustine and Fort Marion. Sidney
Lanier, the great poet of the Georgia coast, witnessed their arrival and
characterized them as "proper men . . . weary and greatly worn [with] a
large dignity and majestic sweep about their movements that made me
desire to salute their grave excellencies. . . . [Yet] they are confined—by
some ass in authority—in the lovely old fort, as unfit for them as they are
for it."[132] Though the poet is characteristically romantic in his impulse
to salute those he paints as the typical nineteenth-century noble savages, proud but fatigued in defeat, he nonetheless hits upon two very
real truths. The decision to confine these Indians as prisoners of war was
both cruel and counterproductive—the order of "some ass in authority."
And the seventeenth-century fort was an unfit place of confinement.

Fort Marion was never meant to be a prison. There were no cells. The
prisoners were housed in the casemates of the old fortress, cramped,
windowless, dungeon-like rooms beneath the parapets. Most of these
had "very dirty sand floors." There was little or no ventilation. For their
first few days at the fort, it rained constantly, and water dripped from
the ceiling of the casemates. They were forced to sleep on the floors.
Compounding already multiple problems, the Indians arrived in coastal
Florida at the high heat of summer.

Pratt gave the inmates colored pencils and sheets of paper from ledger books. They made pictures about their now lost lives on the plains,
of daily events in their prison, and, as already noted, of the journey to
that awful place. The most devastatingly moving image, bar none, produced during their years of confinement is one done by Zotom. It depicts
the Indians the day after their arrival. They are shown standing on the
parapet, their backs to the viewer. Two armed guards flank them. Maybe
they still have their shackles on. They look out on Matanzas Bay to the
Red Atlantic. A steamship chugs away in the distance. At the right of
the frame is a lighthouse. The casemates and parade ground are visible
beneath the Natives. According to Pratt, "The only outlook besides the
sky the prisoners could have was by going to the terreplein under the
charge of the guard, which was done several times each day. Otherwise
they were confined to the court below and the casements in which they
slept."[133] To what sort of place had they been fetched?

Today at the Castillo de San Marcos National Monument, you can
walk the parade ground and poke your head into those casemate dun-

geons. You can stand on the ramparts exactly where Zotom's fellow con-finees stood and look out at the ocean, as I have. There has been some development in the intervening decades, but the lighthouse is still there. In many ways the view is unchanged from Zotom's picture. What sort of place indeed?

Pratt was a career army officer. He dressed the Fort Marion prison-ers in uniforms and imposed military-style discipline on them. He was their jailer. Yet something else was also going on. We will never know the precise moment, but at some point, either while observing the Indians on the long trip to Florida or sometime shortly after arrival, Pratt was seized by the same notion that so tightly gripped Robert FitzRoy: he would see that his charges were educated as a means of betterment for all their people. In part, this was so they could serve as cultural media-tors between their people and whites. He favored "promoting English speech . . . in order to bring the Indians into best understanding and relations with our people."[134] But his urge ran much deeper than a rudi-mentary desire to facilitate communication.

In addition to military drill, art, and English, Indians were instructed in various mechanical arts and the Christian religion. Among the white visitors who regularly passed through Fort Marion was the writer and former abolitionist Harriet Beecher Stowe, the author of *Uncle Tom's Cabin*. In articles for the periodical the *Christian Union*, she wrote that the younger prisoners wanted "to remain and go anywhere they could get an education that would fit them to go back and teach their people the arts and trades of civilized life." Amplifying on the theme, she added that the Indians wished "to learn farming, blacksmithing, and other use-ful arts, as well as to carry on the study of the English language and lit-erature, with a view of being useful to their own people."[135] Though it is Stowe speaking here, she is clearly ventriloquizing Pratt. In her words, one can also hear the failed dreams of FitzRoy for his "Fuegians."

Once they arrived in Florida, the prisoners adapted readily to life on the Atlantic littoral. They enjoyed beachcombing, collecting "sea beans," palm seeds that washed up on the beach, which they polished and deco-rated. They also collected alligator teeth. Initially, they sold these to local merchants who resold them to tourists. They then realized that they could cut out the middlemen and sell them directly, making a greater profit. They especially liked fishing from the beach for sharks—which they called "water buffaloes."[136]

The Indians even ventured out onto the ocean, as well, albeit not very far. Pratt chartered local boats for sailing excursions. Later, he purchased the yawls from a wrecked schooner. The Natives learned how to row and sail these vessels and began to take tourists out for pay. Pratt also allowed the prisoners to sail to Anastasia Island, the barrier island separating St. Augustine from the ocean, and camp, sometimes unsupervised. All these activities of quotidian life on the Red Atlantic were captured with pencils and paper by Zotom.

One of Pratt's greatest educational successes was Making Medicine (Okuh hatuh or Oakerhater). In his memoirs, Pratt writes that Oakerhater was one of the leaders of the Red River War and lists his age as thirty-three. Mann, however, says that the Cheyenne oral tradition maintains that he was not a participant in the outbreak but rather a little boy who insisted on following his older brother into exile. Though the army tried to pull him away, he so clung to his sibling that they relented and took him to the prison as well.[137]

Like Zotom and Cohoe (or Lame Man), among others, Oakerhater took to drawing and became a prolific artist during his imprisonment. Art was, of course, known and practiced by Natives prior to any encounter with whites or experience of their educational processes. Oakerhater, however, also adopted that most pervasive of European imports across the Red Atlantic other than contagions: he became a Christian.

In considering the Native American experience, we often think of Christianity as a purely negative force, a "vehicle of white oppression." In her article "'Everything Necessary for Our Salvation,'" April Middeljans characterizes this position vis-à-vis Christian religion: "Its missionaries and rituals are portrayed as agents of a [theological imperialism] that, confident in its own superiority, aggressively colonizes Indian identities, cultures, and ecology."[138] Certainly there is plenty in the historical record and in the lived lives of Natives—from the *reducciones* in Latin America advocated by Bartolomé de Las Casas to the boarding or residential schools in the United States and Canada—for it as a force destructive of both Native cultures and individuals. Choctaw historian Homer Noley, in his seminal *First White Frost*, says that too often missionaries confused their own culture with the religious message for which they advocated and forgot that the gospel was good because the gospel was good, not because Native cultures and religious traditions were bad.[139] George Tinker goes so far as to call what transpired a "missionary conquest," albeit for Tinker an inadvertent one.[140]

While on the scales of history the balance tilts overwhelmingly toward the negative effects of Christianity, there are nevertheless counterexamples. Native Americans, both as individuals and, collectively, as cultures, were and are highly adaptive, capable of absorbing anything that seemed to them to have power. According to Middeljans, "After hearing of the Jesuit religion from a band of Canadian Iroquois around 1820, the Salish sent four separate deputations (in 1831, 1835, 1837, and 1839) more than 1600 miles through perilous wilderness and enemy territory to St. Louis to solicit a 'Black Robe' for their community. Their stubborn singleness of purpose, which even the Protestants could not deter, indicates that something about this branch of Christianity resonated with Salish beliefs and needs."[141] In recent times, the late Vine Deloria Jr. is the Native scholar most implacably critical of Christianity. Yet his great-grandfather, as a chief of the Yankton Sioux, first invited Episcopal missionaries to come among his people, and he sent his own son, Tipi Sapa (Black Lodge), into the Episcopalian priesthood, becoming in the process Philip Deloria. From William Apess in the 1820s to Oakerhater to Homer Noley and beyond, North American indigenes have appropriated Christianity and made it their own.[142]

In 1877, Mary Douglas Burnham, an Episcopalian deaconess, sponsored prisoners to serve as sextons in church. In April 1878, all the surviving prisoners were released. Burnham arranged for Oakerhater and three others to go to St. Paul's Church in Paris Hill, New York. Funds were provided by George Hunt Pendleton, U.S. senator from Ohio, and his wife, Alice. Burnham also arranged for Oakerhater's wife, Nomee, to join him. The parish priest, Father J. B. Wicks, took them in as members of the family and continued Oakerhater's education. Within six months, Oakerhater accepted Christian baptism and was confirmed shortly thereafter. He took the Christian name David after the ancient Israelite king of the Old Testament. He took Pendleton as a surname in honor of his benefactors.

In Paris Hill, the four former prisoners became popular with the townspeople. As they had in Florida, they made a little money by selling things they made, such as handmade bows and arrows, and then teaching archery. The success of the Paris Hill group and of a larger contingent at the Hampton Normal and Agricultural Institute for Negroes in Virginia convinced Pratt that his great experiment in Native education had indeed succeeded and could be replicated on a larger scale. He began to lobby for federal funds to start an Indian school. Oakerhater's sponsor, Senator Pendleton, shepherded legislation through Congress. In 1879, the Carlisle Indian Industrial School opened in Pennsylvania with Richard Henry Pratt as its superintendent. This first boarding school and all those that came after it—for good and for ill—are directly traceable to the experience of the Red River War prisoners on the Red Atlantic.

David Pendleton Oakerhater was ordained as a deacon in the Episcopal church in July 1881. Shortly after his ordination, Pratt sent him to Indian Territory and the Dakotas to recruit students for Carlisle. According to Brad Lookingbill in his book *War Dance at Fort Marion: Plains Indian War Prisoners*, three of the most zealous "Florida boys," Oakerhater, Zotom, and Telling Something, arrived back in Indian Territory on June 7, 1881 (not in July). They were accompanied by Oakerhater's mentor and friend from Paris Hill, John Wicks, to establish Episcopal missions. Lookingbill notes that Oakerhater's employment by the mission liberated him from dependency on the Indian agency's ration system, writing, "Untethered from both the agency and traditional chiefs, the former dog soldier was free to become a new kind of holy man." Confronting the participants and onlookers at the traditional Cheyenne sun dance, Oakerhater reminded his audience of his history as a warrior: "You remember when I led you out to war, I always went first and what I told you was true. Now I have been to the east and I have learned about another captain, the Lord Jesus Christ, and he is my leader. He goes first and all he tells me is true. I come back to my people to tell them about him, and I want you to go with me now in this new road, a war that makes all for peace and where we never have only victory."[143] The Red Atlantic had unquestionably worked its work on him.

In 1887, Oakerhater began serving the newly built mission in Bridgeport in Indian Territory. In 1889, he moved to the Whirlwind Mission near Watonga on the Cheyenne Reservation. He retired in 1918 but continued to preach and serve as both a Cheyenne chief and medicine man until he died in 1931.

In 2012, the Mohawk convert Kateri Tekakwitha was canonized by Pope Benedict XVI. At the time, it was commonly said that she was the first Native American saint. This ignores Juan Diego, the Nahua peasant who saw the apparition of the Virgin of Guadalupe and was made a saint in 2002—if he existed at all and the entire visitation story was not merely an elaborate evangelizing hoax perpetrated by the Catholic church. It also overlooks Oakerhater, who was canonized by the Episcopal church in 1985.

Ourehouaré was a forced participant on the Red Atlantic, shipped to France as a slave to pull on the oars of the king's galleys on the Mediterranean. The Red River War captives were sent to the Atlantic littoral as prisoners of war—as soldiers (some like Oakerhater and Cohoe were Cheyenne dog soldiers)—again involuntarily. Yet many Indians willingly voyaged forth on the Atlantic, both as sailors and soldiers. It is to these volunteers that we now turn our attention.

2

⚺

In the Service of Others
Soldiers and Sailors of the Red Atlantic

IN *THE BLACK ATLANTIC*, Paul Gilroy notes that ships are a central or-
ganizing principle for him. He writes, "The image of the ship—a living
micro-cultural system in motion—is especially important for historical and theoretical reasons. . . . Ships immediately focus attention on
the middle passage, on the various projects for redemptive return to
an African homeland, on the circulation of ideas and activists as well
as the movement of key cultural and political artefacts: tracts, books,
gramophone records, and choirs."[1] Sailing vessels naturally also figure
prominently in Peter Linebaugh and Marcus Rediker's *The Many-Headed
Hydra*, their history of the "revolutionary Atlantic." They are no less important to the Red Atlantic. They carried the wealth of the Americas
away to Europe, and they transported Indians in a variety of capacities
back and forth. Yet they also provided for the circulation of Native ideas
and technologies (like quinine and aspirin) around the Atlantic basin.
They carried Native words for these things into English, Spanish, and
French—hammock, poncho, canoe, tomato, potato, hurricane, barbecue. And they brought European ideas and technologies to the natives
of the Americas whether or not they themselves traveled on the Atlantic.

Perhaps the most basic capacity in which ships carried American indigenes was as sailors who manned those vessels themselves. They also
carried Native soldiers across the Atlantic to fight in the wars of European powers. In fact, most of those who sailed the Red Atlantic did so in
the service of others, though not always. One, in fact, rose through the
ranks of sailors to own and command not just one ship but an entire
fleet of his own. And in the late seventeenth and eighteenth centuries,

Wabenaki Indians of New England took up piracy. According to historian Matthew Bahar, "For nearly two centuries, Wabanaki Indians responded to the most threatening and most opportunistic effects of colonialism by orchestrating acts of maritime violence and theft. When their long-standing conception of the ocean ran up against European—and later primarily British—efforts to forcefully consolidate the Atlantic into a co-herent and far-flung imperial network, native marine-warriors shrewdly exploited several colonial conflicts in order to decimate European ships and sailors and reinforce their command of the waves."[2] The Wabenaki took advantage of King Philip's War and the French and Indian Wars to exact seagoing revenge and reap profit, in the process, as English colonial officials complained, devastating the North Atlantic fishery.

On the Briny Bosom of the Red Atlantic: The Two Paul Cuffes

It is not coincidental that Herman Melville named his whaling vessel with its mixed-race crew in his novel *Moby-Dick* the *Pequod*. Pequots, Wampanoags, and other Natives, particularly those of mixed African ancestry, crewed the whalers that sailed out of New London, New Bedford, Nantucket, and other New England ports in the eighteenth and nineteenth centuries.

As an aside, these and other sailors were among the earliest adopters of the avocado, a fruit (literally) of the Red Atlantic. They called it a "butter pear"—a pear because, obviously, it is shaped somewhat like a pear, the other because they used it as a substitute for the dairy product to smear upon their bread. Sailors used it to ward off scurvy, the avocado having as much vitamin C as the onion, which, for instance, Lenin used for the same purpose during the Russian Revolution. They also called avocados "alligator pears," the nickname for the rough-skinned, brown-green fruit speaking for itself.

Ourehouaré wound up a slave at the oars of the Sun King's galleys, plying the Mediterranean. Similarly, a primary route into maritime labor for Natives was indenturing.[3] The experience of the Wampanoags of Nantucket is exemplary.

Did New England Natives hunt whales at sea prior to European contact? In his book *Leviathan: The History of Whaling in America*, Eric Jay Dolin takes up the question, noting that the only written documentation of Indian whaling is in the account of George Weymouth's expedition of

1605 (which captured Tisquantum and his compatriots). Dolin writes, "Although this account is fascinating, and it appears to be a reasonable description of how a whale hunt could be prosecuted, it is not entirely convincing on its own. And, as [historian Elizabeth Little] notes, it 'does not appear to be first-hand,' casting further doubt on its reliability."[4] Still, the notion that New England Natives whaled is not entirely beyond the realm of possibility. Peoples with similar technologies—the Inuit in the Canadian Arctic and the tribes of the Northwest Coast on the Pacific— definitely had pre-Contact whaling traditions. Dolin concludes: "As for being able to approach a whale in its element and react to and defend against its fury, the coastal Indians of New England possessed the canoe-handling talents to have done so. Still, if the New England Indians had an independent whaling tradition, it most certainly would have continued after the colonists arrived. Yet none of the accounts of the region written by Europeans during the early years of colonization mention Indian whaling. The lack of evidence, of course, does not prove that Indians didn't have a tradition of whaling, rather it simply means that we cannot say with any confidence that they did."[5] The first solid proof of whaling among the Wampanoag dates to almost a century after first contact and definitely involved white men.

In 1690, Ichabod Paddock of Yarmouth visited Nantucket and taught the island's settlers how to kill and process whales. According to Mark Nicholas, in his article "Mashpee Wampanoags of Cape Cod, the Whalefishery, and Seafaring's Impact on Community Development," "island colonists soon formed their own companies and launched their own vessels. To create a steady labor force, Nantucket merchants reaped the benefit of a trade with local Native Americans. In order to pay off debts to Englishmen, Indians from the island filled the lowest positions of Nantucket whaling crews up until the early 1770s."[6] He notes that by the middle of the eighteenth century, Nantucket whalers ventured forty to fifty miles from shore in search of cetaceans. These whalers became increasingly dependent on Natives and men of African ancestry to crew their vessels. Then they moved on to exploit the deep-sea whalefishery, which was more profitable. Nicholas continues:

By the 1750s, islanders had installed on-deck tryworks on their vessels that allowed blubber to be boiled at sea. Nantucket had the largest whaling fleet in the world in 1775 that brought in thirty thousand barrels of oil. To meet the international demands for oil, ships in search of the profitable sperm whales moved farther away from New England, pursuing these cetaceans in waters from Canada to South America. . . . By the 1770s, more than one hundred Nantucket whaling vessels, set for voyages of four months or longer, competed for laborers from an almost extinct Native population from the island. Men from the island and Vineyard—blacks, Indians, and Yankees—thus came to fulfill most of the labor of an industry in which captaincies and mateships were the "exclusive preserve" of white Nantucketers.[7]

For all its many values, Nicholas's article, as demonstrated in the extended quote above, falls victim to two traps: the vanishing narrative of New England Natives ("an almost extinct Native population from the island") and the common belief that the upper ranks on whalers were occupied exclusively by whites. Natives perdured in coastal New England, and while "captaincies and mateships" were overwhelmingly taken up by whites, they were occasionally held by Natives. Both statements are belied in the person of a single individual, Paul Cuffe.

New England Natives not only provided the labor for the whaling industry but also were shaped by their participation in the wage economy and by their travels around the Red Atlantic. Cuffe was one of those so molded. Though not discussed by Gilroy, Cuffe, like Crispus Attucks, represents a quintessential participant in both the black and Red Atlantics, demonstrating the inextricable intertwining of the two.

Paul Cuffe was born on January 17, 1759, on Cuttyhunk Island, Massachusetts. His father was Cuffe Slocum, an Ashanti from Ghana originally known as Kofi, who was transported to America as a slave at ten years old and later purchased his freedom. His mother was Ruth Moses, a Gayhead Wampanoag. At sixteen, Paul shipped out as an ordinary seaman on a whaling bark to the Gulf of Mexico. He made subsequent voyages on whalers and cargo vessels. According to Sheldon Harris, a contemporary biographer: "Cuffe's horizons as well as his knowledge of seamanship expanded enormously because of these youthful experiences. He not only became familiar with the navigational hazards normally encountered in the Gulf of Mexico, in the Caribbean, among the West Indies, off South America, and the like, but he was introduced to different societies and their mores. These early voyages served as a kind of apprenticeship period for Paul Cuffe. He was learning his trade under the watchful eye of professionals; he was also acquiring knowledge concerning the white man's prejudice as it relates to black-skinned inhabitants of the Western Hemisphere."[8]

Captured and imprisoned by the British for three months in 1776, Cuffe resumed his sailing career in 1778. The following year, he and his brother built a small boat and plied the coastal trade, perhaps engaging in blockade running as well. From that first open skiff, he expanded throughout the 1780s and 1790s until, by 1806, he had a fleet of oceangoing ships, including the 268-ton *Alpha*. He excelled as a captain, both whaling and hauling cargo. Most of the time, he sailed with a crew composed solely of blacks and Natives. He married a woman from his mother's tribe. In 1780, he engaged in tax resistance, petitioning the Massachusetts government concerning his unpaid taxes because, as an Indian, he was not enfranchised, and it was thus taxation without representation.[9]

Cuffe became the wealthiest man of color in the United States. He counted among his friends and supporters Benjamin Rush (a signer of the Declaration of Independence), Albert Gallatin (the U.S. secretary of the Treasury), and William Wilberforce (a member of the British Parliament and the leading abolitionist of his day). In 1812, he achieved another first when he met with President James Madison at the White House, becoming the first black man so received—but not the first Native (Indian delegations had been meeting with U.S. chief executives since George Washington).

Sheldon Harris, in his biography, writes of Cuffe's "racial perplexity" as a mixed-race person in colonial and early republican America. In 1808, Cuffe underwent a Christian conversion and joined the Quaker meeting in Westport, Massachusetts. After that, he became increasingly dedicated to the cause of Africa. Harris says that in this move, he resolved his "racial ambiguity."[10] There is absolutely no evidence, however, that Cuffe ever turned away from his Indianness.

The Algonkian-speaking Wampanoag were matrilineal. As the son of a Gayhead woman, Cuffe had a clan within the tribe. In this regard, his marriage to a Wampanoag woman is significant. It ensured that his children would have the same status.

Sierra Leone had been established by the British beginning in 1787 as a place to resettle self-emancipating enslaved Africans who had fled the American colonists and African American sailors captured during the

American Revolution. By 1806, however, the Sierra Leone Company was bordering on bankruptcy, and in 1807, Britain took it over directly as a crown colony. Cuffe first sailed there in early 1811 to survey conditions. From there, he traveled to England, where he took in the sights and met with the leading figures of the time. His plan was to transport skilled freedmen to Africa as a leaven to raise the level of African civilization and to carry back African resources and goods to pay for the enterprise. He purchased a home in Freetown but held no hope of moving there permanently because his Wampanoag wife refused to relocate.[11]

By 1816, Cuffe came to believe that large-scale relocation was the only hope for African Americans. According to Harris: "Many forces and influences that worked on him over the years coalesced in 1816 to convince Cuffe that the only hope—nay, the only prospect for salvation—for America's Negroes was their complete removal from this country and subsequent relocation elsewhere. He did not abandon the notion of saving Africa, but now the plight of the black man in the United States assumed first place in his hierarchy of priorities. If he was not the father of black nationalism, by this decision Paul Cuffe became a leading contender for the distinction."[12] Even in his espousal of contemporary African recolonization, Cuffe was ahead of his time. He advocated not one but two venues. Harris explains, "A site somewhere in Africa would offer a welcome for those blacks searching for an African identity, while another center could be established along the western fringes of the Louisiana Purchase for Negroes disinterested in African return. In this fashion a black could have freedom of choice in selecting the setting for his exile."[13] In this, Cuffe anticipated those who saw what is today the state of Oklahoma as a future situs for red and black resettlement and cohabitation.

Cuffe died on September 7, 1817, his dream of mass resettlement of African Americans largely unfulfilled. Liberia, another place designated for recolonization of freed blacks (this time from the United States), would not be settled until four years after his death.

Despite his Nativeness, it is ironic that Paul Cuffe has come down to us today solely as an African American man—who just happened to have an Indian mother and an Indian wife. And until now, no one has attempted a serious recovery of him as a Native American. The fault is not really that of Sheldon Harris. Writing his biography in 1972, at the height of the Black Power movement, it was important for him to paint his subject as the "father of black nationalism," to use his phrase. Nor does it lie with other biographers writing in the same era or somewhat later, such as George Salvador (*The Black Yankee*, 1969) and Lamont Thomas (*Rise to Be a People: A Biography of Paul Cuffe*, 1986).[14] Instead the origins of this received perception go back to 1811 and Cuffe's first biographer.

Wilson Armistead was a British Quaker abolitionist from Leeds who authored several antislavery tracts and books over his career with titles like *500,000 Strokes for Freedom*, *Garland of Freedom*, *Clouds of Witness Against Slavery and Oppression*, and *The Negro Is a Man*. Armistead met Cuffe in 1811 when he came to England after visiting Sierra Leone. After talking with him and based on additional information he garnered from newspaper articles published at the time, Armistead published *Memoir of Captain Paul Cuffe, a Man of Colour* that same year. Though called a "memoir," the brief book is told in the third person. Cuffe himself had no idea that he was being "interviewed" and was reportedly miffed when he found out that someone was using his name and exploiting his story, though—admittedly—there is no known account of whether he felt he was being misrepresented.

Armistead's goal, as a fervently committed abolitionist, was to minimize Cuffe's Native identity and enhance as much as possible his African identity. For instance, in discussing his subject's parentage, Armistead writes of his father: "The father of Paul Cuffe was a Native of Africa, whence he was brought as a Slave into Massachusetts.—He was purchased there by a person named Slocum, and remained in slavery a considerable portion of his life.—He was named Cuffee, but as is usual in those parts, took the name of Slocum, as expressing to whom he belonged. Like many of his countrymen, he possessed a mind superior to his condition, and although he was diligent in the business of his Master, and faithful to his interest, yet, by great industry and economy, he procured the means of purchasing his personal liberty."[15] Of Cuffe's mother, by contrast, he says only, "At that time the remains of several Indian tribes, who originally possessed the right of soil, resided in Massachusetts; Cuffee became acquainted with a woman descended from one of those tribes, named Ruth Moses, and married her."[16] Armistead then pivots immediately back to the father. As an industrious son of Africa, Cuffee Slocum was worthy of the author's attention. Ruth Moses was merely "descended" from the degraded remnant of an unnamed tribe. She was of no interest to the abolitionist.

What Armistead wanted in latching onto Paul Cuffe's budding interest in Sierra Leone was a narrative of emancipation and racial uplift. In 1848, he published a full-length book, *A Tribute for the Negro: Being a Vindication of the Moral, Intellectual, and Religious Capabilities of the Coloured Portion of Mankind; with Particular Reference to the African Race*. The purpose, according to its author, was to show by biography that the Negro was the equal of whites. Of the Indians of Tierra del Fuego—encountered by Robert FitzRoy—he writes that although they are "much lighter than the Negro," they are inferior in intellect.[17] He dedicated the book to a number of notable black abolitionists, including Alexander Crummell and Frederick Douglass. In it, he profiles Africans or persons of African ancestry like Olaudah Equiano, Ayuba Suleiman Diallo, Phillis Wheatley, Benjamin Banneker, Frederick Douglass, and Toussaint L'Ouverture. Among the many lives limned is that of Paul Cuffe, thirty-one years after his death. He details Cuffe's time in Liverpool with his "sable" crew.[18]

Despite the fact that Paul Cuffe was from the United States and his father was from the Gold Coast in Africa, not Sierra Leone, Armistead erases the former and homogenizes the latter, writing, "On Paul Cuffe's arrival in his native land, he was joyfully welcomed by his family and friends, and every comfort awaited his command. But the sufferings of his fellow-creatures, groaning under cruel oppression, and groping in the dark and horrible night of heathenish superstition and ignorance, were indelibly stamped on his mind. He could not rest at ease; nor think of enjoying comfort and repose whilst he might be instrumental in the hand of Providence in meliorating their sufferings."[19]

Mining a similar vein, while pressing his theme of racial uplift and advancement, Armistead ends his profile of Cuffe:

We have now concluded the sketch of this interesting descendant of Africa;—we have followed him in gradual rise, through a host of difficulties and prejudices to which the unfortunate descendants of Ethiopia are subjected; from a state of poverty, ignorance, and obscurity, to one of wealth, influence, respectability, and honour. Having thus elevated himself with an unsullied conscience by native energy of mind, we have seen him devoting the whole of his time and talents to pious and benevolent purposes: we have beheld him traversing the globe, at the risk of his own life and property, in endeavouring to promote the happiness of his fellow-creatures:—we have seen that his motives were pure and disinterested, for he dispensed his thousands of dollars at once when occasion required:—we have seen him indeed, a man, and a Christian, maintaining a higher standard than that of many professors, refusing to deal in anything, however lawful or lucrative, that could injure his fellow men:—we have heard that he was a good neighbor, an affectionate husband, and a kind parent:—we have beheld him crossing the mighty deep, visiting the land of his forefathers, carrying with him the light of science and religion, and diffusing it through those vast benighted regions; so that the untutored tribes of Ethiopia learnt to consider him as a father and a friend:—we have seen also that the philanthropists of Great Britain and America were not ashamed to seek counsel and advice from this son of a poor African Slave![20]

William Lloyd Garrison meets Horatio Alger! We can learn nothing about Paul Cuffe's self-perception from Wilson Armistead.

In the above quotation, Armistead refers to Cuffe as "a kind parent." Paul Cuffe's son, Paul Cuffe Jr., followed him to sea. In fact, he made his first voyage with his father aboard the *Alpha* in 1808, when he was twelve years old.

In 1839, at age forty-two, the son authored an autobiography, *Narrative of the Life and Adventures of Paul Cuffe, a Pequot Indian: During Thirty Years Spent at Sea, and in Travelling in Foreign Lands*. The text, penned by the subject himself and told in the first person, could not be more markedly different from the "memoir" of his father authored by Armistead. First, it announces Paul Jr. as Native immediately in its title. On the first page of the narrative, Cuffe amplifies this, calling himself "a descendant of an Indian family, which formerly resided in the eastern part of Connecticut and constituted a part of that fierce and warlike tribe of Indians called Pequots, of whose exploits in the early Wars of New England, the reader may become acquainted by perusing 'Trumball's History of the Indian Wars.'"[21]

Anthropologist Jack Campisi, in his introduction to the 2006 reprint of Cuffe's book by the Mashantucket Pequot Museum and Research Center (which also reprinted Armistead's book about his father), states, "Little is known about Paul Cuffe, Jr. beyond what he tells us in [his] brief memoir."[22] Further research will be necessary in order to determine why he identified as Pequot rather than Wampanoag. The Pequot tribe is part of the Algonkian language family, closely related to the Wampanoag and found, as Cuffe suggests, in eastern Connecticut. Once powerful, the Pequot confederacy was shattered by the Pequot War in 1637, more than 150 years before the birth of Paul Cuffe Jr. and more than 100 years before the birth of his parents. As noted in the prior chapter, survivors of the Mystic Massacre, the signal event of that war, were distributed among the Mohegan and Narragansett and sold into slavery on Bermuda and in the Caribbean.

A clue to the answer of this mystery may perhaps be found, however, in that single first sentence of the autobiography. Campisi, based solely on Armistead and Lamont Thomas (according to his footnotes), writes, "By contrast [to Paul Jr.], his father identified more strongly with his African ancestry."[23] The anthropologist calls Paul the younger's identification as Pequot a simple mistake. I think, however, we must be careful before we call it a mere error that a son misidentifies the tribe of his father, mother, and grandmother. Instead, I believe the misidentification may have been deliberate and strategic.

There is nothing in the memoir to indicate that Paul Cuffe Jr. ever made landfall in Africa, though he reports visiting the Cape Verde Islands off the west coast of Africa, as well as Haiti, Santo Domingo, and Brazil (three New World locales with significant African-descended populations). There is also nothing to suggest that the author identified at all with his African ancestry, instead strongly preferring the Native. It is possible, of course, that these choices may have been the product of editorial interference. Assuming, though, that they reflect the author's attitudes (as I believe they do), the clue may be found in that first sentence and the reference to the Pequot as "fierce and warlike." Jack Forbes, in his brief discussion of Paul Cuffe Sr., writes, "Cuffe was interested in the idea of colonizing free people of color in Africa. Subsequently, the colonization of persons of part-African or African descent occurred in Sierra Leone and Liberia. Some of these persons could, of course, have been part-American in ancestry (since the white racism of the period did not always distinguish between a Red-Black mixed-blood and a 'pure' African)."[24] The Pequot had been dominant in southern New England; that is precisely why they were targeted by the English colonists in the Pequot War. Having identified with his Native side, Paul Jr. decided to align himself with the biggest, baddest, meanest junkyard dog on the block. He was definitely and definitively Pequot.

Paul Cuffe Jr.'s life during his seafaring days was one of brief stays at home on land and extended voyages. He was always happy, as he described it, "to launch out upon the broad Atlantic's briny bosom."[25] Though he refers to his stays with his "dear parents" with affection, this nurturing, maternal language for the Red Atlantic indicates where he saw his true home place.[26]

He first shipped out on his father's vessel the *Traveller*. Over the ensuing years, he sailed all over the world, from Europe to the Caribbean to South America and beyond. In the Pacific, he visited Chile, the Juan Fernandez Islands, the Galapagos, Rapa Nui, and French Polynesia. In his autobiography, he reports encounters with Napoleon's army in Portugal, run-ins with pirates and the British navy during the War of 1812, and, above all, the dangers of the sea, including a capsizing on his first voyage on the *Traveller*.

Cuffe details a trip to Baffin Island and the fishery that so immediately attracted fishermen after John Cabot's voyage, writing, "In May 1819, I shipped aboard the brig *Traveller* again, on a cruise to Cape Harrison [in Labrador], in latitude 65 degrees north, where we took in twelve hundred quintals of codfish. While here we killed four white bears. Wild geese were very plenty. We saw Esquimaux Indians a number of times sailing in their skin canoes."[27]

Aboard the *Atlas*, he reports, Cuffe anchored off Corvo (which he calls Carvo), the smallest of the Azores, at the northern end of the archipelago. There they took on 500 bushels of potatoes and 100 bushels of onions. As I have suggested previously, the onions would have been used to ward off scurvy. The potatoes would provide a stable, long-lasting food staple. It demonstrates the diffusions that took place across the Red Atlantic. Some 300 years after the Inca first introduced Spaniards to the tuber, the crew of an American sailing vessel thought nothing of putting into the Azores in the mid-Atlantic to take on stores of potatoes. Another time, Cuffe discusses obtaining onions, potatoes, and pumpkins, the latter two exports of the Red Atlantic.[28]

The *Atlas* was a whaler. While during his career, Paul Cuffe Jr. engaged in both hauling cargo and whaling, he is remembered principally as a harpooner on whaling ships. Upon arriving at the Brazil Banks, he writes, "Here we commenced fishing for whale, but for a time we had bad luck, owing to the drunken habits of our Captain. We sunk twelve whales before we caught one. Then we caught six more in the course of two weeks. I harpooned all these, and assisted in taking and towing them along side the ship."[29] Cuffe was a harpooner. It is widely assumed that he was Herman Melville's model for Tashtego, the Gayhead Wampanoag harpooner in *Moby-Dick*.

Campisi is correct that there is much we do not know about the younger Paul Cuffe. One of the key unknowns is what happened to him and what he did after the events he reports in his autobiography. In the spring of 1838, he shipped out of Buffalo, New York, aboard the Great Lakes steamer *Wisconsin*. In June of that year, while taking on wood in Cleveland, Ohio, he injured his foot. When he was still, in his own words, "continuing lame" after his return to Buffalo, he traveled to Stockbridge, New York, where he seems to have taken on various casual labors. The area was a location where the Stockbridge Indians, Algonkian-speaking Mohicans, relocated in the late eighteenth century, around 1780, at the invitation of the Oneida and assisted by Christian missionaries. White settlers, however, began to enter the area in 1791, and the Stockbridge band was relocated to Wisconsin in 1833, five years before Cuffe's arrival.

There, Cuffe's memoir concludes. The last paragraph reads, "I now take my leave of those who may hereafter peruse this relation of events through which the writer has passed, during his stay among earth's travellers. May heaven's choicest blessings ever be theirs, together with innumerable comforts which are the attendants of an earthly pilgrimage. Good bye. PAUL CUFFE. Stockbridge, N.Y. March 18, 1839."[30] After this rather sad but valedictory closing, Paul Cuffe Jr. disappears from history. Perhaps his disability persisted, making a return to life at sea impracticable or impossible, and he remained in Stockbridge, which he describes in idealistic terms in his book. Certainly, he should have inherited a tidy sum from his father. We, however, do not know.

The two Paul Cuffes unite the Red and black Atlantics. There are other connections, some of which have already been mentioned in passing: Ayuba Suleiman Diallo, Òlaudah Equiano, Crispus Attucks. Additional links could be made: the Black Carib of St. Vincent and their resistance to British imperialism from 1763 to 1797; the Seminole of Florida and their incorporation of self-emancipating enslaved Africans from Georgia and Alabama; the interactions of Natives and African creoles on the Miskito Coast of Nicaragua.

Regarding the last group listed, it is worth noting that the Atlantic coast of Nicaragua was colonized by Britain. It was not united with the

Spanish-speaking portion of the country until 1894, when Nicaraguan president José Santos Zelaya invaded and seized the region. Prior to that time, the British had maintained a protectorate over this outpost of the Red Atlantic. They supplied the Miskito with arms and coopted them as their surrogate policemen on the coast against other native tribes. They also employed them to capture slaves to be delivered to Jamaica.[31]

The two Paul Cuffes are simply two of the many Native sailors upon the Red Atlantic. As I hope I have made clear, such Natives worked as maritime labor in significant numbers, both in hauling cargo and whaling. During the War of 1812, some were impressed by the British, a fate Paul Cuffe Jr. narrowly escaped. With the surrogacy of the Miskito in British Nicaragua from the early eighteenth century until well into the nineteenth century, we now turn from Indians as sailors to Indians as soldiers.

Indians as Soldiers

The British use of the Miskito to police the Atlantic coast of Nicaragua and to otherwise do their bidding is merely one example of European powers (and the United States and Canada as their successors in North America) making use of Western Hemispheric indigenes as soldiers in their service, and although it began in the late seventeenth century and was formalized (according to British ideas of law) in 1740 in the Treaty of Friendship and Alliance between King George II of Britain and the equally endowed King Edward I of the Miskito, it was hardly among the earliest.

Between 1688 and 1763, Indians in North America fought as allies and as pawns in four intra-European wars, collectively known as the French and Indian Wars, as they sought (with increasing desperation) to maintain historian Richard White's inherently unstable middle ground that they occupied between the British and the French. Each of those conflicts was the American reflection of a war waged far away on that other continent. King William's War (1688 to 1697) was the American reflection of the War of the Grand Alliance in Europe. Queen Anne's War (1702 to 1713) paralleled the War of Spanish Succession. King George's War (1744 to 1748) was known in Europe as the War of Austrian Succession. And what we know popularly as the French and Indian War (1754 to 1763) was the North American alter ego of the Seven Years' War. That last conflict effectively ended French aspirations in North America. A few years after the last of these colonial wars, the American Revolution tested longstanding allegiances. It also tore Native confederacies apart. Some Iroquois remained faithful to the "covenant chain" that bound them to Britain, while others threw in their lot with the rebellious colonists.

Since the inception of the United States, Native Americans have always fought in their conflicts in numbers disproportionately greater than their percentage of the overall population.

In his 1829 autobiography, *A Son of the Forest*, Pequot writer, activist, and Methodist clergyman William Apess describes running away from his indenture-owner in Connecticut at fifteen and joining the New York militia to fight the British in the War of 1812. (Apess expected to work his passage on a brig to New York City but was repeatedly thwarted by the presence of the British fleet off the coast. Walking most of the way, he finally got a ship in Kingsbridge, in what is today the Bronx, for his brief foray onto the Red Atlantic.)[32] Cherokees, including such current or future luminaries as The Ridge, John Ross, and George Lowrey, joined a combined Native force of Lower Creeks, Choctaws, and Yuchis to fight for the United States under Andrew Jackson in a sidelight to the War of 1812 known as the Creek War.[33] The Cherokees saved the Americans' bacon at the Battle of Horseshoe Bend. Cherokee chief Tsunulahunski (better known in English as Junaluska) literally saved Jackson's life at the Horseshoe, despite a name translated as "One Who Tries But Fails." Tecumseh and his warriors fought alongside the British (albeit for his own Native nationalist reason), and Tecumseh gave his life at the Battle of Thames.

During the American Civil War, Ely Parker, a Seneca, served as adjutant to General Ulysses Grant. In that capacity, he physically wrote the surrender document that Robert E. Lee signed at Appomattox Courthouse. (When Grant became president, he named Parker as his Commissioner of Indian Affairs, the first Native to hold that post.) On the other side, Stand Watie became a Confederate general, commanding an Indian brigade in the West. He was the last Confederate general to surrender in the field, more than two months after Appomattox.

Native Americans, many of them former students at Richard Henry Pratt's Carlisle Indian Industrial School, served significantly in the Spanish-American War. Others, like Paul Teenah, had ties to the Apaches imprisoned at Fort Marion in the late 1880s, following the close of the Apache Wars.

In the First World War, large numbers of American Indians and Canadian First Nations citizens sailed the Red Atlantic to fight for the Allies. One of these, Francis "Peggy" Pegahmagabow, an Anishinaabe (Ojibway), became the top sniper in the Canadian army and the most decorated Native in Canadian history.

In the remainder of this chapter, we will examine some of these, particularly Teenah and Pegahmagabow, among others. First, however, we must return almost to the beginning of European conquest and colonization in the Western Hemisphere.

A Fighting Writer

At first blush, it might seem odd to include El Inca Garcilaso de la Vega in this chapter, which deals primarily with soldiers and sailors. He is known principally as a writer and might more logically seem to fit in chapter 5, on literature. A mixed-blood Quechua, born in sixteenth-century Peru, he traveled to Spain, not to fight in new wars but rather to seek recompense for past ones. Yet nonetheless he found himself a warrior in the physical sense, just as his forebears on both sides of his lineage had been. And much of his writing was given to chronicling the exploits of both Inca warriors and Spanish conquistadores.

Garcilaso was born Gómez Suárez de Figueroa in Cuzco on April 12, 1539, the illegitimate son of Don Sebastian Garcilaso de la Vega Vargas, a conquistador, and his Inca princess concubine, Chimpa Ocllo. Chimpa was the daughter of Auqui Huallpa Túpac, the puppet Inca ("Inca" refers both to the people and to their rulers) appointed by Francisco Pizarro after the conquistador's execution of Auqui Huallpa's brother Atahualpa in 1533. She was the granddaughter of Túpac Inca Yupanqui, who ruled from 1471 to 1493. It was Yupanqui who, according to Inca legend, led a voyage of exploration into the Pacific circa 1490.[34]

Garcilaso grew up speaking both Spanish and Quechua in a household dominated by his mother and her Inca relatives. Talented and intelligent, he depicted his Latin teacher, the canon of Cuzco, Juan del Cuellar, as desirous of seeing a dozen Inca boys exposed to the academic marvels of Salamanca in Spain, at whose university the great founder of international law, Francisco de Vitoria, taught and Alonso de la Vera Cruz studied. The idea fired an intense yearning in the youth.

The archives of the Council of the Indies in Seville contain a license to come to Spain, issued to Don Sebastian Garcilaso by the Audencia de Lima in mid-1557 (when his son was eighteen) and good for three years.[35] Don Sebastian asked for the permit to return "for personal reasons," but doubtless he wanted to defend himself against intimations that he had been disloyal to the crown. He asked leave to return without forfeiture of his encomienda. King Felipe II signed a decree, granting permission on the requested terms. Yet, for some reason, Don Sebastian never used it. He died in 1559.[36]

The son's burning desire to visit Spain could not be fulfilled until after his father's death. Using his inheritance, he left for Europe in 1560. Some sources suggest that the idea was Felipe II's, who feared the rising influence of this young mestizo Inca "prince" among his mother's people.

According to Jonathan Steigman, a professor of Spanish at the U.S. Military Academy at West Point, "Very little is known about Gómez's [he did not use Garcilaso as a name until he came to Spain] life in Spain. When he arrived, he traveled to the Spanish province of Extremadura, Captain Sebastián Garcilaso de la Vega's ancestral homeland, to meet his paternal relatives. Indications are that these relatives did not receive with great enthusiasm the mestizo son of [the conquistador]. He was accepted by a great-uncle, Alonso de Vargas y Figueroa of Montilla. He resided in his uncle's home in Montilla, in the province known as Córdoba. There are strong indications that being a mestizo was not a social liability there and that he was well accepted by the citizens of the town."[37] Garcilaso secured an audience with Felipe and the Council of the Indies. His purpose was to present a memorial, asking for additional compensation for his father's service to the empire. The sight of a dark-skinned, well-appointed mestizo created a spectacle in the court, and the Council of the Indies received his petition with sympathy. It languished, however, and after several years was denied. Garcilaso came to the attention of Bartolomé de Las Casas, but when the Dominican found out that he was from Peru rather than Mexico or Guatemala, he lost any interest in him.

In order to support himself, Garcilaso joined the army. It was in this effort that he first distinguished himself. Steigman writes, "Military accomplishments characterized Gómez's paternal ancestral lineage. One ancestor, Garcia de la Vega [the original Garci Lasso], assisted Fernando I in his battle with the Moors in Andalucía during the reconquest of the

Iberian Peninsula. In Peru, Captain Sebastián Garcilaso de la Vega was accepted into the ruling class and was rewarded with estates, slave Indians, and the royal administrative office of *regidor* of Cuzco."[38]

In 1568, the Moriscos (Muslims who had converted to Christianity to avoid the expulsion order by Ferdinand and Isabella in the wake of their Reconquista) in the Alpujarras, a jumble of valleys in Andalucía south of Granada, were forced into rebellion by Felipe II's obstinacy and repression. Garcilaso assumed a command, fighting for Felipe. He thus found himself battling Moors around Granada, just as his father's ancestor had fought for Ferdinand during the reconquest of the Iberian Peninsula. Biographer John Grier Varner muses that it was probably during this period that he decided to refer to himself as "El Inca."[39] Through this rhetorical move (an addition to his appropriated Spanish name), he linked himself not only to the Spaniards of his father but to the Inca royalty of his mother. The Morisco Revolt lasted until 1571.

After his discharge, he remained bitter, claiming at one point in his *Royal Commentaries* that "because of the old reproach against his father [concerning the supposed disloyalty to the crown in Peru] he was unable to obtain satisfactory recognition for his own military service and as a result left the army so naked and impoverished that he dared not appear again at Court."[40] Weary and disillusioned, he retired to Cordoba and took up writing. Despite the entreaties of friends to try to petition Felipe, he refused, believing it to be futile.

While in retirement in Cordoba, Garcilaso's first major work was a history of the military expedition of conquistador Hernando de Soto through what is today the American Southeast, *La Florida del Ynca*. The Inca of the title is Garcilaso himself. In his book *La Florida del Inca and the Struggle for Social Equality in Colonial Spanish America*, Steigman argues persuasively for the book as an indigenous work. Although an account of a Spanish conquistador, Garcilaso's real purpose was to tell the story from two points of view in order to demonstrate that the Indians de Soto and his men encountered were equal actors in the events that ensued. The book was published in 1605. As with Bartolomé de Las Casas and Alonso de la Vera Cruz, writing half a century earlier, El Inca was attempting to influence events by affecting discourse. He sought to replace a narrative of total oppression with one of social equality.

Though he also produced a family history, *Relación de la Descendencia de Garci Pérez de Vargas*, about the descendants of the original Garci

Lasso, Garcilaso's magnum opus was his *Comentarios Reales* (*Royal Commentaries*), a general history of Peru and the Inca. A mammoth work, the book begins with a history of the Inca kings, based on the oral tradition he heard growing up among his mother's relatives. The second part deals with Peruvian history after the coming of the Spaniards. As with *La Florida del Ynca*, Garcilaso's purpose was one of establishing Indian dignity and equality. By relating Inca history from its origins through the Conquest, he created a continuity. The greatness of the Inca was perfected with the coming of the Spaniards bearing Christianity.

Unfortunately, the Spanish censors thwarted Garcilaso's intention. Though they permitted the publication of the first part in 1609, they held up the issuance of the second, thus breaking up the story that the author wanted to be told as a single account. Garcilaso died in Cordoba in 1616, still embittered. He was interred in that city's cathedral, the former grand mosque. The second part of his *Royal Commentaries* would not be permitted publication until the following year.

Yet his *Royal Commentaries* was destined to have a surprising second act, crossing the Red Atlantic back to Garcilaso's homeland. When the rebellion of Túpac Amaru II broke out in 1780, King Carlos III of Spain banned the distribution of the books in Peru, seeing them as inciting. Nevertheless, copies continued to circulate. The Inca leader, revolting against Spanish colonial oppression, was inspired by the books and carried them with him during the rebellion.

Our Caughnawagas in Egypt

In 1889, Rudyard Kipling was sent by his editor at the *Allahabad Pioneer* on a tour of the United States to write feature articles for the newspaper. The editor thought it best to get the young journalist out of India. He had become popular but embarrassing for his "stories and articles that lampooned high officials in the Indian Congress and the [British] imperial government."[41] The extensive trip took Kipling across the continent. He published his dispatches as his *American Notes*, first appearing without his permission in 1891.

While in Yellowstone, Kipling struck up a conversation with two U.S. cavalry officers, a captain and a lieutenant. According to the author: "The Lieutenant had read everything he could lay his hands on about the Indian army, especially our cavalry arrangements, and he was very full of a scheme for raising the riding Red Indians—it is not every noble savage that will make a trooper—into frontier levies—a sort of Khyber guard. 'Only,' he said ruefully, 'there is no frontier these days, and all our Indian wars are nearly over. Those beautiful beasts will die out, and nobody will ever know what splendid cavalry they can make.'"[42] Kipling continued, "The Lieutenant made a statement which rather amazed me. He said that, on account of the scarcity of business, many American officers were to be found getting practical instruction from little troubles among the South American Republics."[43] The writer's amazement is reminiscent of Charles Dickens's stunned surprise at receiving a calling card from the Choctaw Peter Pitchlynn nearly fifty years previous. Dickens had carried his stereotype of "wild Indians" with him when he crossed the Atlantic and did not expect to find an educated, cultured specimen like Pitchlynn. Similarly, Kipling, like many Europeans (albeit in this case one born in India), came to the West expecting to still see "riding Red Indians" roving over the landscape, threatening white settlers as the stalwart cavalry stood in their way.[44]

In 1889, neither Kipling nor his conversation partner apparently knew that something like the "scheme" the lieutenant proposed had already been tried. As noted above, there were all-Native units during the American Civil War—on both sides of that conflagration. And unlike black regiments (which were commanded by whites), these were commanded by Native officers, as the experience of Stand Watie (among others) demonstrates. The closest corollary, however, was just a few years before Kipling's chance encounter in Yellowstone. It involved not Apaches from Arizona but Mohawks from Québec.

In September 1884, the British prepared to mount an expedition to relieve Khartoum, the capital of Anglo-Egyptian Sudan. The city was threatened by Mar Mullah. Proclaimed the Mahdi, the "guided one" or messiah foretold by Mohammed, he had launched an insurrection in the Sudan the previous year. General Charles George "Chinese" Gordon had been dispatched to assist the Khedive in evacuating garrisons from the country. Now Gordon and his men were themselves trapped and in need of rescue. General Garnet Joseph Wolseley was ordered to undertake the relief.

General Lord Wolseley was, at fifty, a venerable presence in Her Majesty's army, the veteran of colonial wars in far-flung corners of the empire. Born in County Dublin, Ireland, in 1833, he entered the army in 1852 and first saw action in Burma. He subsequently fought in the Crimean War and the Sepoy Rebellion in India and commanded British forces in the Chinese War in 1860. In 1861, he was sent to Canada as assistant quartermaster general, rising to deputy quartermaster in 1865.

A "typical British imperialist," Wolseley considered anyone with Native blood a "savage."[45] He saw his role in British North America as one of pacifying the Indians and keeping American annexationists at bay. In 1870, he commanded the force sent to put down the Red River Resistance of Louis Riel and his Métis. He wrote in his diary, "Hope Riel will have bolted, for although I should like to hang him from the highest tree in the place, I have such horror of rebels and vermin of his kidney that my treatment of him might not be approved by the civil powers."[46]

The Métis are a group of mixed-blood people of Indian and, primarily, Scottish and French ancestry. Originally, the term was a catchall for any person of mixed ancestry, but it increasingly came to define a specific people. These persons worked principally as hunters in what is today western Canada.

Unlike the United States, Canada never experienced a civil war. The closest thing to such a conflict was one between two rival mercantile companies, the Hudson's Bay Company and the Northwest Company. The Métis worked for the Northwest Company. The signal engagement of that conflict was the Battle of Seven Oaks in 1816 at which Métis under Cuthbert Grant defeated Hudson's Bay Company forces. Though the Northwest Company was eventually merged into the Hudson's Bay Company, it was largely out of that encounter that the Métis began to coalesce as a distinct Native people.[47]

Louis Riel was a Métis born in 1844. He rose to lead his people in two uprisings against Canadian and British authority, the Red River Resistance in 1869 and 1870, in which General Wolseley played a part, and the Northwest Rebellion of 1885, both continuing Métis opposition to the Hudson's Bay Company. Between those events, Riel had a religious revelation. The Métis were overwhelmingly Catholic. Like David Pendleton Oakerhater, Riel took that most European import across the Red Atlantic—Christianity—and made it his own. His appropriation, however, was far more radical than Oakerhater's.

The 1885 rebellion, thanks to Riel, had a distinctly millenarian and apocalyptic cast. This stemmed from the vision he had experienced in 1876. He identified himself as the biblical King David, and his revelation was distinctly postmillennialist. Riel believed that humanity was living in the third and last epoch of the Kingdom of God, the epoch of the Holy Spirit (after the epochs of the Father and the Son). The new era dawned in 1876 (when he began his messianic mission). At that time, spiritual leadership and authority passed from Rome to Montreal, the first residence of the Holy Spirit in the New World. After 457 years, it would move to St. Vital or St. Boniface in Manitoba. The Métis would be delivered from their present state of oppression. They would lead Manitoba, which would become the leading place in the new order. Catholics and Protestants would be reconciled and world peace established after a series of disastrous wars. The "true religion" would triumph. All this would culminate in Christ's return. That second coming would take place after 457 years plus 1876, or 2333 years. The date of Christ's Parousia was thus set for 4209 c.e.[48]

The most ambitious attempt to study Riel's religious thought is that of Thomas Flanagan in his book *Louis "David" Riel: Prophet of the New World*. While informative, the work is nonetheless seriously flawed. Flanagan does not really take his subject seriously, and he does not take the Métis seriously as Natives, a mistake in my opinion. Further, he sees Riel as simply mentally ill or delusional. He views the Métis as ignoring or humoring his psychoses without actually believing in them, because of his value as a political leader. But Riel's vision and the Northwest Rebellion are so inextricably intertwined that it is impossible to separate the two. Riel's vision was one of unifying the Métis. He was leading a revolt to overthrow the perceived oppression of his people, and victory would usher in God's kingdom on earth. North America would be at the center of salvation history, and the Métis would be liberated as God's chosen people.

A far more sympathetic view of Riel and his new religion is given by Canadian métis writer Joseph Boyden in his dual biography of Riel and his fellow leader in the Northwest Rebellion, Gabriel Dumont.[49] In his final speech at his trial for treason, Riel defended his vision, saying, "I wish to leave Rome aside, inasmuch as it is the cause of division between Catholics and Protestants. I did not wish to force my views. . . . If I could have any influence in the new world it would be to help in that way, even if it takes 200 years to become practical . . . so my children's children can shake hands with the Protestants of the new world in a friendly manner. I do not wish those evils which exist in Europe to be continued, as much as I can influence it, among the (Metis). I do not wish that to be repeated in America."[50] He spoke for himself and all his Métis people, declaring, "Life, without the dignity of an intelligent being, is not worth having."[51] Like Peter Pitchlynn (and countless other Natives), Louis Riel participated in the cross-cultural Columbian Exchange of the Red Atlantic without ever traveling it physically.

For his part, General Wolseley—that "typical British imperialist"—regarded Riel not only as a rebellious savage varmint but as, quite simply, insane. Three years after helping quell the Red River Resistance—before Riel's "delusion" set in—Wolsley led the campaign against the Ashanti in Africa. And in 1882, he defeated and captured Arabi Pasha in Egypt and was raised to the peerage as Baron Wolseley as a result.

Now, in late 1884, with Gordon threatened in Khartoum, Wolseley suddenly recognized the worth of Natives—even as the discontent of Riel's Métis reached the boiling point once again. Realizing that if Khartoum, which lies on the Blue Nile near its confluence with the White Nile, were to be relieved, his expedition would need boatmen experienced at shooting rapids to negotiate the cataracts of the Nile, he personally directed that Mohawks from Kanawake, a small reserve (the Canadian term for reservation) in Québec, be recruited to form part of the Canadian contingent, expressly to perform this function. Their story would be told by their commander—one of their own—Captain Louis Jackson in his book *Our Caughnawagas in Egypt* (Caughnawaga is an older rendering of Kanawake).

Thus it was that "in spite of discouraging talk and groundless fears," a unit of fifty-six Mohawk volunteers found themselves aboard the *Ocean King* bound for Alexandria, being bidden farewell by the governor general, the queen's own representative in Canada himself.[52] Once in Egypt, the Mohawks worked with Egyptian boatmen and conveyed men and matériel up the Nile, performing their jobs in exemplary fashion, with the loss of only two men. On February 6, 1885, just a month before Riel's Northwest Rebellion erupted, the Mohawks departed from Alexandria to voyage back across the Red Atlantic. Upon his return, Jackson penned *Our Caughnawagas in Egypt*. His subtitle is both descriptive of content and a clever rhetorical device to establish not just the importance of the Mohawks to the campaign but also their primacy: "A Narrative of what was seen and accomplished by the Contingent of North American Voyageurs who led the British Boat Expedition for the Relief of Khartoum up the Cataracts of the Nile."

In an introductory preface, T. S. Brown reflects what Robert Warrior has called the rhetoric of novelty, the impulse to always see any act or creative production of a Native American as the first of its kind. Commending the book, Brown writes, "There is something unique in the idea of the aborigines of the New World being sent for to teach the Egyptians how to pass the Cataracts of the Nile, which have been navigated in some way by them for thousands of years, that should make this little book attractive to all readers."[53] Herman Melville implicitly makes a similar claim in his narrative poem *Clarel*, based upon his travels in Egypt and Palestine. In it, American travelers are surprised to find Ungar, a Cherokee Confederate veteran (presumably of Stand Watie's brigade), "[d]rilling some tawny infantry" on the banks of the Nile and conversing with Turkish naval officers in Jaffa as mercenary for the sultan. It is the same shock of discovery experienced by Kipling when he heard that former U.S. cavalry officers were freelancing in South America as the Indian Wars in the West wound down.

Yet, as Hilton Obenzinger points out in his book *American Palestine*, such sights were "altogether plausible" and far from unique:

> In 1868, the khedive of Egypt, eager to modernize his country, particularly his military, against the pressures of the Ottoman sultan's dominance and European penetration, engaged Thaddeus Mott to employ American advisors. Mott, employing William Tecumseh Sherman as advisor, recruited Charles P. Stone, veteran of the Mexican War and survivor of McClellan's intrigues, as the Egyptian chief of staff; and as a brigadier general Stone selected William W. Loring, who had fought Indians, Mexicans, and Mormons, as well as Union troops, to join both Union and Confederate armies. Many of the American mercenaries considered their service a contribution to the independence of an emerging nation against the tyranny of the sultan, while the Egyptians, finding the United States' lack of geopolitical interest in the region particularly appealing, valued American experience in the exploration of Western territories and the conquest of indigenous tribes for their own quest for expansion and modernization.[54]

The Mohawks of the Khartoum expedition may have been volunteers, but their recruitment reflects a consistent pattern of empires employing one colonized Other against another. Jackson's "boys" may have been no less savages to Wolseley than Louis Riel, but they had a valuable skill to be exploited in adventuring in the Sudan.

Another ground on which Brown recommends Jackson's account is explicitly ethnographic. He writes that the book will interest "especially as it is written by one born and bred in Caughnawaga, who, with the quick eye of an Indian, has noticed many things unnoticed by ordinary tourists and travellers." Then, attesting to the authenticity of the Native voice in the text, he states, "It is written off-hand and goes forth to the public as it came from the pen of the writer, to be judged in its style and the matter contained, by no standard but its own."[55] The addition of eight attractive engravings, depicting, among other subjects, Egyptian boats, irrigation techniques, the Sphinx, and the pyramids at Giza, heightened its appeal. The book is part professional memoir of a military campaign, part "fish-out-of-water" story of what it was like to be a North American indigene in Egypt, and part ethnographic travelogue.

Jackson notes at the outset the "groundless fears" the Indians held of their trip to Africa while still in Canada. These apprehensions continued after they arrived. The contingent departed the wharf in Alexandria on October 8, 1884. Jackson writes, "After leaving Alexandria I was surprised to see people standing up to their necks in swamps, cutting some kind of grass. I saw also cattle lying perfectly still in the water with just their heads out. This sight scared my boys as to what the heat might be further south."[56] The different natural environment made the Mohawks, so fearless at home on the St. Lawrence, uneasy.

Crocodiles apparently were a special concern for these Red Atlantic travelers, alluded to no fewer than three times in the brief text. On October 26, the flotilla arrived at Wady Halfa. Jackson relates, "One of the voyageurs while wading must have stepped on some seam, he jumped quickly back into his boat, leaving behind his moccasin and said he was bitten by a crocodile, which all of us were kind enough to believe and we advised him not to wade any more."[57] In fact, one of the few virtues Jackson found in the 175 Dongolese whom he had under his command was their familiarity with the landscape. He wrote, "It proved lucky for these men that the Nile does not scare them, for they had to swim for it on more than one occasion."[58] Finally, late in the navigation of the river, the water had fallen, exposing hundreds of rocks upon which "crocodiles could be seen by the dozen, sunning themselves." Jackson notes that one "brute" was twenty-five feet long.[59]

The North American Indians were on a military mission, but they were also eager tourists. Jackson was shown a "sacred tree" by a Coptic Christian, the dozens of nails driven into the trunk attesting to the many healings it had wrought. He notes the regret of himself and his men at having to "pass such famous places as Thebes and Luxor," even though they camped "quite close to Thebes and there were guides waiting with candles to show us over the place but we had no time to spare and so were not permitted to wander about."[60] And when they reached Abu-Simbel, "the boys" formed an "exploring party" for sightseeing; Jackson was prevented from accompanying them, though, since he had to remain in camp and deal with supplies. It was at the end of their service, however, that the Mohawks proved their mettle as tourists and not soldiers. Arriving in Cairo on February 5, 1885, and scheduled to depart the following day, the group undertook what could only have been a whirlwind tour. Jackson writes that "an opportunity was given to us to visit the following places of interest: Kass el-Nil Bridge, Kass el-Nil Barracks, Abdin Square and Palace, The Mosque Sultan-Hassan, the Citadel, the Mosque Mohamet-Ali, the Native Bazaar, the Esbediah Gardens, and finally Gizeh and the Pyramids."[61] In fact, the entire nature of tourism was changing even as these Red Atlantic visitors made their mad dash through the sights of Cairo and its environs. Once the opportunity of a determined elite, at this time it was becoming increasingly accessible. Upon reaching Assiout, some 240 miles from Alexandria, Jackson observed that "Mssrs. Cook and Son the great tourist agents had just commenced to build a large hotel, which when returning home I found already finished. I noticed a sign over a mud house door 'Egyptian Bank.'"[62]

In his text, Louis Jackson proves himself a keen observer of the Egyptian landscape and its inhabitants. He provides good descriptions of houses, boats, customs, agricultural details, and a local funeral. Often he compares what he saw to what he and his men knew from back at Kanawake. Brown writes that the volume "is written with a most excellent spirit that might wisely be imitated by other travellers. The writer finds no faults, blames nobody."[63] Yet, despite such encomia, Jackson is not without his ethnographic biases when it comes to his observations (though they are biases that doubtless would be shared by his Anglo-Canadian readership). In reaching the first Egyptian settlement where the expedition camped after leaving Alexandria, he notes, "I saw more rats at a glance than I had ever seen before in all my life." At Assiout, when the Mohawks saw a group of "Nubian prisoners," Jackson describes them as "black, ugly and desperate looking fellows chained together with large rusty chains round their necks." And at the same locale, he saw that "there were flies in the children's faces and eyes beyond description."[64] In the end, Jackson states, "I have not seen the place yet where I would care to settle down."[65] Likewise, he found difficulties with the locals. He notes, "It was a pity that we could not get the slightest information from the Egyptian crew with us, who seemed very adverse to us so much so, that I could not even learn their names far less any of their language."[66] About the "Dongolese" under him, he writes, "To give an idea of the trouble we had, I need only say that these Dongolese generally understood just the contrary of what they were ordered to do. They would pull hard when asked to stop or stop pulling at some critical place when hard pulling was required."[67] Later he observes of them, "Scolding was of no use, they neither understood nor cared. I may mention another peculiarity of theirs. I had noticed many scars on their bodies, but could not account for it, until one of them fell sick when the others cut his skin to bleed him, and filled the cut with sand."[68]

The job of "our Caughnawagas" ended at the Dal cataract. Their orders became to assist in "passing boats up the . . . cataract, until the last boat passed."[69] That final vessel passed the rapids on January 14, and the following day Jackson received orders to return to Wady Halfa, bringing the Mohawks' active service to a close. Brown in his preface declares that Jackson was "generous in his acknowledgements for every act of kindness and proper consideration shown to him and his party, by Her Majesty's Officers of all ranks in command of the expedition."[70] Indeed he was. Near the end of his book, he writes, "I cannot conclude without expressing my satisfaction at the handsome treatment accorded us by the British Government, and should our services be of assistance in the proposed Fall campaign in Egypt, they will be freely given. We were allowed just double the amount of clothing stipulated in the contract, the overcoats being given to us at Malta on our way home."[71]

So, clothed in their new topcoats, compliments of Her Majesty, the Mohawks arrived home, "well pleased with what we had seen in the land of the Pharos and proud to have shown the world that the dwellers on the banks of the Nile, after navigating it for centuries, could still learn something of the craft from the Iroquois Indians of North America and the Canadian voyageurs of many races."[72] The main British force reached

Khartoum two days too late to save Gordon and his men, but upon his return to England, General Lord Wolseley was created Viscount Wolseley and made commander in chief of the British army. New coats versus a promotion for leading a failed operation—from the very beginning, such were the unequal wages of the Red Atlantic.

The Atlantic Littoral Redux

Years before Rudyard Kipling had his conversation with the two cavalry officers in Yellowstone, the Indian Wars were already winding to a close. The Lakota and Northern Cheyenne had been subjugated in the wake of their victories over the U.S. Army at the Rosebud and the Greasy Grass (Little Bighorn). Quanah Parker's Comanche and the other tribes of the Red River War had surrendered, the leaders shipped off to Fort Marion on the Atlantic littoral. The Apache, however, remained unsubdued.

The Apache, "riding Red Indians" in the Southwest, had been at war with the United States since 1861, though conflict had arisen periodically for over a decade prior. Chiefs like Mangas Coloradas, Cochise, Victorio, and Geronimo struck fear in the hearts of those living on the Arizona and New Mexico frontier and of the newspaper-reading public in the East who still nervously waited for word from the West. Distrust and fear were constant on both sides. Rumors were rife. Even in times of relative calm, tensions rippled just below the surface.

In his memoirs, James Kaywaykla, a Warm Springs Apache and grand-nephew of the chief Nana, describes the volatile situation:

> Tzoe and Chato [two Apaches who had surrendered and become scouts for the U.S. Army] were very close friends, and both were heartily disliked and distrusted by our people. They were responsible for rumors that Kaytennae had been killed, and that Geronimo, Nana, and Chihuahua were to be imprisoned or killed. They and Mickey Free kept the Chiricahua and Warm Springs expecting trouble all the time.
>
> Nana reminded both that not one of the three had been loyal to his own people—if Mickey *had* any people—and that, inevitably, all would betray the White Eyes as they had us. They were not to be believed under any circumstances, and it was probably not true that Kaytennae was dead. It was not true, either, that the chiefs were to

have their heads chopped off as Chato was continually indicating. Our men knew, though, that as first sergeant, Chato had power over the scouts under him; and that some really liked him. . . . He was in a position to cause us much trouble, even as he had Kaytennae.[73]

As Kaywaykla points out, however, other than "the dread of betrayal," the Apaches were in relatively good shape. They had plenty of food and clothing, and they had raised corn for bread and for *tiswin*, a traditional fermented beverage made from either corn or the pear of the saguaro cactus.[74]

The army and the scouts began interfering in what the Apaches saw as their private lives and internal affairs. At a meeting when a junior officer lectured a drunken Chief Chihuahua for his indulgence in *tiswin* (in the manufacture of which he was reportedly expert), the leader stormed away. Nana did likewise, followed by every leader save one. They held a council, expecting mass arrests. Tensions escalated and nerves frayed.

On May 17, 1885, somewhere around 150 Apaches, fewer than 40 of whom were warriors, left the reservation. They included important men: Chihuahua, Nana, Geronimo, Naiche (son of Cochise), Ulzanna, and Istee (the son of Victorio). They broke hard for Mexico and the Sierra Madre. General George Crook, army commander of the Department of Arizona, put a huge force into the field—eighty companies of cavalry and infantry—to bring them back in. In the pursuit, he used Apache scouts like Chato; he likened the process to using "diamond dust to polish a diamond."[75] Crook was sympathetic to the Apaches, believing all their outbreaks had been the fault of false dealing by whites.[76] Yet he pursued them into Mexico. According to Kaywaykla, "There came a time when the Warm Springs Apaches were so reduced in numbers and equipment that Geronimo permitted Lozen to go to [the army] and arrange for a meeting."[77] Lozen was Victorio's younger sister, a warrior in her own right, and an Apache holy woman.[78]

The army officers agreed and promised safe passage under a flag of truce. Initially, there was still reluctance to come in. Chihuahua refused because his family was being held at Fort Bowie in Arizona. He demanded proof that they were safe, which he received. Crook met with the leaders of the outbreak on March 25 and 27, 1886. On March 29, he sent a dispatch to Lieutenant General Philip Sheridan, saying that he had negotiated surrender terms: "In conference with Geronimo and the other Chiricahuas . . . the only propositions they would entertain were these three. That they should be sent east for not exceeding two years, taking with them such of their families as so desired . . . or that they all should return to the reservation on their old status; or else return to the warpath with all its antecedent horrors. As I had to act at once, I have today accepted their surrender upon the first proposition."[79]

Chihuahua, in charge of by far the largest number, and Nana agreed to give up the fight and follow Crook to Fort Bowie. Geronimo and Naiche initially consented, too, but at the last minute turned back to the Sierra Madre. As Geronimo told it later, "We started with all our tribe to go with General Crook back to the United States, but I feared treachery and decided to remain in Mexico. We were not under any guard at this time. The United States troops marched in front and the Indians followed, and when we became suspicious, we turned back."[80] As it turned out, Geronimo's suspicions were well-founded, suspicions not of Crook but of the wheels within wheels that turned inside the U.S. government.

Crook arrived at Fort Bowie a day later, on March 30. Waiting for him was a reply from General Sheridan. President Grover Cleveland had rejected the surrender terms that Crook had negotiated. The message ran, "The President cannot assent to the surrender of the hostiles on the terms of their imprisonment East for two years with . . . their return to the reservation. He instructs you to enter again into negotiations of the terms of their unconditional surrender, only sparing their lives. . . . You must make at once such disposition of your troops as will insure against further hostilities by completing the destruction of the hostiles unless these terms are acceded to."[81]

Crook responded immediately, telling his superior that he would not impart his new charge to the Apaches. It would be completely counterproductive. Unless the war were terminated by the surrender on the terms agreed to, it would continue for years to come.[82] Disgusted by the continued bad faith and outright perfidy of the general government, discouraged, and bone-weary, Crook asked to be relieved of command rather than carry out his orders.[83]

On April 2, Sheridan named Nelson Miles as the new commander of the Department of Arizona, ordering him to organize as large a force as he deemed necessary and pursue the remaining renegades in Mexico. He warned, "These must be followed up until they are killed or captured."[84] The "hostile" Indians to whom Sheridan referred numbered only thirty-three. In his memoir, Kaywaykla joked that they were so few that he could call them all by name.[85] Many of them were women and children. There were only twenty warriors. Even so, it took Miles 5,000 troops and five more months. The remaining Apaches were exhausted and finished as an effective military force. Geronimo and Naiche finally agreed to treat with General Miles.[86]

Following the Red River War, seventy or so so-called leaders and criminals had been sent to Fort Marion for three years of confinement. Chihuahua, Geronimo, and the other Apaches who surrendered after the outbreak expected similar punishment. General Crook had agreed to their surrender terms that included only a two-year absence in the East (Geronimo in his surrender negotiations with Miles's command proposed these same original terms). What happened, however, was of a very different character in both quality and quantity.

According to Geronimo, General Miles told him, "The President of the United States has sent me to speak to you. He has heard of your trouble with white men, and says that if you will agree to a few words of treaty we need have no more trouble. Geronimo, if you will agree to a few words of treaty all will be satisfactorily arranged."[87] Instead, Miles's order was that *all* the Chiricahua and Warm Springs Apaches—men, women, and children, a total of 500 persons—were to be deported to Florida. The order included the Apache army scouts. Kaywaykla, again exhibiting his usual mordant wit, observes in his memoirs, "The government gave Chato a medal and sent him to jail. From our point of view that was fully in accord with the inconsistencies of White Eyes, and the imprisonment justly deserved by Chato."[88] What we would now call "ethnic cleansing" would ensure that Arizona would forever be free of further Apache wars.

Most were sent to Fort Marion—a fort never designed to be a prison and that could barely accommodate seventy-two inmates after the Red River War now was forced to house many more—and not just warriors but whole families, most of whom had never done anything. Geronimo and his last holdouts were sent to a different outpost of empire in the Red Atlantic, Fort Pickens on Santa Rosa Island in the Gulf of Mexico off Pensacola. Later, these would be transferred to Mount Vernon Barracks near Mobile, Alabama.

The humidity of the Atlantic coast worked upon the Arizona Natives. There were many deaths. As Geronimo taciturnly put it, "We were not healthy in this place, for the climate disagreed with us."[89] As with the Red

River War veterans, there were also acts of self-inflicted violence. Fun, one of Geronimo's group, killed himself and his wife. Another shot his spouse and then himself. She survived, but he died.[90] Ironically, many of those imprisoned joined the U.S. Army as Indian scouts; these included Naiche, Chihuahua, and Perico (Geronimo's brother).

The Apaches' captivity lasted twenty-seven years. In 1894, the survivors were sent to Fort Sill in the recently created Oklahoma Territory. Chihuahua died there in 1901. Geronimo followed him in 1909. In 1913, some were allowed to move to the Mescalero Apache reservation in New Mexico. None were ever permitted to return to Arizona.

In Florida, the Apaches' children were taken from them. Some were sent to Hampton, but others were sent to Carlisle, continuing Fort Marion's association with Richard Henry Pratt. Among those sent to the latter were James Kaywaykla, Paul Teenah (also called Paul Tee), and Emily Chihuahua, the daughter of Chief Chihuahua and his wife, Ilth-Gozey. Emily had been born in captivity at Fort Marion in 1889. Teenah and Emily would later be married.

Much about Paul Teenah's life is subject to conjecture. Records are partial, some having been destroyed, and we must be careful in interpreting them. One might assume that he and Emily Chihuahua knew each other before Carlisle. Paul, however, was born in 1878 and was about the same age as James Kaywaykla, who was sent away to the Pennsylvania boarding school at age nine. That was before Emily was even born. It seems more likely, therefore, that Paul and Emily met at school. He predeceased her in 1907 at about twenty-nine years old. She died two years later at only twenty. They are buried together in the Chihuahua cemetery at Fort Sill.

On April 25, 1898, when the United States declared war on Spain, formally initiating the Spanish-American War, Paul Teenah would have been about twenty years old. We know he participated in the Red Atlantic, joining the army and winding up in Cuba. We do not know, however, if he participated in the Cuba campaign or if he was sent later as a garrison soldier. The one photograph we know with certainty is of him was taken in 1900 at Camp Road MacKenzie in Cuba. The invasion force had begun to withdraw in August 1898. Information written on the back in a crude hand reads only "Pvt. Paul Teenah, I Troop."

General Order No. 28, issued by the army command on March 9, 1891, provided that Troop I of each U.S. Army infantry regiment would be created by enlisting Indians from west of the Mississippi. Troop L in each cavalry unit would have a similar composition. Company I of the Twelfth Infantry contained a significant number of Apache internees, though historian Thomas Britten states that the last of the segregated Indian units, Troop L of the Seventh Cavalry, was mustered out on May 31, 1897.[91] Is the picture of Paul Teenah of an earlier vintage than the proposed 1900 date at Camp Road MacKenzie? The available evidence suggests that Teenah did serve in Cuba. His uniform is that of an infantryman of the period, too. Did he scrawl "Troop I" on the back of his photo to honor the Apaches who served before him? The designations of Troops I and L were resurrected during the Spanish-American War for units with Indian troopers (although they were not segregated). This seems the most likely explanation.

The photograph of Teenah shows him looking directly in the camera, standing at attention in front of tents in the background. The soldier holds his rifle smartly at his side. He is dressed in a light khaki jacket and slightly darker khaki pants. A cartridge belt cinches his waist. He wears gauntlets on his hands, tightly wrapped puttees around his ankles, and a broad-brimmed hat on his head. As for the man himself, he is darkly handsome, with an open and expressive face. A slight smile on his face suggests to me not smugness but pride. He looks proud to have his picture taken in his uniform, proud to be soldier. Perhaps the picture was meant to be sent back to Fort Sill, his home (albeit involuntarily). To Emily?

Like so many Native Americans, even at the dawn of the twentieth century, much else about Teenah's life remains speculative. Even his gravesite is subject to conjecture. There is a grave for Private Paul Teenah in the Fort Bayard National Cemetery in New Mexico. The birth and death dates match those on the tombstone at Fort Sill.

Fort Bayard was built in southwestern New Mexico Territory in 1866 to protect settlers from the Apache. In 1899, it was destined for decommissioning, when army surgeon George Stemberg proposed transferring the post to the medical department. Because of the high altitude and dry climate, it became the first military hospital for the treatment of pulmonary tuberculosis, a major problem for Spanish-American War veterans. Did Teenah contract consumption in Cuba? Was he sent to the

Fort Bayard hospital and died there? Is his tombstone at Fort Sill simply a marker with his wife in the family graveyard, a mere cenotaph?[92] We do not know. Questions outnumber answers.

The lieutenant with whom Kipling spoke in Yellowstone dreamed of a cavalry unit composed of the "riding Red Indians" of the West. When the Spanish-American War erupted, there were renewed calls to enlist segregated Native units. The same yellow press that fanned the flames of a U.S. war with Spain carried wild and untrue stories that William "Buffalo Bill" Cody, at the time fifty-two years old, had raised a force of 600 Lakotas ready to fight. In reality, Native Americans did enlist in significant numbers, though their service is poorly documented. Some, like Paul Teenah (regardless of his year of enlistment), joined to get away from undesirable situations. Others did so to prove their worth to white Americans. Still others did so to fulfill in their own minds the Indian warrior tradition. Many were students or alumni of Pratt's Carlisle Indian school.

On April 22, 1898, after the American blockade of Cuba began—but before the formal declaration of war—Congress passed the Volunteer Army Act. The bill authorized the raising of army units "possessing special qualifications." With the signed law in hand, Secretary of War Russell Alger authorized three new cavalry regiments. The First Volunteer Cavalry Regiment, organized by Captain Leonard Wood, who had served with Nelson Miles (now commanding general of the army), and Theodore Roosevelt, was composed of cowboys and Indians from the Twin Territories (Indian and Oklahoma), as well as from Arizona and New Mexico. The Second was raised from Wyoming and the Third from the Dakotas. Neither the Second (the Rocky Mountain Riders) nor the Third (Grigsby's Cowboys) were to see action. Only the First, known to history as the "Rough Riders," would.[93]

Although the fact is largely forgotten today, a number of Roosevelt's Rough Riders were Indians. Among them was a Cherokee farmer named Bert Holderman, who served as Roosevelt's cook. According to Britten, "After a long day of fighting the Spanish, a very tired Roosevelt slumped into camp. Holderman responded by wrapping his commander in dry blankets and putting him to sleep on a nearby table."[94] More than just a cook, a sympathetic Holderman performed the role of comforter and "body man."

Frank and Joseph Brito, Yaqui (Yoeme) from Arizona, were Rough Rider privates. Roosevelt called Frank "Monte," short for Montezuma—

apparently the lieutenant colonel's equivalent of what became a time-honored, if demeaning, army tradition of calling Native recruits "chief."[95] Unlike Holderman, they never made it to Cuba. Instead, they were halted at the Atlantic littoral in Tampa. They were part of the third of the regiment left to care for the regiment's horses, which also had to remain in Florida. Jon Ault writes, "As privates in Troop H, the Brito brothers spent that summer battling malaria and dysentery." Frank recalled his part in the conflict: "It was no honor to stay behind. Tampa was a hell-hole. We were there, waiting, thinking we could get over to Cuba, or maybe Puerto Rico, and nothing happened. . . . We were there over two months, with nothing to do but get sick and get mad."[96] Holderman and the Britos performed essential roles, if noncombatant ones. Other Native Rough Riders were in the thick of the fighting. Among them were Thomas Isbell, a Cherokee, and William Pollock, a full-blood Pawnee.

Isbell, serving in the Rough Riders' Troop L, was selected by Sergeant Hamilton Fish to be "point," at the head of the advancing American column. At least through the Vietnam War, this was a standard procedure, choosing an Indian soldier to walk point, the justification being the supposed superior tracking skills of the Native troops. Of course, those in the front also drew a disproportionate amount of the fire (with casualty rates to match). When the Spanish rear guard ambushed the Americans in the Battle of Las Guásimas, Isbell killed one of the enemy but was wounded seven times within thirty minutes. In his best-selling memoirs of the war, *The Rough Riders*, Theodore Roosevelt describes Isbell's actions and his injuries in detail:

> Thomas Isbell, a half-breed Cherokee in the squad under Hamilton Fish, was among the first to shoot and be shot at. He was wounded no less than seven times. The first wound was received by him two minutes after he fired his first shot, the bullet going through his neck. The second bullet going through him in the left thumb. The third struck near his right hip, passing entirely through his body. The fourth bullet (which was apparently from a Remington and not from a Mauser [that is to say, from friendly fire]) went into his neck and lodged against the bone. . . . The fifth bullet again hit his left hand. The sixth scraped his head and the seventh his neck. He did not receive all of the wounds at the same time, over half an hour elapsing between the first and the last. Up to receiving the last wound he had declined to leave the

firing-line, but by that time he had lost so much blood that he had to be sent to the rear.[97]

Such was the lot of soldiers on point. Roosevelt concludes, "The man's wiry toughness was as notable as his courage."[98]

Similarly, the future president praised the Pawnee Pollock, writing that he was "one of the gamest fighters and best soldiers in the regiment." In the battles for Kettle and San Juan Hills, Roosevelt noticed him "among the men . . . leading in the charges and always being nearest the enemy."[99] Roosevelt describes him as the stereotypical stoic Indian, silent and solitary. Demonstrating that Pollock was as adept in his understanding of the Red Atlantic as Peter Pitchlynn, while Roosevelt was as uncomprehending as either Dickens or Kipling before him, Roosevelt notes, "I never suspected him of having a sense of humor" until in Cuba he turned to a soldier serving as the regiment's barber. "Eyeing him with unmovable face Pollock asked, in a guttoral voice: 'Do you cut hair?' The man answered 'Yes'; and Pollock continued, 'Then you better cut mine,' muttering, in an explanatory soliloquy: 'Don't want to wear my hair long like a wild Indian when I'm in civilized warfare.'"[100]

Bert Holderman and William Pollock died in Cuba. Tom Isbell survived his many wounds to later join Buffalo Bill's Wild West show.[101]

As noted above—and as Roosevelt states in his memoirs—many of the Indians fighting in the war were Carlisle alumni. One, Joseph Dubray, a Lakota, enlisted in the Sixth Massachusetts and sailed for Cuba from Virginia aboard the U.S.S. *Yale* on July 5, 1898. Though he arrived too late to take part in the fighting, he witnessed the final shots and the surrender of Santiago de Cuba. Later that month, he participated in the Puerto Rican campaign, during which he and his fellow soldiers knew they were "going to be targets for the Spanish bullets!"[102]

Before the war began, on March 29, 1898, students at Carlisle debated a U.S. declaration of war against Spain. The *Indian Helper*, the weekly newspaper of the school, reported on the debate: "The entire list of speakers wanted to be on the affirmative side, and it shows that peace principles have been well-taught in the class and that both sides have been thoroughly studied, for Edgar Rickard and Myron Moses spoke in favor of non-declaration of war, when it was directly in opposition to their feelings."[103] The nonintervention side actually took the day. After the war, Richard Henry Pratt, in his annual report to the U.S. Department of the Interior, praised the Carlisle alumni who fought, averring that it proved the success of his experiment in Indian education and assimilation. He wrote: "Early in the year, when the first rumors of war electrified our country, our young men were eager to prove their loyalty to the Government, and expressed their wish to enlist should there be a call for volunteer troops. The military government and drill used at the school especially qualified them for such service. . . . The interest they show by asking to take an active part in the grave operations, even to laying down their lives if need be, suggests that if in time of war such a oneness of interest is aroused, then in time of peace, universal enlistment can be made in an intelligent and industrious service for the welfare of the nation by adding their energies to its growth of culture and industry."[104] Even as Pratt reported the vindication of his methods to the federal government, his graduates continued to serve.

In the aftermath of the war in the Pacific, a war erupted between the U.S. occupation forces and Philippine nationalist guerrillas. According to the November 17, 1899, issue of the *Indian Helper*, Abram Mumper, a veteran of that rebellion, visited Carlisle and spoke to the students. Reflecting on the grim slog that lay ahead in pacifying the islands and a problem with counterinsurgency that persists to the present day, the paper reported, "Mr. Mumper believes there will be no Waterloo or Gettysburg, but there will be a system of warfare continued for a long time which will take thousands of men and money to conquer."[105] In the wake of Mumper's visit, several Carlisle students volunteered for service abroad. One of them was William Colombe, like Joseph Dubray a Sioux, who served in Troop I of the Fourth Cavalry. In February 1900, Colombe wrote back to his alma mater, both detailing the death of Brigadier General Henry Ware Lawton (whose killer he apparently claimed to have slain) and complaining about the conditions under which American soldiers fought the insurrection. He wrote, "General Lawton was killed about twenty yards from where I was shooting at a man who was shooting from a tree, and I think that was the very man who killed the General. But we kept shooting until he fell from the tree. I don't think he will live to tell the tale to his friends that he killed our good General. It is hard on this Island. Sometimes we do not get anything to eat for three or four days. I don't understand why the Filipinos don't quit fighting, because so many of them get killed in every fight that they go into, and not many are lost on our side."[106]

On the one hand, Colombe's lament at the end of his missive sounds like the questions asked by every ordinary soldier called upon to fight a faceless enemy in a popularly inspired colonial war (think Vietnam or Afghanistan). On the other hand, that a Sioux, whose people fought a long, ultimately futile battle against American expansionism, asked such a question is ironical. There is indeed high irony in the fact that the man who may have gotten the man who killed Henry Lawton—one who those who actually helped capture Geronimo, who fought 5,000 American troops with twenty warriors—entertained such thoughts (even though in his situation they are understandable). The final irony, Ault points out, is that the man who killed Lawton was named Geronimo.[107]

Other Native Americans who waged the war against Filipino *insurrectos* in the Philippine-American War included Clinton Rickard, an Iroquois who would go on to become chief of the Tuscarora, and Joseph Brito. Like his brother Frank, Brito had been stopped at Tampa, never seeing action in Cuba. But he fought and died in the Pacific.

In the story of the Red Atlantic, even as the narrative is recentered on Western Hemisphere indigenes, women can easily remain marginalized. Yet women were nonetheless actors in the Red Atlantic, though men were far more prevalent. King Philip's wife was sold into slavery in the Caribbean. Senauki, the spouse of Tomochichi, was part of his delegation to England. Lozen accompanied Geronimo to prison. More Apache women went into captivity at Fort Marion. Pocahontas and E. Pauline Johnson made transatlantic transits. Yet the involvement of women was far more extensive than I convey and deserves separate, more extensive study. And women played a part in the Red Atlantic during and after the Spanish-American War.

Jon Ault describes how the Daughters of the American Revolution Hospital Corps enlisted four Lakota Catholic nuns from the Congregation of American Sisters at Fort Pierre in South Dakota. When the war was declared, they offered them as nurses, despite their lack of formal training. Throughout the brief conflict, they tended the sick and wounded on the Atlantic littoral at Camp Cuba Libre in Jacksonville, Florida, and on the marge of the Atlantic at Camp Onward in Savannah, Georgia.[108] Ault points out that, for the time, the quartet were paid quite well: newly recruited nurses were paid ten dollars a month, while male hospital stewards earned forty-five. In comparison, the Sioux women made thirty dollars per month.[109] At war's end, they were awarded the

Cross of the Order of Spanish-American War Nurses and discharged on February 1, 1899. Afterward, they went to work in an orphanage in American-occupied Cuba. Susan Bordeaux (Reverend Mother M. Anthony) died there of pneumonia. There were limits, however, to gender parity: Ault relates that, although she was given a military funeral, the request to have her buried in Arlington National Cemetery was refused.[110]

For men, though—again within the context of the time—the situation was different and more clear. Theodore Roosevelt, speaking for the First Volunteer Cavalry Regiment but also for other mixed-race units, says that the Indian soldiers in the Rough Riders "lived on terms of complete equality" with their white comrades.[111] This easy camaraderie, born of the shared dangers and sacrifices of combat, and relative equality are of great importance in the history of the Red Atlantic. Native soldiers in World War I shared this same experience. Veterans of these two foreign conflicts at the turn of the twentieth century would return home unwilling to accept an inferior status after the comparative freedom they experienced abroad. They would be the moving force behind Indian activism for a generation to come.[112]

A Man Called Peggy

At least in the United States, the first three decades of the twentieth century were a kind of interstitial period. The Indian Wars had come to a close. The aggressive assimilationist policies established in the 1880s were breaking down, but nothing would replace them until 1934. This does not mean, however, that nothing was going on in Indian Country. There was a great deal of activism, even if much of this was invisible to the wider publics in the United States and Canada. For instance, Clinton Rickard, a Tuscarora veteran of the Philippine-American War, in 1926 founded the Indian Defense League of America "to guarantee the unrestricted passage on the continent," protesting the tightening of the U.S.-Canadian border that split the territory of the Iroquois Confederacy in two.[113] And 1914 saw the beginning of the last large-scale event of the Red Atlantic. That event encompasses both the topic of this chapter, soldiers and sailors, and the diplomacy examined in chapter 3.

Thousands of North American Natives sailed the Atlantic to fight in the Great War. Among them was my great-uncle Elmer Price from Oklahoma, the son of a Cherokee mother, Bettina Lowrey, and an Anglo-

American father. Price was mustard-gassed in France. Responding to a questionnaire after the war, Jacob Russell, a Winnebago who served in the 130th Field Artillery of the Thirty-Fifth Division, described a similar experience, haltingly writing:

> I was gassed little the morning we were making attack at Cheppy Sept 28, 1918. And I was very glad to come out a live [*sic*] again. There is many of my comrades fell dead beside of me. The brave boys that I will never see again.
>
> Well we all done our big and little jobs so far. But never forget the dead ones which we left behind over there.[114]

Like Russell, Elmer Price survived, but he came home a spent man.

A great deal of very good work has been done on the service of North American indigenous persons in World War I. These include *American Indians in World War I* by Thomas Britten; *North American Indians in the Great War* by Susan Applegate Krouse; *For King and Kanata: Canadian Indians and the First World War* by Timothy C. Winegard; and the more expansive *Indigenous Peoples of the British Dominions and the First World War*, also authored by Winegard.[115] In addition, Diane Camurat produced a master's thesis at the University of Paris VII (Diderot), "The American Indian in the Great War: Real and Imagined," which is based on extensive research of materials that other scholars have not considered.[116]

In sheer numbers, only enslavement and captivity exceeded World War I in terms of involvement in the Red Atlantic, and slaves and captives experienced it not in a single event but over almost a thousand years. Determining, however, exactly how many North American Natives went to Europe has proved difficult. Photographer and pro-Indian activist Joseph Kossuth Dixon, who in the immediate aftermath of the war sought to document and interview veterans, put the number in the U.S. Army at 17,000, apparently based on information supplied by acting secretary of war John Weeks, but this almost certainly is based on the total number that registered with the Selective Service. (Krouse's book is based on Dixon's work.) Native American studies scholar Russel Barsh accepts the figure (17,313 precisely) but states that just over 6,500 Natives were drafted and that another 8,500 volunteered, bringing the number to roughly 15,000. Britten puts the number at perhaps 10,000. Krouse suggests that it may be 12,000. If we accept Dixon's figure (17,000), we can assume that certainly not all of these served overseas. Sifting through all the available data and estimates, it appears that anywhere from 8,000 to 12,000 Native Americans went to Europe (Barsh says the figure may be as low as between 2,000 and 4,000). In addition, Winegard estimates that more than 4,000 Canadian Natives served in theater as part of the Canadian Expeditionary Force between 1914 and 1918. This does not include some number of U.S. Indians who joined the Canadian army to get into the fighting before the United States entered the war in 1917.[117]

As Camurat makes clear, the above figures do not include those who went to Europe in non-military roles, both men and women. Some Native men went as ambulance drivers and attendants. According to Commissioner of Indian Affairs Cato Sells, six Indian women served overseas as nurses. Two Cherokee women, Anne Ross (a descendant of famed Cherokee principal chief John Ross) and Iva Rider, traveled under the auspices of the Young Women's Christian Association. Ross worked in a canteen. Rider entertained, performing under the name "Princess Atalie." Similarly, a Muscogee woman named Tsianina Redfeather entertained troops in the theater of operations.[118]

Some, like Elmer Price and Jacob Russell, served in the army in combat, but one did not have to go overseas to participate in the war and the Red Atlantic. Those who served in the United States or Canada supported the war effort, as well. They acted as trainers and did jobs that freed others to go to the front. According to Krouse, Dixon said that no Natives served in the U.S. Navy or the U.S. Air Service. This may be true if one sticks to a strict definition of service as serving in the theater of war. Britten, however, says that a thousand Indians served in the navy. Most served in escort or transport duty, but given German submarine warfare, they too put their lives at risk. Wesley Youngbird of the Eastern Band of Cherokee Indians was a sailor on the battleship U.S.S. *Wyoming*. Leon Wolfe, a Canadian Cree, served as a gunner aboard the U.S.S. *Utah*. Britten also states that an Oklahoma-born Native named Floberth Richester joined the Lafayette Escadrille, American aviators who fought in France before the United States entered the war, and became an ace with seven credited kills. Camurat, however, researching in France, notes that Richester's Indian identity has been questioned and that his name does not appear in the rolls of the Escadrille—though she acknowledges that he might have enlisted in a British squadron and thus been counted in the Lafayette Flying Corps, "an honorary grouping of all American aviators attached to units of the Allied Forces before the United States entered the war."[119] Virginia Mathews, the daughter of Osage writer John Joseph Mathews, wrote the introduction to the 1988 edition of his novel *Sundown*. In it, she says her father served as an instructor in night flight and later flew in France. Krouse, though, says he never got overseas.[120] Krouse seems certainly to be correct: *Sundown* is in large part autobiographical. In the novel, Mathews's alter ego, Chal Windzer, is told by his fellow officer that he has been appointed as an instructor in night bombing. Mathews imagines the fictional incident: "Chal stood a moment then said, 'Tad—Lieutenant, I hope this appointment won't keep me from goin' across—I want to get across as soon as I can.' Tad looked up at him in scorn. 'Lieutenant, we don't reason or question in the service of the United States army—we do—you are now an officer of the post—good day.'"[121] Though Mathews would become a leading Native American cosmopolitan, being awarded a Rhodes Scholarship (which he declined, attending Oxford on his own resources) and traveling extensively in North Africa and the Middle East, neither he nor Chal made it to France during the war.

Of course, even civilians played their part in the war effort. Cherokees in Tahlequah, Oklahoma, collected scrap metal. Elsewhere, Natives on the prairie grew the wheat that helped feed the troops. They assembled Model-Ts at the Ford Motor Company in Detroit that became ambulances in France. They worked in shipyards and at docks, where they built and loaded the ships bound for Europe, keeping the army supplied. They volunteered with the Red Cross. They bought $15 million in Liberty bonds ($50 per capita for every Indian in the United States) to finance the conflict: among the purchasers, according to Commissioner Cato Sells, were Geronimo's widow and sons, as well as the son of Victorio— all veterans of incarceration in Florida.[122] These, among countless other contributions, are also parts of the story of the Red Atlantic.

When Great Britain declared war on August 4, 1914, Canada was automatically brought in as well, since at the time Great Britain controlled its dominion's foreign policy. "When Britain is at war, Canada is at war. There is no distinction" was the rule of the day.[123] Indian leaders immediately offered support, and Natives went to enlist. There was, however, a question as to whether they should be permitted to join the armed forces. Indians had been barred from service in the Boer War (1899–1902), though, as Timothy Winegard points out, a handful managed to evade the ban and cross the Red Atlantic to fight in South Africa. Walter White, a Huron (Wendat), died there at the Battle of Paardeberg.[124] According to Winegard, "Under the British North America Act and the Indian Act, Canadian Indians did not have the rights and responsibilities of citizenship; therefore, the government of Canada did not expect, or need, them to take up arms in a foreign war."[125]

Four days after Britain's declaration of war, the minister of militia, Sir Sam Hughes, received a question from one of his district commanders, asking, "Is it intended that Indians who are anxious to enlist for service Overseas are to be taken on the Contingent?" Sir Sam responded the same day, writing, "While British troops would be proud to be associated with their fellow subjects [Indians], yet Germans might refuse to extend to them the privileges of civilized warfare, therefore it is considered . . . that they had better remain in Canada to share in the protection of the Dominion."[126] The irony here is that had Hughes known anything about his German enemies, as we will see in chapter 5, he would have known that these literary children of Karl May revered the "Red Indian."

Unlike the firm ban during the Boer War, there was never an official exclusionary rule, barring Native service, during World War I. Indians, however, were to be discouraged from enlisting. Besides, everyone knew that the war would be over by Christmas: there would be no need for Indians in the army. It was only more than a year later, in December 1915, after suffering massive casualties, that Canada officially authorized Native recruitment.

Duncan Campbell Scott, deputy superintendent of Indian Affairs, favored Canada's aggressive policy of assimilation. He looked forward to the day when there would be no "Indian problem," "no Indian question, and no Indian Department." When enlistment was finally formally authorized, he saw service across the Red Atlantic as a means to help fulfill that dream. Reflecting on the issue after the war, Scott wrote:

> These men who have been broadened by contact with the outside world and its affairs, who have mingled with the men of other races, and who have witnessed the many wonders and advantages of civilization, will not be content to return to their old Indian mode of life. . . . Thus the war will have hastened that day, the millennium of those engaged in Indian work, when all the quaint old customs, the weird and picaresque ceremonies, the sun dance and the potlatch and even the musical and poetic native languages shall be as obsolete as

the buffalo and the tomahawk, and the last tepee of the Northern wilds give way to a model farmhouse. In other words, the Indian shall become one with his neighbour in his speech, life and habits, thus conforming to that world-wide tendency towards universal standardization which would appear to be the essential underlying purport of all modern social evolution.[127]

Neither the paternalism nor the cultural imperialism in the statement needs discussion. Scott, however, was right about one thing: the returning veterans would not be content with the status quo.

In 1922, just four years after the armistice, western writer Zane Grey published *The Vanishing American* in serial form in the *Ladies' Home Journal*. It appeared as a book in 1925 and was filmed by George B. Seitz for Paramount that same year. The plot centers on Nophaie, an American Indian on a reservation run by corrupt whites. When war is declared, he and his fellow Natives enlist. In battle they distinguish themselves. Nophaie is awarded the Distinguished Service Cross at Château-Thierry (one of the first battles in which the American Expeditionary Force participated). The Native soldiers come home, shattered in both body and mind. They resolve, however, not to accept the abusive conditions of the reservation.[128]

In 1917, when the United States finally entered the war, there was no thought about whether Native Americans would be permitted to fight, though there was a brief question about whether or not only Indians who were citizens should be subject to the draft. Richard Henry Pratt, always looking to validate his experiment in assimilative education, advocated for Natives in the front lines.[129] Instead, the debate in the United States centered on whether Indians would serve in segregated, all-Indian units (except, of course, for their officers) or be integrated with white troops. Among the most ardent supporters of the first position was anthropologist Francis La Flesche, an Omaha who worked for the Bureau of American Ethnology within the Smithsonian Institute, who saw it as a way for Indians to prove their worth to their fellow Americans. Joseph Kossuth Dixon testified before the House Committee on Military Affairs, reading thirty pages of testimony advocating for all-Native units (à la Kipling's conversation partnership in Yellowstone). In it, he pointed out the successful experience of Great Britain and France with segregated units of South Asian Gurkha, Nigerians, and Senegalese. He reminded the members of Congress of President Woodrow Wilson's support for self-determination for the world's minorities. On the other side of the argument were Pratt and Commissioner of Indian Affairs Cato Sells, both of whom saw integrated service as a way to more fully incorporate Natives into American society. Sells called the segregationist proposal "not in harmony with our plans for developing the Indian's citizenship." Rather, he averred that the indigenes should serve "as the equal and comrade of every man who assails autocracy and ancient might, and to come home with a new light in his face and a clearer conception of the democracy in which he may participate and prosper."[130] Pratt agreed. After the war, expressing assimilationist sentiments remarkably similar to Duncan Campbell Scott's in Canada (though less culturally imperialistic), he wrote to U.S. secretary of war Newton Baker, "If through perilous army service they have proven they are after all not so unequal to us in ability and patriotism and are ready to die for the country it demonstrated the highest attributes of citizenship. If shoulder to shoulder and comrades in war, why not shoulder to shoulder and comrades in peace?"[131] In the end, the integrationists would carry the day. There would be no segregated Indian units.

North American Indians saw action in battles at places with names that, nearly 100 years later, are fast fading into the mists of history, obscure in the popular memory, places like Ypres, Cambrai, Somme, Passchendaele, Vimy Ridge, Meuse-Argonne, St. Mihiel, and Montbréhain. Contemporary Anishinaabe writer Gerald Vizenor has written a powerful recent novel of their experiences, *Blue Ravens*, based on his two great-uncles Ignatius and Lawrence Vizenor. Barely a month before the Armistice, on October 8, 1918, Ignatius was killed at Montbréhain. He was eighteen years old. Meanwhile, on that very day and less than a hundred miles away, his brother Lawrence was being awarded the Distinguished Service Cross for conspicuous gallantry. Ignatius was given a military funeral at his White Earth Reservation in Minnesota. It was impossible to account for all his body parts.[132] Unlike the two brothers, one of whom perished in France, author Vizenor's characters return home to the reservation. They, however, cannot find work. They go to the city. Ultimately, they opt for recrossing the Red Atlantic for Paris.

For Indians who did see action at the front in the Great War, like Ignatius Vizenor or Elmer Price, the experience was similar to that experienced by Native soldiers during the Spanish-American War. There, they felt the relative equality. Yet they were also disproportionately called upon to be scouts and to take the point. Based upon their supposedly innate skills, they were asked to guide patrols through the hell of no-man's-land, between Allied and German trenches. They were also singled out to be snipers. In his questionnaire completed for Dixon, George Pam-o-thah Masquat, a Kickapoo from Kansas, wrote: "In Camp Doniphan, I practiced sniping, scouting and patrolling no man's land. We entered trenches in Vo[s]ges Mts. June 28, 1918, relieving French Army. I was appointed a Chief Sniper in that sector. In another sector, same Mts., I was appointed a Regimental observer. St. Mihiel and Argonne Forest, I resumed a chief sniper of 1st Batt. of 137th Infantry, taking charge of twelve snipers. I divided them in three sections. I took the left flank of our Battalion during the kick off at the [Vosges Mountains], where we pushed Fritz in the face." An officer formally commended Masquat for his bravery and the "noble race" he represented.[133]

Scouting, patrolling, sniping. The last of these roles assigned Native soldiers—sniper—may have been more than strictly stereotype. Indians from the bush in Canada or the backwoods of the United States were accustomed to hunting to supplement the family table, becoming in the process skilled marksmen. The same would be true of rural whites. It would be natural to employ this talent in the service. One of those so tapped was Patrick Riel, the grandson of Louis Riel, who would record thirty-eight kills before he himself was struck down in early 1916. Another would be a Canadian Anishinaabe named Francis Pegahmagabow.

Francis Pegahmagabow experienced an ill-served, passed-around childhood. He was born on March 9, 1889, on his father's reserve on Lake Huron in Ontario. His father, Michael Pegahmagabow, was a member of the Parry Island Band, and his mother, Mary Contin, was of the Henvey Inlet band. After his father died in 1891, his mother left the reserve, returning to her own Native community. She left him in the care of his father's uncle. When the local Indian agent found out about the situation, questions were inevitably raised. The band council decided to give him to an elderly tribal member named Noah Nebimanyquod, who had raised Francis's father many years earlier, at nearby Shawanaga. His uncle approved of the transfer. He died the following year, anyway. In interviews, Duncan Pegahmagabow and Marie Anderson, Francis's children, say their father "went from family to family," finally spending most of his youth in the family of someone named Frank Kewaquendo.[134]

According to Diamond Jenness, an anthropologist with whom Pegahmagabow worked as an informant in 1929, the boy grew up steeped in
hunting and fishing. A feast would have been held, according to tradition, upon his first kill to ensure the blessing of the *manitouk* (spirits) on
his future endeavors. A somewhat sickly child, Pegahmagabow undertook long-distance runs to build up his endurance. According to his biographer Adrian Hayes, "To harden their bodies, boys were encouraged
to wrestle and run races . . . and every child, boy or girl, had to bathe in
a lake or river at the beginning of each month until freeze-up. In winter
they ran naked to a mark on the ice, or were driven out in a snowstorm
and rubbed with snow."[135] Amid his multiple households, Pegahmagabow
still managed a traditional Anishinaabe upbringing. He also received a
perception of himself as special or set apart, marked for greatness.

This was no doubt largely attributable to the woman that Pegahmagabow referred to as his "foster mother" (most probably Kewaquendo's
wife), who was a traditional medicine woman and taught him her ways.
Describing his early childhood many years later, he referred to himself
in the third person: "A native orphan boy at Shawanaga . . . had often
gone to pray and cry by the graves of his dead parents. One time, he fell
asleep there. At the dawn the next morning someone said to him, 'Awake
my boy, do not cry anymore, you are now a great person. You have been
blessed to save your tribes from slavery.' He kept that to himself. Then
another day came an age-old native [who] was about to die. The foster
mother was informed by the old age to take good care of the same orphan boy. 'He has a special, wonderful blessing. He will save our tribes
from slavery when he get [*sic*] to be a man.'"[136] Throughout his childhood
and as an adult, he believed he received supernatural protection.

As a small baby, he was bitten by a snake. People thought he would
surely die, but a *kusbindugeyu* (a seer and curer) divined the cause of his
illness and healed him. When older, he was again threatened. As he described it, "When I was a young man at Shawanaga a *medewadji* [spirit]
tried several nights in succession to carry away my soul. I am sure it was a
conjurer who was trying to harm me, because my father and grandfather
had offended some of the Indians on Lake Huron, and these Indians
destroyed every member of their families except myself." Finally, after
his enlistment, as he was poised to embark for Europe, an aged Native,
whom he did not know, recognized him and gave him a medicine bundle
for his protection, "saying I would shortly go into great danger. The bag

was of skin, tightly bound with a leather thong. Sometimes it seemed to be hard as a rock, at other times its appeared to contain nothing. What was really inside I do not know. I wore it in the trenches."[137]

War was declared by Britain (and hence Canada) on August 8, 1914. On August 13, Pegahmagabow went to the recruiting center of the Twenty-Third Northern Pioneers militia regiment to join up. Adrian Hayes speculates, "For Pegahmagabow, the hostilities probably presented an opportunity to leave a painful childhood behind and distinguish himself as a warrior in the tradition of his forefathers. So strong was this determination that he wrote to Indian Affairs after being wounded in the fall of 1916, pleading to get back into combat so he could earn more medals." In a 1919 newspaper interview, Pegahmagabow himself said simply, "I went to war voluntarily just as quick as the white man."[138]

A short time after Pegahmagabow enlisted, the Northern Pioneers were absorbed into the First Battalion, Western Ontario Regiment. Though hundreds of men were turned away as unneeded in the first overseas contingent, the young Native was accepted. Hayes notes that it is unknown whether those in charge were aware of the informal policy of dissuading Indians from service or simply chose to disregard it.[139] Whatever the case, "Peggy," as he was called, was one of the few Native Canadians who served through the entire war.

The First Battalion, and Peggy with it, crossed the Atlantic, arriving in England in late September or early October 1914. By November, the Native had written to Duncan Fraser Macdonald, the Indian agent at Parry Sound, complaining about the inaction. As Macdonald described it, "I had a letter from Francis Pegamaga [*sic*] at Salisbury Camp. He is getting tired waiting for to get away to try his hand at shooting. He may thank his stars that he is where he is at present. Well, it's rough and will be rougher before it is quieted down."[140] Pegahmagabow would soon get his wish for combat.

The unit crossed over to France in February 1915. In April, the entire Canadian First Division was sent to the Ypres Salient in Belgium. Pegahmagabow would fight in Ypres, Givenchy, Festubert, Passchendaele, and Second Arras. He earned a reputation as a sniper and was promoted to battalion sniper, a designation that allowed him to operate independently to snipe and gather information on the enemy, directly under the battalion's intelligence officer. He was reportedly fearless. Relying on traditional Anishinaabe ways, he chewed on a dead twig to calm his nerves and as protection in times of danger. He would later recommend the practice to his co-tribesman Levi Nanibush who served in World War II. The latter testified, "I couldn't believe it, but I tried it and it sure enough works alright. . . . I was not afraid of anything because of what he told me."[141]

By the war's end, Pegahmagabow had received the Military Medal (Canada's third highest decoration) three times (one of only thirty-eight Canadians—Native or non-Native—to be so honored). He was unofficially credited with 378 kills and more than 300 captured (unofficial because many were uncorroborated, as he worked alone). He was the most decorated First Nations soldier in the Canadian Expeditionary Force. In a ceremony in Toronto after the war, Pegahmagabow received his medals directly from Edward, Prince of Wales, the future King Edward VIII.[142]

Shot in the leg at the Battle of the Somme in September 1916, Pegahmagabow's wound was severe enough that doctors considered amputating the limb. He spent five months recuperating in England. It was at this time that he wrote to Indian Affairs, "Awarded a medal last June. I want another while I have a chance."[143] He was again sidelined for five months, hospitalized in December 1917 with severe pneumonia.

After he returned to his unit, Peggy became a disciplinary problem. He developed a persecution complex. He came to believe—correctly, as it turned out—that he had been awarded the Military Medal, rather than the higher Distinguished Conduct Medal or Victoria Cross, simply because he was an Indian.[144] His behavior became erratic. On September 12, 1918, he was ordered to report to the field hospital for observation. While there, "he apparently held a Canadian medical officer at gunpoint and accused him of being a German spy because he was near a well and yet had no instrument for testing water."[145] Modernly, we would say that the soldier was suffering from post-traumatic stress disorder. The syndrome was most commonly called "shell shock" in the First World War (and "battle fatigue" in World War II). Sent back to Britain less than two weeks before the Armistice in November 1918, he was diagnosed as having "exhaustion psychosis."[146] Peggy's war was over. He recrossed the Atlantic for home.

Though he was invalided out of the Canadian army, Pegahmagabow remained in the militia. He served in World War II on the home front. He also entered politics. In 1921, he was elected chief of the Parry Island Band and reelected in 1924. During his tenure, he repeatedly clashed with both the Canadian administrative bureaucracy and some in his own tribe. He was finally ousted in an internal power struggle, resigning in August 1925. When he ran for his old post in January of the following year, he received just a single vote—his own.[147] He, however, remained an activist in Indian affairs until his premature death in 1952.

Joseph Boyden, like Gerald Vizenor, had a relative who served in the Great War. He used Peggy's wartime experiences as the seed for his first novel, *Three Day Road*. The book tells the story of Xavier Bird. Like his real-life Anishinaabe model, he comes home wounded in both body and spirit. Unlike Pegahmagabow, however, Bird makes it back not only with "exhaustion psychosis" but as an amputee, addicted to morphine. Xavier's aunt Niska, an Anishinaabe medicine woman, fetches him upon his return. The novel shifts between the 1919 present and the horror of the trenches, narrated alternatively by Niska and Bird. Their canoe journey back to the bush is itself a healing ceremony, as Niska, having collected the physical shell of his body, recovers him mentally and spiritually as well.[148]

Like countless Natives before him, Francis Pegahmagabow continued to negotiate the Red Atlantic long after he traveled it physically. In the summer of 1923, frustrated by his continual conflicts with the Canadian government, he undertook a tour of various bands in his region, trying to get them to sign onto a petition directly to British king George V that would bypass the Department of Indian Affairs. John Daly, the Indian agent at Parry Sound, alerted the DIA of the chief's "seditious campaigning," and futile attempts were made to rein him in.[149] This effort was just a small manifestation of Red Atlantic diplomacy on both sides of the United States–Canadian border during the Great War and its immediate aftermath. Much of that maneuvering would involve the Haudenosaunee (Iroquois) Confederacy, also known as the Six Nations.

When the war broke out, the Iroquois, like most other nations, supported it. The Haudenosaunee, however, perhaps more than any other Natives, have always been fiercely protective of their sovereign status. This was especially true in the first half of the twentieth century. In November 1914, Canadian colonel William Hamilton Merritt, who had been adopted by the Haudenosaunee, attempted to raise two all-Native companies among the Iroquois. He even proposed to fund them himself. He had failed, however, to consult the council of the Six Nations. According to Winegard, "On November 26 the council rejected the offer to mobilize a distinct regiment, asserting that they would only respond to a request from King George V. By allowing the Canadian government control of a Six Nations regiment, the council would tacitly acknowledge the government's jurisdiction, something they were not prepared to do. While the council supported the war effort, they decided to force the government to recognize the Six Nations Confederacy as a sovereign ally of Britain, equal to the Dominion of Canada."[150]

In the United States, in 1917, the Iroquois followed the lead of their Canadian brethren and insisted on independently declaring war on Germany and Austria (a maneuver they repeated during World War II, refusing to be drafted until, following a conference in Washington, they issued a declaration of war against Japan and Germany). Arthur C. Parker, a Seneca, drafted the declaration. Parker, a founder of the Society of American Indians (an early-twentieth-century assimilationist group), in this instance navigated the fine line between adherence to the American creed and Indian sovereignty, writing, "The American Indian has common cause with the Allies. . . . The Indian fights because he loves freedom and because humanity needs the defence of the freedom loving man. The Indian fights because his country, his liberties, his ideals and his manhood are assailed by the brutal hypocracy [*sic*] of Prussianism. Challenged, the Indian has responded and shown himself a citizen of the world, an exponent of an ethical civilization wherein human liberty is assured."[151] In part, the Iroquois were remembering and reacting to an incident that occurred as the war first erupted: a few Iroquois performers traveling in Germany were trapped in Berlin when war was declared; they were verbally abused, physically roughed up, and briefly detained. Although the troupe was released and given safe passage to Allied lines, Haudenosaunee memory is long.[152]

For Native nations on both sides of the international boundary, asserting their own sovereignty and their right to separately declare war or to demand that another sovereign treat with them apart from the national government that purported to rule over them was a way to attempt to leverage a change in the immediate conditions experienced by their citizens and to create a better set of conditions in the future. Yet by 1917, diplomacy was a centuries-trodden path for Indians across and around the Red Atlantic.

3

—⁓—

Red Diplomats

*Statecraft and Cosmopolitanism
across the Red Atlantic*

INDIANS OF THE AMERICAS were engaged in diplomacy from the moment of first Contact. Every parlay between Natives and Europeans was in some sense a diplomatic meeting, be it major or minor. Because of the crucial role they played, the Indians trained by Europeans to serve as interpreters were diplomats in their own right.[1] Western Hemisphere indigenes' first experience with formal European diplomacy, however, took place in the year 1533. In that year, Spain signed the first treaty between a European power and a Native nation. It ended a revolt on Hispaniola that had helped paralyze the Caribbean for a decade.

Enrique was a Taino *cacique*, known because of his small stature as Enriquillo ("little Enrique"). After his father was murdered during a council with Spanish authorities, he was taken and raised at a Franciscan monastery in Santo Domingo. While there, he was baptized and, of course, became fluent in Castilian Spanish. Upon reaching adulthood, he left the cloister and returned to his home province, where he married.

In 1519, when his encomendero sexually assaulted his wife and stole his horse (a symbol of nobility among the Taino), Enriquillo sought redress through the *audencia*, the local royal judiciary. He was, however, shuffled back and forth among unsympathetic authorities.[2] He was reportedly publicly flogged to make it clear to all Tainos that he, his wife, and his mare were all the property of his encomendero. Humiliated and furious, he withdrew to the mountains with a few followers and refused to return. When the encomendero went with a force to fetch him, a fight broke out. Two Spaniards were killed, and the rest fled.[3]

Tainos and African slaves flocked to Enriquillo's camp in the mountains in an event reminiscent of the slave revolt of Spartacus against the Roman Empire. Soon there were an estimated 300 rebels in the remote area. Avoiding direct confrontation, Enriquillo used his superior knowledge of the mountain landscape and guerrilla tactics to defeat every Spanish force sent to break the revolt. The costs of subduing the ragtag army of slaves mounted. The colony was panicked and on the verge of chaos. At one point, the Council of the Indies, the Spanish crown's administrative arm for the Americas, intervened directly, sending a force of 200 to capture the rogue *cacique*—all to no avail. Commerce came to a near standstill. After more than thirteen years of asymmetrical warfare, the Spaniards approached him with an offer of peace. According to historian Daniel Castro, "Enriquillo seems to have succumbed to the exhaustion of all those years of struggle, finally agreeing to sign a peace treaty with Captain Francisco de Barrionuevo in August of 1533."[4] The terms of the resultant treaty did not, in reality, give the reluctant warrior much—amnesty for all rebels and the bestowal of the honorific title of "don" on Enrique—but it was enough under the circumstances.

It was at this point that a Spaniard who keeps turning up in the Red Atlantic like a bad penny comes back into our story. Bartolomé de Las Casas contacted Enrique and asked for safe passage to visit him in his mountain camp. The Dominican friar wanted to convince the *cacique* to come out of his stronghold. As Las Casas described the encounter to the Council of the Indies:

> I went—with only the grace of God and a companion friar, provided to me by the Order—to Baoruco, and reassured Don Enrique and confirmed him in the service of the Emperor our lord. I was with him a month . . . and relieved them [Enrique and his followers] all of their very just fears. I would not leave from there, until I took him with me to the town of Azúa, where he was embraced by the citizenry who made merry [with] them. . . . And in truth, noble sirs, had the Dominican Order not sent me, to serve God and his Majesty, and had I not gone there, it might be a hundred years before Don Enrique would have been seen outside the impregnable peaks and highlands where he was born and possesses his patrimony.[5]

One cannot miss the extreme self-justifying satisfaction in Las Casas's words to the council. In fact, for all his advocacy on behalf of Indians, other than his time with his childhood companion Juanico, his experience with Enrique represents one of Las Casas's few extended experiences of Native peoples in the flesh.[6]

Spanish scholar Ramón Menéndez Pidal sums up the importance of Enrique's revolt and its outcome for the story of the Red Atlantic, despite its limited real gains for his Taino people: "With all the moderation and generosity possible in a war, [Enriquillo] fights a powerful state for thirteen years and wins, having his individual rights recognized; his is a splendid triumph, seeing himself recognized and invited to make peace by the great Emperor Charles V."[7] Enrique called himself Don Enrique until he died, less than a year after the treaty, from respiratory illness.

Though Enrique inaugurated formal statecraft in the period of the Red Atlantic, he himself never actually voyaged upon it. Many after him would do so, however. Red diplomats and other cosmopolitans crisscrossed the Atlantic with such frequency that we cannot discuss them all in this book. Haudenosaunee, Cherokee, Muscogee, and Anishinaabe delegations visited England. Osage, Otoe, and Missouria deputations traveled to France. By the close of the Red Atlantic in 1927, among the notables who had ventured forth were Oconostota (Groundhog Sausage), Attakullakulla (Little Carpenter), Ostenaco (Mankiller), Joseph Brant, Peter Jones, and Levi General (better known to history as Deskaheh). Alden Vaughan estimates that from 1500 to 1776, approximately 175 Western Hemisphere indigenes went to the British Isles alone.[8] The bulk of these did not go as diplomats, but many did—as they also traveled to France and Spain.

The Lord of Roanoke

In the summer of 1564, the French established Fort Caroline on the Atlantic coast of North America under the auspices of Admiral Gaspar de Coligny, a Burgundian nobleman. The local Timucua welcomed them. Twice, when the colonists were short on food, Outina, a Timucuan chief, coaxed the French into participating in attacks on villages of his rival, Potano, to seize surplus corn. In the spring of 1565, again starving, the French requested corn and beans from Outina. The chief, already adept at Red Atlantic diplomacy, refused, saying that the tribe needed its stocks for seed. According to anthropologist Jerald Milanich, "To force French demand, Chief Outina was taken hostage and held for a ransom of food, which the Indians said they could not pay. After two weeks of skirmishes and one all-out battle, Outina was released."[9] Unable to supply their own food, the French demonstrated that they did not yet know the New World, and their treatment of Outina in attempting to coerce him into providing what they lacked (and the fact they were forced to capitulate and let him go without having achieved anything) shows they did not understand the Red Atlantic, where—at least temporarily—Indians still held the upper hand. Within a few months of Outina's liberation, the colony at Fort Caroline was massacred by the Spaniards.

The destruction of Fort Caroline prevented any of Outina's fellow tribesmen from enjoying the same "hospitality" at the hands of the French or being taken to France. The failure of the French colony, however, set the stage for the first red diplomats to travel to England.

With French designs on North America temporarily thwarted, the only challengers to English settlement on the lower Atlantic coast were the Spanish, who established Saint Augustine the same year that Fort Caroline perished. Spaniards had, in fact, been exploring the mainland of North America since 1513, when Ponce de León claimed the region for the Spanish crown. In order to stake their own claim to temporal primacy on the continent, Elizabethans invented the myth of Prince Madoc, a Welsh nobleman who shipwrecked in Mobile Bay in 1170 and trekked with his crew through what is today the American Southeast. The first complete account of this fictive expedition is given in Humphrey Llwd's 1559 *Cronica Walliae*. The story quickly took hold. A petition for a royal charter was submitted to Queen Elizabeth in 1580, which stated that "the Lord Madoc, sonne of Owen Gwynned, Prince of Gwynned, led a Colonie and inhabited in Terra Florida or thereabouts" in 1170. George Peckham picked up the story in his *A True Report of the late Discoveries of the Newfound Landes* in 1583, and David Powel repeated it the following year in *Historie of Cambria*. Richard Hakluyt, an important advocate for colonization, followed suit in *Principall Navigations, Voiages and Discoveries of the English Nation* in 1589.

The same year that that Powel's treatise appeared, Sir Walter Raleigh, not Madoc, was granted a royal patent to settle North America. In the spring of that year, he dispatched an exploratory expedition, commanded by Philip Amadas and Arthur Barlowe. The explorers investigated Pamlico and Abermarle Sounds and identified Roanoke Island as a preferred location for settlement. The Englishmen were well received by the local Indians, and "to prove the truth of their reports," Amadas and

Barlowe returned to England with two Roanoke-area Natives, Manteo and Wanchese, curious to see this other land.[10]

The pair were not the first indigenes to travel to England. A few captives had been brought in 1576 and 1577. Also, in 1577, Martin Frobisher arrived back, bearing four Inuit captives.[11] Alden Vaughan observed, "Despite a slow start compared to its European rivals, England . . . gradually discovered the novelty and then the efficacy of imported Americans."[12] One of the quickest to seize upon the idea was Richard Hakluyt. The colonization promoter urged would-be colonists to learn the Natives' language so that they might "distill into their purged myndes the swete and lively liquor of the gospel." Until such time as Englishmen could learn the Atlantic coast Indians' autochthonous tongues, Hakluyt contended that Indians should be brought back to be taught English, so that they might serve as interpreters. The Roanoke Natives were his test cases.[13]

The two were from different tribes, Manteo from Croatan and Wanchese from Roanoke. Manteo was a higher-status person than Wanchese. He was a Croatan *werowance* (chieftain). The English would later bestow on him the honorific title "Lord of Roanoke," "the first and only red American to be so honored in England."[14]

Manteo and Wanchese were installed in the center of London at Durham House, a royal property given to Raleigh's use. Thomas Harriot, an Oxford graduate in Raleigh's employ, acted as their English tutor. Vaughan muses, "One can imagine Hariot exchanging with Manteo and Wanchese an eclectic assortment of information about each other's culture through sign language, halting English, and a few Algonquian words until, toward the end of their eight months in London, conversations in English became reasonably fluent."[15] Between lessons, the Indians went sightseeing. One can only imagine Londoners stopping to stare at the coppery visitors dressed up as faux Englishmen, just as people in Spain fought to catch a glimpse of the captives brought home by Columbus.

Besides learning English and providing Harriot with intelligence about their homeland, Manteo and Wanchese also served a more economic purpose. As Vaughan puts it, "Before long, Manteo and Wanchese were wooing potential investors and colonists for Raleigh as his associates. Some Englishmen took the bait, though not always with a clear eye."[16] In April 1585, Raleigh dispatched 600 to Roanoke on his first colonizing mission. Among those sailing was Thomas Harriot, who had learned a little of "the Virginian language" (as he referred to the Algonkian dialect) while he taught English.[17] So were Manteo and Wanchese, who had been his pupils. Like Robert FitzRoy's "Fuegians," according to reports, they continued to wear their English clothes. Having completed their circumnavigation, with their Western dress and command of English, the two Carolina indigenes were only the first of a steady stream of Natives traversing the Atlantic to conduct diplomacy and investigate the opposite shore.

Of utmost interest is the disparity between Manteo's and Wanchese's reactions to their experience of the Red Atlantic. Manteo seems to have grown increasingly attached to his English friends, assisting them in their colonial efforts. Wanchese, however, opposed any colonization. The two thus represent the two opposite poles of the spectrum, Manteo collaborating and Wanchese encouraging resistance. Though we cannot know the precise reasons for Wanchese's fervent opposition, Vaughan is most surely correct when he writes, "[A]fter seeing England up close, Wanchese probably knew that colonists would disrupt the Roanokes' lives. . . . While Wanchese's precise role in intracultural and intercultural relations remains obscure, his determination to thwart English settlement is palpable."[18]

In the New World, Manteo helped the English make first contact and establish friendly relations. Though we know he continued to be involved, the details of that involvement are hard to glean. At any rate, the good start in international relations that he aided in creating soon went terribly wrong. In an event reminiscent of FitzRoy's obsession with his missing whaleboat, the English commander, Sir Richard Grenville, demanded that the Indians return a silver cup stolen by "one of the Savages." When he failed to get satisfaction, he explained, "we burnt, and spoyled their corne, and Towne, all the people being fledde."[19] Without Indian assistance or resupply from England, most of the colonists abandoned their settlement in 1586 when a passing Sir Francis Drake offered to let them hitch a ride back to England. Fifteen were left behind to establish a continuous English presence.

Manteo returned with the departing English. Soon he was helping Raleigh and Harriot plan another attempt at a colony. Harriot, based on his experience as a participant in the failed 1585 Roanoke colony, is sometimes said to have introduced the potato—one of those important products of the Red Atlantic—into England. We cannot know for sure. We do know, however, that when Raleigh's second Roanoke colonizing expedition departed in the spring of 1587, Harriot was not among the colonists—most probably because of that first, miserable experience. He was lucky.

Manteo once again accompanied the new colonists, completing his second round-trip on the Red Atlantic. When the company arrived at Roanoke, they found the settlement overgrown and dilapidated and no sign of the fifteen colonists left behind in 1586 to garrison it, except for the "bones of one." Again, Manteo's interventionist diplomacy with his Croatan people helped the new Roanoke colonists settle. As Vaughan observes, however, just as it did two years previous, Manteo's ability to prevent the English from provoking mischief proved limited. The colonists' leader, John White, decided to mount a punitive raid against the Roanoke for the deaths of the fifteen. Manteo accompanied the avenging force. Unfortunately, the Indians they found and attacked were Croatan, not Roanoke. White would state, "Although the mistaking of these Savages somewhat grieved Manteo, yet he imputed their harme to their owne follie." A few days later, Manteo accepted Christian baptism, becoming the first Indian to convert to Anglicanism. Again, according to White, "[O]ur Savage Manteo, by the commandment of Sir Walter Raleigh, was christened in Roanoak, and called Lord thereof . . . in reward of his faithfull service."[20]

Ultimately, Manteo succumbed to the same temptation that would lure Ourehouaré to abandon his people, politically if not geographically. He was co-opted into collaboration against them.

Raleigh established his second colony on Roanoke in 1587. Sometime between then and 1590, it disappeared, going down in history as the "Lost Colony." The Virginia Company received a new patent from King James I in 1606, establishing Jamestown the following year. Jamestown was the first successful British colony in North America. It set the stage for yet another red diplomat in England.

Did Manteo perish with his white friends at the Roanoke settlement? Did he lead them to safety? We do not know. His fate, like that of the colonists, is unknown.

Lady Rebecca Rolfe

William Shakespeare's play *The Tempest* was first produced in 1611, four years after the founding of Jamestown. It is thus the first major attempt in England to come to terms literarily with the indigenes of the Western Hemisphere and the reality of the New World, a subject we shall explore in greater detail in chapter 5.

While most today tend to think of the play as set on some vaguely identified or totally imaginary island, it in fact takes place on "Bermoothes," that is to say, Bermuda. Caliban, the dark indigene whom Prospero and Miranda dispossess of his island (and whom the former desperately fears will sexually violate the latter), is identified in the dramatis personae as "a salvage [that is, savage] and deformed slave." His name is an anagram of "canibal" (the contemporary spelling of "cannibal"), which is, in turn, a corruption of "Carib," the indigenous people who lent their name to the Caribbean (that they were far to the south of Bermuda, which, like Roanoke, is off the coast of the Carolinas and nowhere near the Caribbean, is of little import). One of Shakespeare's inspirations was the 1609 shipwreck of the vessel *Sea Venture* on Bermuda. The ship was bound for Jamestown, and after it went aground, survivors were stranded for nine months.

Others, in particular the late Ronald Takaki in his essay "'The Tempest' in the Wilderness: The Racialization of Savagery" and Peter Hulme in "Prospero and Caliban" in his book *Colonial Encounters: Europe and the Native Caribbean, 1492–1797*, have written extensively about *The Tempest* in this context.[21] Takaki notes, "Although the theatergoers [in 1611] were given the impression that Caliban could be acculturated, they received a diametrically opposite construction of his racial character. They were told that Caliban was 'a devil, a born devil' and that he belonged to a 'vile race.' 'Descent' was determinative: his 'race' was signified an inherent moral defect. On the stage, they saw Caliban, with long shaggy hair, personifying the Indian."[22] He also writes:

> Like Caliban, the native people of America were viewed as the "other." European culture was delineating the border, the hierarchical division between civilization and wildness. Unlike Europeans, Indians were allegedly dominated by their passions, especially their sexuality. . . . To the theatergoers, Caliban represented what Europeans had been when they were lower on the scale of development. To be civilized, they believed, required denial of wholeness—the repression of the instinctual forces of human nature. A personification of civilized man, Prospero identified himself as mind rather than body. His epistemol-

ogy was reliant on the visual rather than the tactile and on the linear knowledge of books rather than the polymorphous knowledge of experience. With the self fragmented, Prospero was able to split off his rationality and raise it to authority over the "other"—the sensuous part of himself and everything Caliban represented.[23]

Much more has been and can be written about Shakespeare's drama as it previews European reactions to the Red Atlantic. As noted above, I will turn to other such responses in chapter 5. For the moment, let us turn back to Jamestown and diplomatic traffic across the Red Atlantic.

Among those who were marooned on Bermuda by the wreck of the *Sea Venture* in 1609 was John Rolfe. This colonist was destined to play a major role in the history of the settlement of Virginia. He would survive to become the husband of Pocahontas.

Much has been written about Pocahontas, even if she has often remained less than three-dimensional. Just as Joseph Boyden wrote a dual biography of Métis leaders Louis Riel and Gabriel Dumont, the late Paula Gunn Allen (Laguna Pueblo) wrote a biography of the Powhatan princess from a Native perspective in order to, in a sense, recover her indigenous identity.

First of all, her name was not Pocahontas. Her proper name was Matoaka. Pocahontas was a childhood nickname. That name is of uncertain meaning, but "those who acted as informants to the English" translated her name as "frisky" or "mischief."[24] Was she, as we might say today, "a handful" when she was a girl? The historical confusion as to her true name undoubtedly stems from Jamestown colonist John Smith, who heard her nickname when she "saved" him from "death."

The incident with John Smith is at the center of the Pocahontas story in American history. In fact, it is almost all most Americans know of her. Disney did not help. Neither, however, have many U.S. historians. That Perry Miller, one of the preeminent historians of his generation, could write a book on American colonial history in 1956 called *Errand into the Wilderness* with only half a dozen pages devoted to indigenous peoples— almost all of those given over to a recitation of the Pocahontas story—is remarkable. John Smith didn't help matters either.

We have only Smith's own account of Pocahontas's intervention to prevent his execution, and he was a relentless self-promoter. The Indian girl does not appear in his earliest version of his near-death experience.

She pops up only in his version written in 1624, seven years after her death during her much-publicized visit to England, which established her place in the Red Atlantic.

On an expedition outside of Jamestown in December 1607, John Smith and his party stumbled on a large hunting party of Pamunkey (or possibly a mixed group from several related tribes). The Native group was led by Opechancanough, the brother of Wahunsencawh, the *mamanatowick*, or paramount chief, of the Powhatan Confederacy (commonly referred to in history as Powhatan, the personification of the people he led). Smith was captured and held captive under comfortable conditions, while the Indians continued their hunt. Afterward, he was brought before Wahunsencawk, Powhatan himself.

Powhatan welcomed the Englishman with honor because, as historian Rebecca Anne Goetz puts it succinctly, it had become "ever more clear to [Powhatan] that the English did not intend to live among them, and they did not intend to leave."[25] The two communicated as best they could. Powhatan wanted to know the purpose of the English in taking up residence in his domain. Smith dissembled, saying that their ships had been damaged and that they were merely taking refuge from the Spaniards. The chief offered to take the newcomers under his protection and, knowing that they could not feed themselves, provide them with corn and meat. In return, the newcomers would supply him with metal goods. As anthropologist Helen Rountree puts it in her book *Pocahontas's People*, "Smith glibly promised that the English would, in effect, become Powhatan's vassals."[26] What happened next is the core of the Pocahontas myth.

Smith, writing about himself in the third person, states that "two great stones were brought before Powhatan: then as many who could lay hands on him [Smith] dragged him to them, and thereon laid his head, and being ready with their clubs to beate out his braines, Pocahontas the King's dearest daughter, when no intreaty could prevaile, got his head in her armes, and laid her owne upon his to save him from death."[27] The Indians, who a moment before were intent "to beate out his braines," relented and spared him.

What just happened? There is significant doubt that it occurred at all—remember that Smith did not say anything about it until almost twenty years after the fact. There is general agreement among scholars who have examined the evidence, however, that if it did, in fact, actually happen, Smith's cultural confusion led him to totally misunderstand what transpired.

Matoaka—still Pocahontas—was only eleven or twelve years old, not a mature, young woman as she has often been depicted. Any intimation of romance or physical attraction should be dismissed. What Smith experienced was a ceremony orchestrated by Powhatan, an adoption or initiation ceremony, "in which Smith was symbolically killed and then reborn, marking a passage from his old existence as an Englishman to his new life as an Anglo-Powhatan. Pocahontas merely played her role as she was instructed, very likely a far less dramatic part than Smith describes."[28] Symbolically, Matoaka "redeemed" Smith. The ritual sealed the pact between Powhatan and Smith, the sacred covenant by which the English agreed to a subordinate position in the Powhatan Confederacy in exchange for protection and succor. What one sees is a sort of inversion of the Jemmy Button affair: John Smith became a Powhatan. There was no longer a "John Smith" to them. He was now Nantaquod.

In 1608, the Jamestown colonists believed they had discovered gold. All productive labor—growing food, maintaining the fort, hunting—stopped; "everything was abandoned in the frenetic search for gold." A skeptical Smith complained that "there was no talke, no hope, no worke, but dig gold, wash gold, refine gold, [and] loade gold."[29] In April, a ship laden with "ore" set sail for England. On board were Edward Maria Wingfield, the disgraced former president of the Jamestown council, and an Indian named Namontack, Powhatan's personal ambassador. As Powhatan put it, "I purposely sent [him] to King James [and] his land, to see him and his country, and to returne me the true report thereof."[30]

There is no record that Namontack was given a royal audience. He was treated very well, however, and entertained. The Spanish ambassador, more accustomed to Indians as slaves, scoffed to his monarch, King Felipe III, that he was "amused by the way they honour him, for I hold it surer that he must be a very ordinary person."[31]

Though Powhatan considered the Jamestown colonists his subjects, upon his return Namontack helped persuade the Indian leader to accept an English "coronation" as a vassal of King James. Later, Powhatan complained that when he was "crowned," he was not given a coach and three white horses, because "hee had understood by the Indians which were in England, how such was the state of great *Werowances*, and Lords in England, to ride and visit other great men."[32] This must surely have been intelligence he acquired from his envoy Namontack.

Smith objected to the whole affair, saying such a ceremony would make the Native monarch "overvalue himselfe." He may have, in fact, had a point. Powhatan's reason for participating in the event and his interpretation of it were quite different from what the colonists intended. Horn explains, "The coronation had cost him nothing. He had made the English come to him, he had accepted their gifts, and in return he had given them nothing. . . . And he had confirmed his prestige in the eyes of his own people by inverting the meaning of the ritual: It was he who received the tribute of the English, not the other way round."[33] Powhatan himself never traveled the Red Atlantic physically (preferring instead to send his personal representatives), but he understood its dynamics very well and negotiated it accordingly.

Less than two years after his captivity, death, and rebirth as Nantaquod, Smith, like Edward Wingfield, would depart Jamestown. A freak gunpowder explosion had burned him. So severe were his injuries that it was decided to send him back to England where he could receive proper medical attention.[34] The colonists told Matoaka that he had died. He never returned to Virginia, though he would sail to what is today the coast of Maine and Massachusetts in 1614. He would, however, have one more reprise performance in the Red Atlantic.

During the next several years, relations between the colonists of Jamestown and their Powhatan "overlords" deteriorated. The English, still unable to feed themselves in the New World, raided the Indians to steal corn when they could not purchase it. For their part, the Natives engaged in small-scale raids against the expanding colonists. Finally, in 1611, for the first time, the newcomers were able to raise "an indifferent crop of good Corne," using the forced labor of Indian captives to tend the fields.[35] By 1613, things had reached a sufficiently dire state that Samuel Argall seized Matoaka, planning to ransom her for Powhatan's English prisoners, captured weapons, and "a great quantitie of Corne."[36]

Much to the bafflement of Argall, who saw the kidnapping as a way to bring hostilities between the two peoples to an end, and the Jamestown leadership, Powhatan took three months to respond. At that point, he returned seven of eight captives and some broken muskets, promising 500 bushels of corn and eternal peace and friendship with the English if his daughter were returned.[37] In her biography, *Pocahontas: Medicine Woman, Spy, Entrepreneur, Diplomat*, Paula Gunn Allen casts doubts that Matoaka was the paramount chief's actual, biological child, instead a "daughter" only in the sense that she was his subject.[38] If she is correct, it might help explain what is otherwise a seemingly inexplicable delay on Powhatan's part (though he might simply have refused to seem weak). At any rate, Jamestown leader Thomas Dale rejected the offer, refusing to believe that the pitiful collection of ruined firearms was all that remained of what the Indians had stolen. According to the account, the colonists heard nothing more from Powhatan for another year.[39]

During her prolonged, enforced sojourn in Jamestown, Matoaka was instructed in English customs and Christianity. One of her tutors was John Rolfe, whose wife and daughter had died in Bermuda after the wreck of the *Sea Venture*. The two fell in love. When informed, Powhatan sanctioned a marriage and sent a delegation to witness the ceremony. Matoaka converted to Christianity and was baptized Rebecca Rolfe. With the wedding, peace was sealed between the two warring peoples. The following year, Matoaka gave birth to a boy, Thomas Rolfe.

In 1616, with peace secured, Sir Thomas Dale organized a delegation from the Virginia Colony to England, where it was hoped he could raise a desperately needed capital infusion for the venture. He took with him several thousand pounds of "exceedinge good tobacco," plus potash, sassafras, sturgeon caviar, and "other such lyke commodyties," the material wealth of the Red Atlantic.[40] Immediately upon docking in Plymouth in early June, Dale wrote to Sir Ralph Winwood, King James's secretary of state, detailing these prizes. Yet something else went unremarked upon. According to Allen, "With Pocahontas, Indian paragon of missionary zeal and cash crop, indicator of solid investment opportunity, firmly in tow, Sir Dale must have anticipated a warm welcome and highly successful outcome. . . . The aptly named *Treasurer* set sail in 1616, carrying its precious cargo: Lady Rebecca, her husband, and their son, Thomas, and her dozen or so attendants."[41] Lady Rebecca's entourage was no product of accident. Just as Powhatan had dispatched Namontack with Wingfield, on Dale's voyage, the paramount chief helped shape the delegation so that he could have eyes on the ground to report directly and only to him.[42]

On this trip, that person was Uttamatomakin, Matoaka's brother-in-law. His mission was to find John Smith (reports of whose demise

Powhatan disbelieved), see King James (lending credence to the probability that Namontack had failed in this regard), see the English god (who Matoaka now professed to follow), and to count "both men and trees." As Helen Rountree points out, however, "Unfortunately, for him, Powhatan record keeping consisted of notched sticks. Dale's ship landed in Plymouth and the party crossed southern England—the most heavily populated part of the country—to reach London; Uttamatomakkin [*sic*] soon had to give up his enumeration."[43] Although he was unable to tabulate English trees and population, Uttamatomakin largely succeeded in what was essentially an espionage mission: he found John Smith (Powhatan was right), and he did meet King James (whom he dismissed as stinting and unimpressive).[44] He failed to see the Englishmen's god, but he saw his dwelling place, St. Paul's Cathedral, which was very near their lodgings, the appropriately named Belle Sauvage Inn.

Lady Rebecca was a sensation in London. Queen Anne assigned Lord and Lady De La Warr to be her and her party's guides to show them the city's sights and introducing Lady Rebecca to the right people. While there, she met with Samuel Purchas, George Percy, Thomas Harriot, and Sir Walter Raleigh. The available evidence, though not conclusive, suggests she also was introduced to Ben Jonson, John Donne, and Henry Wriothesley (the Earl of Southampton, who was Shakespeare's patron). She might have gotten to meet the Bard of Avon himself, but Shakespeare had died a few weeks before the *Treasurer* arrived.[45] Though she missed meeting the author, she was taken to performances of *Twelfth Night* and *The Tempest*. Did she recognize that the latter was inspired in part by her husband's experience while he was shipwrecked on Bermuda? Did he?

Lady Rebecca and her entourage also were treated to an audience with King James and Queen Anne, who hosted them at a performance of *The Vision of Delight*, a Twelfth Night masque by the queen's favorite playwright, Ben Jonson, designed by Inigo Jones. As Paula Gunn Allen writes, "The entry of Lady Rebecca—first Christian, Anglicized Indian princess, a model of what they called 'civilizing'—was choreographed to maximize public interest in the venture and secure the means [for Virginia] to expand."[46] Believing Lady Rebecca to be a genuine "princess," James I was reportedly extremely displeased with John Rolfe for marrying her. He feared Rolfe might assert some future claim on his Virginia colony for having married royalty.[47]

Her stay in England also reunited Matoaka with John Smith. The meeting did not go well. She turned her back to him and refused to speak to him for some time, until finally pulling him aside to berate him. The standard interpretation of her bitter reaction to seeing him again is that she resented being brought face-to-face with a former, if unrequited, love, whom she believed was dead. Her reaction was nothing of the sort; Smith's own account of the encounter reveals that. Matoaka said to him, "You did promise Powhatan what was yours should bee his, and he the like to you called him father being in his land a stranger, and by the same reason so must I doe you." She concluded her speech by pointing out that the paramount chief had so distrusted the Jamestown residents' statement that Smith was dead that he had sent his own emissary to find him: "They did tell us always you were dead, and I knew no other till I come to Plimouth; yet Powhatan did command Uttamatomakkin to seeke you, and know the truth, because your Countriemen will lie much."[48] The implication of her remarks seems clear enough: she was accusing Nantaquod of deserting and betraying Powhatan by breaking the sacred covenant he had made with him. The alliance between the English and the Confederacy had collapsed in his absence.[49]

Alden Vaughan writes, "The pity is that Powhatan's most successful representative to the Court of St. James did not live to share with her father what she had seen and heard for she seems to have envisioned a Virginia that expanded, rather than displaced, her natal society."[50] The Powhatan princess never returned home. Taken ill, she died in Gravesend before she could set sail. Her cause of death is unknown, but the most likely seems influenza, which was epidemic in England during the last month of her stay.[51] She was buried under the chancel of St. George's Church in Gravesend. The church was destroyed by fire in 1727.

John Rolfe left the young Thomas in England with relatives. Powhatan's grandson would remain there for more than twenty years. At least two of Lady Rebecca's Powhatan female attendants remained behind, as well, possibly because they too were too ill to travel (records of the London Company indicate that one had contracted tuberculosis). By 1621, the London Company was still supporting "the two Indian Maydes," whom they called Mary and Elizabeth, and they were looking to shed the expense. In July of that year, the "two Virginian virgins" were shipped off to Bermuda with a servant apiece and a letter to the English governor, asking him to find them suitable husbands and gainful employment. The ultimate scheme in the company's thinking was that after being converted to Christianity, married, and having children, the women and their families would be sent to Virginia as missionaries.[52]

Unfortunately, the consumptive Mary died during the voyage. Elizabeth, however, made it to Bermuda, where a husband was found. The governor personally gave a reception for the newlyweds at his residence for more than a hundred people. His motives, however, were less than purely philanthropic. Just as the London Company hoped for a missionary, he wished that upon the bride's return to her native land, she would report on the bounty of Bermuda. There is no record whether Elizabeth (her Native name, like Mary's, is unknown) ever sailed the Red Atlantic again back to Virginia. But from her new island home, she was not quite done with the Red Atlantic: the Bermudan governor had the Christian Indian write a letter (as a precursor to her arrival in person) attesting to her good treatment to her brother who had become *werowance* of his tribe. Exactly which tribe in the Powhatan Confederacy is unknown, as is his reaction to the missive.[53]

Uttamatomakin returned across the Red Atlantic adamantly opposed to the English. The nature of his report to Powhatan is unknown. Powhatan died a year after his beloved daughter, and his brother Opechancanough succeeded him. The new paramount chief "forged an alliance among his peoples . . . united by their hatred of English settlers and their determination to be rid of them."[54] On March 22, 1622, Opechancanough launched a coordinated attack in force against English settlements and plantations, killing 400. Contrary to Opechancanough's expectations, however, the Virginia colony survived.

In 1635, Thomas Rolfe, now an adult, sailed to his American birthplace with his wife and one of his two daughters (the younger was left behind, as Thomas himself had been, with a relative). He came to claim his handsome inheritance from his father. In 1641, despite dicey relations between the colonists and the Indians, he asked the governor to grant him leave to visit his "kinsman Opecancanough [*sic*]." Today, through Thomas Rolfe, several prominent American families, including the Lees, the Randolphs, and the Symingtons, as well as many Britons, trace their lineages back to Matoaka—3 million descendants—an enduring legacy of Lady Rebecca's trip on the Red Atlantic.[55]

Historian Colin Calloway points out that the son of the only other Native American woman commonly remembered in U.S. history also crossed the Red Atlantic. Jean Baptiste "Pomp" Charbonneau was the child of Sacajawea and Toussaint Charbonneau, born in 1805 during the Lewis and Clark expedition. When he was eighteen, he met Friedrich Paul Wilhelm of Wurttemburg, who was on a tour of the American West. He returned with the German prince and spent the next six years living and traveling with him through Europe and North Africa before returning home.[56]

Groundhog Sausage and the Little Carpenter

The Croatan and the Indians of the Powhatan Confederacy were "early adopters" of transatlantic diplomacy by necessity. They were among the first to encounter the English on a sustained basis as permanent colonization of North America began in the late sixteenth and early seventeenth centuries. These tribes beneath the Fall in the initial contact zone with the English enjoyed both the benefits of engagement with the Red Atlantic (metal tools and implements, for one) and suffered the brunt of the burdens brought by the newcomers—new diseases and ever-increasing numbers of settlers encroaching on more and more Native land.

Increasingly, the Red and black Atlantics intertwined in this process. In 1531, William Hawkins returned from delivering African slaves to South America. He carried with him "one of the savage kings . . . of Brasill." The chief, according to Hakluyt, was interested in seeing the new land, and Hawkins left one of own men behind as hostage against the Native's return. The indigenous "king" met with King Henry VIII and remained for almost a year. Unfortunately, he succumbed to European disease on the voyage home.[57]

About fifty Indians dribbled into England between 1620 and 1710 for a variety of purposes. In 1629, three Mi'kmaqs—the sagamore (chief) Segipt and his family—arrived; Segipt came to meet with King Charles I, seeking protection from the French. The Miskito, who served as England's allies and surrogate policemen on the Atlantic coast of Nicaragua and Honduras, sent a number of representatives and rulers beginning in 1618 and continuing until at least 1775. Beyond 1710, the Anglican Church's Society for the Propagation of the Gospel in Foreign Parts—the same organization that brought Reverend Thomas Bluett into contact with Ayuba Suleiman Diallo—brought a Yamasee "prince" to England to be educated at its expense in 1713. He remained a year and a half, during which time he met King George I. Unfortunately, the youth returned in 1715 in the middle of the Yamasee War, in which the English colonists of the lower Carolinas were in the process of crushing and routing his people. The boy, christened George, remained loyal to the British. His fate is unknown.[58] Despite these and others, however, by the late seventeenth and early eighteenth centuries, two powerful tribal groupings began to dominate statecraft in the Red Atlantic.

The Cherokee, the southernmost anchor of the Iroquoian language family, and the five—later six—tribes of the Haudenosaunee Confederacy, the Cherokee's northerly cousins, were among the most numerous and important Indian tribes in British North America. They became the Red Atlantic's preeminent diplomats.

Today we tend to think of the French and Indian War as a single, singular conflict in the imperial struggle between Britain and France for supremacy in North America. In reality, as already noted, it was only the last of four wars between the colonial powers, each corresponding to a European war at the same historical moments. Great Britain based its claim to the continent on John Cabot's single landfall in 1498. France relied on Jacques Cartier, who sailed into the Gulf of St. Lawrence in 1534 and up the St. Lawrence River the next year. Regarding the contested western territories deep in the continent's interior, Britain's rival pointed to the 1673 joint exploration of Jacques Marquette and Louis Jolliet and to René-Robert Cavelier de La Salle in 1682. The first of what have come collectively to be called the "French and Indian *Wars*" (known as the "Intercolonial Wars" in contemporary French Canada) commenced in 1688.[59]

During these wars and after, Haudenosaunee and Cherokee deputations traveled to England with a fair regularity. The Haudenosaunee forged an alliance with the British that was known as the "covenant chain," a bond that like its actual metal counterpart in the metaphor needed to be periodically burnished to renew its luster.

Initially, royally financed delegations from the Americas to England were rare. In 1696, however, a deputation of Mohawks (members of the Haudenosaunee Confederacy) was brought to England during King William's War. The blatant and over-the-top show the English put on for Natives, "with displays of military, political, economic, and cultural achievement," was a deliberate attempt to impress them with the power, wealth, and pomp of England and create a "counterpoise" to France. That same

year, the French brought six "eminent and enterprising" Canadian sachems to Versailles and Paris "to amaze and dazzle them with the greatness and splendour of the French court and army." England had to outdo
its adversary in wooing the Iroquois.[60]

During Queen Anne's War, in 1710, the so-called Four Indian Kings—
three Mohawks and one Algonkian-speaking Mahican, all from New
York—crossed the Red Atlantic.[61] The stage for their visit was set the
previous year. In 1709, Britain had promised an invasion of Canada. Five
Mohawks came to Boston to observe the military preparations. Though
they were treated to the spectacle of a mock battle from the deck of the
H.M.S. *Dragon*, no British naval squadron and no invasion materialized.
Colonel Samuel Vetch warned that unless affirmative steps were taken,
they would "Intirely lose the five Nations of Indians [the Haudenosaunee
Confederacy], who have been so long the barrier betwixt us & the french."
Plans began to bring an Iroquois deputation to London.[62] From the Native point of view, the purpose of the delegation was simple—greater
military assistance against the French and a request for Christian missionaries to instruct their people. From the British side, it was equally
elementary: with the 1696 delegation, it was to show the Indian allies, according to Vetch, "as much of the Grandure and Magnificence of Britain
as possible" or, as a chronicler of the embassy put it, the "Grandeur, Pleasure, and Plenty" of their European ally.[63] Although Indians had come to
London before, never had they been received as royalty on a state visit.[64]

The trip was deemed a success by both sides. At a public audience
with Queen Anne at St. James Palace, the ambassadors made their pleas,
which they felt were favorably received. Queen Anne sat on her throne
when receiving them, "which was just as well, since standing was almost impossible for her. Gout, obesity, and other health problems had
left her essentially immobile."[65] The four "swarthy Monarchs" were
"Cloath'd and Entertain'd at the Queen's Expence." Food and drink in
large amounts were easily forthcoming, demonstrating the empire's generosity and abundance. The Indians had their portraits painted by John
Verelst. They were taken to performances of Shakespeare's *Hamlet* and
Macbeth (during which they were seated onstage), plus other plays and
a number of operas. In all they were "mightily pleased with their kind
reception" over five weeks.[66] I find it a little incomprehensible, however,
that, if the goal was to impress, the Indians were taken to view a work-
house and the Bedlam insane asylum. (To me, it is reminiscent of Sitting

Bull, who while participating in Buffalo Bill's Wild West show in 1885 was impressed by both the number of people and the industrial might he observed in the East, yet could not understand why Americans treated their poor so badly.)[67] At any rate, upon their return, the "kings" influenced the Haudenosaunee Confederacy to fight alongside Queen Anne's forces against the "common enemy" (the French). Vetch and others say that it led directly to British conquest of Acadia (Nova Scotia) and the establishment of a foothold for the Society for the Propagation of the Gospel among the Mohawk.[68]

If the Iroquois were the key to British designs in the north, the Cherokee were the preeminent tribal nation in the south. In 1730, the latter assumed the "imperial limelight."[69] Sir Alexander Cuming, a Scottish eccentric—and, if the truth be told, a bit of a confidence man—assembled a delegation of seven Cherokees to travel to Britain, even though he had no authority to do so. The youngest of them was a warrior—dubbed a "general" by the British—Attakullakulla ("Little Carpenter," though at the time called Oukaneekah).

Despite Cuming's lack of permission, the reception of the Cherokee legation, twenty years after the "Four Kings" and coming during a lull in the French and Indian Wars, was even more lavish (and Cuming connived to convince the crown to pay their expenses). The Natives, with Sir Alexander, set forth in early May 1730 from Charles Town (Charleston), South Carolina, aboard the H.M.S. *Fox*, arriving about a month later. Although most official Indian delegations were lucky to have one meeting with the reigning monarch, the Cherokees, who were present for five months, enjoyed no fewer than four. On the second, they presented King George II with a collection of scalps.

The Natives were taken to all the usual sights—including Bedlam. They saw numerous entertainments, including Christopher Marlowe's *Doctor Faustus* and Aphra Behn's *Oroonoko*. At the theater, they assumed an importance equal to the entertainment on the stage. Rather than watch the play, the English audiences turned to watch the Indians watching the play. Wherever they went, they were the subject of public fascination, as people jockeyed to catch a glimpse of them. They were exhibited like circus attractions when they ate, took tea, or sat in a pub. Merchants hiked their prices to take advantage, and one advertisement invited the public to see them eat "at Mr. Figg's, at One O'Clock, upon the Stage." Attakullakulla, for one, rankled at the discourteous public scrutiny, but, demonstrating the agency that foreigners so often failed to recognize in their Native visitors, relished that the situation permitted *him* to observe thousands of Britons up close.[70]

There is a persistent legend among the Cherokee today that the most enduring legacy of the 1730 delegation was not the treaty they executed (and subsequently renewed in 1733 and 1744) but something more material. The Cherokee men arrived naked "except an Apron about their Middles" (a breechcloth). They also practiced facial and scalp tattooing. Sir Robert Walpole, King George's prime minister, thought them far too fierce-looking to present to His Majesty. Fortunately, a delegation from India had been at court sometime in the recent past and had left their turbans. The Cherokees' brows were crowned with the abandoned headdresses, which they asked to keep. Henceforth the turban became traditional Cherokee male headgear.[71]

The story may be apocryphal. Turbans certainly were Cherokee men's headwear; there are contemporaneous depictions of Sequoyah and George Lowrey (among others) wearing them. Vaughan implies that the group was in Native dress for all four royal meetings. Yet we know the British "had put fine Cloathes on their Backs" and that they were always decorously dressed in public. Their group portrait, which circulated widely as an engraving, shows them in rather flamboyant Western dress but no turbans.[72]

By the time the French and Indian War broke out in 1754, Attakullakulla was the only member of the 1730 embassy still living. The British invoked the treaty he and his compatriots signed, demanding that the Cherokee fight with them against the French. Though the Indians were not unsympathetic, they worried about the security of the Overhill Towns (those on the western side of the Appalachian Mountains), which would be vulnerable to attack if their warriors left to aid the British. After both Virginia and South Carolina built forts in the Overhill area, the tribe did send several hundred men, who fought with distinction on the frontier.[73]

Unfortunately, relations deteriorated at the end of the decade. Some returning Cherokee warriors were attacked and killed by Virginia colonists. The Cherokee retaliated by attacking Carolina settlements, which were closer and more easily accessible than those in Virginia. In Cherokee law and diplomatic thinking, such a move was perfectly acceptable, given how the Cherokee understood their relationship toward British colonists. The Cherokee could take revenge upon those actually responsible or (in the event they were unavailable) on members of their clan; Carolinians' settlements were satisfactory surrogates for Virginians'. South Carolina did not see it that way. In an effort to avert further conflict, Oconostota (Groundhog Sausage), the Cherokee Great Warrior ("famous for having, in all his expeditions, taken such prudent measures as never to have lost a man"), "led a peace delegation to Charlestown [Charleston] in 1759 to offer reassurances of Cherokee loyalty. But the delegation was marched back to Cherokee country in chains, accompanied by 1,300 militia." Oconostota enjoyed hospitality very similar to that experienced by Outina at the hands of the French at Fort Caroline. William Henry Lyttelton, South Carolina governor, offered to ransom the delegation in exchange for the twenty-four Cherokees who, to white lights, had murdered Carolinians. *This* was contrary to Cherokee law—handing over Cherokees for execution when, in Cherokee eyes, they had committed no crime. Finally, three were exchanged for several of the delegation, including Oconostota. Twenty-two members of the peace delegation were executed. This meant war between the Cherokee and the British.[74]

After the force of provincials entered Cherokee territory "as an act of intimidation," Attakullakulla signed a treaty with Governor Lyttelton on December 26. It made no difference. General Jeffrey Amherst sent 1,650 British regulars, who destroyed the Cherokee Lower Towns of Little Keowee, Estatoe, and Sugar Town. The war continued until 1761, when a treaty was signed by the Cherokee "emperor" Kunagadoga (Standing Turkey). As part of the negotiations, Standing Turkey "had one more favour to beg of them [the British], which was, to send an officer back with them to their country, as that would effectually convince the [Cherokee] nation of the good intentions and sincerity of the English toward them." Obviously, what Standing Turkey was requesting was a hostage; should the British break the peace, under the Cherokee law of "corporate responsibility" (the same reason it had been perfectly acceptable to attack Carolina for the actions of Virginia), the hostage would be killed. Henry Timberlake, an officer in the Second Virginia Regiment, in effect drew the short straw.[75]

Timberlake spent less than three months, from December 20, 1761, until March 10, 1762, in the Overhill area, a guest in the home of Ostenaco (Utsidihi, or Mankiller). He observed that when he arrived in

Cherokee country, "I found the nation much attached to the French" because the French courted them, while British military officers were "disgust[ed]" by them. All the "headmen" expressed a filiation with the French "except Attakullakulla, who conserves his attachment inviolably to the English."[76] Such were the profitable fruits of the Red Atlantic for European powers.

Timberlake departed with Ostenaco and 165 warriors for Williamsburg, the capital of colonial Virginia. At Chota, the Cherokee capital, the chiefs told everyone "to remind the English of their promises of friendship, and to press the Governor of Virginia to open trade; for the Indians to behave well to the inhabitants when they arrived, as that was the only way to keep the chain of friendship bright; that we should keep a good look-out, as the enemy were very numerous on the path."[77]

As they neared the colonial capital, Timberlake tried to send the bulk of the party back, but none would turn around. In his memoirs, the soldier reports, "On my arrival, I waited on the Governor, who seemed somewhat displeased with the number of Indians that had forced themselves upon me. Orders however were issued out for their accommodation, and a few days after a council was called, at which Ostenaco, and some of the principal Indians, attended."[78] So far, so good, but as the Cherokees were preparing to depart, what turned out to be a momentous invitation was extended.

James Horrocks, a professor at the College of William and Mary,

> invited Ostenaco and myself [Timberlake] to sup with him at the College, where amongst other curiosities, he shewed him the picture of his present Majesty [George III]. The chief viewed it a long time with particular attention; then turning to me, "Long," said he "have I wished to see the king my father; this is his resemblance, but I am determined to see himself; I am now near the sea, and never will depart from it till I have obtained my desires." He asked the Governor next day, who, tho' he at first refused, on Ostenaco's insisting so strongly upon it, gave his consent. He then desired, as I had been with him so long, that I might accompany him to England; this I was to do at my own expense; but the Governor told me he would recommend me to the minister of state, which he did in as strong terms as I could desire.[79]

In reality, Ostenaco's desire to travel to England was far from the spontaneous whim it seemed to Timberlake. The chief had been negotiating the Red Atlantic for many years—before he arrived at Hampton Roads and the Atlantic littoral, even before he experienced British hospitality in Charleston.

Participation in a delegation to Europe increased one's prestige among one's tribe. Ostenaco and Attakullakulla were rivals within the Cherokee Nation. The former insisted on meeting the British monarch because the latter "owes all his power and influence to his having visited king George." Indeed, "When I was in England . . . " became a stock introductory phrase for Attakullakulla anytime he offered an opinion on any subject. In his conversations with Virginia governor Francis Fauquier, the Cherokee demonstrated his understanding of the dynamics of the Red Atlantic. When Fauquier initially declined his request, he said that if Virginia refused his demand, he would simply go to New York. He thus forced Fauquier's hand. In the end, the Virginia council recommended that the warrior be allowed to see for himself "the number of our people the Grandeur of our King and the great Warlike powers we had at our Command."[80] In the end, therefore, British motives in bringing Ostenaco and the two others who accompanied him were the same as they had been with every Indian delegation since the 1696 Haudenosaunee emissaries. They also wanted to cement the peace recently concluded with the Cherokee. The Anglo-Cherokee war was over, but the Seven Years' War—and its North American counterpart, the French and Indian War—continued.

Ostenaco's bluff worked. In May 1762, Cunne Shote (Stalking Turkey), Ostenaco, and Woyi (Pigeon) boarded the H.M.S. *Epreuve*, bound for England. Just as Bartolomé de Las Casas saw Christopher Columbus's arrival in Spain with his Indian captives, a young William and Mary student named Thomas Jefferson witnessed the Cherokees' departure. Years later, in 1812, Jefferson, by then an old man, wrote to John Adams, reminiscing, "I was in his camp when he made his great farewell oration to his people the evening before his departure for England. The moon was in full splendor, and to her he seemed to address himself in his prayers for his own safety on the voyage, and that of his people during his absence." In reality, of course, Jefferson understood not a word of Cherokee (the language of the address). He nevertheless was deeply moved by the sonorous quality of the speaker's voice and "the solemn silence of his people at their several fires."[81]

Jefferson may not have understood Ostenaco's speech, but his incomprehension did nothing to affect the Cherokees' mission. Far more consequential was the death of the party's interpreter on the voyage over. The only recourse was Timberlake, whose Cherokee language skills can best be generously described as imperfect. The situation greatly cramped the delegation's visit.[82]

The Cherokees were treated to a display of British naval might, both on the voyage and upon arrival in Plymouth, where they were taken aboard the H.M.S. *Revenge*, "a seventy-four gun ship, with which they were equally pleased and surprised."[83] After Plymouth, the Indians were conveyed to London, where they cooled their heels. They had arrived in England on June 16. Even accounting for several days' travel to the kingdom's capital, it would be more than two weeks before they could gain an audience with King George, the delay primarily occasioned by the search for a more suitable interpreter than Timberlake. The Cherokees grew impatient. According to Timberlake, "As several days passed . . . the Indians became extremely anxious to see the King. 'What is the reason," said they, "that we are not admitted to see the Great King our Father, after coming so far for that purpose?' I was obliged to reply, 'That his Majesty was indisposed, and could not be waited on till perfectly recovered,' which in some measure pacified them."[84] Like the 1730 delegation, however, this deputation would eventually get multiple royal visits, a rarity.

Other than two royal audiences, Ostenaco and his companions were treated to the usual rounds—entertainments, sightseeing, and visits with dignitaries. Upon meeting the novelist and playwright Oliver Goldsmith, Ostenaco locked him in a bear hug such that his face was "well bedaubed with vermillion" paint.[85] The Indians had their portraits done by Joshua Reynolds. And, as usual, they attracted crowds "at which they were so much displeased, that home became irksome to them." In fact, they were the "largest, pushiest crowds in two centuries of documented public reaction to Americans abroad." So unruly were the eager mobs that one observer remarked, "Our Nation is remarkable for its Greediness after Novelty, which requires continually to be fed with fresh Matter."[86] In a geopolitical lesson, the Natives were also taken to a prison for French prisoners. While the Cherokees remarked on the "perfidious and cruel" treatment that their people received at the hands of the French, they also "with uncommon Curiosity, [made] several Enquiries about the State and Condition of the Prisoners."[87]

The first audience with King George occurred on July 8 and lasted more than ninety minutes. It was awkward, however, because of the language barrier. In addition, Ostenaco, who had pushed for the embassy, delivered prepared remarks (badly translated by Timberlake) in which he asked only for "a firm peace and quietness between his people and mine," according to Timberlake.[88] The second meeting took place a month later on August 6. Once again, Ostenaco expressed Cherokee fealty:

> Some time ago my nation was in darkness, but that darkness is now cleared up. My people were in great distress, but that is ended. There will be no more bad talks in my nation, but all will be good talks. If any Cherokee shall kill an Englishman, that Cherokee shall be put to death.
>
> Our women are bearing children to increase our Nation, and I will order those who are growing up to avoid making war with the English. If any of our head men retain resentment against the English for their relations who have been killed, and if any of them speak a bad word concerning it, I shall deal with them as I see cause. No more disturbance will be heard in my Nation. I speak not with two tongues, and I am ashamed of those who do. I shall tell my people all that I have seen in England.[89]

(Since Timberlake could not be relied upon for an accurate interpretation, the speech was translated upon the delegation's return and sent back across the Atlantic to King George.) Though the Cherokees had been instructed in etiquette before meeting the British monarch, Ostenaco prepared his pipe and started to offer it to His Majesty. Timberlake, interpreting the offer as "according to the Indian custom of declaring friendship," nonetheless intervened, telling the Indian that "he must neither offer to shake hands or smoak with the King."[90]

Much has been made by Alden Vaughan and others of Ostenaco's use of subservient language when speaking about the British king. He referred to King George as "Father" and said that the monarch treated him as one of his own "children." This has been taken as proof of the Cherokee's recognition of their subordinate status. Certainly the British understood it that way. But this is a fundamental misunderstanding of Ostenaco's words and deeds. The chief used the expected forms of address of subalterns, but his actions say otherwise. His tight clinch of Goldsmith, a luminary (though not a government official), was a natural Cherokee greeting. He offered the pipe to King George in a symbol not of mere friendship but of statecraft. The two acts, like his repeated reference to the Cherokee as a "nation," were meant to represent the Indians as equals to the British, not as inferiors.

Ostenaco was one of the most adept red diplomats. He coerced Virginia into arranging a delegation to Britain after an initial rebuff by threatening to go to New York. The trip cemented peace between the Indians and the British after the recent Anglo-Cherokee war. The trip also enhanced Ostenaco's status both within his tribe and with colonial officials. As the 1730 deputation had for Attakullakulla, the 1762 trip made Ostenaco a lifelong friend of England. So from the Cherokee point of view, the trip was a great success. In contrast, and despite these seemingly tangible gains, the British looked upon it as a colossal, extravagant waste, even if many of the debts were laid on Timberlake himself.[91]

In 1764, an Overhill chief named Chucatah, whom Timberlake had met during his stay among the Cherokee, importuned the Englishman to take him and four of his tribesmen to Britain. The group wanted to appeal to George III to enforce his 1763 Proclamation Line. The Royal Proclamation of 1763 established the Appalachian chain of mountains as the "permanent line of white settlement" in North America, but the line was violated daily as foreigners came into Cherokee territory. Timberlake at first declined, "citing his financial embarrassment and public humiliation two years earlier," but ultimately agreed. This unauthorized delegation was an unmitigated disaster. Two of the Cherokees died. No royal audience could be arranged. Lord Halifax, George Montagu Dunk, the secretary of state, refused to pay their expenses, telling Timberlake that "since I had brought the Indians here, I should take them back, or he would take measures as I should not like." The surviving Indians were quietly shuffled off back to America at the government's expense, and Timberlake wound up in jail for unpaid debts.[92]

There is debate in Cherokee studies circles as to whether Oconostota, a war chief of Chota, ever went to Britain. As in other cases, there is confusion here. Oconostota is often confused with Cunne Shote (Stalking Turkey), Kunagadoga (Standing Turkey), even with Ostenaco. Carolyn Thomas Foreman notes that there are differing accounts as to whether and when he traveled to England.[93] We do know that Oconostota was in New Orleans when Ostenaco, Cunne Shote, and Woyi sailed for Britain. After Ostenaco returned from participating in the 1762 delegation, Oconostota and Attakullakulla requested permission to go to Britain, but their request was refused.[94]

Even so, there is some evidence that Oconostota did visit Britain, where he was fitted with a pair of spectacles.[95] When his grave was excavated in the 1970s to move it before completion of the Tellico Dam flooded the site of Chota, he was found buried with a large knife and eyeglasses. Those glasses, however, most probably were brought back by the 1762 delegation. Among the bills with which Timberlake was saddled in the wake of that trip was an astounding fifty pounds from an optician.[96]

If Oconostota did travel to Britain, it would logically have been sometime between 1764 and the commencement of the American Revolution. In 1765, the British government banned Native delegations without explicit prior approval. Still, if there was some perceived advantage, such permission was granted. Only *unnecessary* Indians were barred. In addition, privately funded Indians continued to come. Britain's Indian strategy paid off. According to Vaughan, "When the time came for the native nations to take sides in Britain's North American civil war, most major Indian communities favored the empire, often spurred to that decision by leaders who had been respectfully treated in London, the epicenter of empire."[97] It certainly worked in Attakullakulla's and Ostenaco's cases.

The possibility of an Oconostota visit to Britain has given rise to a persistent piece of misinformation of uncertain origin, now viral on the Internet. This has it that Oconostota had been one of those on the 1730 embassy and that after the death of his wife, he invited one Lucy Ward, a former lady-in-waiting to Queen Charlotte whom he met during that delegation, to join him in Chota, where they were married.[98] The source of this fairy tale would appear to be a piece of bad reporting in 1730. A London newspaper stated that one of the Cherokees was courting "a Lady of great Beauty and Merit." That woman would actually marry Colonel George Chicken, one of the Indians' non-Native traveling companions.[99]

Throughout the early 1760s, the Cherokee suffered frequent raids by the Haudenosaunee. In October 1765, Oconostota's nephew, Go-ohsohly, was taken prisoner near Fort Pitt (the former Fort Duchesne). James Kelly explains, "Sir William Johnson, British Superintendent for Northern Indian Affairs, was asked to arrange a peace conference between the Cherokees and the six tribes of the Iroquois Confederacy." Oconostota, his cousin Attakullakulla, and their sons, plus six other Cherokees, were escorted to Charleston.[100]

On November 27, 1767, Oconostota ventured forth onto the Red Atlantic for probably the first time (his cousin for the third). The Cherokee party (minus Oconostota's and Attakullakulla's sons) boarded the sloop *Sally* for New York City. Kelly continues: "After a brief stay there, where they saw a performance of *Richard III*, the party set out for Johnson Hall, which they reached on sledges on December 29. Oconostota, white wampum in hand, told Johnson they had come by water for fear of the overland route. They had come, he said, 'from the White Council House, which is at Chota, and here is our Emperor's belt to you, to shew you that we are fully empowered by him and all our people to come and treat about Peace, and crave your assistance.'"[101] The chief proffered eight more belts of white wampum: one for each of the Six Nations, one from Cherokee women to their Haudenosaunee counterparts, and one from Cherokee children to Iroquois youth. A peace was concluded on March 17, 1768, and Oconostota departed for Charleston, arriving on April 28.[102]

During the American Revolution, Oconostota was instrumental in negotiating peace with the new nation. In 1782, Colonel John Sevier rampaged through Cherokee country, burning towns to punish the Chickamaugas. According to Joel Koenig, in his *Cherokee Chronicles, 1540–1840*, "After a lopsided battle at Lookout Mountain, they proceeded to destroy abandoned towns, including Spring Frog, Ustenali, Ellijay, and Coosawatie. Sevier did not find the newer Chickamauga towns and instead headed back to Chota. He met with Oconostota, Old Tassel, and Hanging Maw before heading back to Nolichucky."[103]

More than twenty-five years after that parlay, in 1810, John Sevier wrote to Amos Stoddard, reporting:

> In the year 1782 I was on campaign against some part of the Cherokee; during the route I had discovered traces of very ancient, though regular fortifications. Some short time after the expedition I had an occasion to enter into a negotiation with the Cherokee Chiefs for the purpose of exchanging prisoners. After the exchange had been settled, I took an opportunity of enquiring of a venerable chief called

Oconostota, who was then, as he had been for nearly sixty years the ruling chief of the Cherokee Nation, if he could inform me what people it had been which had left fortifications in their country. . . . The old chief immediately informed me: "It was handed down by the Forefathers that the works had been made by the White people who formerly inhabited the country now called Carolina; that a war existed between the two nations for several years. . . ." I then asked him if he had ever heard any of his ancestors saying what nation of people these Whites belonged to. He answered: "He had heard his Grandfather and Father say they were a people called Welsh; that they had crossed the Great Water and landed first at the mouth of the Alabama River near Mobile and had been drove up to the heads of the waters until they arrived at Highwassee River by the Mexican Indians who had been drove out of their own country by the Spaniards."[104]

At first blush, this letter is preposterous. Oconostota's narrative neatly parallels Robert Southey's poem "Madoc." According to Sevier, the chief also told him of a Cherokee woman named Peg who had in her possession an old book given to her by one of the Welsh tribe. Unfortunately, before Sevier could himself examine the tattered text (which would have been produced nearly 300 years before the Gutenberg press), it was destroyed when Peg's house burned to the ground.

Why would an elderly Cherokee chief, in the immediate wake of prisoner negotiations, engage in cordial conversation about a fictional Welsh explorer? Let us assume, however, that Sevier did not make up the story out of whole cloth. By the time Oconostota sat down with Sevier in 1782, he had possibly (though not probably) been to Britain himself. Regardless, he knew quite well both Attakullakulla and Ostenaco, who unquestionably had visited England (and, as we saw, Attakullakulla enjoyed talking about his experience there endlessly). Oconostota had sat in the audience in New York and watched William Shakespeare's *Richard III*, which culminates with the Welshman Henry Tudor (who becomes Elizabeth I's grandfather, Henry VII) defeating Richard on Bosworth Field. During these and other encounters with English colonialists, I would claim that it is probable that the Cherokee became well acquainted with their fascination with Prince Madoc and a dreamt-of primacy in North America. Sevier's conversation, as limned in the Stoddard letter, suggests that the chief was following Sevier's leading questions perfectly and knew exactly what he wanted to hear. Whether Oconostota was enjoying a joke at the colonial soldier's expense or playing to his prejudice for some strategic effect, we cannot know.

The Covenant Chain and a Gold Ring

By the beginning of the American Revolution in April 1775, the passage of red diplomats from North America to Europe had greatly decreased. France had lost New France in the French and Indian War (and would sell the remainder of its North American holdings to the United States in 1803). In 1765, England banned unauthorized delegations. Britain's North American insurrection curtailed a lot of travel, and after the revolution ended in 1783, its American empire was drastically reduced. All of this decreased both the need and opportunity for Native statecraft across the Red Atlantic. But although opportunities obviously narrowed, they were never forestalled completely. Diplomatic travel to Europe by red diplomats would continue right up to the close of the Red Atlantic.

The best-known red diplomat of this period is probably Thayendanegea (called Joseph Brant in English). Though there were others of importance—two of whom we will examine in the remainder of this chapter—he was unquestionably the most successful. In a sense, he was born and raised for statecraft, part of a long line of Haudenosaunee diplomats that extends far beyond the historical limits of the Red Atlantic right to the present day.

Joseph Brant was probably the grandson of Sa Ga Yeath Qua Pieth Tow, one of the Four Indian Kings feted in London in 1710. From that red diplomat, who was baptized Brant, he inherited his surname.[105] In 1752, his sister Mary (always called Molly) married William Johnson, the British Indian superintendent, in a Native ceremony.[106] The younger brother became the influential Johnson's protégé, and Johnson took the youth into battle during the invasion of Québec during the French and Indian War. In 1761, Samson Occom, the Christian Mohegan who was the first Indian educated by Eleazar Wheelock at what would become Moor's Charity School in Connecticut, hand-carried an invitation to Johnson Hall. After his success with Occom, Wheelock, like so many others after him, saw great possibilities in educating Native Americans. The request Occom delivered was for Johnson to select some potential interpreters to be trained at Moor's. The superintendent chose Brant, then about nineteen, and two other war veterans. While the other two proved problematic students, Brant showed such aptitude that Whee-lock considered sending him on for higher education—first considering the College of New Jersey (later to become Princeton University) and then King's College in New York (today Columbia University), though neither ever eventuated.[107]

After Sir William Johnson died in July 1774, Brant became secretary to Guy Johnson, his successor as superintendent (as well as the elder Johnson's nephew and son-in-law). With the outbreak of the revolution in April of the following year, the younger Johnson made plans for a trip to Britain for himself and Brant. Before their departure, hoping that the Mohawk could still be swayed to the side of the rebellious co-lonials, Eleazar Wheelock contacted Brant, urging either neutrality or active participation on behalf of the rebels. The former pupil wrote back a carefully crafted letter, recalling the happy time he spent at Moor's and summoning up the prayers to which he listened during devotions. One petition, he said, would be forever etched in his mind: "that they might live as good *subjects*—to fear God, and HONOR THE KING."[108] Years later, after the peace of 1783, Brant sent a letter to Sir Evan Nepean, under-secretary of state for the Home Department, writing, "When I joined the English in the beginning of the war, it was purely on account of my forefathers' engagements with the King. I always looked upon these en-gagements, or covenants between the King and the Indian nations, as a sacred thing: therefore I was not to be frightened by the threats of the rebels at that time; I assure you I had no other view in it, and this was my real case from the beginning."[109] The seeds the British had sown in 1710 with Brant's ancestor bore fruit more than half a century later. From the beginning, Brant was pledged to polish the covenant chain.

Johnson's delegation, composed of Brant, Peter Johnson (Brant's nephew, Molly and Sir William's oldest child), and another Mohawk, John Hill, plus Johnson himself and a retinue of other non-Natives, de-parted from Québec City in November aboard the H.M.S. *Adamant*. In a below-decks brig in chains was a recently surrendered Yankee general, Ethan Allen. Johnson and Brant both wanted to reassure the central gov-ernment of Indian support against the revolutionaries. Brant also wanted to press Haudenosaunee land claims. As had other Native ambassadors before him, Brant caused a sensation. This Indian, however, was differ-ent. He was fluent in English and, for the time, highly educated. Writer

Frank Waters states, "As a Pine Tree Chief of the Iroquois, he wore knee-high moccasins and a blanket draped over one shoulder. And as Col. Guy Johnson's secretary, he was equally at home in starched linen and broadcloth."[110] According to Johnson, when in the company of "gentlemen of rank and station—statesmen, scholars, and divines— . . . he wore European dress, there was nothing besides his color to mark wherein he differed from other men."[111] When presented to King George III and at other official ceremonies, he wore traditional Native dress—it was, after all, what people expected of him. He has been called "the most presentable Indian who had ever been seen in London."[112] He had his portrait painted in Indian costume by George Romney.

Though Brant would press Haudenosaunee complaints and land claims with Lord George Germain, the colonial secretary, at the audience with King George he pledged, "I will lead three thousand braves to battle for the cause of England . . . and with our assistance, there can be but one end of the war—England will conquer." The British promised to give the Haudenosaunee land in Québec in exchange for their support.[113] Mohawk poet Maurice Kenney has written a cycle of poems about Molly Brant. In a brief one about her younger sibling, he writes simply: "I love the English. I give them everything."[114] Nineteenth-century scholar S. C. Kimm, in his history of the Iroquois, is no less direct, quoting ethnologist Henry Rowe Schoolcraft as saying of Brant that "he hated the Americans as Attila did the Romans."[115]

Brant made the usual social rounds and sightseeing, accompanied by Johnson. James Boswell, who would later become famed for his biography of Samuel Johnson, persuaded Brant to sit down to be interviewed for a magazine profile. Though William Stone, Brant's early-nineteenth-century biographer, says they developed an "intimacy" and Foreman says the author "became the devoted friend of Thayendanegea," Boswell's assessment of the Indian chief was decidedly cooler in the *London Magazine*. Interviewed at his lodgings at The Swan with Two Necks Inn, Brant wore a green jacket, pants, and hard shoes. Boswell wrote that "there did not seem to be any thing about him that marked preeminence" and that the Indian lacked "the ferocious dignity of a savage leader; nor does he discover any extraordinary force either of mind or body." While in England, Brant also became a Freemason, installed at the Falcon Lodge and accepting his apron from King George himself.[116]

During his 1775–76 embassy, Joseph Brant unquestionably polished the covenant chain binding the Haudenosaunee to the British. But his most poignant act in Britain was the purchase of a gold ring. He had it engraved with his full name, "Joseph Thayendanegea Brant," so that he might be identified should he be felled in battle during the conflict waging in North America, to which he had pledged his allegiance to King George.[117]

Back in North America, Brant made good on his promise to the British monarch. The war tore the Haudensaunee Confederacy asunder. Most Cayugas and Senecas joined Brant's Mohawks on the side of the British. Many Oneidas and Tuscaroras allied with the rebels. The Onondaga attempted to remain neutral. However, in 1779 George Washington ordered a punitive expedition against the English-allied Indians. Led by Major General John Sullivan and Brigadier General James Clinton, the campaign closely resembled that of John Sevier in Cherokee country. Sullivan and Clinton rampaged not only through Mohawk, Cayuga, Seneca, and Tuscarora territories but through Onondaga country, as well. The result was thousands of homeless refugees who fled to Canada.[118] The Iroquois named George Washington "Conotocaurious" or "Town Destroyer," a name still in use today.

The Treaty of Paris, ending the war in 1783, ignored Indians entirely and drew a line through the middle of Iroquoia. Ultimately, in 1784, the British governor of Québec, Frederick Haldimand, gave the loyal Iroquois a large reserve in what is present-day Ontario, and about half of the Haudenosaunee people relocated there, including Joseph Brant, who resumed his diplomatic efforts. According to historian Daniel Richter in his important book *Facing East from Indian Country*, "From that base, [Brant] worked with Native leaders from throughout the Ohio Country and *pays d'en haut* to create a Western Confederacy to coordinate the struggle against the United States and insist that the Ohio River become the border between Indian country and the new republic."[119] In sum, Brant's plan was to gather all the northwestern Native nations into a single grand confederacy. The plan was thus akin to Pontiac's twenty years earlier and Tecumseh's two decades later.

A major motivating factor was the Treaty of Fort Stanwix between the Haudenosaunees and the new United States. Negotiated in Brant's absence, the treaty surrendered all Iroquois claims to land in Ohio and ceded remaining Indian lands in Pennsylvania. The Grand Council of the Haudenosaunee Confederacy refused to ratify the treaty, contending that those who did negotiate it were not authorized to sign away such large tracts of land.[120]

In late 1785, Brant recrossed the Atlantic, arriving in England in December. A dispatch, dated December 12, was published in a London newspaper: "Monday last, Colonel Joseph Brant, the celebrated King of the Mohawks, arrived in this city [Salisbury] from America, and after dining with Colonel De Peister, at the headquarters here, proceeded immediately on his journey to London. This extraordinary personage is said to have presided at the late grand Congress of confederate chiefs of the Indian nations in America, and to be by them appointed to the conduct and chief command of the war which they meditate against the United States of America. He took his departure for England immediately as that assembly broke up; and it's conjectured that his embassy to the British Court is of great importance."[121] Brant biographer William Stone points out that it is unknown whether war was "meditated" or not: "Still, he could not but look upon hostilities, in the event of the formation of his confederacy, as more than probable."[122]

Brant's original mission was the adjustment of Mohawk claims against the British, seeking indemnity for losses they suffered as a result of fighting for the crown. The Treaty of Fort Stanwix, however, increased the urgency of the visit. According to Stone, "At all events, it soon appeared that, coupled with the special business of the Indian claims, was the design of sounding the British government, touching the degree of countenance or amount of assistance which he might expect from that quarter, in the event of a general Indian war against the United States."[123] Though he would be disappointed in the long run, in the immediate, Brant's embassy was a guarded success.

Brant wrote to Thomas Townshend, Lord Sydney (then home secretary), regarding the desired indemnification and subsequently gained a meeting with him. At the meeting, in early January, the Mohawk demonstrated just how skilled he was in the Red Atlantic's language of diplomacy. Addressing the secretary, Brant reminded him of the service the loyal Haudenosaunees had done for the British, having "taken in their favor in every dispute they have had with their enemies." All the more so then that "we were struck with astonishment at hearing we were forgot in the treaty. Notwithstanding the manner we were told this, we could not believe it possible such firm friends and allies could be so neglected by a nation remarkable for its honor and glory, whom we had served with so much zeal and fidelity." Brant said that they had applied to the king's superintendent-general in Canada for reparations but had received no reply. Thus the need for Brant, representing his people, to return to England.[124]

Brant then turned, ever so obliquely, to the touchy other object of his mission. The former colonists had not respected the treaties the Haudenosaunee had made with His Majesty: "[T]hrough their encroaching disposition, we have found they pay little regard to engagements, and are therefore apprehensive of immediate serious consequences. This we shall avoid to the utmost of our power, as dearly as we love our lands. But should it, contrary to our wishes, happen, we desire to know whether we are to be considered as His Majesty's faithful allies, and have that support and countenance such as old and true friends expect." He concluded by begging that the secretary, by his answer, relieve the king's Native subjects' "very troublesome and uneasy suspense."[125]

Brant had to wait three months for a reply. On April 6, Lord Sydney sent a reply. The secretary told him that "no country, however opulent it might be," could afford to compensate every individual for the depredations suffered at the hands of an enemy during a war. After consultation with King George, however, the payment of those claims already certified by the superintendent-general had been authorized, and that "favorable attention" will be given to other claims. As to the other matter referenced by the Mohawk leader, Sydney was as indirect as the chief himself. He stated that he hoped the "liberal conduct" of the king in the settlement of Iroquois claims

> will not leave a doubt upon the minds of his Indian allies that he shall at all times be ready to attend to their future welfare; and that he shall be anxious, upon every occasion wherein their happiness may be concerned, to give them such farther testimonies of his royal favor and countenance, as can, consistently with a due regard to the national faith, and the honor and dignity of his crown, be afforded to them. His Majesty recommends to his Indian allies to continue united in their councils, and that their measures may be conducted with temper and moderation; from which, added to a peaceable demeanor on their part, they must experience many essential benefits, and be most likely to secure to themselves the possession of those rights and privileges which their ancestors have heretofore enjoyed.[126]

Although he seemed to offer Brant everything for which he asked, Sydney instructed Lieutenant General Henry Hope in Québec "to give no open satisfaction to the savages, but not to abandon or estrange them, for the peace and prosperity of the province" depended upon them.[127]

At his audience with George III, Brant reportedly further endeared himself to an amused monarch by refusing to kiss his hand as a sign of obeisance, since he too was called a king. He said that he would, however, gladly kiss the hand of Queen Charlotte. It was a deliberate breach of royal etiquette reminiscent of the Cherokee Ostenaco's, who also ignored his pre-audience coaching.

The remainder of his stay in the imperial capital was the usual social whirl accorded Indian delegations. There were balls and banquets, and Brant had his portrait painted by both Gilbert Stuart, the artist who would go on to become famous for his portraits of George Washington, and John Francis Rigaud.[128] As with other deputations, "no pains were spared to render his residence in London one of uninterrupted gratification."[129] The Mohawk's stay was, however, in two qualitative respects different from those of other red dignitaries who had preceded him. First, it was not only George III who apparently took a shine to the "dusky Chief" but also the Prince of Wales, the future George IV. Second, Brant was cagey enough to exploit the latter relationship to further the Haudenosaunee cause.[130]

According to reports, the prince "took great delight in his company; sometimes inviting him in his rambles to places 'very queer for a prince to go,' as the old chief was wont to remark in after-life." He was also a guest at the prince's table, "among the splendid circle of wits, orators, and scholars, who frequently clustered around the festive board of the accomplished and luxurious heir apparent." Among those Brant interacted with most often were Edmund Burke and his fellow Whig members of Parliament Richard Sheridan and Charles James Fox. He also renewed his acquaintance with Boswell. A brief side trip to Paris did not please the English, but as Vaughan notes, by this point, Brant "was now sufficiently independent and important to do pretty much what he liked."[131]

Despite the cordial reception and all the politesse on both sides, Brant's second mission to Britain accomplished much less than he hoped. In 1797, he sought a third embassy, but the government was cool to the idea. Instead, for this attempt at Red Atlantic statecraft, he had to settle for a trip to the American capital of Philadelphia to meet with the

British ambassador. While in the city, he sat for yet another portrait, this time by noted painter Charles Wilson Peale. (Ironically, given his fidelity to Great Britain and his antipathy toward the United States, it is today in the collection of Independence Hall in Philadelphia.)

Powerless and Wingless

Oconostota did not marry an Englishwoman of beauty and quality, but Peter Jones most certainly did. Jones was an Anishinaabe chief, diplomat, and Christian missionary who made multiple round-trips across the Red Atlantic on behalf of his people. Just as, until the 1990s, William Apess received little scholarly attention, Jones, another Native Christian, was virtually ignored. He is still overlooked in Native American studies, widely viewed as a fully assimilated Christian Indian, thoroughly absorbed into dominant cultural structures—the same sort of "mouthpiece" for whites that Apess has been accused of being.[132] This inattention is all the more a puzzlement when one considers that Jones was part of a remarkable family whose members were deeply involved in Native community, passionate defenders of Native rights, and participants engaged in the Red Atlantic, albeit with mixed results.

Jones half-brother, George Henry, was a Methodist clergyman who became disenchanted with Christianity because of denominational factionalism and left the church. He went on to become a translator, to form a traveling Indian dance troupe, and to author a number of works about North American Natives—most of them related to his company's touring in Britain, Ireland, France, and Belgium.[133] Jones's niece, Catherine Soneegoh Sutton, was a tireless advocate for indigenous rights in lectures, petitions, and letters, "one of the few women of her time [1823–65] to work [within the dominant culture] for the rights of her people."[134] When in Britain, Sutton had an audience with Queen Victoria with which she was well pleased, though the meeting made less of an impression on the head of state. Writing in her diary on June 19, 1860, the same day she met with two Maori chiefs from New Zealand, Victoria said of Sutton vaguely, "She is of the yellow colour of American Indians, with black hair, and was dressed in a strange European dress with a coloured shawl and straw hat with feathers. . . . She speaks English quite well and is come on behalf of her Tribe to petition against some grievance as regards their land. A worthy Quakeress, Mrs. Alsopp, with whom she is living, brought her. She seems gentle and simple." Flint encapsulates the meeting when she writes, "In fact, Queen Victoria's private attitude toward Native Americans does not seem to have differed significantly from that of the average, minimally informed middle-class Victorian."[135] Jones himself produced a dictionary and hymnal in Ojibway and translated the books of Genesis, Matthew, and John and a portion of the Methodist *Discipline* into the language. He also rendered the book of Luke into Mohawk. He is best known for his *Life and Journals* and the *History of the Ojebway Indians*, both published posthumously.

Peter Jones was born on January 1, 1802, "at the heights of Burlington Bay, Canada West" (present-day Hamilton, Ontario).[136] His father was an American surveyor of Welsh descent who had come to Canada for work, and his mother was Tuhbenahneequay, the daughter of Wahbanosay, a chief of the Mississauga Ojibway. In the autobiographical sketch that precedes his published journals, a volume compiled by his widow, Jones states that he had four brothers and five sisters. However, initially he names only his older sibling, Tyenteneged ("but better known as John Jones"), and notes that this name was given to the brother by "the famous Captain Joseph Brant."[137] In these few opening paragraphs, in a manner similar to William Apess, Jones rhetorically accomplishes a number of things. He establishes himself as both American and Canadian— but above all as an Indian, of a "royal" family. By introducing his older brother first by his less-familiar Indian name, he stresses his own (as well as his brother's) Indianness. The effect is heightened by the reference to his family's connections to Brant, one of the most prominent Native chiefs and diplomats of the era. Years later, on a trip to England, Jones was stung by an article that appeared in the *York Courier*, which claimed he was duping the British "by pretending that I was an Indian Chief, when I was not an Indian Chief, nor even an Indian at all."[138]

Much like Garcilaso de la Vega, Jones's early care was left largely to his mother, who, preferring traditional Anishinaabe religious practice, raised her children in that custom. Though it is commonly said that Jones rejected Native religious traditions after his conversion to Christianity, his relationship to his people's traditions, and indeed to Christianity, is much more complex and nuanced. Brought up among the Anishinaabe until he was fourteen, he lived completely the life of a traditional Indian. At an appropriate age, his grandfather held a feast for him, dedicating him to the guardian care of the *animekeek*, or thunder *manitouk*.

He was given the name Kahkewaquonaby, or Sacred Waving Feathers. At the ceremony, he was given a war club and a bundle of eagle feathers, representing, respectively, the power and flight of the thunder gods. In his autobiography, it is significant that Jones notes, "I have long since lost both, and consequently became powerless and wingless."[139] He in some sense lost not only his traditional religion but part of his identity.

When he was fourteen, his father reasserted himself and sent the boy to an English school, where he read the Church of England cate- chism and the New Testament, "but the words had no effect upon my heart."[140] In 1820, his father induced him to receive baptism from an Anglican clergyman among the Mohawk. In an unpublished autobio- graphical manuscript, Jones notes his reasons for agreeing, stating, "The principal motives which induced me to acquiesce with this wish, were, that I might be entitled to all the privileges of the white inhabitants."[141] Baptism was thus a way of grasping at equality with Euro-Americans and perhaps of filling in some of the gaps in his own identity. As Homer Noley states, however, he "was very sensitive to the commitments he was 'induced' to fall into. He was dissatisfied with his baptism experience and began to doubt that it would help him, since it didn't seem to help or change the whites for the better."[142] Jones writes, "Sometimes whilst reading the Word of God, or hearing it preached, I would almost be per- suaded to become a Christian; but when I looked at the conduct of the whites who were called Christians, and saw them drunk, quarreling, and fighting, cheating the poor Indians and acting as if there were no God, I was led to think there was no truth in the white man's religion, and felt inclined to fall back again to my old superstitions. My being baptized had no effect upon my life."[143]

Significantly, it was not whites but Indians, particularly those in his family, who led to Jones's ultimate conversion. In 1823, he attended a prayer meeting at the home of Mohawk chief Thomas Davis, where the Bible was read and prayers were offered in Mohawk. He writes, "It is quite evident that the Spirit of the Lord has already begun to move upon the hearts of this people," probably referring more specifically to him- self and, in retrospect, to John Wesley's doctrine of prevenient grace.[144] A short while later, he accompanied his sister Mary to a Methodist camp meeting: "I was prompted by curiosity to go and see how the Methodists worshipped the Great Spirit in the wilderness."[145] While there, "[s]ome strange feeling came over my mind, and I was led to believe that the

Supreme Being was in the midst of his people who were now engaged in worshipping him."[146] He began to believe that the preachers were addressing him directly. When his brother John arrived and ridiculed the religious enthusiasts, Peter argued that what was happening was of the Great Spirit.

Near the end of the encampment, Jones withdrew by himself into the forest. He described the incident: "Towards evening I retired into the solitary wilderness to try to pray to the Great Spirit. I knelt down by the side of a fallen tree. The rattling of the leaves over my head with the wind, made me uneasy. I retired further into the woods, and then wrestled with God in prayer, who helped me resolve that I would go back to the camp and get the people to pray for me."[147] A voice came to him, saying, "Do you wish to obtain religion and serve the Lord?" It was the voice not of the Christian god but of a non-Native preacher named Reynolds. Though Jones replied in the affirmative, upon his return to camp, his heart hardened against the imported religion once more. Later that night, after he had gone to bed, a number of the preachers woke him up, crying, "Arise, Peter, and go with us to the prayer meeting, and get your soul converted. Your sister Mary has already obtained the Spirit of adoption, and you must seek the same blessing."[148] Determined to have the same experience, he went to his sister, and it was her exhorting that finally converted him. Natives often converted as families, and it was Jones's Indian fidelity to family that worked in his case.

Though he went on to become a highly successful Christian worker in both the United States and Canada, it is clear from both his writings and his praxis that his conversion did not conform entirely to the Western norms expected by missionaries. He undoubtedly wanted Christianity and "civilization" for Natives. He occasionally uses terms like "superstition" and "pagan" to refer to traditional religious practice. At the same time, however, he also speaks of it in positive terms. In his autobiographical material, he mentions the "pleasure" he experienced in participating in a sacred bear-oil feast at the present site of Rochester, New York, where he nonetheless had to "drink about a gill of what was not any more palatable than castor oil."[149] In all his writings, he employs the terms "Great Spirit," "Good Spirit," and "Supreme Being" interchangeably with the Christian word "God." He notes that Natives believe that the same Great Spirit created all nations of humanity and placed the Indians in the Americas, giving them their own distinct languages, complexion, and religions and telling them that it "would be wrong and give great offense to their Creator, to forsake the old ways of their forefathers."[150] His use of pejorative terms for Native religion in his writing, like his use of the "poor Indian" meme, must be viewed as part of his address to a white audience, whom he hoped to influence. His conversion, however, conforms to anthropologist Joseph Epes Brown's description of Native adaptation to Christianity generally. As Brown puts it, "The historical phenomenon is thus not conversion as understood in the exclusivistic manner by the bearers of Christianity, but rather a continuation of the people's ancient and traditional facility for what may be termed nonexclusive cumulative adhesion."[151] It is the phenomenon, quite common among indigenes, that I prefer to call religious dimorphism.

In his written work, Jones is a vociferous critic of whites both for their failure to conform to the dictates of their imported religion and for their treatment of Natives in general. In his *History*, he writes, "Before the treacherous Spaniard made his appearance in our country the Indian could sleep peacefully in his wigwam without fear of being hunted by bloodhounds; as if the owners of its soil were beasts of prey rather than men of like passions with themselves; or as if the rich mines of Mexico were of greater value than the lives and souls of the poor aborigines, whom the Good Spirit had made lords of the land where His providence had seen fit to place them. The real man is gone, and a strange people occupy his place."[152] Like Apess, he thus asserts not only inherent Native sovereignty over all of North America (after all, the Spaniards came nowhere near Anishinaabe territory) but also a primacy in the order of Creation.

Europeans were at first welcomed, Jones notes, but they wanted more and more. Finally, Indians were forced to defend what was theirs. "Goaded to despair, they clutched the deadly tomahawk, and sought to wield it against the encroaching whites; but, instead of conquering, the act only afforded to the calculating, remorseless foe, a pretext for a more general slaughter of the defenseless natives. Then, as if disease and the musket—both imported by whites—could not mow down the Indian fast enough, the fire-waters crept in and began to gnaw their very vitals, debasing their morals, lowering their dignity, spreading contentions, confusion, and death."[153]

Alcohol—along with disease probably the most destructive passenger across the Red Atlantic from Europe—comes in for special attack by Jones, as it did for Samson Occom and William Apess before him. Repeatedly he condemns Europeans for the introduction of liquor. He declares: "Since my conversion to God, one thing has made my heart very glad, and which is, that amidst all temptations and examples of drunkenness to which I was exposed, I never fell into that vice, although most of my young companions did. I always viewed drunkenness as beneath the character of an Indian. If at any time I was persuaded to take a little of the fire-water, I always felt sorry for it afterwards, especially when I reflected how much evil it had done to my poor countrymen, many thousands of whom have had their days shortened by it, and been hurried to destruction. Oh the miseries of drunkenness! Would to God that Indians had never tasted the fire-water!"[154] In the end, Jones concludes that—for manifold acts and introductions, an entire catalog of evils—whites have more to atone for in their treatment of Indians than they ever will be able to do.

In his praxis as well as in his writings, Jones championed Native communities. He was elected a chief in 1829. In that capacity, he authored much protest literature. In June 1830, he wrote to Sir John Colborne of the Canadian governmental authorities on behalf of the St. Clair Indians, voicing their request that they be permitted to remain on their ancestral lands "in as much, as the graves of their fathers were placed here and that it was their wish to lay down by the side of them." In the same letter, he advised of the St. Clair rejection of European ways and stated his agreement with their objections to conversion to Christianity. The following year, he assisted the Anishinaabe chiefs of Lake Huron in drafting a petition to King William IV. The document listed a long series of grievances against whites and commissioned Jones to act as the chiefs' ambassador to take up the matter with the monarch.[155] Before he left for England, he met with Chief William Yellowhead of Lake Simcoe, who was perhaps naive about the expanse of the Red Atlantic and the reach of the British Empire. Yellowhead charged him, "I shake hands with our Great Father over the great waters; when you see him tell him my name; he will know who I am, as he has often heard of me through our fathers the governors and Indian agents, who have sent my messages to him. Tell him I am still alive."[156]

The embassy coincided with a financial crisis afflicting the Methodist mission in Upper Canada. Jones, a dedicated Methodist, departed for England in the spring of 1831. He would remain for a year. His trip was split between his diplomatic mission and Methodist fund-raising. While in Britain, he gave a hundred public lectures and preached sixty-two sermons. He raised more than £1,000.[157]

Jones was mightily impressed with the mercantilism, industrial might, and agricultural fecundity of England. Like other Indian delegates, he met with an assortment of eminent personages, though most of Jones's meetings were religiously related. He did the de rigueur sightseeing, being particularly impressed with Westminster Abbey. When going about the streets of English cities, he dressed in sophisticated Western clothes. In Kingston upon Hull, a man approached him and, after gaping at him for some time, cried out, "Poh, he's been a Hinglishman hall the days of his life!"[158] Of all his meetings and the sights he saw, the one that made the deepest impression on him was an affluent young woman, a devout Christian, Eliza Field. Over his year in Britain, he courted her and, before his departure, proposed.

Jones had to wait for his audience with King William and Queen Adelaide until April 5, 1832. The event at Windsor Castle was inconsequential and unsatisfactory vis-à-vis the petition he bore. He was presented in the company of a Mi'kmaq chief from Nova Scotia and his son, who were in the country to purchase farming implements. The king addressed them first. They were Catholics, a denominational difference upon which the monarch remarked. William also remarked on Jones's traditional garb— "a real Chippewa costume"—and noted that he considered the Mi'kmaq youth "a model of the American Indian." Jones gave the sovereign a copy of the Gospel of St. John that he had translated into Anishinaabe. The king opened it and said, "Very good." After thirty minutes of questions and genial but vacant conversation, the Indians were escorted to a lunch with some members of the court. The meal featured "roasted chickens, beef, potatoes, tarts, wine &c. and they ate out of silver dishes." Toasts were made to the royal couple, and Jones remembered hearing one of the lords jocularly saluting "the King's squaw." Jones effused of the monarch and his consort, "Long may they live to be a blessing to their nation and people! May God direct them in the good and right path of righteousness! God bless the King and Queen!"[159]

Jones returned to Britain twice, in 1837–38 and again in 1844–46.[160] The earlier of the two is of special interest to us. He had drafted a petition on behalf of his people at River Credit in Upper Canada relating to their land claims. As he was preparing to depart, the governor, Sir Francis

Bond Head, decided to intervene. The administrator wrote a letter to the colonial secretary, Lord Glenelg, designed to poison the well against the Indians' entreaty by disparaging Jones as the messenger. The letter stated, "Mr. Peter Jones who in the power of Attorney of which he is the bearer has the double title of *Chief* and *Missionary* [Jones had by this time been ordained a Methodist minister] of the Mississagua [*sic*] tribe of the Chippewa nation of Indians is the son of an American surveyor who living in open adultery had children by several Indian Squaws deemed it admirable to bring up one of them as a Missionary!"[161]

Despite the governor's intervention, in March 1838, Jones did meet with Lord Glenelg to present the petition. During the meeting, Jones explained, "So long as they [the Mississauga] hold no written document from the British Government to show that the land is theirs they fear that the white man may at future day take their lands away from them, and the apprehension is constantly cherished by observing the policy pursued by the United States Government." The secretary was sympathetic. A short time after the interview, he promised to help the Indians get written deeds.[162]

An audience with Queen Victoria was supposed to occur the following month but was postponed by the crown until September. In his *Life and Journals*, Jones relates a funny incident that occurred immediately prior to the royal meeting. As requested, Jones arrived early at Windsor to discuss with Glenelg what he would wear to meet the queen. Jones wore an English suit but told the secretary he preferred to meet the queen in traditional dress, which he assured was a "perfect covering."[163] Glenelg withdrew to discuss the matter with William Lamb, Lord Melbourne, the prime minister. As Donald Smith describes it in his biography of Jones, "For several minutes two of the world's most powerful leaders discussed the Ojibwa national costume. The colonial secretary asked Lord Melbourne whether he thought the Canadian Indian costume was court dress. But the leader of the British Empire, fearing any impropriety before the young queen, advised a cautious policy—the Indian should present himself dressed in his English tailored suit."[164] Glenelg returned to Jones, asking him to gather his outfit for inspection. Back went the Native to his lodgings. Upon seeing it, the secretary finally pronounced it suitable.

When he met with the queen, Jones presented the petition he had previously shown to Lord Glenelg, requesting "title-deeds" for her "red

children." In his journal, he wrote that after presenting it, "I then proceeded to give her the meaning of the wampum [that was attached]; and
told her that the white wampum signified the loyal and good feeling
which prevails amongst the Indians towards Her Majesty and Her Government; but that the black wampum was designed to tell Her Majesty
that their hearts were troubled on account of their having no title-deeds
for their lands; and that they sent their petition and wampum that Her
Majesty might be pleased to take out all the black wampum, so that the
string might be all white."[165]

Jones was plagued by recurring bouts of ill health for many years, but
that did not stop his activities on behalf of his people. In 1847, after his
third trip to Britain, he attempted to resign his chieftainship, but his
community refused to accept his resignation. He died on May 28, 1856.
Eliza completed publication of his autobiography, journals, and history.

Another Missisauga Ojibway who was seemingly born for the Red Atlantic was George Copway. When Copway was a youth, he had a dream.
In his autobiography, *The Life of Kah-ge-ga-gah-bowh* (his Anishinaabe
name), he says that in his sleep he saw a man walking toward him in the
air. The figure instructed him to gaze upon a tall pine tree while he sang.
After the man sang, he told the young Copway to repeat his song:

> I commenced as follows:—
>   "It is I who travel in the winds,
>   It is I who whisper in the breeze;
>   I shake the trees,
>   I shake the earth,
>   I trouble the waters."

The wind shook the mighty tree; the land heaved up; the waters roared
and tossed upon their banks. Then the spirit said, "I am from the rising of
the sun [that is, the east, the direction of the Atlantic]; I will come to see
you again. You will not see me often; but you will hear me speak." Then
he walked away from whence he had come. When the boy told his father
about the experience, the elder interpreted the vision: "My son, *the god
of the winds* is kind to you; the aged tree, I hope may indicate a long life;
the wind may indicate that you will travel much; the waters which you
saw, and the winds, will carry your canoe safely through the waves."[166]
The vision would prove prophetic.

Copway had much in common with Jones. Like him, he would experience a traditional Anishinaabe upbringing, and like him he would become both an Ojibway chief and a Methodist minister. Finally, he would follow in his fellow Anishinaabe's wake in traveling to Europe as a diplomat.

In 1850, Copway met Elihu Burritt, a philanthropist and peace activist. Two years earlier, Burritt had founded a precursor organization, of sorts, to the League of Nations, an International Peace Congress, and he invited the Anishinaabe chief to be a delegate at the fourth congress, to be held in Frankfurt. In 1851, Copway published a diary of his trip to Europe, *Running Sketches of Men and Places*, largely a travelogue.

The Native devoted two chapters to the Atlantic. He writes, "Old Ocean! Here it is surrounding me on all sides!—To the limit of human vision this expanse is illimitable, except that it is bound by the horizon, which forever recedes as we approach it. How appallingly is the mind impressed in contemplating these huge domains."[167]

During his tour of Europe and his time at the peace conference, among the luminaries whom he saw and with whom he interacted (and of whom he offers his "sketches") were, in addition to Burritt, Benjamin Disraeli, Lord John Russell, Richard Cobden, and Baronet Anthony de Rothschild. In England, he even managed to take in a concert by Jenny Lind, the Swedish Nightingale, about whom he rhapsodizes euphoric. At the congress, the indigenous delegate, who of course appeared in Native dress, was welcomed "with plaudits almost equal to those which hailed the entrance of Cobden." He offered a resolution: "This Congress acknowledging the principle of non-intervention recognizes it to be the sole right of every state to regulate its own affairs."[168] Whether the white delegates knew it or not, the motion had direct relevance to Native nations, which the United States was continuing to pressure for land cessions. The resolution passed.

Copway participated in a group that is sometimes thought of as paving the way for the League of Nations, following World War 1. The last red diplomat we will examine sought to influence the league itself.

The Spirit of Geneva

Following the Great War, the Canadian government, which until then had been largely content to deal with the Iroquois as a separate sovereign government, decided to pursue its aggressive policy of Indian assimilation and abrogate the 1784 treaty made by Frederick Haldimand, granting the loyalist Iroquois their Grand River reserve. Ottawa effectively wanted to end Iroquois self-governance and destroy their territorial integrity. As a means of crippling the Six Nations' government, it withheld monies that were rightfully theirs. According to the late Seneca historian John Mohawk, "The Iroquois soon knew that the majority in the legislative halls of the Canadian capitol planned further inroads on their rights as citizens of a separate country known as Grand River Land."[169]

The Haudenosaunee response, as it so often was, was diplomatic. Because the 1784 Haldimand Treaty had been made with Great Britain, which had provided the Indians with the guarantees to the Grand River territory, it was with Great Britain that the Six Nations had government-to-government relations. It was therefore to the British government that they would appeal.

In August 1921, Levi General (better known as Deskaheh), the Tadadaho (or Speaker) of the Iroquois Grand Council at Grand River, using a passport issued by the Six Nations, traveled the Red Atlantic to London. His goal, as he stated it, was to make "earnest application to the Imperial Government of Great Britain for the fulfilment on its part of its said promise of protection, and for its intervention thereunder to prevent the continued aggressions upon the Six Nations practised by the Dominion of Canada." In sum, the Haldimand Treaty had been signed on the authority of George III, and Deskaheh was asking that King George V stand by it and act upon it. Unfortunately, His Majesty's government declined to get involved in Canada's "domestic problem," and the Native went home empty-handed and disillusioned.[170]

In the wake of the failure of Deskaheh's deputation to Britain, things grew worse. The dominion government closed the traditional longhouse and proposed an elected government in place of traditional Haudenosaunee governance. It then cajoled and bribed a "fifth-column" of Grand River Iroquois to support its scheme. As Mohawk puts it, "It was easier still to get the new minority to ask for protection. It was easiest of all to order a detail of the red-jacketed Royal Canadian Mounted Police to ride into the Grand River country to protect the 'loyalist' Indians and 'to keep the peace.'"[171] Deskaheh, alerted to the impending raid, slipped over the U.S.-Canadian border to New York. Many resistant Iroquois were arrested. The Mounties built a barracks on the reserve to establish a permanent Canadian presence. Grand River became an "occupied nation."[172] At this point, Deskaheh, assisted by George Decker, the non-Native attorney for the Six Nations, hit upon a desperate—but thoroughly Haudenosaunee—strategy. He would take their case to the League of Nations.

The League of Nations, a predecessor to the United Nations, grew out of the Treaty of Versailles, ending World War I. A central element of President Woodrow Wilson's Fourteen Points, the aim was to create a forum of countries to meet, debate, and legislate global peace. The league held its first meeting in Paris in January 1920. Moving to Geneva, it held its first General Assembly in November the same year.

In 1829, African American abolitionist David Walker wrote *An Appeal to the Coloured Citizens of the World*, addressing persons of African descent around the black Atlantic. Four years later, during the Mashpee Revolt in Massachusetts, William Apess reversed Walker's language in his "An Indian's Appeal to the White Men of Massachusetts."[173] Whether Deskaheh was aware of Apess's text is unknown, though it seems likely. Echoing but universalizing the Pequot's title, with Decker's help, he authored "The Redman's Appeal for Justice" ninety years later. A precise and legalistic document, it was masterfully designed as a memorial to the league. It was subsequently published as a pamphlet in London.

Article I of the Covenant of the League of Nations provided, "Any self-governing State, Dominion or Colony . . . may become a Member of the League if its admission is agreed to by two-thirds of the Assembly, provided that it shall give effective guarantees of its sincere intention to observe its international obligations." Though the Haudenosaunee believed that they met the conditions for admission as a member, Deskaheh and Decker's simple but nonetheless brilliant plan was to bypass Article I and instead rely on Article XVII, which stated, "In the event of a dispute between a Member of the League and between States not Members of the League, the State or States not Members of the League shall be invited to accept the obligations of membership in the League of Nations."[174] The lawyer and his client saw that the second clause was essentially a back door to membership.

The Haudensaunee appeal outlined the Indians' manifold grievances against Canada and Great Britain. It stated, "The Six Nations of the Iroquois crave therefore invitation to accept the obligations of Membership of the League for the purpose of such dispute; upon such conditions as may be prescribed."[175] If the league took up the Haudenosaunee complaint, win or lose, it would be international recognition of their independent sovereignty.

There was, however, an obstacle: in order to have their petition considered, the Iroquois needed a member nation to sponsor them. In late 1922, Deskaheh and his counsel traveled to the United States to meet with the chargé d'affaires of the Netherlands in Washington. They appealed to the Dutch queen to present the Haudenosaunee case before the league. Holland's government agreed and forwarded the appeal. For Canada, just trying to establish its independent existence in foreign affairs from Great Britain, the Iroquois application was a major embarrassment. In May 1923, Sir Joseph Pope, the under-secretary of state for foreign affairs, replied (in part), "The claim that the Six Nations are an organized and self-governing people so as to form a political unit apart from Canada is to anyone acquainted with the actual conditions an absurd one."[176] Great Britain lodged a formal protest over the Dutch "uncalled for interference" in Canadian domestic affairs.[177] Behind the scenes, maneuvering began to bury the entire matter. Iroquois opponents had, however, underestimated Deskaheh.

The whole affair was almost forgotten. Then, in September 1923, Deskaheh and Decker surprised everyone by showing up in Geneva, the Tadadaho traveling on the same Haudenosaunee passport he had used to go to Britain. He brought with him "The Redman's Appeal for Justice." Dated August 6, 1923, the document was essentially a reworking of the appeal passed along by the Dutch government. According to scholar Joëlle Rostkowski, "The familiarity with international procedures has been the key to success or failure of Indian representation in the diplomatic field and, in that respect, Deskaheh's action is no exception. International civil servants have to play by the rules of the game and Deskaheh's patience and dogged determination might finally have led—if not to international recognition for the Six Nations—at least to a discussion of their case by the Assembly or the Council of the League, and to an assessment of the substance of their complaints."[178] While the first part of her statement is undoubtedly true, the second misjudges the sophistication of the Cayuga chief's plan—as did those who had sought to block him before the league.

Deskaheh sent his "Appeal" to the secretary-general. The league administrator declined to intervene, reminding the chief that he had lost the sponsorship of the Netherlands and that he needed a member nation to bring his case forward. Deskaheh had anticipated this. He had widely circulated the "Appeal" and secured not one but four sponsors: Estonia, Ireland (no friend of Great Britain), Panama, and Persia. The quartet requested that the Iroquois complaint be put on the agenda of the assembly. They also asked that the matter be referred to the Permanent Court of International Justice in The Hague to determine if the case was proper for them to consider under Article XVII of the covenant. The president of the assembly demurred, pointing out that their session was just days away from adjournment. Prince Arfa-ed-Dowleh, the Persian delegate, pressed the Iroquois case, but league bureaucrats again stalled.

Deskaheh tirelessly continued to seek support and an audience before the league. He wrote to his family, "I have no time to go anywhere, only sitting on the chair from morning till night, copying and answering letters as they come, and copying the documents, and I have many things to do."[179] Among those "many things," in addition to meetings, was making himself a public figure in Geneva. Like his predecessors in England, he was willing to embrace expectations by appearing in Indian dress. When he did not, he inevitably disappointed. A Geneva journalist admitted his desolation at finding him "wearing a neat brown business suit and at his side no moccassined [*sic*] brave but a vulturous paleface lawyer." A reporter from Hungary, while elated to see "his first American Indian," was disappointed that the Cayuga did not possess "the typical Indian profile, the nose not the aquiline nose [he] had expected."[180]

Time wore on. Outmaneuvered in the arcane procedures of the League of Nations, Deskaheh began to despair. He called upon the *orenda* of the Haudenosaunee Confederacy. *Orenda* is a spiritual force or essence possessed by every object or being on earth. A rock has *orenda*. A tree has *orenda*. Each person has a portion of *orenda*. Any individual's *orenda* is small, but the collective *orenda* of the Haudenosaunee Confederacy is great and powerful. In May 1924, Deskaheh wrote to his brother, Alex General, saying: "I believe it will be a good thing to have a meeting in one of the Longhouses, but you must [combine] all the good people and the children of the Longhouse, only those that are faithful believers in our religion and no other, and it must be very early in the morning to have this, so that our God may hear you and the children, and ask him to help us in our distress at this moment, and you must use Indian tobacco in our usual way when we ask help to our Great Spirit . . . and you must have a uniform on . . . and also ask God you wish the religion will keep up for a great many years to come and the Indian race also."[181] As a representative of the entire confederacy, Deskaheh possessed the corporate *orenda* of all Iroquois by proxy.

Back in North America, the Canadian government pushed on in its illegal campaign for the dissolution of the Haudenosaunee Confederacy's independent government. It seized the Six Nations' Council House (the seat of that government) and announced a "free election" to replace traditional governance. It placed an armed guard around the Council House. Its police broke open a safe and stole the nation's sacred wampums. In November 1924, Deskaheh wrote to a Swiss journalist, "It is the heart broken that I must affirm that since several months I am against the most cruel indifference. . . . My appeal to the Society of Nations has not been heard, and nothing in the attitude of Governments does not leave me any hope."[182] Confirming him in his despair, the secretariat informed him that not only would his people's case not be heard but, in fact, he and George Decker would be barred from even sitting in the gallery of the assembly.

In a last desperate ploy, Deskaheh and Decker booked the Salle Centrale in Geneva for the chief to make a public address. Several thousand people, journalists, and ordinary individuals—but no representatives of the League of Nations—showed up. Deskaheh, not disappointing, appeared in full regalia and passionately presented his case. Although the crowd roared its approval, it did no good. By the end of the year, Deskaheh recrossed the Red Atlantic, spent physically and mentally, but unbowed.

Unable to enter Canada, he went to the house of Clinton Rickard, that Iroquois veteran of the Philippine War, in New York. On March 25, 1925, he delivered a last radio address. Still defiant, he declared, "Over in Ottawa they call that policy 'Indian Advancement.' Over in Washington, they call it 'Assimilation.' We who would be the helpless victims say it is tyranny. . . . If this must go on to the bitter end, we would rather that you come with your guns and poison gas and get rid of us that way. Do it openly and above board." Less than three months later, he died. His family in Canada was prevented from coming to his bedside, but in that final speech, he told the Iroquois that their case "has gone into the records where your children can find it when I may be dead."[183]

Iroquois diplomacy across the Red Atlantic began in 1696. It continued through Deskaheh's futile mission to Switzerland at the close of that era. Though the Red Atlantic ended in 1927, the tradition of Haudeno-saunee diplomats has continued uninterrupted. In 1977, a delegation, including Oren Lyons, faithkeeper of the Grand Council, journeyed to Geneva to address the United Nations, joining other Natives to discuss indigenous rights with the global community. They entered the buildings, once the domain of the League of Nations, to which Deskaheh had once been denied admission. They traveled on the deerskin passports of the Haudenosaunee Confederacy. Their position papers, authored by John Mohawk, became the core of the important book *Basic Call to Consciousness*. In 1993, Lyons led a delegation of nineteen indigenes to the U.N. headquarters in New York for the International Year of the World's Indigenous People. Their speeches marked a path directly to the United Nations' adoption in 2007 of the Declaration on the Rights of Indigenous Peoples. In 2000, Thom White Wolf Fassett (like John Mohawk, a Seneca), general secretary of the United Methodist Board of Church and Society, brokered an end to the Elián Gonzalez crisis, traveling to Cuba to negotiate with Fidel Castro and hiring, through his agency, Elián's father's attorney, Greg Craig.[184] These are but a few of the critical interventions of Iroquois diplomats upon the international stage.

The Haudenosaunee Confederacy continues to issue its own passports. They are honored by Switzerland and a number of other nations, but not by Canada or the United States. During the summer of 2010, twenty-three members of the Iroquois National Lacrosse Team attempted to travel on their Haudenosaunee passports to participate in the sport's international championship. Upon the advice of the U.S. State Department, Britain barred them from entry.[185]

4

—⁓—

A Gazing Stocke, Yea Even a Laughing Stocke
Celebrity Indians and Display across the Red Atlantic

AT THE OUTSET OF THIS BOOK, I noted that the demarcations between its various categories are far from hard and fast. They tend to bleed into one another. Garcilaso de la Vega, who, if he is remembered at all, is thought of as a writer, is presented in this book as a warrior—which he certainly was. Tisquantum was a captive and a slave, yet he was also the consummate diplomat. Deskaheh went to Geneva as a diplomatic representative of the Six Nations Iroquois, but he was unafraid to make himself a stereotypical spectacle in order to try to achieve his objective. As Alden Vaughan observes of the Natives traveling to England, the "painted 'savages' en route to Whitehall or St. James's Palace who dazzled London crowds proved powerful negotiators inside those stately buildings with Britain's commissioners of trade, privy councilors, and monarchs."[1] Yet those same Natives became celebrities, their comings and goings—often their every move—followed by press and public. From the first Taino captives brought back by Columbus straight through to Deskaheh, Indians became sensations wherever they traveled. Indians literally stopped traffic.

Yet other indigenes came or were brought to Europe more explicitly as spectacle and as entertainers. Many know that William Cody brought Indians to Europe as part of Buffalo Bill's Wild West show. Cody came eight times between 1887 and 1892 and between 1902 and 1906. His first tour, in 1887, coincided with Queen Victoria's Golden Jubilee and included two command performances for the British monarch. The highlight of the second came when Albert, Prince of Wales, along with the kings of Belgium, Denmark, Greece, and Saxony, plus the future Kaiser

189

Wilhelm II, boarded the Deadwood Stage. With Buffalo Bill himself in the driver's seat, the coach raced around the arena while Cody's Indians "attacked."

Among the ninety-seven Indians in the company during that first tour were Black Elk and Red Shirt. The pair officiated at the funeral of Surrounded by the Enemy, who succumbed to a lung infection while in England. Among the other dignitaries who saw the Natives during their European tours were President Sadi Carnot of France, the celebrated German author Karl May, and Pope Leo XIII, who conveyed a special blessing upon them.[2]

The late Blackfeet writer James Welch used the touring company for his 2000 novel, *The Heartsong of Charging Elk*, focusing on an Indian who gets left behind in France. In the original version of the novel, there was a framing device (discarded before publication) in which an accultur- ated, and in many ways deracinated, Lakota university professor travels to France. There he encounters Charging Elk's descendants. In these Frenchmen, he discovers people who are yet thoroughly Sioux and know more about what it means to be Lakota than he does.[3]

Despite the familiarity of many people with Buffalo Bill, Natives had been coming to Europe as part of spectaculars for centuries before Cody ever launched his Wild West show. One of the most lavish such displays took place in Rouen, France, in 1550. Fifty imported Tupinambá from Brazil took part in an enormous moving *tableau vivant* for King Henri II and Catherine de Medici. They joined around 250 nude painted French in a recreation of life in their homeland, complete with monkeys and parrots. According to Vaughan, "The painted participants staged two mock battles—one for the king, the other upon the queen's arrival a day later—in which [the constructed] villages were intentionally destroyed, thus bringing the festivities to a symbolic climax with civility's victory over savagery."[4]

Though history does not record what happened to the Brazilian Indians, Vaughan wonders if some of them were the three whom the great French writer Michel de Montaigne encountered as a young man. In 1562, Montaigne, then a courtier of King Charles IX, witnessed the three in an audience with the monarch in Rouen. Nearly twenty years later, he would recall the incident in his essay "Of Cannibals." The French king reportedly spoke to the three at some length. Then, as with scores of other indigenes whom European metropoles wanted to impress, "they were shown our ways, our splendor, the aspect of a fine city." Montaigne writes:

> After that, someone asked their opinion, and wanted to know what they had found most amazing. They mentioned three things, of which I have forgotten the third, and I am very sorry for it; but I still remember two of them. They said that in the first place they thought it very strange that so many grown men, bearded, strong, and armed, who were around the king (it is likely that they were talking about the Swiss of his guard) should submit to obey a child [Charles would have been eleven or twelve years old], and that one of them was not chosen to command instead. Second (they have a way in their language of speaking of men as halves of one another), they had noticed that there were among us men full and gorged with all sorts of good things, and that their other halves were beggars at their doors, emaciated with hunger and poverty; and they thought it strange that these needy halves could endure such an injustice, and did not take the others by the throat, or set fire to their houses.[5]

As would so many Red Atlantic travelers after them, these Indians wondered at the wealth disparity and poverty they witnessed. These three come off as sagacious in previsioning the French Revolution yet more than two centuries in the future. One wishes Montaigne could have remembered their third observation. If the three were among the fifty in Henri II's tableau, perhaps they were remembering the destruction of their faux villages in their reference to French peasants' setting fire to the chateaux of the wealthy. Montaigne says that he "had a very long talk" with one of the group but that it was hindered by the French interpreter's "stupidity in taking in my ideas."[6]

Cases of intentional, "commercial display" of Natives were relatively few, though they, of course, did occur. In 1759, the "Famous Mohawk Indian Warrior" (who, we do not know), in face and body paint, with "Scalping-knife, Tom-ax, and all other Implements of War," was displayed for money and advertised as "a Sight worth the Curiosity of every True-Briton." As Vaughan observes, whether from "ignorance or avarice," he was also called the only Indian to visit Britain since Queen Anne's Four Indian Kings.[7] Two Mohawks, Synchnecta and Trosoghroga, were brought to England for public display in 1764, causing confusion and consternation during Henry Timberlake's unauthorized Cherokee delegation the same year. Afterwards, the Mohawks were taken to the Netherlands and displayed in The Hague. Synchnecta was sold in Amsterdam to the owner of the "Blauw Jan Inn," who continued to show him until public opinion forced his emancipation.[8] Apparently, Indian display was profitable enough to spawn a cottage industry of Englishmen painting themselves and posing as Indians. Kate Flint notes that, as time wore on, Indians crossing the Atlantic were "increasingly multifunctional," acting as both emissaries and entertainers. For example, in 1818, seven Senecas came to England to discuss land claims but also appeared in theaters in Leeds, Liverpool, London, and Manchester.[9]

Occom's Razor

Did Samson Occom shave? His portrait shows no hint of shadow. In his depiction, he resembles nothing so much as an ever so slightly dusky Dr. Johnson. "Occom's razor" refers, in this case, neither to a straight-edged blade nor to the rule of logic and theology but to the precise, careful, and razor-like manner with which he employed the only tools at his disposal—a shrewd intellect, a gift for words, and his own celebrity—in order to promote Native values across the Red Atlantic, critiquing the white power structure of his day even while being a marginal figure in it.

Occom was born in 1723 near present-day New London, Connecticut, a member of the Mohegan Nation, which had split off from the Pequot in 1631, a few years before the latter were virtually destroyed (with Mohegan cooperation). Though he began to learn to speak and read English from Christian ministers as early as 1733, he knew little or nothing of Christianity until the summer of 1739, when missionaries began to proselytize more systematically among his people. He "Continued under Trouble of Mind" for about six months, but within a year he had "a Discovery of the way of Salvation through Jesus Christ, and was enabl'd to put my trust in him alone for Life and Salvation. From this Time the Distress and Burden of my mind was removed, and I found Serenity and Pleasure of Soul, in Serving God."[10] He began to read the Christian scriptures and developed a desire to gain further education in order to teach his fellow Indians how to read. In 1743, when he was nineteen, at his own request, his mother sent him to Eleazar Wheelock, who operated Moor's Charity School for indigent young men in Lebanon, Connecticut. The arrival of Occom convinced the Congregationalist minister that his preparatory school might serve a missionary purpose. Occom expected to stay two or three weeks, but he remained four years, until his impaired eyesight made further studies impossible.[11]

Occom's remarkable ability "inspired his teacher with a vision of educating many Indians and sending them to spread salvation among their respective tribes."[12] Wheelock's dream, however, never materialized. He continued for twenty-five years, educating some notable young men like Joseph Brant, but in 1769, he moved to Hanover, New Hampshire. He reorganized Moor's there and founded Dartmouth College. Wheelock once again began to train non-Natives. Though education of Natives was written into Dartmouth's charter, Indians made up only a small percentage of the student body, and this number rapidly dwindled. The shift was to cause a final rupture between Wheelock and his former pupil.

Occom was licensed to preach shortly after leaving Moor's. For ten years, however, he remained unordained. He experienced significant success teaching and evangelizing among the Montauk and Shinnecock of New York's Long Island and eventually made missionary visits to the Oneida, as well.

In December 1765, in the company of Reverend Nathaniel Whitaker, Occom sailed to Britain from Boston to raise funds for the education of Indians at Wheelock's new college, arriving in February. News of their journey and Occom's reputation preceded the pair. Because the colonies were roiled with opposition to the Stamp Act and because of supposed opposition to the mission, an English friend warned that the Indian was "Expected and much Talkt of here. . . . Pray let him come to London by Coach privately & unseen, & let him first see Mr. Whitefield."[13] Occom and Whitaker did as suggested and stayed with George Whitefield, one of those who had been a friend of Tomochichi, remaining under wraps at his home for several days.

Indeed, Whitefield seems to have orchestrated much of the pair's early stay. Occom wrote, "Mr. Whitefield takes unwearied Pains to Introduce us to the religious Nobility and others, and to the best men of the City of London—Yea he is a tender father to us, he provides everything for us, he has got a House for us—the Lord reward him a thousand and Thousand fold." Whitefield even furnished their house and provided a maid for them. Occom preached his first sermon in Britain at Whitefield's church.[14]

Among the "religious Nobility" and "best men" to whom Occom and

Whitaker were introduced were William Legge, a member of the Privy Council and president of the Board of Trade, and the archbishop of Canterbury. Though King George III contributed £200 to Occom's cause, the Native gained no audience with the monarch. He was permitted, however, to observe him putting on his raiment in the robing room of Parliament.

While Occom kept a journal during his trip, it is somewhat fragmentary and the entries cursory. This is due, in part, to lengthy and repeated bouts of ill health and to the fact that his poor eyesight often made it painful for him to write.

Like the Brazilian Indians whom Montaigne observed at the French court two centuries previous, Occom remarked upon the extreme economic disparity and poverty, noting both the bustling hubbub of London but also "the poor Begars Praying, Crying, Beging upon their knees."[15] Most of his time was taken up with his primary mission, preaching to crowds that numbered into the thousands to raise funds for Moor's. Even so, he and Whitaker had time to take in the usual attractions: the Tower of London, Westminster Abbey, Bedlam, and Gravesend (the site of Pocahontas's demise). He also preached in locales as far-flung as Liverpool and Scotland. By any measure, the two-year stay was an unqualified success, raising £12,000.[16]

Upon his return in 1768, however, Occom was angered that he had collected money for an enterprise that was already being largely abandoned by Wheelock in favor of education of whites. His correspondence with Wheelock reveals his disillusionment, his commitment to Native peoples, and his skill with English letters. He complained, "Hoping that it may be a lasting Benefet to my poor Tawnee Brethren, With this View I went [to Europe] a volunteer—and I was willing to become a Gazing Stocke, Yea Even a Laughing Stocke, in Strange Countries to Promote your Cause," but he was betrayed. Wheelock had turned his back on the community to whom Occom was committed. In a wicked and incisive pun, Occom wrote, "I am very jealous that instead of your Semenary Becoming alma Mater, she will be too much *alba mater* to Suckle the Tawnees.—I think your College has too much Worked by Grandeur for the Poor Indians, they'll never have much benefit of it." He goes on to accuse his mentor of sending him to England as part of an elaborate fraud.[17]

The same year, Occom wrote an autobiographical essay to correct "several Representations . . . made by Some gentlemen in America Concerning me."[18] Occom had already proved himself quite adept of self-representation on the page. When a white neighbor accused him of alcoholism, he wrote back, "You represent me to be the vilest Creature in Mohegan. I own that I am bad enough and too bad, Yet I am Heartily glad I am not that old Robert Clelland [the author of the accusation], his sins won't be charged to me and my Sins won't be charged to him, he must answere for his own works before his Maker and I must answere for mine. You signify, as if it was in your Power to do me harm. You have been trying all you can and you may [do] your worst, I am not concerned." As literary critic David Murray states, Occom's closing is both a permission to Clelland "to 'represent' him *and* a way of totally rejecting it: 'I am, Sir, just what you Please, S. Occom.'"[19] Likewise, while in London, he found a way of expressing indigenous powerlessness in the face of colonial encroachment and of affirming Natives' innate superiority, declaring, "I am afraid the poor Indians will never stand a good chance with the English in their land controversies, because they are very poor, they have no money. Money is almighty now-a-days, and the Indians have no learning, no wit, no cunning; the English have all."[20]

We have already seen in chapter 3 the motif of the "poor Indian" in Peter Jones's writings. As a reference to Native peoples, it is common to all Occom's works and, in fact, to works by many other Indian writers of the period. At first glance, this self-abasing language would seem to run counter to what I have in the past labeled "communitism," that is to say, a proactive commitment to Native community. (This neologism is a combination of the words "community" and "activism.") As Murray observes, however, "When this [formulaic] humility is accompanied by a sense of grievance, as it is quite often in the case of Samson Occom, the same gesture of abasement can carry a sting in the tail." Murray illustrates his point with a letter in which Occom complains bitterly of his own inadequate funding for a missionary endeavor but nonetheless vows to go "tho no White Missionary would go in such Circumstances." Occom closes, "In a word I leave my poor Wife and Children at your feet and if they hunger, Starve and die let them Die there. Sir, I shall endeavor to follow your Directions in all things. This in utmost hast and with Sincere obedience is from . . . Your Good for Nothing Indian Sarvant."[21]

In his autobiography, Occom delineates the difficulty he had making ends meet in his undertakings and the shabby treatment he received at the hands of whites. Whereas a white missionary was paid £100 a year, plus £50 for an interpreter and £30 for an "introducer," Occom, who needed no such extraneous personnel, received only a total of £180 over a dozen years. He writes:

> What can be the Reason that they used me after this manner? I can't think of any thing, but this is as a Poor Indian Boy Said, Who was Bound out to an English Family, and he used to Drive Plow for a young man, and he whipt and Beat him almost every Day, and the young man found fault with him, and Complained of him to his master and the poor Boy was Called to answer for himself before his master, and he was asked, what it was he did, that he was So Complained of and beat almost every Day. He Said, he did not know, but he Supposed it was because he could not drive any better, but says he, I Drive as well as I know how; and at other Times he Beats me, because he is of a mind to beat me; but says he believes he Beats me for most of the Time "because I am an Indian." So I am *ready* to Say, they have used me thus, because I Can't Influence the Indians so well as other missionaries; but I can assure them I have endeavoured to teach them as I know how:—but I *must Say*, "I believe it is because I am a poor Indian." I Can't help that God made me So; I did not make myself so.[22]

With that, he breaks off his account entirely. The parable, and the work that contains it, is more than simple self-vindication. Like other works by Occom, it is a communitist vindication of Indians in general.

Occom is best known for his "Sermon Preached at the Execution of Moses Paul, an Indian." First published in 1772, it became an early best seller, running through several editions on both sides of the Red Atlantic. Moses Paul converted to Christianity but fell into drink while first in the army and later the navy. While intoxicated, he committed a pointless murder. As Murray explains, "His execution was therefore an opportunity to contemplate not just one Indian's downfall but to make him symbolize the particular weaknesses and susceptibilities of Indians. By having the sermon actually preached by a virtuous Indian (though one who also had shown his weakness for alcohol . . .), it was possible to stage a sort of moral tableau which encapsulated the moral capacities and disabilities of the Indians."[23] Occom was asked to deliver the sermon, supposedly by Paul himself, and the resulting oration demonstrates that he was more than "just a pawn in a white game."[24]

In a preface to the printed version of the talk, Occom writes that he hopes that it will benefit his people and, indeed, other people of color, saying, "I think they [common people] can't help understanding my talk: little children may understand me. And poor Negroes may plainly and fully understand my meaning; and it may be of service to them. Again, it may in a particular manner be of service to my poor kindred the Indians. Further, as it comes from an uncommon quarter it may induce people to read it because it is from an Indian."[25] In the sermon itself, the preacher alternately addresses both Indians and whites, making the white audience "overhearers" of a "pre-arranged conversation between Indians." He tells Paul, and presumably his white listeners as well, that he (and the whites) have had the advantage of education and the Christian gospel and "therefore your sins are so much more aggravated." Calling Paul "bone of my bone, and flesh of my flesh," he argues, "You are an Indian, a despised creature; but you have despised yourself." As Murray accurately claims, Occom thereby implies that because they are despised, Indians have "an obligation not to live up, or rather down" to others' expectations. Then, in a complicated rhetorical maneuver and with only a slightly veiled manner, Occom blames whites for Indian alcoholism. He cries, "And here I cannot but observe, we find it in the sacred writ, a woe denounced against men, who put their bottles to their neighbours mouth to make them drunk, and that they may see their weaknesses; and no doubt there are such devilish men now in our day, as there were in the days of old." Murray does not go far enough when he states, "I am certainly not claiming an overall subversive purpose here, but when we link the possible ironies shown here with those found in his letters and the letters of some of Wheelock's other pupils an impression emerges of self-expression both *within* the conventions of Christian piety they had been taught and also *beyond* them."[26] I would argue that the intent is clearly subversive. Occom uses the occasion to affirm Native personhood, and the overall message is meant to be more accusatory of whites who created the situation by introducing liquor and by hating Indians than it is of the condemned and unfortunate Paul.

Unfortunately, Occom met with a fate not that different from the condemned Indian he both admonished and eulogized. For the next decade, he acted as local minister and tribal consultant to the Mohegan and to other Indians in the area, including the new Christian Indian community of Brotherton (also called Brothertown), which he helped found. He "also succumbed to occasional bouts of self-pity and heavy drinking—behavior that further identified him as an Indian in the eyes of both red and white observers."[27] He died in 1792.

White Shamans and Plastic Medicine Men

Contemporary Native Americans like to refer to "white shamans" and "plastic medicine men." The first term denotes non-Natives who practice Native American religious traditions, acting as holy persons for white "congregations." The second references actual Natives who cater to the same audiences, lending an air of authority to those practices and making audiences feel like they are involved in something authentic. Both are part of the religious phenomenon known as the New Age movement. In 1996, a documentary, popular among Native Americans, with the title of this section, was made for public television.[28] It might not be wholly accurate as a title for a discussion of George Catlin's "Indian Curiosities," but neither is it entirely inappropriate. Catlin put them on display as a kind of (retro)spectacle of the vanishing American while he performed somewhat the role of the white shaman for his European audiences. His tours of Europe also intertwined his story with that of George Henry, who called himself Maungwudaus (Great Hero), Christian missioner, impresario, and performer, who became a kind of plastic medicine man.[29]

Catlin is today recognized as a major American painter of the West, particularly of Indians. Between 1830 and 1838, he made a number of trips, visiting almost seventy different tribal nations. Returning to the East, he displayed his paintings and the artifacts he had collected throughout American cities. In 1839, he took his collection across the Atlantic for an extended tour. He self-published a memoir of his time in Europe in 1848 in two volumes entitled *Catlin's Notes: Or, Eight Years' Travels and Residence in Europe, with His North American Indian Collection.*[30]

Initially the gallery consisted only of Catlin's paintings and objects. He established an exhibition hall at Waterloo Place in London. For four years, he lectured throughout the United Kingdom and displayed his collection in London in an attempt "to inform the English people of the true character and condition of the North American Indians, and to awaken a proper sympathy for them."[31] Then he had a stroke of great good fortune—three separate troupes of Natives came to Europe.

In his memoir, Catlin is quick to point out that he had nothing to do with bringing these Indians across the Red Atlantic; they "had come avowedly for the purpose of making money, (an enterprise as lawful and unobjectionable, for aught that I can see . . . as that of an actor upon the boards of a foreign stage)." Describing how the connection was forged, he writes:

> These [three] parties successively, on their arrival, (knowing my history and views, which I had made known to most of the American tribes,) repaired to my Indian Collection, in which they felt themselves at home, surrounded as they were by portraits of their own chiefs and braves, and those of their enemies, whom they easily recognised upon the walls. They at once chose the middle of my Exhibition Hall as the appropriate place for their operations, and myself as the expounder of their mysteries and amusements: and, the public seeming so well pleased with the fitness of these mutual illustrations, I undertook the management of their exhibitions, and conducted the three different parties through the countries [of Europe].

In other words, the Indian participation increased the British public's interest in Catlin's enterprise. Since the Indians themselves had come to England to earn money, he felt no compunction about exploiting them for everyone's joint profit. He concludes, "I considered my countenance and aid as calculated to promote their views; and I therefore justified myself in the undertaking, as some return for the hospitality and kindness I had received at the hands of the various tribes I had visited in the wildernesses of America."[32] By his efforts, he said he meant no offense.

Before the arrival of the real Indians, to illustrate his lectures, Catlin dressed white Englishmen up in Native garb "so that they might bring the costumes to life, sing an Indian song, and give 'the frightful war-whoop'—a gesture straddling the line between educational innovation and publicity gimmick."[33] The Natives' presence and willing participation was thus a serendipitous boon to Catlin. He was about to give up and return to the United States when the Indians—at least figuratively—rode to his rescue. The first group, in 1843, was made up of nine Anishinaabes brought by Canadian entrepreneur and politician Arthur Rankin, who secured a performance before Queen Victoria. Though it began auspiciously, the partnership between Rankin and Catlin turned acrimonious and broke up. Fortunately for the latter, fourteen Siouan-speaking

Iowas arrived at just the right time. The third group comprised a dozen Anishinaabes brought by George Henry in 1844.

Catlin's Notes provides nearly no sense of the interiority of the Indians who participated, no sense of what they thought about the experience. Catlin displayed the Natives as a kind of freak show, and in his memoir he portrays them as simple primitives. When the 7-foot 8-inch Robert Hales and his 7-foot 2-inch sister Mary—the so-called Norfolk Giants—visited Catlin's Indian show during its Iowa iteration, the Natives insisted on measuring the pair with string, lest their fellow tribesmen not believe them when they returned home. Flint, borrowing a phrase from Bernth Lindfors, calls it "ethnological show business." She quotes former director of the National Museum of the American Indian Richard West, who calls Catlin the "emblematic exploiter of native peoples. . . . Taking his canvases, artefacts, and live Indians on tour to a host of venues, including European cities where the show's 'red men' inspired a familiar combination of awe and condescension, Catlin can be seen today as a cultural P. T. Barnum, a crass huckster trading on other people's lives and lifeways."[34] We can learn but little from Catlin about "his" Indians. We have, however, another primary source about the third Indian troupe. As Louis Jackson did, after the failed expedition to relieve Khartoum, George Henry published a brief book about his experiences. In 1848, the same year Catlin published his *Notes,* Henry brought out *An Account of the Chippewa Indians, Who Have Been Travelling among the Whites, in the United States, England, Ireland, Scotland, France and Belgium.*

George Henry was the younger half-brother of Peter Jones.[35] Unlike Peter, however, whose father was white, Henry's father was Native, and his parents raised him totally as Indian until he converted to Christianity in 1825 around the age of fourteen. He became a candidate for the ministry in the Methodist church, taught Sunday school, acted as an interpreter for white missionaries, and translated a hymnal into Anishinaabe. He was respected by his own people (who invited him to become a chief) and by whites, who considered him to be among the best Indian exhorters. One clergyman referred to him as "a clever, respectable looking young man, a good speaker, said to be a good divine, a tolerable poet, and an excellent translator."[36]

Then, in 1840, this Renaissance man, fed up with the strict nature of Methodism and repulsed by denominational infighting, left the church. Despite the fact that his departure was motivated in part by attacks on

Jones by whites, the move opened up a breach with his half-brother. The rift widened in 1844 when Henry formed his Indian dance troupe to tour the United Kingdom. Peter disapproved of Indians performing in Wild West shows. The thought of Natives in flashy regalia "for the sole object of dancing and shewing the wild Indian before the British public for the sake of gain" mortified Jones. He thought such displays actually lowered whites' opinions of Natives.[37]

The company Henry formed comprised his own family and some St. Clair Anishinaabes from the Walpole Island reserve. He booked Egyptian Hall in Piccadilly. Jones's biographer, the historian Donald Smith, speculates that, despite his opposition, Jones possibly could not resist taking in a performance during his second trip to England. Giving a flavor for what he would have seen, Smith quotes the show's handbill advertisement:

> A Grand Indian Council
> In front of the Wigwam, when
> the whole Party will appear in
> FULL, NATIVE COSTUME,
> Displaying all the Implements
> of War—the Chief will Address
> the Council—and the whole of
> the Forms of declaring War will
> be gone through.
> The INTERPRETER will Deliver
> A LECTURE
> Descriptive of Indian Character.[38]

As I said, this is speculation, but it is a fair one. We do know that the breach between the brothers was mended during Jones's trip even though, during his sojourn in England, Henry had converted to Catholicism, much to the ire of the Methodist Jones, who remarked that he had "never discovered any real difference between the Roman Catholic Indian and the pagan, except the wearing of crosses."[39]

As with his stage show, in his self-published memoir, Henry had a fine eye for marketing. As an author, he makes no mention of George Henry, styling himself only with his self-given name, Maungwudaus. Though he had attended a mission school at Mississauga after his conversion, he describes himself as "the Self-Taught Indian of the Chippewa," heightening the exotic appeal to readers. Finally, the subtitle promises a kind of ethnography for whites on both sides of the Red Atlantic: "With Very Interesting Incidents in Relation to the General Characteristics of the English, Irish, Scotch, French, and Americans, with Regard to Their Hospitality, Peculiarities, Etc."

Regarding hospitality, while in England, Henry was treated very well indeed and feted by the English upper crust. He took tea regularly with Sir Augustus d'Este, Queen Victoria's cousin. Taken to Windsor Castle, he writes of the experience, "Mr. Harris took us into the Queen's house. She is a small woman but handsome. There are many handsomer women than she is. Prince Albert is a handsome and well built man. Her house is large, quiet country inside of it. We got tired before we went through all the rooms in it. Great many warriors with their swords and guns stands [*sic*] outside watching for the enemy."[40] The Indians were entertained and presented with gifts by the Duke of Wellington. William Hawley, archbishop of Canterbury, gave them a personal tour of his cathedral. They also, as usual, saw the sights: Lord Nelson's flagship, the H.M.S. *Victory*; St. Paul's Cathedral; Parliament (where they saw Prime Minister Robert Peel and opposition politician Lord John Russell speak). Henry commented on the great disparity in wealth between rich and poor and the sooty color of the great buildings because of all the smoke. He also said that the English drank too much, causing corpulence and "noses [that] look like ripe strawberries."[41]

In the autumn of 1845, Henry hooked up with Catlin. He writes: "We went to France; stayed five months in Paris with Catlin's Indian Curiosities. Shook hands with Louis Phillippe and all his family in the Park, called St. Cloud; gave them little war dance, shooting with bows and arrows at a target, ball play; also rowed our birch bark canoe in the artificial lake, amongst swans and geese. There were about four thousand French ladies and gentlemen with them. We dined with him in the afternoon in his Palace. He said many things concerning his having been in America, when he was a young man. He gave us twelve gold and silver medals; he showed us all the rooms in his house."[42] In other words, after an alfresco command performance for Louis-Philippe, the last king of France, and his guests, they enjoyed an intimate, private audience with the monarch. Plaster casts were made of the Indians' heads. The king had court artist Jean Gudin paint their portrait for his palace.

Henry found Paris much cleaner than London. The Natives were particularly struck by the Frenchmen's beards and mustaches. Proof of

Henry's rapprochement with his brother is a letter he wrote to Jones on October 19, 1845 (addressed to "My Dear Brother"), describing the same events outlined above. In particular, the Anishinaabe war chief Sasagon, who was part of the troupe, said one of their tribe would be hard-pressed to locate a Frenchman's mouth amid all the hair, which made a Frenchman with facial hair "look like one of our Indian dogs in North America when running away with a black squirrel in his mouth."[43] Unfortunately, for all the gaiety of France, tragedy was about to strike.

From France, Catlin took his third and last group of Indians to Belgium, where in Brussels they met with King Leopold, who "was very kind to us."[44] However, three of the Native company, including Sasagon, had refused inoculation for smallpox while in England, claiming that they did not trust white men's medicine and that their sacred bundles would protect them. In the Belgian capital, two—Aunimuckwuh-um and Mishimaung—died of the disease. The show pushed on, however, visiting towns on the German border. Then they returned to London, where Sasagon expired from the same disease.[45] In all, eight of the twelve were sickened, but of these, five who had been vaccinated recovered.

In his little sixteen-page book, Henry is not one to dwell on detail or emotion. He moves on immediately to the group's tour through England. After visiting a number of towns and cities, where they "saw many good people and wonderful things," they sailed from Liverpool to Dublin. Arriving at the height of the Irish potato famine, Henry remarked on the poverty of the people, giving as the cause that "the British government is over them." Nevertheless, the company performed in the Rotunda and at the Zoological Gardens to enthusiastic crowds of 3,000 each night. They then went south before traveling to Belfast and Londonderry.[46]

Scotland was next. They saw Robert Burns's cottage and the William Wallace Oak before going on to Glasgow and Edinburgh. Henry found Edinburgh filthy with a lingering offensive smell all day from the garbage thrown into the streets. Henry and the Natives saw the Scottish crown jewels in Edinburgh Castle and visited the royal residence of Holyrood Palace. They were also taken to the medical school where they observed students performing dissections on cadavers, "skinning and cutting them same as we do with venison."[47]

The coldness of Henry's narrative can be startling and off-putting. After cataloging their activities and a few observations about the Scots, he writes, "At Glasgow, two of my children died, another in Edinburgh;

buried them in the burying ground of our friends the Quakers; and after we visited other towns at the North and South, we went to England again; my wife died at Newark. The vicar of that church was very kind to us, allowing us to bury her remains near the church." Henry then resumes his travelogue, mentioning visits to Shakespeare's and Lord Byron's homes and to the grave of the former.[48] He was not above playing upon sympathies, however, to sell books, mentioning on the title page that he was writing "for the benefit of his youngest Son, called Noodinokay, whose Mother died in England," hoping to induce whoever had twelve and a half cents (the book's price) to help support the boy.[49] The book also contains a "blurb" from Catlin and is rounded out with some of Henry's Anishinaabe hymns.

Seven of the original twelve Anishinaabe died. The five survivors departed England aboard the *Yorktown* on April 23, 1848, arriving back in New York on June 4. Henry writes that they "were very thankful to the Great Spirit for bringing us back again to America"—the five survivors, that is.[50]

Catlin, too, experienced loss during the continental portion of the tour. His wife, Clara, died of pneumonia, and his son George Jr. expired from typhoid. After parting company with the Anishinaabes, Catlin returned to Paris to care for his remaining children. A short while later, Peter Jones crossed the channel and traveled to Paris for a medical consultation on his deteriorating health. While there, he sought out Catlin. Apparently, apart from the October 19, 1845, letter, he had had no news of his brother; Catlin had been the one to inform him of the deaths of the three company members from smallpox.[51] On a subsequent visit to London, Catlin ran into an acquaintance in Piccadilly, who told him that Sasagon's skeleton had been preserved and that he thought the artist might want to see it. Catlin politely declined.[52]

Jones was not impressed with Catlin during his visit. According to Donald Smith, "Peter felt he had little interest in Indians as human beings. In a note to Eliza on 7 March Peter described him as, 'a thorough blue Yankee he makes a great professions of attachment for the Indians.'"[53] Catlin told him that he would not mount any more stage spectacles, saying that the deaths from smallpox too greatly grieved him. His statement was undercut, however, and Jones's impression reinforced, by the fact that No-ho-mun-ya (Roman Nose) from the earlier Iowa contingent had similarly died.[54] Besides, Catlin was quick to point out that the costs of the enterprise were too great, and he needed to support his family.

Back in North America, Henry renounced Catholicism and became a root doctor and herbalist—in other words, a self-styled medicine man. He remarried, and with his second wife, an Anishinaabe named Taundoqua, he reformed the dance troupe, which performed in Toronto in 1851.

The Red Atlantic is, in part, about Natives' encounter and struggle with, and adaptation to, modernity. Flint writes:

> Maungwudaus, like the [other] Indians who traveled alongside Catlin, had been affected by a number of the features that we have come to consider characteristic of modernity. These include demographic up-heavals and the concomitant severance of people not just from their ancestral habitats but from a sense of their traditional connections to both space and time; the expansion of their relationship to capitalist world markets and industrialization, including the growing tourist industry; their role as subjects, rather than agents, in the formation and development of a huge nation-state and their subjection to ex-ternally imposed bureaucracy; their relationship to the growth of the rhetoric of individuality . . . and the articulation of various freedoms, whether these involved self- determination, the ownership of prop-erty, or freedom of speech; and their incorporation into systems of mass communication.[55]

While there is much to what Flint says, she underestimates the role of Natives as agents. There was always room for personal choice, however constricted. Western Hemisphere indigenes were "selves determined," but they were also self-determined. The Red Atlantic constrained, but it also provided opportunities. For some like George Henry, the new reali-ties, such as the tourism industry and the rise of mass communication, provided the chance for self-exploitation and self-invention.

Near the close of *Catlin's Notes*, the author strikes a condescending and fatalistic note, writing of the Indians who performed for him: "Their tour of a year or two abroad, amidst the mazes and mysteries of civilized life, will rest in their minds like a romantic dream, not to be forgotten, nor to be dreamed over again; their lives too short to aspire to what they have seen to approve, and their own humble sphere in their native wilds so decidedly preferable to the parts of civilized life which they did not admire, that they will probably convert the little money they have made, and their medals and trinkets, into whisky and rum, and drown out, if possible, the puzzling enigma, which, with arguments, the poor fellows have found it more difficult to solve."[56] He concludes, however, "In taking leave of my red friends, I will be pardoned for repeating what I have before said, that on this side of the Atlantic they invariably did the best they could do."[57] Despite its patronizing tone, that is the most and best one can say about the indigenous participants in the Red Atlantic—"they invariably did the best they could."

A Pagan in St. Paul's

Emily Pauline Johnson is best remembered today for her brief appearance as a kind of Banquo's ghost in Thomas King's comic novel *Green Grass, Running Water*, a wraithlike figure who leaves copies of her books as tips in restaurants in the vain hope that she can induce someone to read the largely forgotten volumes. At one time, however, the Mohawk poet was the best-known Indian author in the United States and Canada, lionized by the *New York Sun* as "perhaps the most unique figure in the literary world on this continent."[58] Kate Flint hits upon her importance to the Red Atlantic when she writes, "On both sides of the Atlantic—and again in a triangulated Canadian-U.S.-British space—she emphasized the need for white people to recognize the rights, the feelings, and the needs of the land's original inhabitants and to stop denigrating them as savages, noble or otherwise—a theme that continued throughout her career."[59]

Johnson was born on March 10, 1861, in Brantford, Ontario, with a venerable heritage on both sides of her family. Her mother, Emily Howells, was the English-born cousin of noted American author William Dean Howells. Her father, George Martin Johnson, was a chief of the Mohawk. On her father's side, her family was inextricably bound up with two figures we have already met in our explorations of the Red Atlantic, Sir William Johnson and his protégé and brother-in-law Joseph Brant. As the English Indian superintendent, responsible for keeping Britain's half of the covenant chain burnished, William Johnson was both respected and trusted by the Haudenosaunee and often invited to their ceremonies. In 1758, three years after his appointment as superintendent, he was present at a mass baptism. One of those to be baptized was Tekahionwake (Double Wampum). The parents had selected the Christian name of Jacob for the boy but were undecided on a last name. Johnson stepped forwarded and offered his own surname, and the youth was christened Jacob Johnson. He became E. Pauline Johnson's great-grandfather. Her grandfather, John Smoke Johnson, as a youth fought alongside Joseph Brant and later fought with the British during the War of 1812. He served as a Pine Tree Chief of the Grand Council for four decades.[60]

From an early age, Emily Johnson instilled in her daughter a love of English letters, while her grandfather and father taught her the stories and ways of her Mohawk people. Pauline published her first poem, titled "To Jean," in the New York–based periodical *The Genius of Poetry* in 1881. Over the course of the next few years, she saw several of her poems printed in the United States, Canada, and Great Britain. Her breakthrough came in January 1892, when she appeared at a literary evening at the Academy of Music in Toronto. Her reading of two of her poems, "Cry of an Indian Wife," about Louis Riel's rebellion, and "As Red Men Die," about a Mohawk captive who stoically endures torture and death rather than be enslaved, was a tremendous success. The result was an almost nonstop series of tours in the United States and Canada (with two important trips to Britain) that lasted over sixteen years. She produced three collections of poetry, two of prose, and an anthology of traditional Chinook myths that she collected.

As a performer and a writer, Johnson is often mistaken for the quintessential "White Man's Indian." Canadian literary scholar Penny Petrone sees her as a figure caught between two cultures but as one whose worldview, culture, and literary output were ultimately Western. She writes, "It is difficult to be a woman in one world; it is more difficult to be a woman in two worlds."[61] Daniel Francis, in his study of the figure of the Indian in Canadian culture, *The Imaginary Indian*, portrays her as a complex character but one who ultimately served the myths of white dominance by representing the vanishing Indian and pandering to white tastes for stereotypical noble savages.[62] Likewise, Terry Goldie, another Canadian literary critic, points out that while Johnson "identified herself as a Mohawk and . . . produced a number of texts in prose and verse which present a strong although ideologically undeveloped support of native people," she nonetheless is best known for lyrics that present indigenes as "fairy-like figures."[63] On the other hand, Mohawk writer Beth Brant extols her commitment to Native community and calls her "a spiritual grandmother" of all contemporary Native women writers. As Brant states, "A non-Native might come away with the impression that she only wrote idyllic sonnets to the glory of nature, the 'noble savage,' or 'vanishing redman' themes that were popular at the turn of the [twentieth] century. It is time to take another look at Pauline Johnson."[64]

Certainly, Johnson herself did much to contribute to the view that she was nothing but an entertainer, a "celebrity Indian" in the basest sense, who catered to white expectations and tastes. She allowed her manager to bill her as the "Mohawk Princess." In late 1892, while touring, she adopted an Indian costume that became one of her trademarks. The buckskin, cloth, and fur dress was a pan-Indian fantasy of her own design that became increasingly elaborate as time passed, with additions such as an ermine-tail necklace. She also carried a hunting knife on her waist. Many of her poems employ stereotypical images, such as "The Happy Hunting Grounds," and she was capable of lapsing into stylized, broken "Red English" in her discussions about herself and her people.[65] Once she bitterly complained to naturalist Ernest Thompson Seton, "Oh, why have your people forced on me the name of Pauline Johnson? Why was my Indian name not good enough?"[66] In actuality, of course, her Indian name, Tekahionwake, was that of her great-grandfather Jacob Johnson, which she had adopted for stage purposes.

By 1894, Johnson had saved enough money from her performances to travel to Britain. She journeyed to New York, where she booked passage on the Cunard Steamship Company's *Etruria*. She carried with her two precious cargoes, the manuscript of her first collection of poetry for which she hoped to find a publisher and, in her handbag, a large clutch of letters of introduction (courtesy of her family's connections) to the elite of British society.

According to her biographer Betty Keller, Johnson's physical interaction with the Red Atlantic itself was not a felicitous one. She complained of "the awfulness of the intervening ocean." After suffering constant seasickness during the five-day voyage, she arrived in Liverpool in the rain only to find that hansom cab drivers were on strike. She had to carry her baggage herself to a public omnibus coach to get to her lodgings.[67]

In London, however, she had managed through friends to let a small studio flat in a fashionable neighborhood, which she accented with Canadian Native items. She then began a process of "networking," using her second cargo—the introductions in her purse—to achieve her primary objective, the publication of her first. Building connection upon connection, she became the acquaintance of the lords, ladies, princesses, and peers. She used these to arrange a series of engagements to entertain at various elegant "social evenings" in salon society to support herself. In the process, she became the toast of upper-class society. After one reading, Queen Victoria's son Prince Arthur, the Duke of Connaught, sent an aide to ask what had become of her father's blanket upon which he had knelt when her father made him an adoptive chief of the Six Nations. Proving herself adroit in her understanding of the Red Atlantic, Johnson replied, "Will you tell His Highness that the mantle that I wear was once honoured by his feet!" According to Keller, "She never told him that when her mantle had not been serving as a ceremonial blanket, it had been used as a piano dustcover" in the family home.[68]

The theater season in London when Johnson was there was sparkling with all the stars of the international stage. The Italian actress Eleanora Duse was there in *La Signora dalle Camelie*. The great English thespians Henry Irving and Ellen Terry starred opposite each other in *Faust*. Lillie Langtry opened a new play, *Society Butterfly*. And the renowned Sarah Bernhardt performed in *Tosca* and *Phèdre*, as well as in five other plays. Johnson saw them all. Keller says, "For Pauline, the evenings of theatre were like hours spent in the classroom. She studied the technique of each actress, memorizing the movements and the gestures. But she learned most from the costumes that the women wore, especially those of Lillie Langtry." As a result of this education, she ordered four evening gowns made.[69] Those elegant dresses would play a significant role in Johnson's career in the future.

The whole reason Johnson had come to England was to get a publisher for her poetry manuscript, and she used the contacts she made both through the introductions she brought and through her engagements to work that all-important angle. In this she was successful, though she could not stay in London long enough to see it in print. *The White Wampum* was published in 1895.[70]

Pauline returned to London in April 1906 with her professional partner, Walter McRaye. The trip was significantly different from her first in a number of ways. Instead of a budding performer and poet, E. Pauline Johnson was now famous. She brought with her a letter of introduction from the Canadian prime minister, Sir Wilfred Laurier. There was no first book manuscript to peddle; she and McRaye came only to perform.

They settled into a luxury flat on St. James Square. She was anticipating reading and reciting not in private salons but in large public venues. Still, despite her increased station in life, she was not a wealthy woman, and she and McRaye would need continual employment if they were to support themselves as Johnson envisioned.[71]

During her stay, Johnson published three pieces in the *Daily Express* newspaper: "The Lodge of the Law-Makers," "The Silent News-Carrier," and "A Pagan in St. Paul's." They are "fish out of water" articles. Flint is entirely correct in evoking Philip Deloria's phrase from his book *Playing Indian*—she was "mimicking white mimickings of Indianness." By far, the most popular of the three pieces was "A Pagan in St. Paul's," and it remains one of her best-known writings today.[72]

It is hard to argue with Daniel Francis's assessment of Johnson as pandering to white expectations when one reads pieces like those in the *Daily Express*, especially "A Pagan in St. Paul's," which describes a visit she made to the London cathedral. In the article, she defends Native traditional religious practices. Instead of doing so, however, as the educated, articulate woman she was, she resorts to primitivism. Describing the seat of British imperial power, she writes, "So this is the place where dwells the Great White Father, ruler of many lands, lodges and tribes. I, one of his loyal allies, have come to see his camp, known to the white man as London, his council which the whites call his Parliament, where his sachems and chiefs make the laws of his tribes, and to see his wigwam, known to the palefaces as Buckingham Palace, but to the red man as the 'Teepee of the Great White Father.'"[73] Francis sums up, "Whatever the worth of her argument about Native religion, Johnson was clearly pandering to a stereotypical notion of the Indian as an artless, childlike innocent."[74] While there is no gainsaying Francis's assessment, notice that even in the above statement, she refers to herself and her fellow Indians not as "subjects" but as "allies," thus establishing an equality between them and the British (also, given that Victoria was on the throne, the reference to "Great White Father" is striking). Johnson, in both her writings and her negotiation of the Red Atlantic, was a more complex character than Francis gives her credit for.

Johnson was keenly aware of the problem of self-representation to a white, colonialist readership tipping over into stereotype and exoticism. In 1894, she wrote back to a lawyer who had corresponded, complaining that she played too much to the white audience in her work. She answered, "More than all things I hate and despise brain debasement, literary 'potboiling' and yet I have done, will do these things, though I sneer at my own littleness in so doing. . . . The reason is that the public will not listen to lyrics, will not appreciate real poetry, will not in fact have me as an entertainer if I give them nothing but rhythm, cadence, beauty, thought."[75] In her work, Johnson sought not so much to represent the stereotypical Indian as to (re)present the Native to American and Canadian society. Duplicity was the price she had to pay in order to gain a hearing. According to Francis, "What gave Johnson's work an added poignancy was the belief shared by most members of her audience that they were listening to the voice of a disappearing people. 'The race that is gone speaks with touching pathos through Miss Johnson,' was how the *Toronto Globe* put it. In her stage performances, she personified the Vanishing Race and people strained to hear the final whisper before it faded away completely."[76]

Despite the necessity of catering to white tastes and expectations, Pauline Johnson fought stereotyping. Though she appeared in Indian regalia of dubious origin in her recitals, she always insisted on wearing one of her evening gowns for the second half of her performance. Fluent in Mohawk, she once attempted to introduce readings in her Native language into her performance, but the audience attempted to boo her from the stage. Maintaining her composure, she chastised her spectators, telling them that as she had had to learn their language, the least they could do was *hear* hers.[77] In an interview with a reporter for the *Boston Herald*, she stated, "You're going to say that I'm not like other Indians, that I'm not representative. That's not strange. Cultivate an Indian, let him show his aptness and you Americans say he is an exception. Let a bad quality crop out and you stamp him an Indian immediately."[78] Like William Apess before her, she rejected the generic designation "Indian." He wrote, "The term 'Indian' signifies about as much as the term 'European' but I cannot recall ever reading the story where the heroine was described as 'a European.'"[79] Yet she never thought of herself as anything other than a Native, contending that she was so "by law, by temperament, by choice, and by upbringing."[80] She wrote, "There are those who think they pay me a compliment in saying that I am just like a white woman. My aim, my joy, my pride is to sing the glories of my own people."[81] Johnson skillfully manipulated the image of the "Indian" to carry her message and used every opportunity to "plead the cause of the Native."[82]

Johnson was quite capable of addressing Indian issues with great force and yet with sophistication and subtlety. Flint points out that in her *Daily Express* article "The Lodge of the Law-Makers," subtitled "Contrasts between the Parliaments of the White Man and the Red," Johnson "showed up the weaknesses of Britain and Canada's political system, which refused the rights of citizenship to native peoples, which was inherently unstable and mutable, and which failed to grant women the authority they held in Iroquois society." Reflecting on the role of Haudenosaunee women in councils of governance and their inherent equality within their culture, she concluded with the devastating contrast that "I have not yet heard of fifty white women even among those of noble birth who may be listened to in the lodge of the law-makers here [in Great Britain]." Significantly, perhaps because of the directness of her address in that piece at a time when suffragettes were agitating for women's rights, the *Daily Express* refused to publish a fourth article she penned while in London (it was subsequently published in a magazine in Canada), which ran in part, "In all the trails I have travelled to the white-man's camping grounds I do not see that his women have the importance either in his Council or in his Camp, that we [the Iroquois] have given to our womenkind these many centuries."[83] While she was careful in addressing her white audience in order to gain a hearing, her words could still pack a punch.

Although Johnson wrote seemingly patriotic odes to Canada, Beth Brant points out that they are, in actuality, hymns to the land: "She had a great love of Canada, the Canada of oceans, pine trees, lakes, animals and birds, not the Canada of politicians and racism that attempted to regulate her people's lives."[84] Flint perhaps comes closest to capturing Johnson's allegiances when she describes an interview the writer gave to the *London Gazette* during her first visit in 1894, writing, "Her adherence is neither to the British throne nor to Canada, and less to the United States; she couches herself as a member of an imaginary, pan-Indian nation."[85] Even so, Johnson's commitment was not to a community purely of her imagination. It was rather to a growing sense of unity among all North American Native nations as they struggled with the colonialist modernity at the turn of the twentieth century. As Flint notes, it is a question of "power relations." In that 1894 interview, the Native writer posits what things might have been like had the situation been reversed: "Suppose we came over to England as a powerful people. Suppose you gave us welcome to English soil, worshipped us as gods, as we worshipped you white people when you first came to Canada; and suppose we encroached upon your homeland and drove you back and back, and then said, 'Oh, well, we will present you with a few acres—a few acres of your own dear land.' What would you think of it all? So we think. We are without a country. The whole continent belongs to us by right of lineage. We welcomed you as friends, we worshipped you, and you drove us up into a little corner."[86] In that single response, Johnson encapsulates one history of the Red Atlantic. She demonstrates a commitment to the widest possible definition of North American Native community.

In her poem "The Cattle Thief," Johnson is more direct in her critique of the white, colonial power structure and the looting of the wealth of the Red Atlantic than in much of her writings, in a way more in keeping with the interview cited above:

> Have you paid us for our game? How much have you paid us
>   for our land?
> By a *book*, to save our souls from the sins *you* brought in your
>   other hand.
> Go back with your new religion, we have never understood
> Your robbing an Indian's *body*, and mocking his *soul* with food.
> Go back with your new religion, and find—if you can—
> The *honest* man you ever made from out of a *starving* man.
> You say your cattle are not ours, your meat is not our meat;
> When *you* pay for the land you live in, *we'll* pay for the meat
>   we eat.[87]

Her anger here is reminiscent of the irony-tinged vitriol that dripped from Samson Occom's quill 150 years earlier. Like Occom, like Peter Jones, like Sitting Bull (who reached only the marge of the Red Atlantic in New York City), Johnson was struck by the poverty she saw in the imperial capital. Flint states, "Johnson's first London visit alerted her . . . to the poverty [of] a class of what she termed, with a deliberate double edge, 'city savages.'" In 1896, she wrote "your heathen in Africa . . . is nearer the light of civilization than those wretched Whitechapelites [Whitechapel, the prostitute-ridden London slum where the Ripper murders occurred], that poison the airs of the great clean forest lands, and rot the morals of the simple but blameless Indian." The 1906 visit apparently hit her even harder, though she never put her stark observations and critiques into print.[88]

Johnson's best-known short story, "A Red Girl's Reasoning," was published in 1893, before she ever crossed the Atlantic, but it nonetheless
questions the Christian underpinnings of the Red Atlantic in a sharper
way than a London newspaper piece like "A Pagan in St. Paul's." In it, she
presents a quick-witted, intelligent, and free-thinking Native woman as
its heroine. Her white husband sees her as "simpleminded" and "igno-
rant." When she mentions at a party that her father married her mother
in the traditional Native way, her husband is embarrassed and outraged.
She responds with a stinging defense of Native religious traditions,
which she considers more sacred than Christian ceremonies. When the
husband persists that her father should have had the union sanctified by
a priest, she stands her ground, asking, "Was there a *priest* at the most
holy marriage known to humanity—that stainless marriage whose offspring is the God you white men told my pagan mother of?"[89] She leaves
her husband and, despite his entreaties, refuses to return.

Petrone contends that Pauline Johnson's work appears "dated and
shallow."[90] Yet pieces like "The Cattle Thief" and "A Red Girl's Reasoning"
reveal a startlingly contemporary sensibility. Francis writes, "But Johnson herself only went so far. She presented the plight of the Red Man,
but she demanded little from her White audience beyond sentimental
regret, which was easy enough to give. The land may once have belonged
to her people, but she was not asking for it back."[91] Yet she clearly merits
further consideration and study within the context of the Red Atlantic.
She was in many ways the "revolutionary" Beth Brant depicts.[92] She was
the only voice her white audiences were capable of hearing.

Her health shattered by the rigors of constant touring, Pauline Johnson retired to Vancouver, where she died in 1913. Years earlier, in 1907,
she read on the Chautauqua circuit in the American Midwest. She never
spoke or wrote about the experience. According to her biographer, "The
reaction of Midwesterners to Indians had not changed much since [the
end of the Indian Wars], except that they now allowed Indians to be
either dead or captive. They rather enjoyed seeing one now and then in
a side show or a circus, because it gave them the opportunity to show
their children what the enemy looked like. They treated Pauline as if
she too were a circus freak, though they were a bit awed by her obvious refinement and talent."[93] They were the same upstanding citizens
who, decades earlier, threw rocks and bottles at the Indian prisoners of

war passing through a long-pacified American heartland on their way to Fort Marion for their first glimpse of the Red Atlantic. Her reception was quite different from the one she received in London, where those in her audience were, after all, really no longer responsible for the Natives that had once been their colonial subjects.

5

---*w*---

Fireside Travelers, Armchair
Adventurers, and Apocryphal Voyages

The Literature of the Red Atlantic

SAMSON OCCOM AND E. PAULINE JOHNSON are important figures of
Native American literature. Garcilaso de la Vega is a major author of a
wider Western Hemispheric indigenous literature. Others like George
Copway, Peter Jones, George Henry, and Deskaheh—while important
for the roles they played in the Red Atlantic—are lesser figures when it
concerns writing and letters. In the introduction, I stated that literature is a vital component part of the Red Atlantic. In ensuing chapters,
I have made reference to how some contemporary Native writers like
Paula Gunn Allen, Joseph Boyden, Gerald Vizenor, and James Welch have
reflected upon the experience of Western Hemisphere indigenes abroad.
In the pages that remain, we will see a few more such instances.

The principal literary aspect of the Red Atlantic, however, is how Europeans and, later, Americans came to define themselves in comparison
with, and in contrast to, the indigenous peoples of the Americas. And literature was a primary forum for those comparisons and contrasts. In this
chapter, we will examine how works by authors from European metropoles and the United States figured the Indian in this effort. From Spain, we
will examine Michael de Carvajal's drama *Complaint of the Indians in the
Court of Death*, as well as the theo-juridical writings of other prominent
figures in the so-called indigenist movement—Bartolomé de Las Casas,
Alonso de la Vera Cruz, and Vasco de Quiroga. France will be represented
by Voltaire's *L'Ingenu* and *Candide*. I have already briefly discussed Shakespeare's *The Tempest*, but now I will examine the early English novel *The
Female American*. From the United States, I will discuss Susanna Rowson's 1798 novel *Reuben and Rachel* and Edgar Allan Poe's *The Narrative*

of Arthur Gordon Pym of Nantucket. And finally, though Germany had no colonies in North America, nineteenth- and early-twentieth-century Germany writer Karl May played an unexpectedly important role in shaping opinions about its indigenes on both sides of the Atlantic.

The "Indigenists"

Michael de Carvajal was part of a group that grew up in Spain and Ibero-America in the sixteenth century speaking out in favor of the rights of the Spanish New World's indigenous peoples and struggling for their fair treatment. This group, composed primarily of clergymen, came to be known as the *indigenistas*—the "indigenists"—whose cause was the *indigenista* movement. The best known of this group is our Red Atlantic friend Bartolomé de Las Casas, but it also includes lesser-known figures like Alonso de la Vera Cruz and Vasco de Quiroga.

We actually know very little about Michael de Carvajal. We do not know with certainty who he was. There are multiple possible candidates with that name. There are even more possibilities if we assume his name might really have been Miguel de Carvajal. We do not know whether he was a member of the *indigenista* movement in direct contact with other advocates like Las Casas, or if he was merely a passionate supporter of the cause from the periphery.

In 1557, Luis Hurtado de Toledo published a volume entitled *Cortes de castro amor y Cortes de la Muerte* (*The Court of Chaste Love and The Court of Death*). *The Court of Death* formed an autonomous collection of twenty-three dramatic pieces in which various persons from a variety of stations in life are brought before that ultimate judge, a personified Death. This "moral, highly allegorical court drama" is in the tradition of the *Danza de la Muerte* (*Danse Macabre*).[1] In 2008, Carlos Jáuregui published Carvajal's Cena XIX (scene 19) in a supple translation by himself and Mark Smith-Soto under the descriptive title *Complaint of the Indians in the Court of Death*. Hurtado's *The Court of Death* was addressed to Felipe II, who is called king of Spain and England.[2] Felipe was then only in the second year of his reign. *The Court of Death*, at least Carvajal's scene 19, must therefore be viewed as part of a long *indigenista* line of theo-juridical disputations meant to "catch the conscience of the king" and influence policy in a manner favorable to the indigenous peoples of the Spanish New World. According to Jáuregui, "In effect, Carvajal's

Complaint of the Indians in the Court of Death constitutes a dramatic allegorical *summa* of the modern formation of imperial reason (the political, legal, and theological justification of the empire) and of the moral doubts and debates with respect to the Conquest of the New World and the domination of the Indians."[3] We do not know if the play was ever performed.

In the play, several *caciques* and ordinary Indians come before Death to describe atrocities committed against them by the Spaniards. They also suggest different remedies and punishments. Also present are the World, the Flesh, and the Devil, along with three Christian saints—Augustine, Francis, and Dominic—representing the three mendicant orders evangelizing the Americas. The World, Flesh, and Satan offer a sardonic but gimlet-eyed assessment of the Conquest. The three pietists perform the roles of Job's comforters—who are anything but comforting.

The Natives complain that they have all converted to Christianity after being evangelized by the missionaries who came in the name of the three saints present. What possible basis is there for the horrific treatment they have received at the hands of other supposed Christians? Like Indians in every era of the Red Atlantic, they wonder at the incredible hypocrisy. One supplicant states:

> But how is it, O Lady Death,
> That these people promise you wine
> And sell you nothing but vinegar,
> Exploiting hour by hour
> The poor and suffering Indian?
> How is it possible that Christians
> Could let such things come to pass,
> Which even barbarians would scorn,
> And have the earth not split apart
> At such a horrible sight?[4]

The root cause of the problem is the Spaniards' insatiable lust for gold. A *cacique* rhetorically addresses an absent Claudius Ptolemy, a famous second-century geographer:

> How is it that you failed to notice,
> I ask you, that our lands were there?
> It turns out that the malicious

Cleverness of avarice and evil
Has known better how to find us.
Well, O sad land of ours!
Best start making gold in masses,
Because I am here to tell you
The plundering armies are near,
Come with their greed to destroy you.[5]

The comments are significant. Not only does the chief call the lands of the New World, correctly, "ours," but he links the demand for gold to Indian slavery ("Best start making gold in masses") backed up by military force ("The plundering armies are near,/Come with their greed to destroy you"). The *cacique* invokes the example of the Roman general Marcus Licinius Crassus, "enriched by mining as well as the slave trade," whom the Parthians forced to swallow molten gold, and suggests the same punishment as a remedy to slake the "burning thirst" of Spaniards for gold.[6]

One of the Indians proposes that the solution is that they surrender their lands and go into exile rather than continue to suffer. Ultimately, one of the indigenes suggests to Death that if their tormenters cannot be removed, at least let the Indians die quickly and mercifully.[7]

The World, the Flesh, and the Devil play cynics. Satan points out that the Conquest is simply an economic enterprise. The proselytizing mission was merely a fig leaf:

What? Are they really planning
To keep people away
From plundering the Indies? . . .
Don't they know too well the source
Of all wealth and prosperous business
Flows from the pits of Hell?[8]

For their part, the saints encourage the Indians to continue in their labors, suffering in silence. Suffering is necessary, if not redemptive. Their reward will be in heaven. Death is not unsympathetic, telling them that they "so little deserve" what has befallen them.[9] In the end, Death leaves the matter to God but cautions the indigenes to "watch yourselves against tyrants/Who lay siege outside your walls."[10]

In contrast to the marauding Spanish conquistadores, Carvajal's

Indians "do not care for gold; they are perfectly content with their sense of right and wrong. The Indians suppose that in this respect there might be a different understanding of Christian philosophy in Europe."[11] Michael de Carvajal holds a mirror up to Spain, hoping that in it, Spaniards will see themselves wanting in comparison to the primitive—but pure and not intellectually unsophisticated—Indians they are abusing.

Carvajal unquestionably had read Bartolomé de Las Casas's *Brevissima relación de la destruycion de las Indias* (*A Brief Account of the Destruction of the Indies*). That document was written originally in 1542 and sent to then prince Felipe in an attempt to influence the promulgation of the so-called New Laws to protect the Indians of Ibero-America. It was published as a book in Seville in 1552 in the aftermath of Las Casas's Valladolid debate with Juan Ginés de Sepúlveda concerning the status of those same Indians.

Unlike Carvajal, Las Casas depicts Western Hemisphere indigenes as peaceful, childlike innocents. But other than this tonal difference, though presented in dramatic form, the arguments made by Carvajal are those found in Las Casas. In the *Destruction of the Indies*, the obsession with gold takes center stage. Las Casas's stories are repetitive and formulaic: the conquistadores arrive; the Indians welcome them, feed them, and offer them gifts; the Spaniards demand gold; the Spanish kill the Indians. As I have mentioned before, so singular is the invaders' focus on the yellow metal that Las Casas's Indians quickly become convinced that gold is the Spaniards' true god. Hypocrisy on the part of the supposedly Christian Spanish also plays a major role.

Pope Alexander VI's papal bull *Inter Caetera*, which sanctioned the Conquest months after Columbus's return, led the Council of Castile, in the name of King Ferdinand and his daughter Queen Johanna the Mad, to issue the "Requerimiento," or the "requirement." In satisfaction of the pope's edict that the subduing of the Americas must be an evangelistic mission, the Requerimiento was a document that had to be read to Indians, explaining their rights to them. It stated that they had the right to serve the one true God and his vassals on earth the monarchs of Spain. Should they accept this right, all would be well, and no harm would befall them. Should, however, they refuse or delay in their reply, war would be waged upon them, and they would be enslaved, theirs lands taken.

There was, of course, a built-in flaw with this requirement that worked in favor of the invaders: it was read in Spanish to an uncomprehending population. Even this advantage, however, was not enough. The Requerimiento quickly became the sixteenth-century equivalent of Mirandizing a criminal suspect. Las Casas reports conquistadores whispering the words in the direction of a sleeping village in the wee hours and of them shouting it into a forest before entering. Such ruses were deemed sufficient by those exercising them.

Las Casas tells of the Spaniards (whom, to highlight the gap between professed belief and vile actions, he insists on referring to in his text as "Christians") who hanged Indians in groups of thirteen, representing the twelve apostles and the Lord Jesus Christ, or baptizing them immediately before killing them. Despite such gruesome tales, the definitive story of hypocritical behavior on the part of the Spanish followers of Jesus is Las Casas's account of Hatuey, a Taino *cacique* from Hispaniola who had fled with his people to Cuba in advance of the Spaniards. Resisting only in the face of Spanish pursuit, the chief is nevertheless captured and prepared for execution. When he is tied up to be burned at the stake, a Franciscan friar (acting in the name of the St. Francis in Carvajal's text) approaches the condemned Indian, telling him of Christ and saying that, if he would believe, he would be saved. In a rare showing of sophistication by Lascasian Natives, the *cacique* inquires whether all Christians go to heaven. Assured that the "good ones do," the man does not hesitate but replies that, in that case, he would rather go to hell. Las Casas, holding the same mirror up to the Spanish visage that Carvajal would five years later, concludes, "This is just one example of the reputation and honour that our Lord and our Christian faith have earned as a result of the actions of those 'Christians' who have sailed to the Americas."[12]

Las Casas based his account in part on events he witnessed personally and on eyewitness reports of others. More of it is based on hearsay. In order to make his point, he exaggerated the number of Indians who died (though no one disputes that some areas experienced a demographic collapse of up to 80 or 90 percent). The book is unrelenting. Inadvertently, Las Casas probably did more than any other person to create and cement the Black Legend of Spanish cruelty in the Americas. The text became popular in the metropoles of other colonial contenders—in England, Holland, and France—where citizens were only too happy to believe and repeat its claims. It was first published in England in 1583 in a translation from the French and came out in a new translation by John Philips in 1656 under the florid title *The Tears of the Indians: Being an Historical and True Account of the Cruel Massacres and Slaughters of Above Twenty Millions of Innocent People; Committed by the Spaniards in the Islands of Hispaniola, Cuba, Jamaica, &c. As also, in the Continent of Mexico, Peru, & Other Places of the West-Indies, to the Total Destruction of Those Countries.* A year earlier, England's lord protector Oliver Cromwell, covetous of Spanish possessions in the Americas, declared, "God will have an account of the Innocent blood of so many millions of Indians so barbarously Butchered by the Spaniards." Philips dedicated his translation to Cromwell.[13]

We have already encountered Bartolomé de Las Casas playing a part on multiple occasions in our story of the Red Atlantic—as a child witnessing Columbus's return to Spain from his first voyage, as the recipient of an indigenous slave brought by Columbus on his second, as a keeper of the Admiral's legacy, and as a broker of peace during Enriquillo's rebellion. He first traveled to the Indies in 1502 at the age of eighteen. Though some report that he was a soldier, there is no evidence that he ever took up arms. He did, however, participate in some punitive expeditions against Indians on Hispaniola as a provisioner. For this and in recognition of his father's service with Columbus, he was awarded an encomienda. In 1506, he returned to Spain to resume his studies. He was ordained as a deacon in Seville that year, and the following year he went to Rome, where he was ordained as a priest. In 1509, he returned to Hispaniola with Diego Columbus, the Admiral's son.[14]

In September 1510, the Dominican order arrived in Hispaniola and immediately began to challenge encomiendas. During Advent 1511, Dominican António Montesinos preached a sermon in which he denounced the encomienda system of forced Indian labor as a mortal sin. Though there was a technical distinction between Native *encomendados* and slaves, in practice they differed little. Despite the fiery denunciation, Las Casas remained unconvinced and saw no conflict between his dual roles as encomendero and priest. In 1513, he was asked by his friend Diego Velásquez to accompany the expedition to conquer Cuba in his role as a chaplain. While in Cuba, he witnessed Pánfilio Narváez's massacre at Caonao, where "hundreds, if not thousands," of unoffending Indians were put to the sword. He tried to stop the slaughter, but Narváez was ruthless. Las Casas reported that he saw "a stream of blood running . . . as if a great number of cows had perished." He may also have seen Hatuey burned at the stake.[15] Though he was given a second encomienda in Cuba for his participation in the "pacification of the island," the ghastly experience apparently set in motion an accelerated emotional and psychical turmoil. On Pentecost 1514, he had a prophetic call to defend the indigenes of the New World.[16]

Las Casas renounced his encomiendas. In 1515, he sailed to Spain and gained an audience with Ferdinand, where he appealed for fair treatment of indigenes. He was named "Protector of the Indians" by the crown. From 1520 to 1522, he attempted a peaceful colonization of Venezuela, but the attempt failed. In 1522, he joined the Dominican order. In 1543, he was named bishop of Chiapa (Chiapas) in southern Mexico. He returned permanently to Spain and the Spanish court in 1547. During 1550 and 1551, he engaged in a debate with Juan Ginés de Sepúlveda before the Council of Valladolid, in which—though they were not physically in each other's presence—they squared off over the humanity of Indians and their treatment.[17]

Today, Las Casas is normally remembered only in his role as Protector of the Indians and for his engagement with Sepúlveda in the Valladolid debate—in which, it is commonly agreed, he bested his opponent. The Catholic church began the beatification process in the year 2000, setting him on the road to sainthood. Yet his record is far from spotless, even putting aside his early involvement with encomienda slavery before his "conversion." He was a man of his times and could not transcend that. Las Casas's ultimate vision was of New World colonies without colonists. Indians would become self-colonizing, paying taxes and tribute to the king of Spain under the tutelage of the church. And in 1516, in order to protect his Indian "lambs," he advocated the importation of African slaves. Like other early defenders of the Indians, he considered Africans inferior to Indians. Carlos V first authorized importation of black slaves in 1518. Many years later, Las Casas changed his mind about such slavery. In fact, the Dominican thought he would go to hell for having made the suggestion, but by then it was too late. Though not in a positive way, Las Casas united black and Red Atlantics.

In 1565, Alonso de la Vera Cruz appeared before the Council of the Indies to read a memorial, arguing against granting encomiendas in perpetuity. The document was from Bartolomé de Las Casas, who was too ill to attend.[18] In many ways, Vera Cruz's record is one of stronger support for Indians and greater effectiveness than that of his modernly better-known ally, without the blemishes. He never advocated for African slavery, though by his time it was simply a given, thanks to Las Casas.

Alonso de la Vera Cruz was born Alonso Gutiérrez to well-to-do parents in Caspueñas, near Toledo, in 1507. His family's prominence permitted him a first-class education. He first attended the University of Alcalá and then the University of Salamanca, where he studied under the founder of international law, Francisco de Vitoria. He was held in such high esteem that, following his studies, he was asked to teach philosophy at Salamanca. Already ordained a priest, his life took an unexpected turn when he met Augustinian friar Francisco de la Cruz, recently arrived from Mexico and looking for volunteers to return with him to evangelize the Indians.

In early 1536, Gutiérrez set sail from Seville in the company of Cruz and three other Augustinians, arriving in Vera Cruz (today, Veracruz) in July. Upon arrival, he took Augustinian orders and assumed the name Alonso de la Vera Cruz, after the city of their docking. In 1540, he was teaching in the Tarascan (P'urhépecha) Indian town of Tiripetío in northwestern Mexico, where he established the first library in the New World, using books he had brought with him from Spain four years earlier. On January 25, 1553, the University of Mexico opened in Mexico City (the former Aztec capital of Tenochtitlan), and Vera Cruz was named its first professor of sacred scripture and theology. Less than three months later, the prince, later Felipe II, appointed him to the episcopacy of Léon, Nicaragua. In an unusually candid letter, Vera Cruz replied, "Your Highness . . . I neither accept the honor nor want the bishopric, neither this one or any other, either now or at any other time. . . . There is no need to enlarge on the theme, since Your Highness may be certain that for [naught] in this world nor at the command of anyone—as long as God deigns to keep me in my right mind—would I accept the responsibility of a bishopric, either the one offered to me or any other. Hence, His Majesty and Your Highness should provide at once that diocese with its spiritual shepherd, and in the future not lose time by appointing one who will not accept."[19]

Vera Cruz biographer Ernest Burrus writes, "The life work of Vera Cruz may be summed up in one phrase: the defense of the natives."[20] Unlike Las Casas, Vera Cruz mastered a Native language to engage in evangelism. Burrus correctly states:

With greater calm and scientific depth than his Dominican friend, Bartolomé de las Casas, Vera Cruz defended the rights of the natives and condemned the injustices committed against them. He was careful not to make sweeping and unfounded claims of Spanish cruelty. He was not a proponent of a black or of a white legend: he strove to find out the facts and to correct the undeniable and tragic abuses. He was not so narrow-minded as to think that all Spaniards who crossed the Atlantic were necessarily evil. He was deeply convinced that each of the two ethnic groups had much to give to and share with each other; it was to their mutual advantage to live and work together— even to govern, and to own and till the land together.[21]

He was helped by his strong relationship with Felipe, a relationship that allowed him to speak to the royal as he did when turning down the episcopacy. Before composing his treatise *Relectio de Dominio Infidelium & Justo Bello* (*A Discussion on the Dominion of Unbelievers and Just War*, which Burrus published as *Defense of the Indians: Their Rights*), Vera Cruz had spent seventeen years living and working with the Indians. He is less well known than Las Casas because many of his writings were not published during his lifetime. Between 1968 and 1972, the Jesuit Historical Institute published five volumes of his work in an edition edited by Burrus.

Putting the legal training he received from Vitoria to good use, Vera Cruz, in *Defense of the Indians*, goes further than other defenders of the Indians of the time. He inquires "whether the Indians were really their own masters [prior to the coming of Europeans]; and, consequently, whether they might be deprived of their dominion." After carefully considering the question from every angle, he concludes that "it is perfectly clear that among the natives there existed a government for the good of the commonwealth." Despite the fact that they were pagans, they owned the land, because dominion was independent of faith. He concludes, "It follows that the Spaniards cannot have just dominion since they have despoiled the true owners of their tribute. . . . Therefore, it follows that, since there are *caciques* and governors in the villages, such dominions [of the Spaniards] is unjust."[22] He declares that restitution must be made. Burrus writes, "Nor will Vera Cruz allow the Spaniards to use a subterfuge to get possession of vast tracts of lands which are as yet lying idle, in order to till them at some time in the future. The welfare of the native communities demands that such lands remain in the natives' possession and at their disposal: they are of the nature of necessary insurance for their livelihood and even survival."[23] In expressing such a view, Vera Cruz was, as Burrus notes, far ahead of his time. The Augustinian said whoever takes such lands is a thief, guilty of a mortal sin.

The final two of Vera Cruz's "doubts" (that is, propositions) and their analyses are the longest in *Defense of the Indians*. They deal with "whether the emperor or king of Castile might have declared just war against [the] aborigines" and "[w]hether there is any motive to justify war against the inhabitants of the New World."[24] In answering the first of these questions, he finds all of the stated reasons insufficient. He then writes, "It is commonly asked whether, granting that the motives assigned by some in the preceding question are insufficient to warrant a just war, there is some just cause for war which can be found on the part of the emperor either through his own authority or that of the pope."[25] Burrus writes, "Vera Cruz's purpose is not to drive out the Spaniards and give back the lands and the government of the various countries to the Indians. He is not putting all of his fellow countrymen on trial before the world and in the fashion of his close friend Las Casas accusing them of massive genocide. Instead, he investigates the justice of their historical coming at the time of various discoveries and their continued presence through subsequent explorations and administration. Vera Cruz asks . . . whether there *could have been*, not . . . whether there *were* any such justifying motives."[26] More modulated in tone than Las Casas's works, *Defense of the Indians* was originally delivered as lectures at the University of Mexico during the 1554–55 school year. Through them, Vera Cruz influenced the next generation of colonizers. Burrus published Vera Cruz's treatise *De Decimis* (*On Tithes*) as *Defense of the Indians: Their Privileges*.[27]

Alonso de la Vera Cruz was mentored in the New World by Vasco de Quiroga, the bishop of Michoacán. For nine months in 1542, Quiroga left him in charge of the diocese while he was away.[28] Perhaps that experience explains why Vera Cruz was so quick and emphatic in rejecting the episcopacy when it was offered by Felipe.

Like Vera Cruz, Quiroga was more effective than Las Casas. Whereas Las Casas's attempt at a new model of peaceful colonization in Venezuela failed, Quiroga succeeded.

Vasco de Quiroga was born to a noble family in Castile, probably in 1478. Like his protégé Vera Cruz, he was trained as a lawyer and theologian. During the early sixteenth century, he served as a judge in Spain and in North Africa. In 1526, he returned from Algeria and served at the royal court. He was a friend of Juan Bernal Díaz de Luco, a member of the Council of the Indies. After the first Real Audiencia, the governing body of New Spain (Mexico), was cashiered in 1530 because the colony was in turmoil as a result of the Audiencia's violent subjugation of the indigenous population, Quiroga was selected to become a member of the second Audiencia, which would operate from 1531 to 1535. For the lawyer-theologian, it was a dream opportunity.

Like Las Casas, Quiroga was deeply influenced by Thomas More's *Utopia*. It was More's work that led the former to attempt his colonization of Venezuela. According to Daniel Castro, "Bartolomé de Las Casas envisioned utopias resulting from his proposals, but ultimately he was defeated by the economic dependence of the crown on the contributions coming from the colonies and the inevitable sway of capital, which transformed those utopian dreams into inescapable and unforgiving dystopias."[29] Quiroga went to Mexico determined to make More's vision a reality—real places and not "nowhere."

In 1531, using his own money, he founded Hospital-Pueblo de Santa Fe (Hospital Village of the Holy Faith) at Mexico City. In 1535, he founded a second, Santa Fe de Laguna in Michoacán. These *pueblos hospitales* were meant to be an alternative to encomiendas for Christian Indians and were modeled on More's *Utopia* and the early Christian socialism of the book of Acts.

Similar to the *reducciones*, praying towns for Christian Indians advocated by Las Casas, Quiroga's *pueblos* were designed to protect Christian converts from depredations at the hands of Spanish colonists and from the dangers of "backsliding" as a result of continued contact with their non-Christian kinsmen. According to Juan Miguel Zarandona of the University of Valladolid, "The Pueblos-Hospitales were hospital, asylum, church, school, and charity house at the same time. No private property of land was allowed. Everybody had to devote time to farming, on a rotating communal work basis, and to learning a trade or craft. Extended families were the rule. All had to work, but only six hours a day. Women had the right to work. Physical health was very important. A Christian life-style was promoted. No luxuries were allowed."[30] There was universal education in reading, writing, and music.

The *pueblos hospitales* differed from the reductions in an important respect, their democratic governance modeled closely on More. The most basic social unit was the family, headed by a *padre de familia* (head of household, father of the family). Over every thirty families was a *jurado* (jurist). Above every ten *jurados* was a *regidor* (alderman). Above these were two *alcaldes ordinaries* (ordinary mayors) and one *alcalde mayor* (major mayor). Natives held all these governing positions and were selected by popular suffrage. At the top of the hierarchy was a Spanish *corregidor* (chief magistrate, a replacement for the encomendero), appointed by the Audiencia.[31] Quiroga's fullest explication of his concept was his *Información en Derecho* (*Investigation on Justice*), penned in 1535 in response to the crown's revocation of the ban on Indian slavery, which he sent to the Council of the Indies, probably to Juan Bernal Díaz de Luco.

In 1547, Quiroga traveled to Europe, where he attended several sessions of the Council of Trent. The last ecumenical council of the Roman Catholic Church before Vatican II, the council established Catholic positions on a number of important issues and condemned the Protestant heresy. Quiroga traveled with a number of Indians, whom he presented at the Spanish court.

While Las Casas's Venezuelan experiment fizzled, Quiroga's project succeeded beyond his wildest expectations. Santa Fe, on the outskirts of Mexico City, swelled to a population of 30,000. Though Quiroga founded only two *pueblos hospitales*, many encomenderos adopted his example. By 1580, fifteen years after Quiroga's death, there were more than 200 such settlements.[32] Together, Vera Cruz and Quiroga influenced more Spaniards and, ultimately, protected more Indians through their measured efforts than Las Casas ever did.

Voltaire's Innocents

The man known to history and letters by his nom de plume Voltaire was born François-Marie Arouet in Paris in 1694 to a minor government official father and a mother from a noble family. He was educated by Jesuits at the Collège Louis-le-Grand. He rejected orthodox Catholicism in favor of deism, which rejects revelation in favor of the belief that reason and observation of the natural world are sufficient to prove the existence of God: God created the universe, established its laws, set it in motion, and remains apart and uninvolved. Voltaire became a consummate philosopher and writer of the Enlightenment. A protean mind and a prolific writer, he produced works in every genre of literature. In 1745, he wrote an opera-ballet with composer Jean-Philippe Rameau. *Le Temple de la Gloire* was addressed to King Louis XV of France and attempted to convince the well-loved monarch that if he would adopt Enlightenment principles and rule in accordance with them, he would be enshrined in the Temple of Glory. Fluent in Spanish, Voltaire kept a copy of Garcilaso's *Royal Commentaries of the Incas* in his library.

Voltaire drew upon Garcilaso's history especially for his best-known novel, *Candide*. The book is a satire of the philosophical optimism of Gottfried Wilhelm Leibniz dressed up as a kind of *bildungsroman*. The young hero, Candide (whose name means "innocent"), and his philosopher companion, Dr. Pangloss, go through a series of absurd adventures. As catastrophe upon catastrophe befall them, the ever cheerful Pangloss, a stand-in for Leibniz, chirps, "Everything happens for the best in this best of all possible worlds." The world of the novel is a haphazard, unreasonable, and pessimistic place. The one exception is El Dorado.

Voltaire modeled the South American realm of El Dorado on Garcilaso's descriptions of the Incas' Peru. Candide and his valet Cacambo travel to the imaginary kingdom and find a paradise. It is the only Enlightened country on earth. The inhabitants are monotheistic, believing in the one true God before the coming of Europeans. When Candide and Cacambo encounter a 172-year-old man, they inquire of the country's religion. The citizens are deists and do not pray: "'We do not pray to him at all,' said the reverend sage. 'We have nothing to ask of him. He has given us all we want, and we give him thanks continually.'"[33] There are no arguments over religion. There are no lawsuits. The citizens are purely rational, and there is a great hall dedicated to science. The king is just and reasonable. Though there is abundant gold, it is of no worth to the inhabitants.

The aged man they encounter tells the travelers, in a passage leaning directly on Garcilaso,

> I am now one hundred and seventy-two years old; and I heard from my late father, who was liveryman to the king, the amazing revolutions of Peru which he had seen. This kingdom is the ancient country of the Incas, who very imprudently left it to conquer another part of the world, and were ultimately conquered and destroyed by the Spaniards.
>
> Those princes of their family who remained in their native country

acted more wisely. They decreed, with the consent of their whole nation, that none of the inhabitants of our little kingdom should ever leave it; and to this wise rule we owe the preservation of our innocence and happiness.[34]

Candide and Cacambo remain for a month. But one cannot remain in Utopia. When the pair tell the El Doradoan king that they wish to depart, he calls them foolish. They ask only to take some of the region's "yellow clay" with them. The king smiles and replies, "I cannot imagine what pleasure you Europeans find in our yellow clay; but take away as much of it as you will, and may it do you much good." Later, Candide, thinking of Pangloss, exclaims, "Certainly, if everything is for the best, it is in El Dorado, and not in the other parts of the world."[35]

Candide was first published in 1759. Eight years later, Voltaire turned again to the Red Atlantic and the image of the Indian to make his philosophical points about France. In that year, he published *L'Ingenu* (another title meaning "the innocent").

Voltaire's novella begins in 1689 with the arrival in France from England of a Huron (Wendat). The young man speaks excellent French. When asked why he had come, he replies simply that he "wanted to see what the coast of France was like, and he was then going back again."[36] He is taken in by a prior and his sister, Mademoiselle de Kerkabon. They note his fair complexion and downy beard. When he shows them miniature portraits of his parents, a mystery is solved. His parents were the Kerkabons' brother and sister-in-law who had gone to Canada twenty years earlier. They failed to return from an expedition against the Huron. Their visitor must have been taken as an infant and raised by the Huron.

Though the young man is French by birth, he is Huron in his worldview. Voltaire uses this son of the forest as a means to critique French society. Because he was raised by the Huron in Canada and never knew his parents, he is uncorrupted compared to the immoral French. He is curious, open, and naive. He converts to Christianity, which he can see in its purity, free from the hypocrisy and false doctrine imposed by the church. He is baptized and takes the name Hercules de Kerkabon.

When an English invasion force crosses the Channel, Hercules jumps in the small boat that he had used to sail from England and goes out to meet the admiral's ship. He "asked whether it was true that they had come to ravage the country without declaring war in an honest manner."

The admiral and his men laugh at him for his innocence. Deeply stung by their laughter, he returns to shore and leads the defense, rallying the French militia, and the English are repulsed. The grateful citizens advise him to go "to Versailles to receive the reward for his services."[37] Thus, like Garcilaso, Hercules de Kerkabon heads to court as a patronage seeker.

En route, Hercules encounters a group of protestant Huguenots, who are preparing to flee France because of the revocation of the Edict of Nantes, which had assured French Protestants' rights. Moved by their stories of persecution, he asks them, "But how is it . . . that such a great king, whose fame has even reached the Hurons, should let himself be deprived of so many folk who would love him with their hearts and serve him with their hands?" The reply comes back that he is being deceived by the Jesuits. Hercules vows to take their story directly to Versailles and Louis XIV himself: "I will see the King and I will let him know the truth. It is impossible not to acknowledge the truth of this once you see it."[38] Unfortunately, the conversation is overheard by a Jesuit spy.

As soon as he arrives at his destination, Hercules naively asks what time the Sun King may be seen. After an interminable wait, he is finally permitted an audience with a first secretary's first secretary. When told that he could purchase himself a commission, he indignantly replies, "What's that you say? I am to put down some money for driving the English off? To pay for the privilege of getting myself killed for you, while you sit here quietly giving audiences? I want a company of cavalry for nothing. I want the King to get Mademoiselle de St. Yves [his beloved] out of her convent and give her to me in marriage. I want to plead with the King on behalf of fifty thousand families, whom I mean to restore to him. In short, I want to be useful, I want to be employed and get on in the world." Confronted with Huronian directness, the secretary concludes that the man before him is not right in the head. For his part, Hercules returns to his inn, where he lulls himself to sleep "with the delicious thought of seeing the King next day, obtaining the hand of Mademoiselle de St. Yves in marriage, commanding at least a cavalry company, and ending the persecution of the Huguenots."[39] The Jesuit spy, however, has made his report. Instead of an audience with the Sun King, the Huron is arrested and thrown in prison.

Hercules's cellmate is a Jansenist, a member of a theological reform movement within the Catholic church opposed by the Jesuits. The Huron complains to him that the French call Natives "savages," "but they are decent folk, and the people of this country are refined blackguards."[40] The novel's author makes clear that Hercules is free of any of the racial prejudice of the French. With the Jansenist as his tutor, he uses his time in jail to read philosophy and science in addition to Molière, Corneille, Racine, and the Greek tragedies, amassing a sizable library behind bars. Voltaire writes, "The Child of Nature was like one of those hardy trees which begin life in unpromising soil and throw out their roots and branches as soon as they are transplanted into a more favorable locality. Strange as it may seem, it was life in prison which provided this locality." And with irony, "The rapid development of his mind was almost as much due to his savage upbringing as to the spirit he was endowed with, for having been taught nothing during his childhood, he had not acquired any prejudices. Since his understanding had not been warped by error, it had retained its original rectitude. He saw things as they are, whereas the ideas we have been given in childhood compel us to see them in false lights all our lives."[41]

Ultimately, Hercules (along with the Jansenist) is freed. The lovely Mademoiselle de St. Yves sacrifices her virtue to a lecherous official to gain his freedom. Though her sacrifice works, the ordeal breaks her emotionally and physically, and she dies after being reunited with her lover. He changes his name, goes to Paris, gets his military commission, and serves with honor. The Jansenist remains by his side the rest of his life, adopting the motto, "Misfortune has its uses."[42]

In *Candide*, Voltaire presents, through Garcilaso's lens, the portrait of an ideal society. But El Dorado is only a brief interlude in a larger satirical narrative. *L'Ingenu*, however, is a quintessential novel of the Red Atlantic. Voltaire projects onto the noble savage all the virtues he sees lacking in a corrupt and decadent Europe—even if, in this case, the Huron was actually a Frenchman.

The Female American

In 1719 Daniel Defoe published *Robinson Crusoe*, sometimes thought of as the first English novel. The book's eponymous hero is on a slaving voyage to Africa when he is shipwrecked and castaway on an Atlantic island, where he spends twenty-seven years. His companion is Friday, an indigene captive whom he saves from cannibals, teaches English, and converts to Christianity. By his presence and in his actions, Crusoe thus unites white, black, and Red Atlantics. Defoe based his novel, at least in part, on true-life accounts of Alexander Selkirk, a Scottish sailor who was marooned on Masatierra in the Juan Fernandez Archipelago in the Pacific for more than four years in 1704.

Defoe's novel was a sensation, inspiring so many imitators that its title was adapted to describe a genre, "Robinsonades." Often these castaway accounts bent gender, substituting a feminine protagonist. During the eighteenth and nineteenth centuries, there were no less than twenty-six "female Robinsonades" published in America, England, France, Germany, and Holland.[43] *The Female American* was one such work. Just as *Robinson Crusoe* purported to have been "written by himself," *The Female American* is ascribed to its heroine, Unca Eliza Winkfield, "compiled by herself." Michelle Burnham, a professor of English, brought the novel back into print in a critical edition in 2001. Despite her best investigations, it proved impossible to determine actual authorship. According to Burnham, the author "articulated for readers on both sides of the Atlantic an often radical vision of race and gender through an account of a biracial heroine who is able to indulge in a kind of 'rambling' mobility and 'extraordinary' adventure precisely because she is, as the title declares, an American female."[44] Published originally in England in 1767 (the same year as the appearance of *L'Ingenu*), there is no intimation and very little possibility that the novel's author was Native American, let alone a female one. It may, however, be *the* quintessential novel of the Red Atlantic.

The "biracial heroine" of whom Burnham speaks—the purported author, Unca Eliza Winkfield—is truly of transnational heritage. The novel begins with a stylized and highly sexualized recapitulation of the Pocahontas–John Smith story. The first-person narrator's grandfather is the son of Edward Maria Winkfield (Wingfield), the first president of the Virginia Colony who sailed back to England in disgrace.[45] William Winkfield, captured by Indians during the Jamestown massacre of 1622, is brought before a Powhatan-style figure for torture and execution. He is, however, saved by the chief's daughter, who claims the Englishman for her spouse. Despite the duress and incomprehension of their meeting, the two fall deeply in love and conceive a daughter. The father goes on, through the largesse of his wife's family, to become prosperous in Virginia.

When the Native mother, also named Unca, is murdered by her jealous sister, desirous, too, of the captive Englishman, father and child decamp for England. Ultimately, however, William Winkfield returns across the Atlantic, and his crossblood daughter joins him. After his death, despite Unca Eliza's claim of America as her "native country," she decides to abandon the continent. She writes: "Having paid my father every funeral honour I could, and having nothing now to attach me to this country, and the bulk of my great fortune lying in England, I determined to embark for that kingdom, and to conclude my days with my uncle's family."[46]

On the voyage "home," however, our heroine rejects the extortionate advances of the ship's captain. When she does, he puts her ashore on an uninhabited Atlantic island, condemned like Crusoe or his real-life model, Selkirk, to live out a solitary existence, slowly to expire. But just like those marooned seafarers, she not only survives but thrives.

John Smith, when he first saw the island named for him in what is today Maryland, declared, "The land is kind," by which he meant that he had never seen a place more fit for human habitation.[47] Forsaken on her island prison, Unca survives because she finds an apparently recently abandoned home of another castaway containing a supply of edible root vegetables. As these run out, she must search for more food, and she, like Smith, comments on the fecundity of the land:

> My next care was to provide a new stock of roots, as those I found in the cell were nearly consumed. It was not long before I found plenty; these I roasted on a fire, and laid them up. If I was now rich in provisions, I was quickly more so; almost every day . . . there was not only plenty of shell-fish on the shore, all of them wholesome, except the black flesh kind, but that every tide left great numbers of other fishes in the holes and shallows. I soon tasted some of each sort, and found them very delicious; particularly, a shell-fish, like what are called oysters in England, and which needed no dressing; others were of the lobster and crab kind; the shells of the latter, being large, were very useful. Besides fish and flesh, I could also help myself to birds of various kinds, particularly some like larks. . . . From several of the trees issued a kind of glutinous matter, which I gathered and besmeared the little low branches and bushes with it, and by that means catched a great many small birds, that used to eat the berries of them. . . . What a plentiful table was here, furnished only at the expense of a little trouble!

At length, however, worry about her plight gives way to fear: Unca becomes feverish and delirious. She has only the strength to drag herself to a stream and drink. Still weak, she sees a female goat, crawls to her, and suckles. Gradually, she regains her strength.

Burnham correctly points to the incident as a rebirth, writing, "After undergoing a kind of inadvert baptism in the island's river, she recovers her strength by nursing at the dugs of a she-goat. As her health returns and she regains the ability to walk, Winkfield is figuratively reborn on this New World island. But that rebirth also increasingly resembles something more like a resurrection."[48] Such a statement is true as far as it goes, but it does not go far enough. It is literally suckling at the teats of the Americas that gives Winkfield reborn life. Initially, the milk's very richness and unfamiliarity makes her ill. She vomits violently, but the milk nonetheless helps cure and *purify* her, as she herself testifies: "For notwithstanding the milk had made me sick, yet I believe it contributed to my recovery, by clearing my stomach." Significantly, the second time she drinks the milk, it agrees with her.

Burnham writes, "*The Female American* ought . . . to be considered with the extraordinary transnational tradition of early eighteenth-century fiction produced about America and its social and cultural possibilities."[49] For the novel's author, as for Defoe, but also more broadly, England can be defined only in relationship to its colonial world, which, at that historical moment, meant America. Published in 1767, the same year as the passage of the Stamp Act, the book stresses the New World as a place of opportunity for reinvention. The previous castaway left a journal, which, with its details about the island, gives Unca the wherewithal to subsist. In narrating his life, the hermit noted that his first thirty years pre-island were profligate and crime-ridden, leading to the loss of his liberty and his transport to the colonies. The shipwreck left him imprisoned on the island, but in that event he ironically regained his freedom. America is a place of *liberty*. The island is contrasted to Jamestown, where, prior to his return to England, Unca's father was compelled to conceal the wealth he received from his Indian in-laws "as many of the colony were not only persons of desperate fortunes, but most of them such whose crimes had rendered them obnoxious in their native country."

Equally if not more important for the author of *The Female American*, however, was the Indian as constitutive of American identity. The figure of the Native looms large in literature popular in Great Britain at the time.[50] In *Regeneration through Violence: The Mythology of the American Frontier, 1600–1860*, Richard Slotkin details how "the Indian comes to represent a symbolic distillation of actual or potential American virtues."[51] Unca's island is uninhabited, but it is utilized for ceremonial purposes by nearby mainland Indians. These Natives have a written language and are apparently her mother's people, because, when Unca finds their inscriptions, she can read them. For the author, Indians are one people—one *American* people.

The attitude toward Natives and colonialism in the novel is one of ambivalence—what one would expect from a book whose protagonist is both colonizer and colonized. Before her father's original departure for Virginia, his elder brother, a clergyman, warns him: "We have no right to invade the country of another, and I fear invaders will always meet a curse; but as your youth disenables you from viewing this expedition in this equitable light that it ought to be looked on, may your sufferings be proportionally light! for our God is just, and will weigh our actions in a just scale." Later, after the father is captured in the Indian attack on Jamestown, the Powhatan figure echoes the sentiment, addressing him: "Our god is not angry; the evil being who made you has sent you into our land to kill us; we know you not, and have never offended you; why then have you taken possession of our lands, ate our fruits, and made our countrymen prisoners? Had you no lands of your own?"

Despite the expression of, by contemporary standards, such enlightened sentiments, the novel also offers a sense of patronizing entitlement regarding the Natives and the wealth of their world. In spite of her filiation with the Natives who use the island, Unca considers the island her own and refers to the Indians in the third person, thus separating herself from them. Yet she does the same with "Europeans." The offspring of an English colonizer and an Indian "princess," Unca Eliza Winkfield is that truly new creation, a hybrid—an American in the modern, Western sense.

As noted above, mainland Indians use the island for ritual. Once a year, they come in large numbers, apparently on the summer solstice to worship the sun. Discovering their temple with its hollowed-out idol, Unca devises a scheme of religious imperialism. She will secrete herself within the statue when the Natives come. From this hiding place, she will use her superior knowledge and reasoning to control and convert them. She declares, "I imagined hundreds of Indians prostrate before me with reverence and attention, whilst like a law-giver, I uttered precepts, and, like an orator, inculcated them with a voice magnified almost to the loudness of thunder."

By this subterfuge, she introduces herself to the Indians not simply as a missionary but as a direct messenger of the Christian god sent to instruct them. She refers to herself as an apostle, waited upon with every need attended to by subservient Natives: "How greatly was my situation changed! From a solitary being, obliged to seek my own food from day to day, I was attended by a whole nation, all ready to serve me." She translates the Bible and the Anglican Book of Common Prayer into the Indian language, teaching the latter to their priests, who, in turn, instruct the indigenous children.

Finally, Unca is found by her cousin John Winkfield. He vows to stay with her, learn the Indian tongue, and help her evangelize the indigenes (for he has been ordained since they last saw each other). The narrator marries her kinsman-rescuer. Unlike Robinson Crusoe, they—and the sea captain who brings him—decide to stay among the savages. But first she strips what she calls "my island" of its abundant gold. She and her new British husband go off to settle their estates in the Old World, buy books, table linens, and place settings, and then return with the first colonists to this Indian community, re-creating the initiative moment of Jamestown.

The cultural exchange is complete. The hybrid progeny of America and Europe recrosses the Red Atlantic bearing civilization. Joining with a pure European son, she remains to finish the incomplete project of colonialism.

Reuben and Rachel

If Unca Eliza Winkfield's return to the New World in *The Female American* brings back the united gene pool of Powhatan and the first president of colonial Virginia, Susanna Rowson in *Reuben and Rachel*, published thirty years later, accomplishes an even more amazing reunion within the expanse of the Red Atlantic.

Unlike *The Female American*, which first appeared in Britain, Rowson's novel was published in Boston in 1798 and reprinted in London the following year. Susanna Haswell Rowson was best known for *Charlotte Temple*, the most popular novel in America until Harriet Beecher Stowe's

Uncle Tom's Cabin appeared more than fifty years later. Born in Portsmouth in 1762, Rowson first came to America five years later, living in Massachusetts until 1778, when she and her British naval officer father returned to England. She published *Charlotte Temple* in 1791 and came back to the United States in 1793 as part of acting troupe. In the ensuing period, she produced a number of disparate works, including a musical farce based on the 1794 Whiskey Rebellion. Stung by criticism that her work was not American, she wrote *Reuben and Rachel* as a defense of the fact that she was, in fact, a true Republican.[52]

The novel begins in sixteenth-century Wales, the homeland of Prince Madoc, where Isabelle Arundel lives with her daughter, Columbia, and Indian maid, Cora. The aptly named Columbia Arundel is the perfect ancestor for Americans. Goaded by Columbia, Cora reveals the family's hidden history. If Unca Eliza Winkfield, in her journey to North America, brings back the genes of a Jamestown founder, in her text Rowson goes one better. Columbia is the descendant of the Admiral of the Ocean Sea himself.

As Rowson tells the story, Cora possesses a bundle of documents, commencing with an October 1490 letter from Columbus to his wife, Beatina, outlining his plans for a transatlantic voyage. After his initial 1492 exploration, Columbus travels back to the Americas with their son Ferdinando. The youth falls in love with an Inca princess, Orrabella. This Native woman becomes the ancestor of Columbia's mother Isabelle.

Historically, Fernando was Columbus's son by his mistress Beatriz Enriquez de Arana. He accompanied his father on his fourth and final voyage to the Western Hemisphere. The closest the pair came, however, to Peru, the site of the fictional Ferdinando's meeting with his beloved Orrabella, is a statue in Lima, depicting the father holding the hand of a kneeling, submissive, and bare-breasted Indian maiden.

According to English professor Joseph Bartolomeo, in Rowson's fiction Columbus "becomes the original founder not only of a new nation, but of the extended family that the novel presents through ten generations. Rowson's treatment was part of the widespread attention to the Columbian origins of American identity in the early Republic, which attempted to distance the United States from Britain by tracing the genealogy back to Columbus."[53]

Columbia Arundel, the product of both Old and New Worlds, marries Sir Egbert Gorges. She gives birth to five children, including a son named for the Columbian ancestor, Ferdinando. With his birth, the colonial enterprise begins to come full circle.

Just as Unca Eliza Winkfield brings her indigenous mother's bloodline, commingled with that of Edward Maria Wingfield, back to the Americas, Susanna Rowson posits that Sir Ferdinando Gorges, the father of colonization of North America (who has already played such a large role in our story of the Red Atlantic, as seen in chapter 1), was the direct descendant of Columbus and a South American indigene. According to Rowson, Gorges's grandson Edward "delighted in conversing" with one of Sir Ferdinando's Indian "servants": "His little heart would bound with transport at the description of vast oceans, immeasurable continents, and climes yet unexplored by Europeans; and seized with an irresistible desire to visit the new world in America, in the year 1632, embarked for New-England." The circle is closed: with Edward Gorges's passage across the Red Atlantic, an heir of Columbus and of American indigenes returns both their bloodlines to the New World.

In its storyline, *Reuben and Rachel* anticipates by almost 200 years a novel by a prominent Native American author. In 1991, in the runup to the quincentennial of the Columbus event, Gerald Vizenor penned *The Heirs of Columbus*. Vizenor's book begins with an annual October gathering of a group of Natives at the headwaters of the Mississippi, at which they compete to share their best stories of Columbus. The novel is supposed to be that year's winning story. In this vision, the Maya traverse the Atlantic in prehistoric times, where they intermarry with Europeans. According to Vizenor's character Stone Columbus, "The Maya brought civilization to the savages of the Old World and the rest is natural. . . . Columbus escaped from a culture of death and carried our tribal genes back to the New World, back to the great river; he was an adventurer in our blood and he returned to his homeland." Vizenor's novel was itself an unintended satire of *The Crown of Columbus* by Michael Dorris and Louise Erdrich, published a month later the same year. It also inadvertently mocks Pliny's account, picked up by Jack Forbes, of "Indos" blown off course to Europe.

Rowson's novel continues through the generations, through King Philip's War and beyond, as the "returning" Natives/colonists cohabit again with Native Americans. Even so, these colonials and their descendants distance or divorce themselves from their indigenous roots. Indian ancestry makes them "true-born Americans," but European blood makes them superior. "Real" Americans are Europeans, indigenized by intermarriage with Natives. In such a context, the Indian, for American colonists and Europeans alike, reemerges as savage, "wreaking havoc on Euro-American farmers who are no longer figured as ruthless colonizers but as virtuous and productive colonists."[54] Bartolomeo concludes, "And while the conception of transatlantic exchange may be narrowed, the process of exchange remains essential to the novel's vision of what it means to be an American."[55] As this book you hold in your hands and its title suggest, that process of Columbian Exchange is also the essence of the Red Atlantic, as well.

Arthur Gordon Pym

Most American readers, if they know anything about Edgar Allan Poe's life, think of him as a man born in Boston who lived and worked in New York and Baltimore and wrote macabre poems and short stories. Yet he was raised in Virginia, spent much of his life there, and never considered himself anything but a Southern gentleman in his sensibilities. As a writer of that location and of his time, Poe wrote more than one would think today about Indians in that era of Indian Removal and Native erasure from the American Southeast. In a 2012 issue of the journal *Native South*, in a piece titled "Mr. Poe's Indians," I examine Poe's images of Indians in short stories like "The Man That Was Used Up" and in other works such as his unfinished novel *The Journal of Julius Rodman*. In the article, I make a case for considering Poe a Southern writer.[56]

In this section, I want to look at Poe's one completed novel, *The Narrative of Arthur Gordon Pym of Nantucket*, perhaps the most racist novel ever produced by a major American author. It is also his one work with direct relevance to the Red Atlantic. Most discussion has centered on Poe's depiction of blacks in the novel. While I will, by necessity, examine that focus as well, I want to look in a much less studied direction—at his depiction of Dirk Peters, the Indian character in the book.

Many modern Poe scholars have struggled to rehabilitate Poe on the issue of race relations. This requires not only exonerating him of pro-slavery views generally but finding nonracist readings of *Pym* in particular. One faction has read it as satire or parody, as "ironic criticism of Southern attitudes and institutions," as "an early jeremiad on the evils of slavery . . . cryptic forebodings of national doom over the sin of slavery."

Perhaps the most expansive recent reading is that of Dana Nelson, who sees it as "a profound satirical critique of American imperialism and ethnocentrism." Frederick Frank and Diane Long Hoeveler, in their excellent introduction to the 2010 Broadview edition of the novel, note that "*Pym* criticism that deals with slavery motifs is frequently characterized by the pitfalls of over-reading a text."[57]

I suspect much of this is rooted in the very human impulse to believe that an artist whose work we like or admire must also be a good person, and by "good" we mean morally good by our own reckoning and standards. For instance, we are dismayed to discover that the same Louis-Ferdinand Céline who wrote *Voyage au Bout de la Nuit* was also a virulent anti-Semite and sympathizer with the collaborationist Vichy regime during World War II. Poe *must* have been opposed (even quietly) to slavery, and there must be an alternative antiracist reading to much that is facially offensive in *Pym*.

Others see in Poe a proto-modernist with little in the way of regional affinities. Poe was not a Southern writer. Still others contend that a writer's or thinker's biography and political views are irrelevant, believing that every artistic or aesthetic creation stands apart and separate, as if creation can be divorced from creator. Is the fact that Martin Heidegger supported National Socialism irrelevant, as his defenders maintain, or, as Emmanuel Levinas contended, does it raise serious questions about his philosophy? Even if Poe held ambiguous or even favorable views toward slavery, does that mean we should read *Pym* through that lens? What about his attitudes toward Indians?

The Narrative of Arthur Gordon Pym of Nantucket was originally published in installments in the *Southern Literary Messenger*, beginning in 1837. What is it in the story and in its depictions of people of color that has led to such a diversity of readings and engendered such sharp critiques and passionate defenses? Central to the discussion of Poe and racism are the mutiny aboard the brig *Grampus* and the events that transpire in Tsalal. I would also add that the character of Dirk Peters, the "half-breed" Indian crewman, is crucial to understanding Poe's socio-racial and political views.

The novel begins when a young man, the eponymous Mr. Pym, stows away on the *Grampus* with the assistance of his friend Augustus Barnard, the son of the ship's captain. Seafaring novels were a popular genre at the time. Here, in Pym's adventures at sea, you have a whaling tale that bears a striking resemblance to Melville's *Moby-Dick*, more than a decade before the latter novel's publication. *Pym* is a remarkable piece of writing in which white, black, and Red Atlantics all merge.

The book is unmistakably Poe in its view of human nature and psychology and in its sense of ominous dread. Yet for most of its length, it is a relatively straightforward and compelling novel of the sea, filled with mutinies, pirates, and shipwrecks, with a vague sense of racialized apprehension—Herman Melville meets H. P. Lovecraft, a sort of *Moby-Dick at the Mountains of Madness*. Then in the last section of the book, it takes a hard, racist, H. Rider Haggard–like turn.

As discussed in chapter 2, mixed-race crews were common in the nineteenth-century maritime industry. Natives, especially those of mixed-African ancestry, routinely sailed out on whalers. Race first enters *Pym* in chapter 4. Not long after the *Grampus* puts to sea, the first mate and seven other crewmen mutiny, seizing the ship and killing the captain. One of the chief instigators is a "negro" cook, "who in all respects was a perfect demon." The rest of the crew is trapped below deck, and the mate orders them to come up one by one. After some time, only one emerges, begging for his life: "The only reply was a blow on the forehead from an axe. The poor fellow fell to the deck without a groan, and the black cook lifted him up in his arms as he would a child, and tossed him deliberately into the sea. . . . A scene of the most horrible butchery ensued. The bound seamen were dragged to the gangway. Here the cook stood with an axe, striking each victim on the head as he was forced over the side of the vessel by the other mutineers. In this manner twenty-two perished." The African American cook is brutal, treacherous, and double-dealing. He participates in a mutiny aboard the ship, killing those crew members loyal to the captain with an ax. He later pretends to side with Peters, a line manager, against the mutineers who want to turn pirate, but he then switches sides.

Peters also participates in the mutiny, though Pym describes him as "less bloodthirsty." Peters is a Native, described as the "son of a squaw of the tribe of Upsarokas, who live among the fastnesses of the Black Hills near the source of the Missouri," and a white fur-trader father. The name of the tribal nation, Upsaroka, seems to be Poe's corruption of Absaroka, the Crows' name for themselves.

We have already seen that Natives were a common source of maritime labor in New England. Yet Poe offers no explanation for why a Crow from the headwaters of the Missouri and the plains would be going to sea. That question aside, what I want to focus on is Poe's extended description of Peters's physical appearance and his character. As to the former, he writes:

> Peters himself was one of the most purely ferocious-looking men I ever beheld. He was short in stature—not more than four feet eight inches high—but his limbs were of the most Herculean mould. His hands, especially, were so enormously thick and broad as hardly to retain human shape. His arms, as well as his legs, were *bowed* in the most singular manner, and appeared to possess no flexibility whatsoever. His head was equally deformed, being of immense size, with an indentation on the crown (like that on the head of most negroes), and entirely bald. To conceal this latter deficiency, which did not proceed from old age, he usually wore a wig formed of any hair-like material which presented itself—occasionally the skin of a Spanish dog or American grizzly bear. At the time spoken of he had on a portion of one of these bearskins; and it added no little to the natural ferocity of his countenance, which betook of the Upsaroka character. The mouth extended nearly from ear to ear; the lips were thin, and seemed, like some other portions of his frame, to be devoid of natural pliancy, so that the ruling expression never varied under the influence of any emotion whatsoever. This ruling expression may be conceived when it is considered that the teeth were exceedingly long and protruding, and never even partially covered, in any instance, by the lips. To pass this man with a casual glance, one might imagine him to be convulsed with laughter—but a second look would induce a shuddering of acknowledgment, that if such an expression were indicative of merriment, the merriment must be that of a demon.

For Poe, grotesque physical deformity (and, for some reason, especially bowlegs) was a particular distinguishing characteristic of both blacks and Indians. Later, he describes Peters as a drunkard.

Three primary stereotypes of Indians dominate literary representations of them: the noble savage (the "good" Indian), the bloodthirsty savage (the "bad" Indian), and the half-breed. The last of these hews closely to the second, the bad or bloodthirsty savage, possessing all the negative qualities the dominant culture hates about itself. But the half-breed stereotype goes further: as the degenerate project of miscegenation, he has no redeeming qualities whatsoever and is distrusted by both whites and Natives. Despite Peters's grotesque—even demonic—appearance and his dipsomania, in the end he proves to be a good man and an ally of the protagonist. Still later, Poe refers to Peters as a "hybrid" rather than as a "half-breed." Unlike the usual stereotype, it appears here that white blood ennobles Peters, giving him redeeming aspects. In this, Poe adheres to a prevailing ideology concerning southern Indians during the era.

On December 29, 1830, in response to President Andrew Jackson's second annual message to Congress, sent earlier that month, the American Board of Commissioners of Foreign Missions, meeting in the Cherokee Nation's capital of New Echota, passed a number of resolutions and statements in support of the Cherokees in their opposition to Removal. The document read in part, "The intermixture of white people with the Indians has undoubtedly been a considerable cause of the civilization of the latter. The operation of this cause upon the descendants of white men we believe is not called into question. . . . That the Indians of mixed blood possess, in a considerable degree, that superior influence which naturally attends superior knowledge, cannot be doubted." In *Democracy in America*, Alexis de Tocqueville goes further, writing of the so-called Five Civilized Tribes inhabiting the American South: "The growth of European habits has been remarkably accelerated among these Indians by the mixed race which has sprung up. Deriving intelligence from the father's side, without entirely losing the savage customs of the mother, the half-blood forms the natural link between civilization and barbarism. Wherever this race has multiplied the savage state has become modified, and a great change has taken place in the manners of the people."[58] Ultimately, such attitudes are testimony to the indigenizing desires and instincts of those in the dominant culture of the settler colony that is the United States.

The mutiny is just the first calamity to befall Pym. In his subsequent adventures, Peters's savage brutality comes in handy as he protects them both and does the dirty work that must be done, thwarting the mutineers and dispatching the unlucky Parker with alacrity when the latter draws the short splinter in a cannibalistic pact among survivors of a shipwreck to save those who remain. In the end, Peters will be rewarded, but first he and Pym must pass through Tsalal.

After mutiny, storm, shipwreck, and cannibalism, only Pym and Peters have survived. At last they are picked up by the topsail schooner *Jane Guy*, outbound from Liverpool "on a sealing and trading voyage to the South Seas and Pacific." Frank and Hoeveler map Pym's adventures and point out the implausibility of the trip. "Poe's voyage is, as described, quite impossible. The various ships that Pym sailed on could not possibly have crossed such distances in the time that Poe claims they did."[59] After a side trip to Kerguelen in the Indian Ocean, the ship returns to the South Atlantic and begins her journey south. It is a journey into increasing whiteness.

On January 17, two days before they reach Tsalal, the crew spot "a gigantic creature of the race of the Arctic bear [polar bear]" on an ice floe. The mate, Pym, and Peters are dispatched in an open boat. According to Pym, "Being well armed, we made no scruple of attacking it at once." Shot, the angered bear plunges into the water and swims to attack its attackers. Once more, it is the savage Peters who acts: "In this extremity nothing but the promptness and agility of Peters saved us from destruction. Leaping upon the back of the huge beast, he plunged the blade of a knife behind the neck, reaching the spinal marrow at a blow. The brute tumbled into the sea lifeless, and without a struggle, rolling over Peters as he fell. The latter soon recovered himself, and a rope being thrown him, he secured the carcass before entering the boat. We then returned in triumph to the schooner, towing our trophy behind us." It is hard to miss the white man here claiming credit for what was almost exclusively the accomplishment of the Indian—"towing *our* trophy behind us." Polar bears, of course, do not exist in the Antarctic, and this one was a huge specimen, measuring fifteen feet in length. Its fur was "perfectly white."

The following day, they retrieve from the water "the carcass of a singular-looking land-animal." The creature was three feet long but only six inches tall, with long claws on its feet. "The tail was peaked like that of a rat, and about a foot and a half long. The head resembled a cat's, with the exception of the ears—these were flopped like the ears of a dog." The body was "covered with a straight silky hair"—once again, "perfectly white."[60]

This voyage into an increasingly albino landscape ends abruptly on January 19, when the sea turned "an extraordinary dark colour." The *Jane Guy* has reached the island of Tsalal. The native Tsalalians are the ultimate villains of the novel, making the black cook of the *Grampus* look redeemable by comparison. These are a people so "jet black" that even their teeth are black. Their souls are so black that they are superstitiously terrified of anything white. Pym observes, "It was quite evident that they had never before seen any of the white race—from whose complexion, indeed, they appeared to recoil." It is not only pale skin that agitates them but also the ship captain's white handkerchief with which he first tries to hail them and the white sails of the *Jane Guy* herself. Later, they are equally disturbed when they see the preserved carcass of the white platypus-like creature that the crew recovered from the sea before arriving at the island.

The Tsalalians initially seem to welcome the white newcomers. In exchange for replenishing the ship's provisions, the whites give the natives "blue beads, brass trinkets, nails, knives, and pieces of red cloth, they being fully delighted in the exchange." Trade is routinized: "We established a regular market on shore, just under the guns of the schooner, where our barterings were carried out with every appearance of good faith, and a degree of order which their village of Klock-klock had not led us to expect from the savages."

Captain Guy is eager to explore the country, "in the hope of making a profitable speculation in his discovery." The whites find that the surrounding waters are abundant in *biche de mer* (sea cucumber), and they decide to exploit this resource using native labor. The captain, however, is also anxious to use the fair weather to continue his ship's explorations to the south. According to Pym, "A bargain was accordingly struck, perfectly satisfactory to both parties." Structures would be erected for curing sea cucumber. The *Jane Guy* would sail on, leaving three men as factors, and huts would be built for them—a permanent mercantile colonialist presence. The natives, for their part, "were to receive a stipulated quantity of blue beads, knives, red cloth, and so forth, for every certain number of piculs of the *biche de mer*." A picul is a measure equal to sixty kilograms. Pym notes that first-quality sea cucumber commanded a price of ninety dollars per picul in Canton.

The Tsalalians' hospitality, however, appears to have been all subterfuge. Before the bulk of the whites can depart, the natives do the unthinkable and commit the unpardonable sin of resisting and aggressively attacking their would-be colonizers. Pym says that their "apparent kindness was only the result of a deeply laid plan for our destruction, and that the islanders for whom we entertained such inordinate feelings of esteem, were among the most barbarous, subtle, and bloodthirsty wretches that ever contaminated the face of the globe." Later, he repeats the sentiment, amplifying upon it: "In truth, from every thing I could see of these wretches, they appear to be the most wicked, hypocritical, vindictive, bloodthirsty, and altogether fiendish race of men upon the face of the globe."

The natives take the *Jane Guy* and set about destroying her. They rip up the decks, take down the sails, and begin removing nails and anything metal. They are quite literally dismantling the master's house, assaulting white civilization itself.

Ultimately, once again only Peters and Pym escape, the former through brute force and the latter with the aid of firearms. The pair seize one of the Tsalalian canoes and take one of the natives captive. Pursued by their black villains, the two decide on a bold plan, sailing south toward the pole. As they do, whiteness returns. The ocean water undergoes "a rapid change, being no longer transparent, but of a milky consistency and hue." Their Tsalalian captive becomes increasingly agitated, then goes into convulsions, and eventually throws himself facedown into the bottom of the canoe and refuses to move as occurrences of whiteness increase, seemingly exponentially.

The narrative ends abruptly. At the pole is a limitless, yawning cataract, into which the canoe is being inexorably drawn. Just as it is about to slip into the abyss, the Tsalalian succumbs, the victim of a surfeit of whiteness. After his death, the narrative continues for only three additional breathless sentences: "And now we rushed into the embraces of the cataract, where a chasm threw itself open to receive us. But there arose in our pathway a shrouded human figure, very far larger in its proportions than any dweller among men. And the hue of the skin of the figure was of the perfect whiteness of snow." It is a white apotheosis, exaltation at the hands of the white Christian god.

Though the captive Tsalalian clearly dies, the fate of the canoe's other two occupants is left unclear. In an epilogic "Note," however, presumably attributed to Poe himself, since Pym discusses his editorial role in the book's preface, the reader is informed that Pym, of course, survived to write the narrative the reader holds in his or her hands. He has in the interim, however, died in an accident, without delivering the last few chapters. Thus the sudden cliffhanger of an ending.

The reader is told that Peters survived and is living in Illinois. He might be able to provide some gap-filling information but "cannot be met with at present." Peters presumably is permitted to participate in the white apotheosis because of his white blood—or perhaps because of his service to Pym. In an essay on the novel, John Carlos Rowe writes: "Suffice it to say that Illinois is a Free State, and the convenience of Peters' status as a 'half-breed' (Native American and white) allows Poe's Pym to liberate a savage without succumbing to the Southern heresy of liberating a perfectly good piece of property, that is a black slave. Having served his murderous purposes—the murder of Parker, the vengeful murder of the natives on Tsalal, the indirect murder of Nu-Nu [the captive Tsalalian in the canoe]—Peters has earned his just desserts [*sic*]: the 'free state' that only the white slave master . . . can award for service against the savagery that threatens him and his kind."[61] Regarding the kidnapping of Nu-Nu, he writes, "With the help of the servile half-breed, the white master affirms his mastery and takes possession of the savagery that so threatens him."[62]

The jet-black Tsalalians are clearly stand-ins for African slaves. Their uprising reflects Poe's and his fellow antebellum Southerners' fears of slave revolts. Nat Turner's rebellion in 1831 was still fresh in their minds. Even earlier revolts like Gabriel Prosser's (1800) and Denmark Vesey's (1822) haunted them in a landscape where they were outnumbered.

Yet the Tsalalians are also coded as indigenes. *Pym* was written in 1837, just as the Cherokee removal crisis was nearing its end, a culmination that would result in the Trail of Tears and the virtually complete ethnic cleansing of Indians from the southern geography (in the minds of the responsible whites, a total erasure). Poe's short story "The Man That Was Used Up," a parody of the Seminole Wars, was published within a few months of the last surviving Cherokee exiles straggling into Indian Territory after the 800-mile forced march of the Trail of Tears. *Pym* and Poe's other depictions of Natives are comments on Indian Removal. Indians, like the Tsalalians, are savages who must be expelled from the presence of civilized men.

Even though I agree with those who read *The Narrative of Arthur Gordon Pym of Nantucket* as an allegory of southern planter society's paranoia of slave revolt (and I would add as a tacit justification for Indian Removal), I acknowledge it as a major American novel nonetheless. It influenced Herman Melville, Jules Verne, and H. P. Lovecraft. Poe is a significant figure of the American Renaissance, even though he has been long marginalized because he was a southerner.

In 2011, Mat Johnson, a writer of black, Muscogee, and white ancestry, published his wildly comic novel *Pym*, at once a sequel, a parody, and an inversion of Poe's book. Johnson's fiction takes as its premise that an African American English professor discovers a manuscript of the memoirs of Dirk Peters, revealing to him that Poe's story is not fiction but instead factual. With Peters's skeleton (retrieved from a descendant) as baggage, the academic leads an expedition of people of color to sail to Tsalal. The voyage goes terribly wrong, however, and the crew find themselves enslaved in Antarctica by a race of giant ice-dwelling "snow honkies," one of whose members saved Pym and Peters at the end of Poe's novel. As an early reflection of indigenous participation in maritime labor, *The Narrative of Arthur Gordon Pym of Nantucket* is an important part of the literature of the Red Atlantic. And Johnson's novel is an equally important comment upon it, just as, for instance, Joseph Boyden's *Three Day Road* and Gerald Vizenor's *Blue Ravens* are critical literary comments on Native doughboys' participation in the Red Atlantic during the Great War.

An Übermensch among the Apache

German author Karl May might, as I indicated at the outset of this chapter, seem an odd choice to include in a discussion of the literature of the Red Atlantic. While he is the most popular German author—in Germany—of all time, his works have been only partially and sporadically available in English. If, however, the heart of the literature of the Red Atlantic is how whites, particularly Europeans, defined themselves in relation to Western Hemisphere indigenes, then Karl May is its very essence. Furthermore, his influential representations are intimately linked to the celebrity Indians of Buffalo Bill's Wild West show. And like Garcilaso's *Royal Commentaries*, which crossed the Red Atlantic from Spain to Peru to influence indigenous rebellion there, May's works came to the United States in translation at an important historical moment to curious effect.

Karl May wrote popular adventure stories involving Old Shatterhand, a German in the American West after the American Civil War, and Kara-ben-Nemsi, an adventurer in the Middle East. May, labeling his stories as *reiseerzahlungen*—travel tales—claimed that they were based upon his own travels and exploits. Old Shatterhand's name was actually Karl, having been given the frontier moniker for his ability to lay out any man with a single punch. Kara-ben-Nemsi simply means Karl, son of the Germans. May did everything he could to encourage the identification of himself with his heroes. He was photographed in buckskins as Old Shatterhand and in orientalist costume as Kara-ben-Nemsi. His trusty *Bärentöter* (bear killer), with studs on the stock (one for every man he killed), is on display at the Karl May Museum in Bamberg.[63] His last novel, the mostly overlooked *Winnetou IV*, published in 1910, begins with his wife, Klara, bringing up the day's mail to his study. Among the envelopes is one from the United States addressed only to "May. Radebeul. Germany." The letter inside reads:

> To Old Shatterhand
>
> Are you coming to Mount Winnetou? I certainly will. Maybe even Avaht-Niah, the one-hundred-and-twenty-year-old. Can you see that I can write? And that I have done so in the language of the palefaces?
>
> Wagare-Tey
> Chief of the Shoshone[64]

The meld is now complete. The elderly May and Old Shatterhand are one and the same.

May claimed to speak forty languages, including many Native dialects. In reality, this claim, like all his others, was as fictitious as the novels he wrote.

May was born in 1842 near Chemnitz, Saxony, the fifth child in a large family headed by a weaver father and professional midwife mother. He went blind from malnutrition and remained so until he was five. The first thirty years of his life were unremarkable. He attended a teachers' training school but was known primarily for minor scrapes with the law, crimes of petty theft, impersonation, and obtaining money under false pretenses. At twenty-three, he was sentenced to five years in prison for insurance fraud and the fraudulent sale of medicines. Within six months of his release in the winter of 1868, he was back in jail for four years for impersonating a police officer. In 1899, a public inquiry revealed that *Dr.* Karl May had purchased his doctorate from the German University of Chicago, a mail-order organization run by a former barber. It also revealed that 1870–71, the period of his supposed adventures in the American West, had been spent in Zwikau prison. The resulting stress led to May's nervous breakdown.[65] His works are thus "travel lies," conforming to the pattern of earlier such writings outlined by Percy Adams in his book *Travelers and Travel Liars*. They are the product of a "fireside traveler," who uses his work not to amuse or to instruct but to deceive "for the sake of money, pride, or a point of view."[66] It is the willful sin, the "lie direct" in medieval church English.[67] May journeyed to America only once, in 1908, four years before his death.

While in prison, May began to write. According to Austrian-born writer Frederic Morton, "May, whose background was so wretchedly unheroic, began to write about a knight-errant of nonpareil ethics and muscle. Known as Old Shatterhand in Indian territory, he battles desperadoes. As Kara-ben-Nemsi, he takes on fiendish emirs in the dunes and casbahs of Arabia. May's experience at that point was entirely and provincially Middle European. He had never been west of the Rhine or south of the Alps."[68] Despite the disclosures about the spurious nature of his claims, however, May's popularity never waned. He recovered his reputation. His books continued to sell. And in 1928, sixteen years after his death, Villa Shatterhand, his home in Radebeul, near Dresden, where he purportedly received the letter from Shoshone chief Wagare-Tey, opened as a museum. Such was his popularity that at the time of German partition in 1945, a replica of Villa Shatterhand had to be built in Bamberg in the western zone to accommodate pilgrimages by his fans.

It is often fashionable to tar May with the fact that he was Adolf Hitler's favorite author. Yet he was also the favorite author of Albert Schweitzer, Albert Einstein, and Hermann Hesse. During the latter years of the Red Atlantic, he was quite simply every German boy's—and not a few German girls'—favorite writer.

Beyond Germany, of course, numerous other writers were representing American Indians and influencing popular images in Europe. We have already examined some of these. Some others influenced May. In France, François-René de Chateaubriand helped cement the stereotype of the *bon sauvage* (noble savage) with works such as *Atala* (1801), which became the first real European best seller, and *René* (1802). Later, Gustave Aimard published a "western" a month at times between 1850 and 1870. James Fenimore Cooper was readily available in translation. May modeled his fabrications closely on Cooper and on French author Gabriel Ferry's *Coureur de Bois* (which he helped edit in a German edition). He may also have had access to John Heckwelder's *Account of the History, Manners and Customs of the Indian Nations* (1819), Cooper's principal source of information.

May's westerns revolve around the relationship between Old Shatterhand (Karl) and the Apache warrior Winnetou. Winnetou is the consummate noble savage. Cultured, he carries around a copy of Longfellow's "Hiawatha," which he occasionally reads. In choosing to make this progressive specimen an Apache, May seems to be responding to Ferry. As the French attempted to regain a foothold in the Americas and to establish and shore up Maximilian in Mexico, French literary interests turned from Canada and the Great Lakes region to the Southwest. Ferry's heroes in *Coureur de Bois* were Comanches. According to Christian Feest, "If the archenemy of the German people was siding with the Comanche against the Apache, the latter had to be the Germans' potential allies. Winnetou, the 'red gentleman' and slightly effeminate Indian chief . . . thus had to be an Apache."[69] In *Satan and Ischariot*, written in 1894–95, May depicts Winnetou visiting Old Shatterhand in Dresden. The warrior orders German beer, which "he likes to drink, but with moderation," and requests a performance of German music. Though the Indian says nothing following the music, May writes, "[B]ut as I knew his personality, I knew quite well how deep an impression the German song had left on his soul." Again, according to Feest: "Although nothing else is reported about the chief's reactions, the message is clear enough—an Apache chief who likes German songs and drinks beer in moderation must be a kindred soul."[70] He is every bit as much the Übermensch as the German narrator.

As with Euro-American representations of Indians, those of May and other European writers have more to do with internal European needs than any "real" or "authentic" Natives. According to the late Kjell Hallbing, a Norwegian writer who wrote over eighty best-selling westerns under the pen name Louis Masterson (a nom de plume mash-up of Louis L'Amour and Bat Masterson), "The so-called Western Myth is a European myth." Or, as Julian Crandall Hollick observes, "The Wild West for many Europeans has been, always will be, a mythical place where Europeans can stage their own quarrels, dream their own dreams. If the Wild West had never existed, then Europe would have had to invent it."[71]

May's Apaches unfailingly fit the noble savage stereotype. Their enemies, whether Yankees or other Natives, are irredeemably evil. The stories reflect May's vaguely pacifistic, muscular Christianity and Christian socialism. His depiction of Apache ritual dispenses with reality completely, and the rites themselves are decidedly Teutonic.

In order to prove his bravery and worthiness before being accepted by the Apache, Old Shatterhand must undergo a series of trials. In the final test, he must swim underwater to a totem pole in the middle of a lake, while the Mescalero chief Intschu-tschuna, Winnetou's father, throws tomahawks at him. Having triumphed, he is welcomed as a "white Apache." The ensuing "blood brotherhood" ritual is purely Teutonic with overt Christian and neo-pagan symbology and language, imagery of the Eucharist and of death and resurrection.

As in much popular literature, there is an element of sexual ambiguity in May's stories (covers of the original Winnetou books designed by Sacha Schneider feature classical, Olympiad-style nudes "disguised" as Indians) and a strong homoerotic overtone in the relationship between Old Shatterhand and Winnetou. The first time Karl sees the Indian, he describes him: "His bronze-colored face bore the imprint of a very special nobility. We seemed to be about the same age. He immediately impressed me as being endowed with an exceptional mind, and an exceptional character. We looked each other up and down. His eyes shone with a dull fire, and I thought I could detect in them the faint light of sympathy. The others told me that Winnetou has accomplished more, though still in his youth, than ten other warriors could hope to accomplish in a whole lifetime. I believed them. One day, his name would be famous through all the plains, and in all the mountains." He states that "the cut of his earnest, beautiful face, the cheekbones of which barely stood out at all, was almost Roman." Likewise, Winnetou says of Shatterhand, "I admired his courage and strength. His face seemed sincere. I thought I could love him." He tells the Aryan that "the Great Spirit has endowed you with an extraordinarily robust body."

In *Winnetou I*, the first of the stories chronologically but not the first written, a female love interest is provided for Karl—Nscho-tschi ("Spring Day"), Winnetou's sister who is smitten with the German. Though extraordinarily beautiful, her beauty for Karl seems to lie primarily in her resemblance to her brother: "Her hair reminded me of Winnetou's—and so did her eyes. Her eyes were soft, and velvety, shining through from under thick, black eyelashes. The perfect, delicate shape of her face was not spoiled by the prominent cheekbones which are a common feature among the Indians. Her nose made her profile seem more Greek than

Redskin. She must have been about eighteen years old." After Nscho-tschi and her father are killed by the evil Yankee Frederick Santer, Shatterhand and Winnetou are left alone, free to pursue their adventures unencumbered by female restraint. May never introduced another love interest in any of the subsequent stories.

Christian notions of a universalizing brotherhood and homoerotic subtexts aside, the original root appeal of May's fiction during the waning days of the Red Atlantic rested in the way it tapped into nascent German nationalism and the ideology of European colonialism. Lisa Bartel-Winkler, an author who, during the Nazi era, would write novels in which the virtuous traits of Indians were explained by their Viking— and hence Aryan—ancestry, wrote in 1924, "In Winnetou Karl May delineates the Indian drama. It is also the German drama. Winnetou is the noble man of his race—he knows about the purity of blood, the longing, and the hope of his brothers, but they have to founder because they are worn down by discord. . . . This is Indian, this is also German. Who has grasped the meaning of the Indian drama has also grasped the meaning of the German drama."[72]

Frederic Morton nuances such an argument and draws out its appeal in May's time, writing, "It's odd, but a country that was to generate so formidable a nationalism in the 20th century had, until the 19th, few heroic figures to call its own. Britain's ran from King Arthur to Lord Nelson; France had a gallery from Roland to Louis XIV. But Germany? The scattered sagas of the Germanic tribes dramatize the end of Rome rather than the dawn of Teutonia."[73] In this mythopoeic nation-building quest, May can be seen as of a piece with composer Richard Wagner. Wagner's tools were music and a reconstructed pre-Christian Teutonic mythology. May deployed pre-Christian, pagan Indians and the wandering Aryan knight Old Shatterhand as his devices. May gave his readers what they longed for desperately, "an epos of the German conquistador bestriding the world at large."[74] This heroic myth is part of the impulse of German colonialism and much of colonialism in general. According to Kjell Hallbing, "When every frontier in Europe was conquered, every wilderness was cultivated, the people still had a need for a dream of something fresh, new, original."[75] Or, as Christopher Frayling puts it, in May it is as if the Code of the West "has been rewritten by Kaiser Wilhelm."[76]

Some have disputed that May is the root source of German fascination with Indians, an interest that continues to our present day. It is true that the image shaped by May was reinforced subsequently (even in his own lifetime) by a variety of sources. Visits by Buffalo Bill's Wild West show, and a homegrown knockoff, founded in 1901 by Hans Stosch-Sarrasani, helped cement May's representations in the popular imagination.[77] The future kaiser, of course, saw Cody's extravaganza in London with his cousins, the British royal Hanovers. The show came to Leipzig in 1890. By 1895, Gustav Wustmann reported that the annual Tauchisher Jahrmarkt had become an institutionalized mass expression of Indian enthusiasm, something that would have been unthinkable "thirty years ago." Though Cody's spectacular may have contributed, it is significant that the other type of costume noted by Wustmann as common was that of Bedouins. Thus, both Old Shatterhand's America and Kara-ben-Nemsi's Arabia are represented. When Cody's spectacle played in Dresden in 1906, May and his wife attended and were invited backstage. Klara May recorded that, when Karl was introduced to the Indians, he immediately began conversing with them in their Native tongues. According to Feest, "After a time, the American image-maker, Cody, interrupted the conversation: 'You are an idealist, my dear,' he said, patting his German rival's back, 'the only valid law is that of the strong and clever!' To Klara it seemed as if the facial expression of the Indian suddenly changed— 'and hate seemed to flash in his beautiful dark eye.'"[78] It is, of course, an exercise in mythmaking: May spoke no Native language.

Interactions such as this continued. Sarrasani chose to build his circus in Dresden. In 1928, at the height of Sarrasani's popularity, the Karl May Museum opened at Villa Shatterhand. Sarrasani visited May's widow, Klara, to pay his respects, and "his Indians" "consecrate[d] their death songs" to May and laid flowers on his grave.[79]

Beyond ethnostalgic identification of a glorious Teutonic past with a fast-receding, noble Native American present, there is concrete reason why Europe, in particular Germany and Karl May, should seize upon the image of American indigenes. It is related to the impulse that caused May to make Winnetou an Apache in contradistinction to Ferry's elevation of the Comanche. In "The Germans and the Red Man," Alfred Vagts writes, "The German reader single[d] out the Indian as the one exotic race with which he was and still seems ready to sympathize, and even to identify himself. That the Germans should have this special relationship, stronger than the French or the English, is traceable, most likely, to the fact that Germany was a latecomer to colonialism, and never encountered the Indian as opposing colonization; that her contact with the Red Man was 'only literature.'"[80] In the colonial enterprise, there is, as Jonathan Boyarin points out, "the tendency, in the respective imperial contexts of America and Europe, to valorize the other empire's vanquished Other."[81] Thus, just as the English promoted the Black Legend of Spanish atrocities in the New World, Germans grabbed the image of the dying Indian, victim of the English, Dutch, French, and Americans, with both hands.

It would be a mistake, however, to assume that May affected the image of the Indian only on the European side of the Red Atlantic. In the late 1890s, Marion Ames Taggart published her unauthorized and heavily edited translations in the United States with Benzinger Brothers, a Catholic publishing house specializing in theological and religious books. *Winnetou I* was pirated as *Winnetou: The Apache Knight. The Treasure of Nugget Mountain* was a drastic reediting of *Winnetou II* and *Winnetou III*. For some unknown reason, Taggart changed the white hero's name from Karl to Jack Hildreth, probably to erase the tracks of his European origin, thus emphasizing his Americanness.[82] Coming on the heels of the closure of the frontier, the books became unexpectedly and improbably popular. It is a simulation of a simulacrum. The completely spurious German depiction of Indians influenced how Americans thought of their own indigenes. Central to this phenomenon, as it was to May's popularity in Germany, was May's embrace of the myth of the vanishing Indian.

At the beginning of *Winnetou I*, May writes:

> The Indian Race is dying. The White Man came with sweet words on his lips but had a sharp knife in his belt and a loaded rifle in his hand. The dying Indian could not be integrated into the White world. Was that reason enough to kill him? Could he not have been saved? I came to know the Indians over the course of a number of years, and one of them still lives brightly and magnificently in my heart. He, the best and most loyal and devoted of all my friends, was a true representative of his race. I loved him as I have loved no other. I would gladly have given my life to protect his, as he risked it countless times to preserve mine. This was not to be. He died to save his comrades, but it is only his body that died, for he will survive in these pages, as he lives in my soul. Winnetou, the great chief of the Apaches.[83]

May, the pacifist crypto-colonialist, thus gets to have it both ways. He can express sentimental regret at the passing of the noble savage, perpetrated by another imperialist power, while being assured that Natives are kept safely in the stasis box of the past. Nothing more is required of him, nor does he require any more from his readers. Winnetou—this "true representative of his race"—may live, but it is a noncorporeal existence in the dead letters of the printed page, his "life" carefully circumscribed by the non-Native voice of the narrator. The same holds true of his American readers, whether through the bowdlerized texts of Marion Ames Taggart or otherwise. While they cannot rest comfortably in the distance of deniability that the crime of Indian extinction was committed by others, they are still reassured that Indians are of the past and that their vanishing was the inevitable result of contact with Western civilization into which they could not be integrated.

May's frontier may be a place where "civilization" confronts innocence, but even as he writes, the outcome of the contest has been decided. It is a foregone conclusion as the engine of Progress moves inexorably on. Even his noble savages, in their more prescient mode, recognize it. Frayling writes, "The more 'cultured' Indians in the 'Winnetou' stories (the chosen ones) are aware that the Twilight of the Gods is approaching, that they are 'The Last of the Tribe.' Intschu-tschuna, for example, is resigned to the fact that 'we cannot stop the white men from coming here and stealing land. First the scouts and the pioneers. Then, if we resist, the army. It is our destiny.' . . . In May's vision, the myth of the noble savage has less to do with 'back to human nature' than 'forward to European culture' (or, to put it another way, 'away from both primitive and Yankee cultures'). But the noble savage is doomed (and knows it), and there is nothing the Siegfried of the Sagebrush can do about it."[84] Writing in 1876, May describes

the site of that desperate fight in which the Indian lets fly his last arrow against the exponent of a bloodthirsty and reckless "civilization." . . . At the beginning of the 19th century the "Redskin" was still master of the vast plains. . . . But then came the "Paleface," the White man drove the "Red brother" from his own hunting grounds and through disease, "firewater" and shotguns dealt out death and destruction in the ranks of the strong and trusting sons of the wilderness. . . . What and how the Indian was not supposed to be, that and so he did become through his Christian brother who carried the scripture of love on his lips and the murderous weapon in his fist, depriving mankind and universal history of inestimable potential for development . . . but traditions will weave their golden gleam around the vanished warrior of the savanna, and the memory of the mortal sin committed against the brother will continue to live in the song of the poet.[85]

Winnetou IV begins with a summons of Old Shatterhand (now truly old) to Mount Winnetou, a mountain in the Rockies named for "the most famous chief of all red nations." The reason is that, as in Michael de Carvajal's drama, "a league of old chiefs and a league of young chiefs have been called to Mount Winnetou to bring the palefaces to trial and to decide on the future of the Red Man." There is talk of a "great, last battle" that would rival anything envisioned by Tecumseh or Joseph Brant—an indigenous Ragnarök—and Shatterhand/May must intervene to prevent it. The novel ends with a kind of apology to American Indians.

May is safely back at Villa Shatterhand. It is Easter Sunday, March 27, 1910, and May has just completed his manuscript. Klara brings him a newspaper from four days earlier. In the paper is an announcement that Lewis Rodman Wanamaker, the Philadelphia department store magnate, and Joseph Kossuth Dixon plan to build a monument to the American Indian to rival the Statue of Liberty in size, on Staten Island overlooking New York Harbor. The proposal was a real one historically, though it never eventuated. May explains, "It is to symbolize the debt incurred by the country against the dying race of the 'first Americans' and to demonstrate the beautiful characteristics of the red race to future generations. The Indian is depicted with outstretched arms, the way he welcomed the first white men that stepped onto American shores." He concludes by writing, "I ask: isn't this interesting?"

At the end of *Winnetou III*, Winnetou is killed. Before he dies, however, he embraces that final symbol of Western civilization, the religion of the conquerors, Christianity. His last words are, "I believe in the saviour. Winnetou is a Christian. Fare well!" Then having heard the strains of the "Ave Maria," he crosses over to life eternal.

Once the noble savage is gone, his story is complete, and the conquest can proceed unimpeded. As Jonathan Boyarin concludes, "Once again the compatibility of the elegiac mode with the smooth history of genocide is reconfirmed."[86] One might feel regret at the Indian's passing, but, if it is the work of ineluctable forces, one need not feel any guilt.

6

—ᴧᴠᴧ—

The Closing of the Red Atlantic
A Conclusion

PERHAPS NO INDIGENOUS PEOPLE was more closely tied to the Red Atlantic than the Inuit, a circumpolar group often lumped together with the Yupik and Iñupiat of Alaska under the collective name "Eskimo." Today they stretch from Denmark to Greenland, to Canada, and on to Alaska and Siberia. Writing in 1875, Danish explorer Hinrich Rink, who spent two decades living and working among the Inuit of Greenland and Labrador, stated, "With the exception of a few small and scattered tribes who may be considered as the only link between the coast people and the inlanders, the Eskimo always have their habitations close to the sea, or on the banks of rivers in the immediate vicinity of their outlets to the sea. Even on their hunting and trading expeditions they seldom withdraw more than twenty, and only in very rare cases more than eighty miles, from the sea-shore."[1] Their traditional sources of subsistence and economy came from the sea. As we saw in the introduction, with Peter Pitchlynn's Choctaw origin story and those of the Cherokee, the Inuit creation myths similarly involve the ocean.

It is often said that the Inuit have no creation myths. Such a view is both erroneous and narrow-minded. In her article "Native American Creation Stories," literary scholar Laura Adams Weaver points out that creation cycles involve three separate but related parts: the creation of the physical world, the creation of the people, and the creation of the culture. In the article, she discusses one of the most widespread and important Inuit creation stories, that of Sedna (She Down There), based on accounts recorded by anthropologist Franz Boas on Baffin Island in 1884 and by Knud Rasmussen in the mid-1920s. As Weaver relates it:

As it was told, an older widower lived with his beautiful daughter Sedna. Although the young woman had many Inuit suitors, she refused to marry any of them because she had been beguiled by the sweet song of a seagull. Despite her father's protests, she agreed to marry the bird-man and return with him to the land of his people. Contrary to her new husband's promises of luxury and beauty, Sedna found his domain repugnant. Their home was a crude tent made of fish-skins that did little to keep the elements out. Her sleeping mat was uncomfortable walrus hide. Instead of delicious meat, she was forced to eat raw fish that the birds brought her. In desperation, she cried out for her father to come get her.

When spring came, the old man went to visit his daughter. Seeing the miserable state of her existence, he determined to rescue her and have revenge upon her husband. When the seagull returned home, the father killed him and fled in his kayak with Sedna. The other gulls, however, pursued the pair and, once they spotted the boat, caused a violent storm to break out on the ocean. Panicking, the old man threw his own daughter overboard in order to save himself, but Sedna clung to the edge of the craft.

The crazed man then took his *ulu* and sliced off Sedna's fingertips. These fell into the water and became whales. Still the woman hung on to the boat. Still the storm raged. Terror-stricken, the father tried again to dislodge his now dreadful cargo, cutting off her fingers down to the first joint and then to the second. They fell into the sea and became seals and walruses.[2]

Sedna fell beneath the waves and drowned. The storm subsided, and the father survived. In her death, Sedna was deified. She became the Mistress of the Sea, responsible for her children, the marine mammals who sprang from her body. If the Inuit anger her, she will withhold the sacrifice of her children, and the Inuit will starve. A prime responsibility of Inuit shamans is to travel to the bottom of the ocean and comb Sedna's hair—because she has no hands—and keep her from becoming displeased.[3]

The first reports of the Inuit date to circa 985 C.E., when the Vikings found evidence of abandoned Dorset culture habitation in southern Greenland. They were first encountered probably at the turn of the eleventh century. By the fourteenth century, the Norse were engaged in sporadic military conflict with them that continued for over a century. Inuit captives were probably taken to Norway (then part of Denmark) around 1420.[4] Martin Frobisher brought a man from Baffin Island to England in October 1576. Though he died about two weeks later, the anonymous Inuit caused a sensation sufficient to entice Frobisher to kidnap three more Baffin Islanders the following year.[5] Official "state colonialism" by Denmark began in Greenland in 1721. The "first large shipments" of Greenlander Inuit began arriving in Denmark in the 1930s after the close of the Red Atlantic. Today, perhaps as much as 10 percent of the Greenlandic population live there, where through the assimilative power of colonial language they have been magically transformed (along with their kin still in Greenland) into "Northern Danes."[6] The point is that throughout the period of the Red Atlantic, there was regular interaction and interchange between the Inuit and Denmark. No one personifies this more than Knud Rasmussen, the "Danish Eskimo."[7]

A White Man Who Was Also an Inuit

Knud Rasmussen was born on June 7, 1879, in Jakobshavn, a Danish settlement on the west coast of Greenland (today known as Ilulissat). He was the son of a Danish missionary father, Christian, and Sophie Louise Fleischer, his mixed-blood Inuit mother. Noted Danish anthropologist Kaj Birket-Smith sought to downplay Rasmussen's Inuit heritage, writing that the "drop of native blood in his veins" no doubt "strengthened his feeling of kinship with the Eskimos and even to some extent left its traces in his appearance, although . . . his features were more like those of an American Indian than of an Eskimo."[8] Such a bigoted statement reflects the casual racism Danes held in past times toward Inuit. In 1923, Birket-Smith contended that they were incapable of abstract thought, even displaying the temerity to cite Rasmussen for the proposition. Birket-Smith relates how the explorer asked a Canadian Inuit which of two paths to a particular destination was the shorter: "Although the man knew the two paths very well and could say how long it took to travel each of them, he could not hold them both in his mind at once."[9]

In fact, the "drop" of Inuit blood was one-eighth, and like the Inca Garcilaso de la Vega and Peter Jones—and countless other crossblood indigenes—Rasmussen's early upbringing and education was left almost entirely to his mother. He spoke Greenlandic Inuit before he spoke Danish. He grew up playing with Greenlanders and learning dogsledding and other Inuit life skills. The films I reviewed of Rasmussen's Fifth Thule Expedition (1921–24) at the National Museum of Denmark reveal a strikingly handsome, genial man who was completely at ease with the Inuits with whom he interacted—something that does not come through in still photographs.[10] The account of his close friend and longtime partner Peter Freuchen, *I Sailed with Rasmussen*, confirms that view. So does French anthropologist and Inuit expert Jean Malaurie in his magnum opus, *The Last Kings of Thule*. He was comfortable with them, not only because he spoke their language fluently but because he was one of them. In his account of the expedition, *Across Arctic America* (published in the United States in 1927, the year the Red Atlantic closed), Rasmussen himself recounts his meeting with the Canadian Inuit leader Igjugarjuk, who declared that he was "the first white man he had ever seen who was also an Eskimo."[11]

Not that Rasmussen's lifelong friend Freuchen, who was married to an Inuit wife, was immune to succumbing to stereotypes concerning the Arctic indigenes. According to Freuchen, the Inuit are either totally impassive or excitable, depending on the situation. Perhaps giving in to Birket-Smith's assessment, he describes them as bad at math, a condition from which he says his friend suffered. Testimonials from various Inuits as to Rasmussen's affinity with them abound in Malaurie and Freuchen. Perhaps the greatest testament comes from Inuit filmmaker Zacharias Kunuk in his 2006 feature *The Journals of Knud Rasmussen* (directed with Norman Cohn), in which he depicts the explorer as an Inuit.

When he reached sufficient age, Knud's Inuit childhood was interrupted. Christian Rasmussen asserted himself and took his son to Denmark to complete his formal, Western education. Freuchen writes that "when Knud actually saw the mountains [of Greenland] disappear and the icebergs in the ocean become fewer and fewer, he experienced his first real loneliness."[12] The father wished his boy to attend his alma mater, the prestigious Herlufsholm School, founded in 1565 for boys "of noble and honest heritage." But Knud failed the entrance examination—because of his innate difficulty with mathematics, according to Freuchen.[13] An alternative school had to be found.

After his schooling was complete, the younger Rasmussen toyed with becoming an actor or an opera singer but finally wound up a journalist. Freuchen writes, "Naturally Greenland lay behind this resolve; he had been born there, after all, and not a day passed without his longing for the land. He wanted to travel in his beloved Greenland and to write about his travels."[14] In this capacity as a reporter, he finagled a trip to Lapland in Sweden to see the Sámi, the indigenous people of Scandinavia. They reminded him of the Inuit, but he found travel by sleigh drawn by reindeer a poor substitute for his native dogsleds.

Since the advent of Danish state colonialism in 1721, Greenland had been a closed land. The only outlanders permitted to travel there were colonial officials and missionaries. It was thought, in a well-meaning but paternalistic fashion, that "it was best for the country and its inhabitants if they were left alone and had as little contact as possible with civilization."[15] In 1902, Rasmussen was invited by his friend and fellow journalist Ludvig Mylius-Erichsen to join a proposed "Danish Literary Expedition" to Greenland, along with physician Alfred Bertelsen and the nobleman painter Count Harald Moltke. Despite the ban on outside travel and the initial opposition of Danish administrators, Rasmussen's status as a Greenlander helped secure approval for the trip. Jörgen Brönlund, a Greenlander Inuit, accompanied the party as interpreter. Though Rasmussen was fluent in the language, he always eschewed acting as an interpreter out of respect for his fellow Inuits.

In Qeqertak, they took time to visit Knud's uncle Carl and aunt Augustine. They also visited his other uncle, Jens Fleischer, renowned as the best dog driver in North Greenland. According to Freuchen, "Whenever the expedition arrived at a settlement, big or small, the inhabitants came rushing out and greeted Knud with loud cries, quite forgetting that there were others in the party."[16] In Upernavik, they met with the Danish governor of Greenland. Making Upernavik the expedition's headquarters, "Knud turned the whole colony upside down. A series of parties and celebrations, the likes of which had never been seen, were arranged, culminating in a carnival."[17] This hero's welcome for a favorite son aside, the expedition was plagued with difficulties. The dogs got sick. Moltke did, as well, and nearly died. They ran short of fodder for the dogs. They made it back, however, and Rasmussen learned from the travails. In this return to Greenland, he also discovered his life's calling.

Returning to Denmark in 1904, Rasmussen became a popular figure on the lecture circuit. In 1908, he published *The People of the Polar North*, a narrative of the expedition, combined with Inuit ethnography.

In 1910, Rasmussen and Peter Freuchen established the Thule Trading

Station at Uummanaq, an Inuit village at Cape York on the west coast of Greenland: "Rasmussen renamed [it] Thule—or Toollay, as the Eskimos say when, as rarely happens, they call it by this alien name. *Uummanaq* means seal's heart; a small mountain stands out in front of the village, and its tabular mesa gives it the shape of a seal's heart."[18] Rasmussen chose Thule as a name because the village was the northernmost inhabited part of the world, and he wanted to evoke Ultima Thule, in ancient European geographical mythology that place in the far north that was beyond the boundaries of the known world.

The trading station was a means for Rasmussen and Freuchen to support themselves, but the real purpose was scientific. Rasmussen wanted to continue ethnographic work with the Inuit. Yet there was still another motive. At the time, Danish sovereignty extended only to the area of Greenland south of Melville Bay. Cape York was on the northern edge of the bay, and Rasmussen wanted to establish a claim for Denmark over the rest of the island. There was cause for concern and a need for urgency: word had reached Denmark that famed Norwegian Arctic explorer Otto Sverdrup (who had crossed Greenland with Fridtjof Nansen in 1888) was planning a similar enterprise in the region. Many years later, in 1931, Norwegian hunters occupied an area of the northeastern Greenland coast. Denmark filed a complaint against Norway with the International Court of Justice in The Hague. Late in his life, Rasmussen testified in the case. Largely through his and Freuchen's work, Danish sovereignty over the totality of Greenland was recognized.[19]

The enterprise almost ended before it began. Just short of their destination, the intrepid pair ran into a terrific gale, tossing their ship against an iceberg, first cracking its rudder and then splintering its propeller. The ship was in danger of foundering. Luckily, the wind shifted and blew them "into a snug little harbor, North Star Bay, which served the Eskimo settlement" of Uummanaq. The Inuits had powerlessly watched as the storm threatened to sink the ship. Now, they rushed to the beach to meet the sailors. According to Freuchen, they exclaimed, "If we had known Knud Rasmussen was on board, we would have realized he would make harbor." A beaming Knud told his friend that an Inuit named Samik "had gone to fetch some rotten meat which was two years old—a feast to mark our coming."[20] This was hardly a welcome for the purely European outsider to whom Birket-Smith would lay claim. During a later trek, Rasmussen himself would describe his fellow Inuit "leaping and capering round me in an outburst of unrestrained natural feeling," the "old easy merriment" showing forth.[21] Neither are these the stereotyped Inuit often described by Freuchen.

During World War I, Thule was more or less cut off from Europe. When the war ended, Freuchen took his Inuit wife, Navarana, to Denmark. Her first reactions to the colonial metropole are instructive about the response of many indigenes traveling across the Red Atlantic to European metropoles. Freuchen writes:

> Navarana, like all Eskimos visiting civilization for the first time, was disappointed. White men are apt to exaggerate the commonplaces of their homeland.
>
> "Oh, I thought the houses were bigger," she said. "They are not much higher than an iceberg."
>
> Only two things impressed her: first, it was winter and the sun was shining; second, she noticed a team of horses eating from their nose bags while being driven about—Navarana considered this device certain proof of white men's intelligence.[22]

On the couple's second day in Copenhagen, they enjoyed an audience with King Christian X. Because Navarana did not speak Danish, Freuchen acted as interpreter. The monarch graciously asked the Inuit what she thought of his country. Her reply: "Is that man really the King we have heard so much about? How can he think for everybody in Denmark if he is stupid to suppose I have any opinions about this magnificent land after only one day's stay?" When Christian inquired as to her response, Freuchen translated "freely": "Your Majesty, she thinks it is wonderful and grand." A smiling and contented sovereign replied, "I thought so!"[23] In fact, Christian, who would so inspire a dispirited nation during the Nazi occupation of World War II, is presented in Freuchen's memoir as a bit of a self-absorbed fool. During a 1921 visit to Greenland—the first by a Danish monarch—he promised to give everyone coffee. The excited Inuits expected the drink of the king to be "extraordinary": "When the drink turned out to be merely plain coffee, the natives were sullen with disappointment."[24]

From their Thule base, Rasmussen and Freuchen launched five ethnographic expeditions among the Inuit, beginning in 1912. By far the most famous and most ambitious was the Fifth Thule Expedition between 1921 and 1924. The expedition investigated the Inuit around Hudson's

Bay in Canada. Then Rasmussen left Freuchen and three others from his party and, with two Inuit companions, traveled by dogsled across Canada to Nome, Alaska. Though he planned to complete the journey by going on to Siberia—and thus traversing the entirety of the Inuit world—the Soviet Union denied him a visa.

Peter Freuchen writes that his colleague's methods were different from those of prior ethnographers: "He first made friends with a people, and got to know their good and bad points before he made judgments about them, and he never acted in a superior or unapproachable manner. He became one of them and was able to break through their shell of custom and get to the real worth that lay behind."[25] Freuchen, however, writing as a white Dane, misses the point: Rasmussen did not *become* an Inuit; he already *was* one of them.

Still, Freuchen admits that Rasmussen made "mistakes." In the end, he was a Christian and viewed Inuit religious traditions through that prism. Writing to a white audience, he refers to the Inuit spirituality as an "old heathen faith." Referring to a shaman's tools, he states, "These charms, quaint or meaningless as they may seem, are used by the Eskimos in all sincerity and pious faith, as prayers humbly addressed to the mighty powers of Nature."[26] Freuchen describes a contest his friend undertook during the Fifth Thule Expedition with a shaman who did not want to part with his collection of "amulets and artifacts" that Rasmussen desired for the National Museum of Denmark:

> "I intend to make water burn," said Knud, who poured some white gas on the floor and applied a lighted match so that a big flame roared up. The man was paralyzed with fright.
>
> "And now I'm going to replace air with fire!" cried Knud, and exploded some photography phosphate powder in a big flash.
>
> Then the man gave up.
>
> "No! No!" cried Knud. "I'm not finished!" He grabbed the man by the hand and ran around the house three times with him. The poor man lost his breath with it all.
>
> "And now I propose to let the roof fly off the house if you still think your spirits are the stronger!"
>
> "Oh, no, no, no!" cried the man. "Rest your powers, and let us remain in here where it is warm. My amulets are poor things and worthless beside yours!" And he then gave up his raven's claw, useful for

finding game even in the middle of winter; his stick of wood, which rendered one insensible to pain; his fox tooth, which made one cunning and ingenious; and all the other magical objects that he owned.[27]

Freuchen makes no comment on the incident. What seemed to the old holy man supernatural was nothing more than a couple of cheap parlor tricks, beneath Rasmussen's otherwise largely remarkable and sympathetic career. Today, the shaman's objects reside in the National Museum in Copenhagen.[28]

Despite these significant shortcomings, Freuchen concludes that "few people have ever judged others so fairly, and I have never known a man who could forget others' faults so quickly and completely and find compensating good points."[29] That assessment was particularly true of his relationship with his mother's people.

Deskaheh's mission to Geneva and Rasmussen's Fifth Thule Expedition were the last major events of the Red Atlantic. Rasmussen produced a ten-volume collection of his findings from the fifth expedition. These were edited into a single book, *Across Arctic America*, published in the United States in 1927, the year that Lindbergh's flight announced the end of the Red Atlantic.

Closure

When I lived in New Haven, Connecticut, I occupied a house in a neighborhood called Beaver Hill, the most significant geographic feature of which was Beaver Pond. The area had been developed in the first decades of the twentieth century, at a time coinciding with the reintroduction of beavers to the state by the Board of Fisheries and Game. The animal had been hunted and trapped into extinction in Connecticut more than 50 years earlier, a process that began over 300 years before that.[30]

In the introduction, I asked you to imagine, in your mind's eye, a prosperous Dutch merchant, sipping chocolate and smoking tobacco, his pockets bulging with wealth gathered from the slave trade. I now ask you to picture a delegation of Native American warriors walking the streets of London. They are the object of intense curiosity. Newspapers carry accounts of their movements day-by-day. People in crowds crane their necks to catch a glimpse of the exotic visitors. Men in beaver felt hats strain to see them above the heads of others. If you have joined me this far in this journey across the Red Atlantic, you know that the scene is not simply hypothetical. Often these indigenous travelers—from Tomochichi to Peter Freuchen's wife, Navarana—were left cold and unimpressed by what they saw in the colonial metropoles. Others like Ourehouaré were beguiled by the experience.

The story of the Red Atlantic, however, like that of the black Atlantic, is about more than the movement of human bodies around and across the Atlantic (though that has been a principal focus of this book). A large part of those histories is also economic. The wealth of the Americas—from timber to gold—saved a resource-depleted Europe and fueled its development for centuries. The Americas' fecundity caused European tables to sag with corn, potatoes, lobsters, and turkeys. Native ingenuity gave Europeans material culture and technologies, including the canoe, the kayak, terrace farming, and rubber processing. Indians enriched both European coffers and their languages. The world after the inauguration of the Red Atlantic, when Vikings kidnapped the Beothuk boys Vimar and Valthof, was forever and majorly different from what it was the moment before. That was true for both colonizer and colonized.

Red and black Atlantics are narratives of its subjects grappling with modernity. For this reason, the Red Atlantic spans a wider period of time than that normally accorded the black Atlantic, as indigenes encountered, contended with, and struggled for a place in modernity and the Western world—from the Beothuk to Deskaheh—much longer than Africans and their descendants did. Much of this involved becoming integrated into modern economic systems. This occurred through plunder, slavery, and trade and through participation in the wage economy via maritime labor. In North America, in the early instances, such involvement meant (most often) participation in the fur trade—which brings us back to beavers.

As we saw in the introduction and in chapter 1, the first North American resources exploited by Europeans were timber and fish. By 1578, there were at least 350 fishing vessels exploiting the Grand Banks fishery off Newfoundland. Drawing the Natives of that island and Labrador into their economy, the sailors from those ships traded European implements with the Indians in exchange for fur pelts. Within a few years, the soft hairs of the underbellies of American beaver furs were becoming a mainstay of French hatters for making felt.

As part of the University of Minnesota's Bell Library's Expansion of

Europe seminar, Ken Mitchell writes, "A taciturn and sedentary animal of the woodlands, the beaver may have seemed an unlikely actor in the development of trade in the early modern world. But as Europeans ventured across the Atlantic to North America in increasing numbers, this industrious rodent became an integral part of Europe's economic and geographic expansion into the northern reaches of the New World of the seventeenth century."[31] Europeans had been using beaver furs for centuries, but by the time of the European colonization of North America, the beaver in Europe was largely played out. This new resource from the other side of the Atlantic was thus a godsend. Initially, it was the French and the Dutch who exploited this trade. As fish had in the earliest instance, the fur trade drew Europeans to North America and determined patterns of settlement and trade. Within the first three decades of the seventeenth century, the English colonies of Virginia and Plymouth were exporting beaver pelts to England.

The industry also continued to draw Indians into the economy with Europeans as they became more and more dependent upon bartering beaver skins for the trade goods upon which they increasingly relied. There was, of course, a built-in profit for Europeans in this process: Indians would trade, for instance, one beaver pelt for one metal ax head, while that same pelt would fetch a price in England sufficient to buy a dozen such implements.

The beaver trade imbricated tribal nations far beyond the Fall with European economies. Dislocations caused by European invasion and the fur trade deeply affected the Ojibway around the Great Lakes. In an effort to come to terms with these new circumstances—as well as with epizootics (epidemics in animal populations) among beavers—the Anishinaabe developed a mythology in which human beings and beavers were engaged in spiritual warfare with one another. The muskets, shot, powder, and iron traps the Indians received in trade from Europeans tipped the balance in this supernatural war in the Natives' favor. The large-scale killing of fur-bearing animals resulted. Beaver populations all over upper North America—as in Connecticut—plummeted.[32]

What the beaver was in the north, the deer was in the south. As beaver populations—and hence the beaver fur trade—dwindled, their place in the exchange economy between Europeans and Indians was taken over by the deerskin trade. Tanned deerskins were employed in Europe for gloves, bookbindings, even leather hats. Deer were so abundant that

Europeans could only marvel. In 1682, Thomas Ashe declared, "There is such infinite Herds, that the whole Country seems but one continued Park."[33] Ashe was writing about the Carolinas. Though Virginia and other English colonies participated in the trade (as did the Spanish in Florida and also the French), it was South Carolina that was the largest exploiter, and Charles Town was the epicenter of the deerskin trade. Carolina traders bartered with the Cherokee and Creek—deerskins for European trade goods—pulling them into the European economy and forging alliances with both tribal nations. Between 1699 and 1715, annual exportation of hides to England from Charleston averaged 54,000. During the height of the deerskin trade, between 1739 and 1761, it is estimated the Cherokee alone killed 500,000 to 1,250,000 animals. During the same period, Charleston witnessed the shipment of 5,239,250 pounds of hides to England. According to historian Verner Crane, the single largest year ran from Christmas 1706 until Christmas 1707 when 121,355 hides were shipped. As late as 1730, the deerskin trade accounted for approximately 30 percent of South Carolina's economy.[34] Though the trade would continue into the 1770s, by the end of the French and Indian War in 1763, the "infinite Herds" witnessed by Ashe were a thing of the past.[35]

Integration into the world economy through the Red Atlantic represented a radical upheaval for indigenous cultures. In addition to furs and hides, the other "singular branch of the business" was the "traffic in Indian slaves." Through the slave trade, some were forcibly integrated into that economy as commodities, while other opportunistic groups, like the Westos, willingly participated, capturing their fellow Natives in Georgia, Florida, and the Carolinas and exchanging them for European manufactures. In 1702, Pierre Le Moyne d'Iberville stated that, in the prior decade, the Chickasaw had captured 500 Choctaws as slaves at the behest of the English, killing three times that number in the process. According to Crane, "The Frenchman was addressing an Indian council, when rhetoric was in order, but the proportion of captives to casualties in these wasting contests was probably typical. By such attrition the slave-trade . . . wore down the barriers to English advance."[36]

Historian Alan Gallay, the leading scholar of the Native slave trade, writes, "Indian slavery was not peripheral in the history of Native America, but central to the story."[37] Brett Rushforth, in *Bonds of Alliance: Indigenous and Atlantic Slaveries in New France*, states that the French and their Indian allies, centered on the St. Lawrence, enslaved thousands of Natives, "keeping them in the towns and villages of New France or shipping them to the French Caribbean." Of course, as the experience of Ourehouaré and many other Iroquois attests, still others were transported to the French metropole as galley slaves. (Louis XIV commanded officials in New France, "I will that you do everything in your power to make a great number of them prisoners of war and have them embarked by every opportunity that will offer, in order that they be conveyed to France.")[38] Spain enslaved thousands in the Caribbean and shipped them to Europe and enslaved more thousands in Florida and Latin America. Thousands also passed through Willemstad in the Netherlands Antilles. Still thousands upon thousands more were enslaved by the Spanish and worked to death in situ in the mines and on encomiendas. In the British American colonies, Gallay estimates that as many as 51,000 southern Indian slaves were captured by the English, or by other Natives for sale to the English, and enslaved before 1715.[39] In the Carolinas, exportation of these Indian slaves "was favored both on grounds of public policy and self-interest."[40] If kept in North America, they simply used every opportunity to escape into the forest, and their presence in any significant numbers in settlements raised the specter of Indian uprisings. The economic impact of all this Indian slavery was a vital component of the Red Atlantic. As Gallay points out, "Slave-produced goods from the Americas took up most of the cargo space on the transit to Europe."[41] In the south, Indian slaves were shipped chiefly out of Charleston. South Carolina became the quintessential Atlantic colony, participating not only in the deerskin trade and Indian slave transshipment but also in the Triangle Trade in enslaved Africans.

These complex economic relations inevitably led to conflict. Beginning in 1702 and continuing until 1713, troops from Carolina joined with Creeks and Yamasees in slave raids into Spanish Florida. Most of the survivors were shipped to the British Caribbean.[42] Beyond trafficking in human beings, competition for the resources of the Red Atlantic—between European colonial powers, between Europeans and Natives, and among Indian tribes themselves—led to friction and warfare. In New England, the Wampanoag, Narragansett, and Mohegan jostled with the Pequot for dominance in the fur trade. For their part, the English wanted to break Pequot domination over wampum production. The ensuing Pequot War in 1637 shattered the Pequot. Hundreds of their survivors were sold into slavery in Bermuda and the West Indies. By 1715, the Yamasee,

previously stalwart allies of British colonists, found it increasingly difficult to provide them with the two commodities they most sought—deerskins and Indian captives. The resulting Yamasee War and its aftermath
had the same consequences for them as the 1637 conflict had for the
Pequot. After King William's War (1688–97), the beaver fur trade fell off
while the deerskin trade soared. The rivalry between Britain and France
for control of trade west of the Allegheny Mountains (the Appalachians)
was a root cause of the French and Indian War (1754–63).

In this study, time and again we have seen links between the black
and Red Atlantics, whether in the persons of figures like Crispus Attucks
and the two Paul Cuffes, or in Bartolomé de Las Casas's advocating of
African slavery in the New World to protect his indigenous lambs, or in
Edgar Allan Poe's bizarre paranoid fantasy, *The Narrative of Arthur Gordon Pym of Nantucket*. Perhaps one of the strangest connections is Olaudah Equiano, an icon of the black Atlantic, who nonetheless merits, like
Attucks, only a single reference in Paul Gilroy's *The Black Atlantic*. Like
Ayuba Suleiman Diallo, Equiano was a black African who was kidnapped
and sold into slavery around 1753, when he was about nine years old. He
was an Ibo from Nigeria. After changing hands a number of times, he
was purchased by Robert King, a Philadelphia merchant who conducted
trade in the Caribbean. King promised Equiano that he could purchase
his freedom for forty pounds, which the African did in 1766. In 1772, after
British Lord Chief Justice William Mansfield ruled that slaves in Great
Britain were to be considered free persons, Equiano went to England,
where he would become an activist in the abolitionist cause. In 1792, he
published his autobiography. It became the prototype for future slave
narratives and was used by abolitionists in the push that eventually led
to the British abolition of the slave trade in 1807.

During his captivity, Equiano converted to Christianity. While in England, he encountered a group of Miskito Indians, who "were brought
here by some English traders for some selfish ends." Although the Natives had been baptized while across the Red Atlantic, Equiano discovered that they had not been taken to church, "nor was any attention
paid to their morals." Appalled by this "mock Christianity," Equiano took
the indigenes, especially a teenager christened George, under his wing
and schooled them in the Christian religion.[43] Were this all there was to
his story, Equiano would be minor footnote in the linkages of Red and
black Atlantics. Like, however, Ourehouaré and Ayuba Suleiman Diallo,

Olaudah Equiano, abolitionist cause célèbre, is an illustration of the dark side of Atlantic world history.

In 1775, Equiano linked up with Dr. Charles Irving in the latter's effort to establish a plantation colony on the Miskito Coast. The ex-slave's role in the enterprise was to purchase African slaves to work the plantation. As if that were not ironical enough, he purchased his own countrymen—Ibos—presumably because of the linguistic ease he felt in communicating with them. The ship on which Equiano and Irving sailed carried the Miskitos back to their homeland from England at government expense. Upon reaching Central America, Equiano "admonished" the Indians, and Dr. Irving gave them "a few cases of liquor." The Natives debarked, were met by a Miskito "king," and were never seen again.[44]

In the establishment of the plantation colony, Equiano acted as Irving's overseer and managed contacts with the local Indians, thus forging more links between Red and black Atlantics. The indigenes would come to Irving for cures and brought "a good deal of silver in exchange" for European trade articles. From them, Irving and Equiano received "turtle oil, and shells, little silk grass, and some provisions." Despite the presence of enslaved Africans, Equiano comments, "They [the Indians] would not work at any thing for us, except fishing; and a few times they assisted to cut some trees down, in order to build us houses."[45] He then proceeds, like any European, to make a few cultural observations about the Natives, in his case comparing them to Africans.

As I have noted on a number of occasions (most fully in chapter 5), literature is a defining element of the Red Atlantic. Writing was a key import from Europe.[46] Within a few years of the conquest of Mexico, Nahuas (Aztecs) wrote their own accounts of their own fall, attempting to come to terms with why this tragedy had befallen them.[47] Though in large measure thwarted by Spanish censors who broke his history of Peru in two, Garcilaso nonetheless told the story of his people. Possibly influenced by his father's experience at the hands of Wilson Armistead, Paul Cuffe Jr. insisted on representing himself in print. Knud Rasmussen produced an extensive and sophisticated ethnography of his mother's people. Contemporary Native writers like Gerald Vizenor and Louise Erdrich continue to reflect on the events of the Red Atlantic and their continued impact today.

It is, however the writings of the Other—in this case, *non-Natives*—that most embody the literature of the Red Atlantic. First Europeans and then the settler colonists of the Americas defined themselves by comparing and contrasting themselves with Western Hemisphere indigenes. In *The Transatlantic Indian*, Kate Flint quotes British historian Linda Colley from her landmark *Britons: Forging the Nation, 1707–1837* that the British "came to define themselves as a single people not because of any political or cultural consensus at home, but rather in reaction to the Other beyond their shores."[48] For Colley, this Other was Catholic continental Europe. Flint expands this notion to interaction and competition with France and Spain in the New World. Yet from the earliest encounters, it was also in opposition to *Indians*. Settler colonists saw themselves as sharing "the courage, the hardiness, the endurance, the nobility, and the *manliness* of the land's original inhabitants."[49] Yet those same settlers also saw themselves as qualitatively different and separate from those same "original inhabitants."

Even so, proximity to those indigenes and "sharing" the American earth with them was working a remarkable alchemy on those who crossed the Red Atlantic from east to west. To be sure, they were quantifiably more "civilized." In 1782, French settler J. Hector St. John de Crèvecoeur, in his highly influential *Letters from an American Farmer*, though he lamented the depredations against and disappearance of Indians, nevertheless spoke of the "improvements" and "superior genius" of the Europeans and of the "new man" being born as colonists tilled the rich soil of North America.[50] In like fashion, in 1797 settler Eliphalet Stark wrote to a relative, "The Yankees have taken care of the wolves, bears and Indians . . . and we'll build the Lord's temple yet, build it out of these great trees."[51] Crèvecoeur's new man—an *American*—would build God's American Israel once the Canaanites were cleared from the land. Then the Americans would be indigenous because there would be no one left to dispute the claim.

In *The Atlantic World*, Thomas Benjamin writes, "For more than three hundred years, Europeans and European-Americans wrote about and lived among native societies that were among the most libertarian and equalitarian in the world. 'Savages' often organized complicated confederations, governed through consensus and highly valued personal autonomy, in contrast to the 'civilized' European manner of monarchical absolutism, religious intolerance, class-based poverty, institutionalized injustice and the hierarchical and economic demands of deference, dependence and servitude."[52] This inevitably had an impact on European philosophy. Not only Montaigne and Voltaire (as we have seen) but also Jean-Jacques Rousseau, John Locke, David Hume, and Thomas Paine were influenced by the figure of the Indian in developing concepts like "the noble savage, the social contract, individual autonomy, religious liberty and natural rights."[53]

John Locke was particularly influenced. Canadian philosopher James Tully writes in *An Approach to Political Philosophy: Locke in Contexts*:

> Locke had extensive knowledge of and interest in European contact with aboriginal peoples. A large number of books in his library are accounts of European exploration, colonization and of aboriginal peoples, especially Amerindians and their ways. As secretary to Lord Shaftesbury, secretary to the Lord Proprietors of Carolina (1668–71), secretary to the Council of Trade and Plantations (1673–4), and member of the Board of Trade (1696–1700), Locke was one of the six or eight men who closely invigilated and helped to shape the old colonial system during the Restoration. He invested in the slavetrading Royal Africa Company (1671) and the Company of Merchant Adventurers to trade with the Bahamas (1672), and he was a Landgrave of the proprietary government of Carolina.[54]

North American indigenes influenced Locke's view of the "state of nature," in which all things are held in common by common consent. Simply because a philosopher was affected by his assumed knowledge of Natives does not mean, however, that he got things right. Anishinaabe philosopher Dennis McPherson has been especially critical of Locke's theories of societal progressive evolution and valorization of private property, with their concomitant and continuing effect on indigenous peoples. He (with his scholarly partner Douglas Rabb) writes:

> Locke was, of course, writing before the theory of evolution and he thought that the Americas were very close to his conception of the state of nature. Though there was . . . agriculture in the Americas prior to contact . . . it was very different from that practiced in Europe with its comparative monoculture, clearing of forest and the widespread plowing of fields. More importantly, vast areas of the Americas were seen by the colonists as completely undeveloped, the Indians' hunting grounds. From a Lockean perspective, these forested lands were unproductive, wasted and certainly could not be the property of the

Indians who hunt in them, any more than fishing the oceans makes the oceans the property of the fishermen.[55]

With a nod to the Red Atlantic, McPherson and Rabb observe that it is not difficult to see why settlers with a "Lockean mindset" would be hostile to Native land claims.[56]

Benjamin Franklin was impressed by the orderly representative democracy of the Haudenosaunee Confederacy: "How different this is from the Conduct of a polite British House of Commons, where scarce a Day passes without some Confusion that makes the Speaker hoarse in calling to order."[57] A small group of scholars still vociferously debate the Iroquois's influence upon the U.S. Constitution, though it seems likely given the circumstances and available evidence that it played some part. More improbably, perhaps, they also influenced the authors of modern Communism, Karl Marx and Friedrich Engels.

Marx in his *Ethnological Notebooks*, notes for a study he did not survive to write, has snippets about a number of different tribal traditions from the Americas: the Anishinaabe, the Shawnee, the Maya, and so on. The most space, however, was given over to early anthropologist Lewis Henry Morgan's study of the Haudenosaunee Confederacy in his book *Ancient Society*. Like Franklin, Marx liked their democratic governance, but he was also attracted to their "primitive" socialism. The notebooks marked Marx's shift from an abstract theory of history to an empirical study of actual human cultures as they existed in history. According to the late leftist historian and artist Franklin Rosemont, Morgan's book "for the first time gave Marx insights into the concrete *possibilities* of a free society *as it had actually existed in history*." Unfortunately, what attracted him most was Morgan's theory of evolution of human society—just as Locke had been lured in 200 years earlier. Again, according to Rosemont, "Morgan's theory of social and cultural evolution enabled him to pursue the problems he had taken up philosophically in 1844 in a new way, from a different angle, and with new revolutionary implications."[58] Though his *Ethnological Notebooks* (actually fragmentary research notes) was not published until the 1970s, approaching a century after the philosopher's death, Engels used the manuscript to write *The Origin of the Family, Private Property and the State*, published in 1884.

The looted wealth of the Americas—their timber, silver, and gold—crossed the Red Atlantic only unidirectionally, flowing to Europe never to return. Technology, material culture, and ideas traveled in both directions. Potatoes, tomatoes, the suspension bridge, and the concepts that fueled the imaginations of European philosophers went from west to east. Christianity, writing, liquor, and firearms ran the other way. Though many indigenes who crossed the Atlantic to Europe never returned home, others managed to do so. Some, like Tisquantum, probably did so multiple times.

As I was researching and writing this book, I met contemporary Luiseño (Payomkowishum) artist James Luna and attended one of his "performative lectures." He introduced me to Pablo Tac, a fellow Luiseño. The Luiseño were so-called Mission Indians, gathered into Spanish Catholic missions in California, in this case San Luis Rey de Francia near present-day San Diego.[59]

Tac was born around 1820 at San Luis Rey. A bright child, he was singled out early on as a likely candidate for the priesthood. In February 1834, Fray Antonio Peyri took Tac and another Luiseño boy, Agapito Amamix, across the Red Atlantic to Spain, arriving in Barcelona on June 21. There he secured admission for both youths to the Collegium Urbanum Propaganda de Fide (College for the Propagation of the Faith) in Rome, in which they enrolled in September of the same year. There they joined three other American Native boys: Patritius Lynch (a Cheraw from South Carolina) and Iacobus McCollion and Guilielmus Monfort, both from Ohio (possibly Shawnees). Both Luiseños proved adept pupils, studying Latin, rhetoric, philosophy, theology, and humanities.

Just as Ayuba Suleiman Diallo helped Sir Hans Sloane organize the British Museum's collection of Arabic manuscripts, Tac worked for Cardinal Giuseppe Mezzofanti, the Vatican's librarian. He wrote a combination of Luiseño grammar and history of the Indians of Alta California. He also produced a Luiseño-Spanish dictionary. The manuscripts were to be tools to aid future missionaries in their proselytizing efforts.

The goal was for Agapito and Pablo to finish their education, be ordained, and return to San Luis Rey as missionaries among their own people. Sadly, the plan never came to fruition. Like so many other indigenous travelers who crossed the Red Atlantic, both youths succumbed to European diseases and died before they could return home, Amamix dying in the fall of 1837 and Tac following him in December 1841.[60]

Hearing Luna tell Tac's story reminded me of another I heard from Frank Brennan, an Australian Jesuit priest and lawyer, two years earlier.

In 1849, Father Rosendo Salvado took two Aborigine boys, Francis Xavier Conaci and John Baptist Dirimera, first to Dublin, then to London, then to Paris, and finally to Italy, where they were to train to be Benedictine monks. When they arrived in Italy, they were presented in an audience to Pope Pius IX.[61] But that is a tale of different oceans and an indigenous story for another day.

NOTES

PREFACE

1. Adolf Augustus Berle, "Introduction," *Berle's Self Culture* (Chicago: Twentieth Century Self Culture Association, 1920), 1:13.

2. United States Hydrologic Office, *American Practical Navigator: An Epitome of Navigation and Nautical Astronomy*, rev. ed. (Washington: Government Printing Office, 1939), 328–91.

3. Unfortunately, I let my father's copy slip from my grasp. As an adult, however, I purchased a replacement copy. The "Ex Libris" plate in the front says it was the property of John H. Beach.

4. Colin Calloway, "Indian History from the End of the Alphabet," *Ethnohistory* 58 (2011): 197–211.

5. Kate Flint, *The Transatlantic Indian, 1776–1930* (Princeton: Princeton University Press, 2009), 25 (emphasis in original).

6. Thomas Benjamin, *The Atlantic World: Europeans, Africans, Indians and Their Shared History, 1400–1900* (Cambridge: Cambridge University Press, 2009), 273. This book, intended it seems as a textbook, contains a list for further reading at the end of each chapter but no footnotes.

7. Walter Goebel and Saskia Schabio, eds., *Beyond the Black Atlantic: Relocating Modernization and Technology* (New York: Routledge, 2006), v–vi.

8. Robert Stam and Ella Shohat, *Race in Translation: Culture Wars around the Postcolonial Atlantic* (New York: New York University Press, 2012, Kindle ed.) (emphasis mine).

9. Jean-Baptiste Duroselle, *L'Europe: Histoire de ses Peuples* (Paris: Perrin, 1990); translated by Richard Mayne as *Europe: A History of Its Peoples* (London: Viking, 1990). Duroselle was my professor of diplomatic history at Paris IV.

10. See, e.g., Jacques Barzun, *From Dawn to Decadence: 500 Years of Western Cultural Life, 1500 to the Present* (New York: HarperCollins, 2000), 862.

11. I have also been privileged to study at both the undergraduate and graduate levels with distinguished historians. In addition to Jean-Baptiste Duroselle, these include Kenneth Jackson, Richard A. Norris Jr., and James Shenton.

INTRODUCTION

1. Alexander VI, *Inter Caetera* (May 4, 1493).

2. David Armitage, "The Red Atlantic," *Reviews in American History* 29, no. 4 (2011): 479.

3. Walter Lippmann, *The New Republic*, Feb. 17, 1917, 60.

4. Qtd. in Bernard Bailyn, *Atlantic History: Concept and Contours* (Cambridge, Mass.: Harvard University Press, 2005), 10.

5. International Seminar on the History of the Atlantic World, 1500–1825, http://www.fas.harvard.edu/~atlantic/index.htm (Feb. 24, 2011; Oct. 1, 2012).

6. Simon Winchester, *Atlantic: Great Sea Battles, Heroic Discoveries, Titanic Storms, and a Vast Ocean of a Million Stories* (New York: HarperCollins, 2010), 448–49.

7. Ibid., 449.

8. W. E. B. Du Bois, *The Souls of Black Folk* (1903; New York: Penguin Books, 1996), 5.

9. Paul Gilroy, *The Black Atlantic: Modernity and Double Consciousness* (Cambridge, Mass.: Harvard University Press, 1993), 126.

10. Qtd. in Ibrahim Sheme, "Leopold Sedar Senghor (1906–2001)," http://allafrica.com/stories/200201040434.html (Jan. 4, 2002; Feb. 3, 2013).

11. Gilroy, 2.

12. Robert Warrior, *The People and the Word: Reading Native Nonfiction* (Minneapolis: University of Minnesota Press, 2005), 181.

13. Armitage, 479.

14. Gilroy, 13.

15. Paul Cohen, "Was There an Amerindian Atlantic? Reflections on the Limits of a Historiographical Concept," *History of European Ideas* 34 (2008): 394.

16. In Leonardo Boff and Virgil Elizondo, eds., *1492–1992: The Voice of the Victims* (London: SCM Press, 1990), 141.

17. Bailyn, 5.

18. Ibid., 12. Hoffman, a professor of history at Fordham University, used the term in a March 1945 essay titled "Europe and the Atlantic Community." He referred to that Atlantic Community as "the mighty geographic, historical and political reality that surrounds us on all sides."

19. Ibid., 83.

20. Qtd. in ibid.

21. Ibid., 83–84.

22. Qtd. in John R. Swanton, *Source Materials for the Social and Ceremonial Life of the Choctaw Indians* (1931; Tuscaloosa: University of Alabama Press, 2001), 30–31.

23. Ibid., 31.

24. Many Natives object to the use of the word "myth" to characterize their sacred stories. This is because, in our contemporary parlance, the word has come to mean a story that is not true, akin to a fairytale. I use it herein, however, in its strictest sense. A "myth" is any story that is foundational to the identity of a people. The United States has many creation myths—the Pilgrims, the American Revolution, the Civil War, Manifest Destiny. All of these actually occurred historically. Yet all have taken on the character of myth.

25. Christopher B. Teuton, "Cherokee Stories of the Turtle Island Liars' Club" (unpublished manuscript, 2011), 71. The book has since been published (Chapel Hill: University of North Carolina Press, 2012), 56.

26. See Enrique Dussel, *The Invention of the Americas: Eclipse of "the Other" and the Myth of Modernity* (New York: Continuum, 1995).

27. See, generally, Sophie D. Coe, *America's First Cuisines* (Austin: University of Texas Press, 1994).

28. Thomas Benjamin, *The Atlantic World: Europeans, Africans, Indians and Their Shared History, 1400–1900* (Cambridge: Cambridge University Press, 2009).

29. Philip J. Deloria, *Indians in Unexpected Places* (Lawrence: University Press of Kansas, 2004), 6.

30. Carolyn Thomas Foreman, *Indians Abroad, 1493–1938* (Norman: University of Oklahoma Press, 1943); Alden T. Vaughan, *Transatlantic Encounters: American Indians in Britain, 1500–1776* (Cambridge: Cambridge University Press, 2006); Kate Flint, *The Transatlantic Indian, 1776–1930* (Princeton: Princeton University Press, 2009). Flint's book picks up where Vaughan's leaves off. It is important to note that both Foreman and Flint carry their studies well beyond the confines of what I define as the Red Atlantic. Foreman's book, as I note, was quite early. As Vaughan states, Foreman is generally reliable regarding the nineteenth and twentieth centuries. He writes, however, "Its treatment of the period before 1776 . . . is incomplete and largely undocumented; the facts and quotations are often inaccurate." Vaughan, xv. I am aware of this, and my use of Foreman has been judicious.

31. This estimate is based on my reading of the British, French, and Spanish sources, as well as on the secondary texts. As I note elsewhere, Gallay says up to 51,000 southern Indian slaves passed through Charleston, and Rushforth speaks of the thousands enslaved by the French. In groups of 1,500 here, 500 there, 1,500 there again, 5,000 forcibly exiled, and so on, it is not hard to reach a minimal 600,000 figure. I have also run the estimate by several historians of

the field who agree that it is reasonable. Total indigenous slavery is estimated at 2–4 million. My estimate is limited to those who experienced some blue water transshipment. The largest portion of these would have been those enslaved and shipped from and to the Caribbean or to Spain or elsewhere by the Spanish, along with those who passed through the Netherlands Antilles port of Willemstad, Curacao. It is part of the perverse logic of Indian slavery that the Spanish, having depopulated the Caribbean, had to import new indigenous slaves.

32. Bailyn, 93–94.

33. Michael Thurmond, *Freedom: Georgia's Antislavery Heritage, 1733–1865* (Atlanta: Longstreet Press, 2002), 14.

34. Ibid., 15.

35. Thomas Bluett, *Some Memories of the Life of Job, the Son of Solomon High Priest of Boonda in Africa; Who was a Slave about two Years in Maryland; and afterwards being brought to England, was set free, and sent to his native Land in the Year 1734* (London: Richard Ford, 1734).

36. Helen Todd, *Tomochichi: Indian Friend of the Georgia Colony* (Atlanta: Cherokee Publishing Company, 1977), 62; Vaughan, 153. Vaughan and Todd differ slightly as to the size of the delegation.

37. Todd, 63.

38. John Perceval, Earl of Egmont, *The Journal of the Earl of Egmont: Abstract of the Trustees Proceedings for Establishing the Colony of Georgia, 1732–38*, ed. Robert McPherson (Athens: University of Georgia Press, 1962), 69.

39. Todd, 67.

40. Vaughan, 154.

41. Ibid., 155.

42. Todd, 71; Perceval, 61.

43. Foreman, 60.

44. Todd, 73–74.

45. Ibid., 75.

46. Perceval, 132; Todd, 98.

47. Charles Colcock Jones Jr., *History of Georgia* (Boston: Houghton-Mifflin, 1883), 1:281.

48. Charles Dickens, *American Notes for General Circulation* (1842; Whitefish, Mont.: Kessinger Publishing, 2004), 150–51 (emphasis in original).

49. Magnus Magnusson and Hermann Pálsson, trans., *The Vinland Sagas: The Norse Discovery of America* (London: Penguin, 1965), 55. See also Gwyn Jones, *The Norse Atlantic Saga*, 2nd ed. (Oxford: Oxford University Press, 1986), 117–20.

50. Magnusson and Pálsson, 57–58.

51. Annette Kolodny, *In Search of First Contact: The Vikings of Vinland, the Peoples of the Dawnland, and Anglo-American Anxiety of Discovery* (Durham, N.C.: Duke University Press, 2012), 99.

52. Heather Pringle, "Vikings and Native Americans: Face-to-Face," http://www.ngm.nationalgeographic.com/2012/11/vikings-and-indians/pringle-text (Oct. 19, 2012; Oct. 21, 2012), 5; Heather Pringle, "Evidence of Viking Outpost Found in Canada," http://news.nationalgeographic.com/news/2012/10/121019-viking-outpost-second-new-canada-science-sutherland/ (Oct. 19, 2012; Oct. 21, 2012), 1–4.

53. Qtd. in Bailyn, 45, 88; Bailyn, 87–88.

54. Qtd. in ibid., 88.

55. Coe, 96.

56. Besides Coe, see, generally, Kenneth F. Kiple, *A Moveable Feast: Ten Millennia of Food Globalization* (New York: Cambridge University Press, 2007).

57. Marcy Norton, *Sacred Gifts, Profane Pleasures: A History of Tobacco and Chocolate in the Atlantic World* (Ithaca: Cornell University Press, 2008), 4.

58. Ibid., 1.

59. Coe, 55.

60. Norton, 3.

61. Though I have played with and enlarged it, I am indebted to my historian colleague Claudio Saunt for sticking this image in my head.

62. Alexis de Tocqueville, *Democracy in America*, trans. Henry Reeve (New York: George Dearborn & Co., 1838), ch. 18.

63. The Maya, of course, possessed "true writing," as opposed to pictographs prior to the arrival of Europeans.

64. Pedro Sarmiento de Gamboa, *History of the Incas*, trans. and ed. Clements Markham (Cambridge: Hakluyt Society, 1907), 91; Pedro Sarmiento de Gamboa, *History of the Incas*, trans. Brian S. Bauer and Vania Smith (Austin: University of Texas Press, 2007), 151. Sarmiento's history was commissioned by Francisco de Toledo, viceroy of Peru. Upon its completion, it was read publicly to more than forty Inca authorities for their input. It was supposed to be conveyed to King Felipe II, but due to its association with Toledo, who fell into disfavor after his execution of Túpac Amaru, it never crossed the Atlantic and was forgotten for more than three centuries.

65. John Howland Rowe, "The Incas under Spanish Colonial Rule," *Hispanic American Historical Review*, 1957, 157–58.

66. Bodega's life gets an excellent account in Freeman M. Tovell, *At the Far Reaches of Empire* (Vancouver: University of British Columbia Press, 2008).

67. Barry O'Connell, "'Once More Let Us Consider': William Apess in the Writing of New England Native American History," in *After King Philip's War:*

Presence and Persistence in Indian New England, ed. Colin G. Calloway (Hanover, N.H.: University Press of New England, 1997), 175–76. Historian Nancy Shoemaker states that Elisha Apes (his preferred spelling) was William Apess's younger half-brother, not his son. Nancy Shoemaker, "Race and Indigeneity in the Life of Elisha Apes," *Ethnohistory* 60, no. 1 (Winter 2013): 27–50.

68. O'Connell, 176.

CHAPTER 1

1. Jack D. Forbes, *Africans and Native Americans: The Language of Race and the Evolution of Red-Black Peoples*, 2nd ed. (Champaign: University of Illinois Press, 1993), 12–13.

2. Ibid., 13.

3. Ibid.

4. Annette Kolodny contends that they might have been Mi'kmaqs or, alternatively, Montagnais or Naskapis (the people now known as Innu). Annette Kolodny, *In Search of First Contact: The Vikings of Vinland, the Peoples of the Dawnland, and Anglo-American Anxiety of Discovery* (Durham, N.C.: Duke University Press, 2012), 91, 96. Jennings C. Wise and Vine Deloria Jr. identify the *skrælings* of the sagas as Mi'kmaqs. Jennings C. Wise, *The Red Man in the New World Drama*, rev. and ed. Vine Deloria Jr. (New York: Macmillan, 1971), 5–7. At any rate, the two peoples are closely related, and DNA evidence demonstrated that they were linked to the same ancestral population, either through intermarriage or a common ancestor.

5. Magnus Magnusson and Hermann Pálsson, trans., *The Vinland Sagas: The Norse Discovery of America* (London: Penguin, 1965), 65–67.

6. Ibid., 102.

7. Jayme Sokolow, *The Great Encounter: Native Peoples and European Settlers in the Americas* (Armonk, N.Y.: M. E. Sharpe, 2002), 49. I say controversial simply because he was accused of plagiarism.

8. Magnusson and Pálsson, 102.

9. Ibid.

10. Sokolow, 49; Jack D. Forbes, *Columbus and Other Cannibals* (New York: Autonomedia, 1992), 37.

11. Wise, 7.

12. Gwyn Jones, *The Norse Atlantic Saga*, 2nd ed. (Oxford: Oxford University Press, 1986), 135.

13. Magnusson and Pálsson, 67.

14. Kolodny, 69.

15. Sokolow, 49.

16. Kolodny, 100.

17. Razib Khan, "Icelanders Descended from Native Americans?," http://blogs.discovermagazine.com/gnxp/2010/11/lcelanders-descended-from-native-americans/ (Nov. 17, 2010; Oct. 16, 2012), 4.

18. Kirkpatrick Sale, *The Conquest of Paradise: Christopher Columbus and the Columbian Legacy* (New York: Alfred A. Knopf, 1990), 15; Hans Koning, *Columbus: His Enterprise*, 2nd ed. (New York: Monthly Review Press, 1991), 27–28. See also Percy G. Adams, *Travelers and Travel Liars, 1600–1800* (New York: Dover, 1980), 3. Columbus's extant books are housed in the Biblioteca Colombina in Seville.

19. Christopher Columbus [Bartolomé de Las Casas], *Journal of the First Voyage to America*, with introduction by Van Wyck Brooks (New York: Albert and Charles Boni, 1924), 25.

20. Christopher Columbus, *Letter of Columbus on the Discovery of America*, trans. Samuel Kettell (1827; New York: Lenox Library, 1892), 1–2.

21. Columbus, *Journal*, 24.

22. Ibid.

23. For information on the Taino, see, generally, Irving Rouse, *The Tainos: Rise and Fall of the People Who Greeted Columbus* (New Haven: Yale University Press, 1992); and Scott M. Fitzpatrick and Ann H. Ross, eds., *Island Shores, Distant Pasts: Archaeological and Biological Approaches to the Pre-Columbian Settlement of the Caribbean* (Gainesville: University Press of Florida, 2010).

24. Columbus, *Journal*, 27.

25. Ibid., 31.

26. Ibid., 26; Sale, 97.

27. Columbus, *Journal*, 29.

28. Columbus, *Letter*, 7.

29. Columbus, *Journal*, 69–70.

30. Ibid., 203. The exact number of captives with Columbus is uncertain, but ten is the commonly accepted figure. Alden T. Vaughan, *Transatlantic Encounters: American Indians in Britain, 1500–1776* (Cambridge: Cambridge University Press, 2006), 264 n. 35.

31. Columbus, *Journal*, 204.

32. Vaughan, 12.

33. Columbus, *Journal*, 205–7; see also Martin Dugard, *The Last Voyage of Columbus* (New York: Little, Brown, 2005), 11–13.

34. Gustavo Gutiérrez, *Las Casas: In Search of the Poor of Jesus Christ* (Maryknoll, N.Y.: Orbis Books, 1993), 86.

35. Columbus, *Journal*, 208.

36. Qtd. in Vaughan, 12.

37. Vaughan, 12–13.

38. Ibid., 13.

39. Koning, 72, 69.

40. Columbus, *Journal*, 27. See Felipe Fernández-Armesto, *1492: The Year the World Began* (New York: HarperCollins, 2009), 200; and Koning, 74–75.

41. Qtd. in Koning, 82.

42. Qtd. in David E. Stannard, *American Holocaust: The Conquest of the New World* (New York: Oxford University Press, 1992), 66–69.

43. Qtd. in Koning, 82.

44. Vaughan, 14.

45. Qtd. in Thomas Benjamin, *The Atlantic World: Europeans, Africans, Indians and Their Shared History, 1400–1900* (Cambridge: Cambridge University Press, 2009), 278.

46. Ibid.

47. Fernández-Armesto, 200.

48. Carolyn Thomas Foreman, *Indians Abroad, 1493–1938* (Norman: University of Oklahoma Press, 1943), 7–9.

49. Vaughan, 34–39. These indigenes may have been brought back by Raleigh in 1595, or they may have come more recently. It is possible they came voluntarily.

50. Foreman, 7.

51. Wise, 6–7.

52. Coll Thrush, personal communication (Jan. 20, 2013).

53. Alan D. McMillan, *Native Peoples and Cultures of Canada*, 2nd rev. ed. (Vancouver: Douglas and McIntyre, 1995), 47; Arthur J. Ray, *I Have Lived Here Since the World Began: An Illustrated History of Canada's Native People* (Toronto: Lester Publishing, 1996), 10.

54. See Peter E. Pope, *The Many Landfalls of John Cabot* (Toronto: University of Toronto Press, 1997), 13–14.

55. Qtd. in ibid., 14.

56. Qtd. in ibid., 15.

57. Ibid., 29.

58. McMillan, 47.

59. Kate Flint, *The Transatlantic Indian, 1776–1930* (Princeton: Princeton University Press, 2009), 59; Pope, 42.

60. Qtd. in Pope, 27.

61. Pope, 56.

62. Ibid., 42.

63. Ray, 143.

64. Jennifer Birch, personal communication (Nov. 3, 2012). The story of the excavation of the Mantle site and the remarkable find is told in the Canadian documentary *The Curse of the Axe*, dir. Robin Bicknell, History Television (July 9, 2012). Dr. Birch participated in the dig.

65. Foreman, 15–16. Others believe that Tisquantum was not captured until 1614.

66. Ibid., 16–17.

67. William Shakespeare, *The Tempest*, 2.2.

68. Foreman, 17. The two Natives returned to England with the ship.

69. "Biography of Tisquantum ("Squanto")," http://www.mayflowerhistory .com/History/BiographyTisquantum.php (Nov. 5, 2012).

70. Caleb Johnson, "Tisquantum, Massasoit, and Hobbamock," http://www .mayflowerhistory.com/History/indians4.php (Mar. 1, 2010).

71. Ibid.

72. Francis Jennings, *The Invasion of America: Indians, Colonialism, and the Cant of Conquest* (New York: W. W. Norton, 1976), 30.

73. See Alfred Cave, "Canaanites in a Promised Land: The American Indian and the Providential Theory of Empire," *American Indian Quarterly*, Fall 1988.

74. Vaughan, 65–66.

75. Ibid., 66–67.

76. John Mason, *Narrative of the Pequot War* (Boston: S. Kneeland and T. Green, 1736), 3:31.

77. Qtd in Foreman, 31.

78. H. C. Burleigh, "Ourehouaré," *Dictionary of Canadian Biography*, vol. 1 (1000–1700), http://www.biographi.ca/009004-119.01-e.php?BioId-34565 (Mar. 16, 2010).

79. Francis Parkman, *The Battle for North America*, ed. John Tebbel (Garden City, N.Y.: Doubleday, 1948), 341.

80. Ibid., 342.

81. Ibid.

82. Qtd. in ibid., 342–43.

83. Qtd. in Francis Parkman, *Count Frontenac and New France under Louis XIV* (Boston: Little, Brown, 1894), 199–200.

84. Ibid., 200–201.

85. Ibid., 201.

86. Foreman, 33.

87. Brett Rushforth, "'A Little Flesh We Offer You': The Origins of Indian Slavery in New France," *William and Mary Quarterly* 60, no. 4 (2003): 777.

88. Ibid. See also, generally, Brett Rushforth, *Bonds of Alliance: Indigenous and Atlantic Slaveries in New France* (Chapel Hill: University of North Carolina Press, 2012).

89. Rushforth, "'A Little Flesh,'" 799.

90. Robbie Ethridge, "English Trade in Deerskins and Indian Slaves," in *The New Georgia Encyclopedia*, http://www.georgiaencyclopedia.org/nge/Article

.jsp?id-h-585 (Mar. 24, 2010). See also Robbie Ethridge and Sheri M. Shuck-Hall, eds., *Mapping the Mississippian Shatter Zone: The Colonial Indian Slave Trade and Regional Instability in the American South* (Lincoln: University of Nebraska Press, 2009).

91. Ethridge explains that she calls them "coalescent" because these new constellations of identity were all, in varying degrees, coalescences of people from different societies, cultures, and language groups. I tend to use the latter term. Either way, a prime example are the Seminole, originally made up of Georgia and Alabama Creeks who drifted south into Spanish Florida (at the time, what is today Alabama was part of Georgia), absorbing into themselves the shattered remnants of a number of Florida Native peoples. They did not "coalesce" as a tribe until around the year 1700.

92. Alan Gallay, *The Indian Slave Trade: The Rise of English Empire in the American South, 1670–1717* (New Haven: Yale University Press, 2003), 299.

93. Nick Hazlewood, *Savage: The Life and Times of Jemmy Button* (New York: St. Martin's Press, 2001), 29.

94. Richard Lee Marks, *Three Men of the Beagle* (New York: Alfred A. Knopf, 1991), 27.

95. Peter Nichols, *Evolution's Captain: The Dark Fate of the Man Who Sailed Charles Darwin Around the World* (New York: HarperCollins, 2003), 47.

96. Ibid., 49–50.

97. Hazlewood, 37.

98. Qtd. in ibid.

99. Marks, 29.

100. Robert FitzRoy, *Voyages of the Adventure and Beagle*, vol. 1, *Narrative of the Surveying Voyages of His Majesty's Ships Adventure and Beagle, Between the Years 1826 and 1836, Describing Their Examination of the Southern Shores of South America, and the Beagle's Circumnavigation of the Globe* (London: Henry Colburn, 1839; Kindle ed., 2012).

101. Ibid.

102. Hazlewood, 41.

103. Ibid., 49–57.

104. Qtd. in ibid., 67.

105. Nichols, 81.

106. Ibid., 85.

107. Marks, 43.

108. FitzRoy, op. cit. Queen Victoria had assumed the throne upon William IV's death in 1837. FitzRoy was writing in 1839.

109. Ibid.

110. Marks, 45.

111. FitzRoy, op. cit.

112. Nichols, 153.

113. Qtd. in Nichols, 161–62.

114. Qtd. in Hazlewood, 131.

115. Hazlewood, 132; qtd. in Nichols, 176.

116. Hazlewood, 144–45.

117. Ibid., 147. But Jemmy Button did not pass entirely from history. English missionaries saw him again in 1855 and 1859. In late 1859, there was a massacre of missionaries, reportedly led by Jemmy and his family. In 1860, he testified at an inquiry into the massacre, denying responsibility. In 1863, British missionary Waite Stirling met Jemmy. Jemmy died in 1864. In 1865, Stirling took one of Jemmy's sons, Wammestriggins (Threeboys), to Great Britain.

118. Nelson A. Miles, *Personal Recollections and Observations of General Nelson A. Miles* (Chicago: Werner Company, 1896), 1:135.

119. "Slaughtered for the Hide," *Harper's Weekly*, Dec. 12, 1874, 1022.

120. Ralph K. Andrist, *The Long Death: The Last Days of the Plains Indian* (New York: Macmillan, 1964), 184–85.

121. Ibid., 188.

122. See Gregory F. Michno, *Encyclopedia of Indian Wars: Western Battles and Skirmishes, 1850–1890* (Missoula, Mont.: Mountain Press, 2003), 274–76.

123. Ibid., 289–90.

124. Herman J. Viola, *Warrior Artists: Historic Cheyenne and Kiowa Ledger Art Drawn by Making Medicine and Zotom*, with commentary by Joseph D. and George P. Horse Capture (Washington, D.C.: National Geographic Society, 1998), 6.

125. Edgar Heap of Birds, personal communication (Aug. 19, 2003).

126. Michno, 274.

127. Henrietta Mann, *Cheyenne-Arapaho Education, 1871–1982* (Niwot: University Press of Colorado), 40–41.

128. Ibid.

129. Stan Hoig, *The Peace Chiefs of the Cheyennes* (Norman: University of Oklahoma Press, 1980), 160–61.

130. Viola, 83–84.

131. Ibid., 8; Mann, 41.

132. Qtd. in Viola, 8.

133. Ibid., 92.

134. Richard Henry Pratt, *Battlefield and Classroom: Four Decades with the American Indian, 1867–1904*, ed. Robert Utley (New Haven: Yale University Press, 1964), 121.

135. Ibid., 138, 158–62; Mann, 41–42.

136. Viola, 95.

137. Pratt, 137; Mann, 64.

138. April Middeljans, "'Everything Necessary for Our Salvation'" (unpublished paper, 2012), 1.

139. Homer Noley, *First White Frost: Native Americans and United Methodism* (Nashville: Abingdon Press, 1991), 191.

140. George Tinker, *Missionary Conquest* (Minneapolis: Fortress Press, 1993), 4.

141. Middeljans, 2.

142. From the Native perspective, religious conversion did not always conform to the model in the mind of the Christian missionaries. To the missionaries, conversion meant to completely swap one religious system for another and, inevitably, to trade Native culture for European or Euro-American culture, as well, as Noley points out. Many Natives, however, converted to Christianity and continued to practice their Native religious traditions, too. It is a process that anthropologist Joseph Epes Brown calls "non-exclusive cumulative adhesion." Others term it simply "religious dimorphism," the practice of two forms of religion, the term I prefer.

143. Brad D. Lookingbill, *War Dance at Fort Marion: Plains Indian War Prisoners* (Norman: University of Oklahoma Press, 2006), 182–84.

CHAPTER 2

1. Paul Gilroy, *The Black Atlantic: Modernity and Double Consciousness* (Cambridge, Mass.: Harvard University Press, 1993), 4.

2. Matthew Bahar, "Pirating Empire: 'Indian Pirets,' 'Savage Mariners,' and the Violent Theft of the Atlantic World" (unpublished article, 2013), 3, forthcoming in the *Journal of American History*. Bahar is doing pioneering work on this unknown chapter of Native maritime history.

3. Mark A. Nicholas, "Mashpee Wampanoags of Cape Cod, the Whalefishery, and Seafaring's Impact on Community Development," *American Indian Quarterly* 26, no. 2 (2002): 165.

4. Eric Jay Dolin, *Leviathan: The History of Whaling in America* (New York: W. W. Norton, 2007), 36–37.

5. Ibid., 38

6. Nicholas, 165.

7. Ibid.

8. Sheldon H. Harris, *Paul Cuffe: Black America and the African Return* (New York: Simon and Schuster, 1972), 18–19.

9. Ibid., 18–21, 35–36.

10. Ibid., 37–38.

11. Ibid., 50–57.

12. Ibid., 66.

13. Ibid., 69.

14. George Salvador, *The Black Yankee* (New Bedford, Conn.: Reynolds-DeWalt Printing, 1969); Lamont D. Thomas, *Rise to Be a People: A Biography of Paul Cuffe* (Urbana: University of Illinois Press, 1986). See also Rosalind Cobb Wiggins, ed., *Captain Paul Cuffe's Logs and Letters, 1808–1817: A Black Quaker's "Voice from within the Veil"* (Washington, D.C.: Howard University Press, 1996).

15. Wilson Armistead, *Memoir of Captain Paul Cuffe, a Man of Colour* (York: C. Peacock, 1811), 5–6.

16. Ibid., 6.

17. Wilson Armistead, *A Tribute for the Negro: Being a Vindication of the Moral, Intellectual, and Religious Capabilities of the Coloured Portion of Mankind; with Particular Reference to the African Race* (London: William Irwin, 1848; Kindle ed.), ch. 5.

18. Ibid., 468

19. Ibid., 469.

20. Ibid., 475. Despite the extreme length of this quotation, note that, as written by Armistead, it is only two sentences!

21. Paul Cuffe Jr., *Narrative of the Life and Adventures of Paul Cuffe, a Pequot Indian: During Thirty Years Spent at Sea, and in Travelling in Foreign Lands* (Vernon: Horace N. Bill, 1839), 3.

22. Jack Campisi, introduction to *Narrative of the Life and Adventures of Paul Cuffe, a Pequot Indian: During Thirty Years Spent at Sea, and in Travelling in Foreign Lands*, by Paul Cuffe Jr. (1839; Mashantucket, Conn.: Mashantucket Pequot Museum and Research Center, 2006), 2.

23. Ibid.

24. Forbes, *Africans and Native Americans*, 58.

25. Cuffe, 5.

26. Ibid., 4.

27. Ibid., 14. A quintal is equal to 100 pounds. Cuffe is speaking of taking 60,000 tons of cod.

28. Ibid., 6, 15.

29. Ibid., 7.

30. Ibid., 21.

31. See, generally, C. Napier Bell, *Tangweera: Life and Adventures among the Gentle Savages* (1899; Austin: University of Texas Press, 1989).

32. Barry O'Connell, ed., *On Our Own Ground: The Complete Writings of William Apess, a Pequot* (Amherst: University of Massachusetts Press, 1992), lxxix, 21, 24.

33. Lowrey would go on to become second chief (or assistant principal chief) under John Ross. He was my great-great-great-grandfather.

34. It was Pedro Sarmiento's account of Yupanqui's expedition that I quote in chapter 1. Pedro Sarmiento de Gamboa, *History of the Incas*, trans. and ed.

Clements Markham (Cambridge: Hakluyt Society, 1907), 91; Pedro Sarmiento de Gamboa, *History of the Incas*, trans. Brian S. Bauer and Vania Smith (Austin: University of Texas Press, 2007), 151.

35. "Licencia para venir a España a Garcilaso de la Vega," ES.41091.AGI/22.9.1574//Lima,567,L.8,F.231V-232R (1557-03-06 Valladolid).

36. John Grier Varner, *El Inca: The Life and Times of Garcilaso de la Vega* (Austin: University of Texas Press, 1968), 158–62.

37. Jonathan D. Steigman, *La Florida del Inca and the Struggle for Social Equality in Colonial Spanish America* (Tuscaloosa: University of Alabama Press, 2005), 15.

38. Ibid., 10.

39. John Grier Varner, introduction to *The Florida of the Inca*, by Garcilaso de la Vega, trans. John Grier Varner (Austin: University of Texas Press, 1951), xxix; Varner, *El Inca*, 20–24.

40. Varner, introduction, xxix.

41. Arrell Morgan Gibson, "Editor's Introduction," in *American Notes*, by Rudyard Kipling (1891; Norman: University of Oklahoma Press, 1981), viii.

42. Rudyard Kipling, *American Notes* (1891; Norman: University of Oklahoma Press, 1981), 98–99.

43. Ibid., 99.

44. Kipling's accounts of exchanges with army officers are used by Kate Flint in her book *The Transatlantic Indian* for a very different purpose. Flint writes, "Although the response to this momentary vision is framed in terms that convey his learned respect for the difference of other cultures, Kipling's words also evoke, more conventionally, both the supposedly vanishing Indian of the closing frontier and the newly minted Indian tourist, displaying a picturesque primitivism that offers a safe yet indisputable counterpart to the forces of modernity." Flint, *The Transatlantic Indian, 1776–1930* (Princeton: Princeton University Press, 2009), 256.

45. Maggie Siggins, *Riel: A Life of Revolution* (Toronto: HarperCollins, 1994), 184.

46. Qtd. in ibid., 195.

47. See Lawrence J. Barkwell, *The Battle of Seven Oaks: A Métis Perspective* (Winnipeg: Louis Riel Institute, 2009).

48. Jace Weaver, *Other Words: American Indian Literature, Law, and Culture* (Norman: University of Oklahoma Press, 2001), 275. See also Thomas Flanagan, *Louis "David" Riel: Prophet of the New World* (Toronto: University of Toronto Press, 1996), 96–99.

49. Joseph Boyden, *Louis Riel and Gabriel Dumont* (Toronto: Penguin Canada, 2010).

50. "Final Statement of Louis Riel at his trial in Regina, 1885," http://www.law.umkc.edu/faculty/projects/ftrials/riel/rieltrialstatement.html (Nov. 25, 2012).

51. Ibid.

52. Louis Jackson, *Our Caughnawagas in Egypt* (Montreal: W. Drysdale and Co., 1885), 5/1. This slim book has long been out of print. I brought it back in print in 1998 by including it in my book *American Journey: The Native American Experience* (Woodbridge, Conn.: Research Publications, 1998), on CD-ROM. In order to make this text as accessible as possible, I include citations to both editions of the work. Thus, "Jackson, 5/1" designates that the information appears on page 5 of the original work and page 1 of the version on CD-ROM.

53. Ibid., 4/1.

54. Hilton Obenzinger, *American Palestine: Melville, Twain, and the Holy Land Mania* (Princeton: Princeton University Press, 1999), 138–39.

55. Jackson, 4/1.

56. Ibid., 6–7/2.

57. Ibid., 18/5.

58. Ibid., 32/10.

59. Ibid., 33/10.

60. Ibid., 13–14/4

61. Ibid., 34/11.

62. Ibid., 9/3.

63. Ibid., 4/1.

64. Ibid., 7–9/2.

65. Ibid., 26/8.

66. Ibid., 12/4.

67. Ibid., 29–30/9.

68. Ibid., 31/10.

69. Ibid., 33/10.

70. Ibid., 4/1.

71. Ibid., 34–35/11.

72. Ibid., 34/11.

73. Eve Ball, *In the Days of Victorio: Recollections of a Warm Springs Apache* (Tucson: University of Arizona Press, 1970), 175. The book is described as narrated by James Kaywaykla. Ball got to know him late in his life and recorded his story, which she then fact-checked with "other members of the Warm Springs and Chiricahua bands." Ibid., xi. The story is told in the first person in Kaywaykla's voice. It must be considered in the long tradition of as-told-to Indian autobiographies.

74. Ibid., 175–76.

75. Jon Ault, "Native Americans in the Spanish American War," http://www.spanamwar.com/NativeAmericans.htm (May 9, 2010), 2.

76. Ralph K. Andrist, *The Long Death: The Last Days of the Plains Indian* (New York: Macmillan, 1964), 332.

77. Ball, 182.

78. Kathleen P. Chamberlain, *Victorio: Apache Warrior and Chief* (Norman: University of Oklahoma Press, 2007), 168.

79. Dispatch, General George Crook to Lieutenant General Philip Henry Sheridan, Commanding General of the Army (Mar. 29, 1886).

80. Geronimo, *Geronimo: His Own Story, the Autobiography of a Great Patriot Warrior* (originally, *Geromimo's Story of His Life*, 1906; New York: Penguin, 1996), 132. This autobiography by Geronimo was as told to S. M. Barrett.

81. Dispatch, General Philip Henry Sheridan, Commanding General of the Army, to General George Crook, Commander, Department of Arizona (Mar. 30, 1886).

82. Dispatch, General George Crook to Lieutenant-General Philip Henry Sheridan, Commanding General of the Army (Mar. 30, 1886).

83. Andrist, 332; Robert M. Utley and Wilcomb E. Washburn, *Indian Wars* (Boston: Houghton Mifflin, 1977), 286.

84. Dispatch, General Philip Henry Sheridan, Commanding General of the Army, to General Nelson Miles, Commander, Department of Arizona (Apr. 2, 1886).

85. Ball, 184.

86. Andrist, 332; Utley and Washburn, 286–87.

87. Geronimo, 135.

88. Ball, 200.

89. Geronimo, 141.

90. Ibid.

91. Thomas A. Britten, *American Indians in World War I* (Albuquerque: University of New Mexico Press, 1997), 18–24.

92. Such markers are actually fairly common. For instance, in the Tahlequah City Cemetery in Tahlequah, Oklahoma, the capital of the Cherokee Nation, former second chief George Lowrey's grave is marked by a large stone obelisk. A small tombstone next to it gives information for his wife, Lucy. Her actual grave, however, is elsewhere. They rest together in death only symbolically. While mine is not the only possible explanation, we can say comfortably that Teenah was not among the Apaches who went to join the Mescaleros. That happened years after his death, and Fort Bayard is more than a hundred miles from Mescalero. The White Sands desert lies between. Alicia Delgadillo states that Teenah was sent to Fort Bayard but then transferred to Arizona to convalesce. Discharged, he returned to Fort Sill, where he married Emily and died of consumption. Alicia Delgadillo, ed. (with Miriam Perrett), *From Fort Marion to Fort Sill: A Documentary History of the Chiricahua Apache Prisoners of War, 1886–1913* (Lincoln: University of Nebraska Press, 2013), 248–49.

93. Britten, 25–26; Ault, 6.

94. Britten, 26.

95. Ault, 7.

96. Ibid.

97. Ibid.; Theodore Roosevelt, *The Rough Riders* (1899; Kindle ed., 2012).

98. Roosevelt, supra.

99. Ibid.

100. Ibid.

101. Ibid.

102. "Our Soldier Boy," *Indian Helper*, Nov. 25, 1898, 1; Ault, 7.

103. Qtd. in Ault, 5–6.

104. Richard Henry Pratt, Report to U.S. Department of Interior (Sept. 28, 1898), qtd. in ibid., 8.

105. Qtd. in ibid., 9.

106. Ibid., 10.

107. Ibid., 9.

108. Ibid., 2. I have visited the site of Camp Onward, which was largely a tent city, in Savannah, Georgia.

109. Ibid.

110. Ibid., 9.

111. Roosevelt, op. cit.

112. See Clinton Rickard, *Fighting Tuscarora: The Autobiography of Chief Clinton Rickard* (Syracuse: Syracuse University Press, 1994).

113. Andrew Bard Epstein, "Unsettled New York: Land, Law, and Haudenosaunee Nationalism in the Early Twentieth Century" (master's thesis, University of Georgia, 2012), 93.

114. Qtd. in Susan Applegate Krouse, *North American Indians in the Great War* (Lincoln: University of Nebraska Press, 2007), 64–65.

115. Britten; Krouse; Timothy C. Winegard, *For King and Kanata: Canadian Indians and the First World War* (Winnipeg: University of Manitoba Press, 2012); Timothy C. Winegard, *Indigenous Peoples of the British Dominions and the First World War* (Cambridge: Cambridge University Press, 2011).

116. Diane Camurat, "The American Indian in the Great War: Real and Imagined," http://www.net.lib.byu.edu/~rdh7/wwi/comment/Camurat1.html (1993, Dec. 1, 2012). The thesis is available on the Internet but has never been peer-reviewed for publication. Though it contains errors in the detail and must be used cautiously, it is nonetheless a good review of the literature.

117. See Britten, 59–60; Krouse, 181; Winegard, *For King*, 137; Camurat, http://www.net.lib.byu.edu/~rdh7/wwi/comment/Cmrts/Cmrt6.html#83 (1993; Dec. 1, 2012).

118. Camurat, http://www.net.lib.byu.edu/~rdh7/wwi/comment/Cmrts/Cmrt6.html#83 (1993; Dec. 1, 2012).

119. Krouse, 181; Britten, 83; Camurat, http://www.net.lib.byu.edu/ ~rdh7/wwi/comment/Cmrts/Cmrt6.html#83 (1993; Dec. 1, 2012).

120. John Joseph Mathews, *Sundown* (1934; Norman: University of Oklahoma Press, 1988), xi; Krouse, 117.

121. Mathews, 214. Though there are differences between Chal and John Joseph Mathews, Krouse, not Virginia Mathews, is correct here. She bases her statement on Mathews's own questionnaire for Dixon. Krouse, 217.

122. Ervan Garrison, a citizen of the Choctaw Nation, and other faculty of the Institute of Native American Studies at the University of Georgia have participated with the Cherokee Nation in an archaeological survey of the site of the Cherokee National Male Seminary, which burned in 1910. Based on the archaeological evidence and other historical research, it appears the iron at the site was salvaged for scrap during World War I. Camurat, http://www.net.lib.byu.edu/~rdh7/wwi/comment/Cmrts/Cmrt6.html#83 (1993; Dec. 1, 2012).

123. Winegard, *For King*, 42.

124. Ibid., 38.

125. Ibid., 44.

126. Qtd. in ibid., 44–45.

127. Qtd. in ibid., 41.

128. The movie inexplicably changes the location of Nophaie's bravery to the Somme. If so, it would have to be the Second Battle of the Somme in 1918. The First Battle of the Somme was fought in 1916, before the United States entered the war.

129. Homer Noley, personal communication (Mar. 15, 2000), based on review of Pratt's papers in the Beinecke Library, Yale University.

130. Britten, 39; Camurat, http://www.net.lib.byu.edu/~rdh7/wwi/comment/Cmrts/Cmrt5.html#85 (1993; Dec. 2, 2012).

131. Qtd. in Camurat, http://www.net.lib.byu.edu/~rdh7/wwi/comment/Cmrts/Cmrt6.html#81 (1993; Dec. 1, 2012).

132. Gerald Vizenor, "Blue Ravens" (unpublished manuscript, 2012), 2; Gerald Vizenor, personal communication (Dec. 1, 2012). *Blue Ravens* has subsequently been published by Wesleyan University Press in 2014.

133. Qtd. in Krouse, 66–67.

134. Adrian Hayes, *Pegahmagabow: Life-Long Warrior* (2003; Toronto: Blue Butterfly Books, 2009), 14–16. There is some question about the year of Pegahmagabow's birth. When he enlisted, he gave his age as two years younger than he probably was.

135. Ibid., 16–20.

136. Qtd. in ibid., 17–20.

137. Qtd. in ibid., 18–19; Winegard, *For King*, 113.

138. Hayes, 27–30.

139. Ibid., 32.

140. Qtd. in ibid., 34.

141. Winegard, *For King*, 113; Hayes, 38–39.

142. Hayes, 40, 54; Winegard, *For King*, 51.

143. Qtd. in Hayes, 43.

144. Pegahmagabow's commanding officer originally recommended him for the Distinguished Conduct Medal, Canada's second highest decoration, but the recommendation was downgraded.

145. Hayes, 49.

146. Ibid., 51.

147. Ibid., 77–78.

148. Joseph Boyden, *Three Day Road* (Toronto: Viking Canada, 2005).

149. Hayes, 70–73.

150. Winegard, *For King*, 52.

151. Arthur C. Parker, "Why the Red Man Fights for Democracy," *American Indian Y.M.C.A. Bulletin* 7, nos. 1–2 (Oct.–Nov. 1917): 1; Camurat, http://net.lib .byu.edu/estu/wwi/comment/Cmrts/Cmrt6.html (1993; Dec. 3, 2012).

152. Camurat, http://net.lib.byu.edu/~rdh7/wwi/comment/Cmrts/Cmrt5 .html (1993; Dec. 3, 2012).

CHAPTER 3

1. See James H. Merrell, *Into the American Woods: Negotiations on the Pennsylvania Frontier* (New York: W. W. Norton, 2000). Merrell discusses the importance of translators as go-betweens and cultural mediators.

2. Daniel Castro, *Another Face of Empire: Bartolomé de Las Casas, Indigenous Rights, and Ecclesiastical Imperialism* (Durham, N.C.: Duke University Press, 2007), 93.

3. Ibid.

4. Ibid., 93–94.

5. Qtd. in ibid., 94.

6. Castro, 97. Gustavo Gutiérrez, although speaking of the Enrique incident as formative in Las Casas's worldview, actually makes little mention of it in his otherwise extensive biography. Gustavo Gutiérrez, *Las Casas: In Search of the Poor of Jesus Christ* (Maryknoll, N.Y.: Orbis Books, 1993), 303–4.

7. Castro, 95–96.

8. Alden T. Vaughan, *Transatlantic Encounters: American Indians in Britain, 1500–1776* (Cambridge: Cambridge University Press, 2006), xi. Vaughan is among those scholars who catalog these important contacts.

9. Jerald T. Milanich, *Florida's Indians from Ancient Times to the Present* (Gainesville: University Press of Florida, 1998), 149–52.

10. Lee Miller, *Roanoke: Solving the Mystery of the Lost Colony* (New York: Arcade Publishing, 2002), ix; Carolyn Thomas Foreman, *Indians Abroad, 1493–1938* (Norman: University of Oklahoma Press, 1943), 15.

11. Vaughan, 17.

12. Ibid., 233. Vaughan notes that by the mid-sixteenth century, France had imported approximately twenty Natives, Spain exponentially more. Meanwhile, England's total was barely one-fifth that of its cross-channel rival. Ibid., 15.

13. Ibid., 21–22.

14. Foreman, 15.

15. Vaughan, 22.

16. Ibid., 23.

17. Ibid., 22.

18. Ibid., 24.

19. Qtd. in ibid.

20. Qtd. in ibid., 27–28.

21. Peter Hulme, *Colonial Encounters: Europe and the Native Caribbean, 1492–1797* (London: Routledge, 1986), 89–134.

22. Ronald Takaki, *A Different Mirror: A History of Multicultural America* (New York: Little, Brown, 1993), 36.

23. Ibid., 31–32.

24. Paula Gunn Allen, *Pocahontas: Medicine Woman, Spy, Entrepreneur, Diplomat* (San Francisco: HarperSanFrancisco, 2004), 255–56.

25. Rebecca Anne Goetz, *The Baptism of Early Virginia: How Christianity Created Race* (Baltimore: Johns Hopkins University Press, 2012), 41.

26. Helen C. Rountree, *Pocahontas's People: The Powhatan Indians of Virginia through Four Centuries* (Norman: University of Oklahoma Press, 1990), 38.

27. James Horn, *A Land as God Made It: Jamestown and the Birth of America* (New York: Basic Books, 2005), 66–68; Allen, 40–50.

28. Horn, 68.

29. Qtd. in ibid., 80–81.

30. Qtd. in Vaughan, 45.

31. Qtd. in ibid, 46.

32. Qtd. in ibid., 47–51.

33. Horn, 207.

34. Allen, 56; Rountree, 52.

35. Qtd. in Rountree, 57.

36. Qtd. in Horn, 212.

37. Horn, 213.

38. Allen, 21.

39. Horn, 213. This version of events by Jamestown settler Ralph Hamor is not the only one, but it seems the most plausible.

40. Qtd. in ibid., 226.

41. Allen, 270–71.

42. Vaughan, 84.

43. Rountree, 62.

44. Ibid.

45. Allen, 282; Vaughan, 88.

46. Allen, 278–79.

47. Foreman, 24.

48. Qtd. in Vaughan, 87–88.

49. See Allen, 293–94.

50. Vaughan, 55.

51. Allen, 297.

52. Vaughan, 93–94.

53. Ibid., 94–95.

54. Horn, 255.

55. See Allen, 304–5.

56. Colin Calloway, personal communication (Mar. 10, 2013); see also "Jean Baptiste Charbonneau, http://en.wikipedia.org/wiki/Jean_Baptise_Charbonneau (Mar. 8, 2013; Mar. 26, 2013). Some scholars question whether Jean Baptiste was not actually a servant of the prince rather than a guest and traveling companion.

57. Vaughan, 11–12.

58. Ibid., 97, 100–101, 182, 200–219, 133–35.

59. Seymour I. Schwartz, *The French and Indian War, 1754–1763: The Imperial Struggle for North America* (Edison, N.J.: Castle Books, 1994), 3. See also Colin G. Calloway, *The Scratch of a Pen: 1763 and the Transformation of North America* (New York: Oxford University Press, 2006), 4.

60. Vaughan, 237, 114.

61. Several books have been written about the "Four Kings." See Richmond P. Bond, *Queen Anne's American Kings* (London: Oxford University Press, 1952); John G. Garratt, *The Four Indian Kings/Les Quatres Rois Indiens* (Ottawa: Public Archives Canada, 1985); and Eric Hinderaker, *The Two Hendricks* (Cambridge, Mass.: Harvard University Press, 2010).

62. Bond, 24–31; Vaughan, 116.

63. Garratt, 3; Vaughan, 118, 133.

64. Garratt, 3.

65. Nelle Oosterom, "Kings of the New World," *Canada's History*, Apr.–May 2010, 26.

66. Vaughan, 129; Garratt, 7–9.

67. Dee Brown, *Bury My Heart at Wounded Knee: An Indian History of the American West* (New York: Henry Holt, 1970; Owl Book ed., 1991), 427.

68. Vaughan, 130, 133.

69. Ibid., 148.

70. Ibid., 240.

71. *Daily Post*, June 24, 1730; Vaughan, 138; Troy Wayne Poteete, personal communication (Apr. 25, 2011).

72. Vaughan, 137–38, 146, 143–44.

73. Duane King, introduction to *The Memoirs of Lt. Henry Timberlake: The Story of a Soldier, Adventurer, and Emissary to the Cherokees, 1756–1765*, by Henry Timberlake, ed. Duane King (Cherokee, N.C.: Museum of the Cherokee Indian Press, 2007), xvii.

74. Henry Timberlake, *The Memoirs of Lt. Henry Timberlake: The Story of a Soldier, Adventurer, and Emissary to the Cherokees, 1756–1765* (Cherokee, N.C.: Museum of the Cherokee Indian Press, 2007), 37; King, xvii.

75. Schwartz, 130, 138; King, xviii–xxv.

76. Timberlake, 37.

77. Ibid., 47.

78. Ibid., 55.

79. Ibid., 55–56.

80. Qtd. in Vaughan, 146–47, 166.

81. Qtd. in ibid., 167–68.

82. Timberlake, 57–58.

83. Ibid., 58.

84. Ibid., 61–62.

85. Ibid., 137.

86. Ibid., 62; Vaughan, 169, 174.

87. Qtd. in Vaughan, 174.

88. Vaughan, 170.

89. Qtd. in Timberlake, 147.

90. Timberlake, 71–72.

91. Ibid., 73–76.

92. Ibid., 21; King, xxviii–xxx; Vaughan, 187.

93. Foreman, 54–55.

94. Duane King, personal communication (Mar. 24, 2010); Vaughan, 150.

95. Brett Riggs, personal communication (Feb. 20, 2010).

96. Timberlake, 73–75.

97. Vaughan, 176ff., 237–38.

98. See, e.g., "Oconostota," http://en.wikipedia.org/wiki/Oconostota (Nov. 17, 2012; Dec. 15, 2012). If it were simply the Wikipedia entry, it would not be worth comment, but this misinformation is replicated at almost every website devoted to the Cherokee chief.

99. Vaughan, 143.

100. James C. Kelly, "Oconostota," *Journal of Cherokee Studies* 3, no. 4 (Fall 1979): 227.

101. Ibid., 227–28.

102. Ibid.

103. Joel Koenig, *Cherokee Chronicles, 1540–1840: From First Contact to the Trail of Tears* (Chattanooga: Town and Country Publishing, 2003), 147.

104. John Sevier to Amos Stoddard, Knoxville, Tenn., Oct. 9, 1810.

105. Garratt, 7; Bruce E. Johansen and Donald A. Grinde Jr., *The Encyclopedia of Native American Biography* (New York: Henry Holt, 1997), 51. There is some uncertainty about this. Although no one disputes that he inherited his name from Brant, Vaughan says it was through a stepfather. Vaughan, 221. Vaughan also says he may have been a great-grandson or "collateral descendant." According to Vaughan, the relational Mohawk word for "grandfather" can also signify great-grandfather, granduncle, or other relationship. Vaughan, 225, 324.

106. Maurice Kenney, *Tekonwatoni/Molly Brant* (Fredonia, N.Y.: White Pine Press, 1992), 207.

107. Vaughan, 222–23.

108. William L. Stone, *Life of Joseph Brant* (New York: Alexander V. Blake, 1838; Millwood, N.Y.: Kraus Reprint Co., 1991), 1:153 (emphasis in original).

109. Qtd. in ibid., 152.

110. Qtd. in Johansen and Grinde, 52.

111. Qtd. in Foreman, 94.

112. Foreman, 94–95; qtd. in Vaughan, 225.

113. Vaughan, 227; Foreman, 95.

114. Kenney, 138.

115. S. C. Kimm, *The Iroquois: A History of the Six Nations of New York* (Middleburgh, N.Y.: Press of Pierre W. Danforth, 1900), 61. Kimm does not give the origin of the Schoolcraft quotation, though the characterization is certainly accurate.

116. Stone, 1:151; Foreman, 94–95; Vaughan, 227–28.

117. Foreman, 95.

118. Daniel Richter, *Facing East from Indian Country: A Native History of Early America* (Cambridge, Mass.: Harvard University Press, 2001), 220.

119. Ibid., 224.

120. Colin Calloway believes that Richter, Brant's biographers, and, by extension, I exaggerate Brant's role in forging the Western Confederacy. He writes, "Iroquois influence among the western tribes was largely shot after the 1768 Treaty of Fort Stanwix, when the Shawnees took the lead in building an anti-British/anti-Iroquois coalition. The [Northwest] confederacy grows out of that and the Revolutionary era coalition, and its prime movers were Miamis and Shawnees." Colin Calloway, personal communication (Mar. 10, 2013).

121. Qtd. in Stone, 2:249.

122. Ibid., 248.

123. Ibid.

124. Qtd. in ibid., 252–54.

125. Qtd. in ibid., 254–55.

126. Qtd. in ibid., 255–56.

127. Foreman, 97.

128. Kate Flint, *The Transatlantic Indian, 1776–1930* (Princeton: Princeton University Press, 2009), 42.

129. Stone, 2:258.

130. Ibid., 251.

131. Ibid.; Vaughan, 230–31.

132. Jace Weaver, *That the People Might Live: Native American Literatures and Native American Community* (New York: Oxford University Press, 1997), 54–59. Choctaw historian Homer Noley made a beginning at recovery from a Native point of view in his book *First White Frost*. I continued it my book *That the People Might Live*. Kate Flint discusses Jones in *The Transatlantic Indian*, as does Carolyn Foreman in her early *Indians Abroad*. There is one excellent biography, Donald Smith's *Sacred Feathers*. While that might seem like an ample amount of attention, it is actually relatively small.

133. George Henry [Maungwudaus], *Remarks Concerning the Ojibway Indians, by One of Themselves Called Maungwudaus, Who Has Been Traveling in England, France, Belgium, Ireland, and Scotland* (Leeds: C. A. Wilson, 1847); *An Account of the Chippewa Indians, Who Have Been Traveling in the United States, England, Ireland, Scotland, France and Belgium: with Very Interesting Incidents in Relation to the General Characteristics of the English, Irish, Scotch, French, and Americans, with Regard to Their Hospitality, Peculiarities, etc.* (Boston: Privately printed, 1848); and *An Account of the North American Indians, Written by Maungwudaus, a Chief of the Ojibway Indians Who Has Been Traveling in England, France, Belgium, Ireland, and Scotland* (Leicester: T. Cook, 1848). Henry is often referred to as Jones's cousin, but he was a half-brother, sharing a common mother, Tuhbenahneequay. See, for example, Penny Petrone, ed., *First People, First Voices* (Toronto: University of Toronto Press, 1983), 94.

134. Penny Petrone, *Native Literature in Canada* (Toronto: Oxford University Press, 1990), 65–66.

135. Flint, 271.

136. Peter Jones, *Life and Journals of Kah-ke-wa-quo-na-by (Rev. Peter Jones), Wesleyan Minister* (Toronto: Anson Green, 1860), 1.

137. Ibid., 1–2.

138. Ibid., 314.

139. Ibid., 2. For a discussion of the thunder gods of the Anishinaabe, see Theresa S. Smith, *The Island of the Anishinaabeg: Thunderers and Water Monsters in the Traditional Ojibwe Life-World* (Moscow: University of Idaho Press, 1995), 68–69.

140. Jones, *Life*, 6.

141. Peter Jones, "Autobiography of Peter Jones" (microfilm, General Commission on Archives and History, The United Methodist Church, Drew University, n.d.), 7. The manuscript is substantially similar, though not identical, to that published by his wife in *Life and Journals*.

142. Homer Noley, *First White Frost: Native Americans and United Methodism* (Nashville: Abingdon Press, 1991), 103.

143. Jones, "Autobiography," 7.

144. Jones, *Life*, 8–9. For Wesley, prevenient (from the Latin for "comes before") grace was God's grace working in an individual before he or she was even aware of it.

145. Jones, "Autobiography," 9.

146. Ibid., 9–10.

147. Jones, *Life*, 11.

148. Ibid., 12.

149. Peter Jones, *History of the Ojebway Indians: With Especial Reference to Their Conversion to Christianity* (London: A. W. Bennett, 1861), 92–93; Jones, *Life*, 3.

150. Jones, *History*, 31. He also notes that the Great Spirit "understands all languages." *Life*, 15. "Great Spirit" is, of course, itself a Christianized term for the Native high gods, in the case of the Anishinaabe, for "Gitchi Manitou."

151. Joseph Epes Brown, *The Spiritual Legacy of the American Indian* (New York: Crossroads, 1989), 27.

152. Jones, *History*, 25.

153. Ibid., 27–28.

154. Jones, *Life*, 7–8.

155. Letter, Peter Jones Collection, Victoria University Library, University of Toronto, qtd. in Petrone, *Native Literature*, 61, 62–63.

156. Qtd. in Donald B. Smith, *Sacred Feathers: The Reverend Peter Jones (kahkewaquonaby) and the Mississauga Indians* (Lincoln: University of Nebraska Press, 1987), 123.

157. Flint, 209–10.

158. Qtd. in Foreman, 152–53.

159. Ibid., 154–55; T. Smith, 138–39; Flint, 210.

160. Flint, 208.

161. Qtd. in T. Smith, 165.

162. Qtd. in ibid., 165–66.

163. Jones, *Life*, 405–7.

164. D. Smith, 166–67.

165. Jones, *Life*, 407.

166. George Copway, *The Life of Kah-ge-ga-gah-bowh* (1847); reprinted in Willis G. Regier, ed., *Masterpieces of American Indian Literature* (Lincoln: University of Nebraska Press, 2005), 30.

167. George Copway, *Running Sketches of Men and Places in England, France, Germany, Belgium, and Scotland* (New York: J. C. Riker, 1851), 21.

168. Ibid., 211, 218.

169. *Akwesasne Notes* [John Mohawk], ed., *Basic Call to Consciousness* (Summertown, Tenn.: Native Voices, 2005), 42. *Akwesasne Notes* is an Iroquois newspaper. John Mohawk was its editor when this book was originally published in 1978. He edited the book and wrote most of it.

170. Deskaheh, *The Redman's Appeal for Justice* (London: Kealeys Limited, 1923), 5; *Akwesasne*, 42; Johansen and Grinde, 110.

171. *Akwesasne*, 42–43.

172. Ibid., 43.

173. Weaver, *That the People*, 56–57.

174. Covenant of the League of Nations (1919).

175. Deskaheh, 1.

176. Qtd. in Joëlle Rostkowski, "The Redman's Appeal for Justice: Deskaheh and the League of Nations," in *Indians and Europe*, ed. Christian F. Feest (Aachen, Germany: Edition Herodot, 1987), 439.

177. Ibid., 440.

178. Ibid.

179. Qtd. in *Akwesasne*, 44.

180. Rostkowski, 445.

181. Qtd. in *Akwesasne*, 44.

182. Qtd. in ibid., 45.

183. Qtd. in ibid., 47; Johansen and Grinde, 111; Rostkowski, 452.

184. *Akwesasne*, 8; Alexander Ewen, ed., *Voice of Indigenous Peoples* (Santa Fe: Clear Light Publishers, 1994), 31ff.; Thom White Wolf Fassett, personal communication (Feb. 6, 1998).

185. Johansen and Grinde, 111; Thomas Kaplan, "Iroquois Defeated by Passport Dispute," www.nytimes.com/2010/07/17/sports/17/lacrosse.html?pagewanted=all (July 18, 2010; Dec. 28, 2012).

CHAPTER 4

1. Alden T. Vaughan, *Transatlantic Encounters: American Indians in Britain, 1500–1776* (Cambridge: Cambridge University Press, 2006), xii.

2. For a good discussion of Cody's show in Europe, see, generally, Robert W. Rydell and Rob Kroes, *Buffalo Bill in Bologna: The Americanization of the World, 1869–1922* (Chicago: University of Chicago Press, 2005).

3. James Welch, personal communication (Nov. 11, 1999). This original manuscript resides in the James Welch Papers in the Beinecke Library, the rare book library of Yale University.

4. Vaughan, 15–16.

5. Michel de Montaigne, *The Complete Works: Essays, Travel Journal, Letters*, trans. Donald M. Frame (New York: Alfred A. Knopf, 1943), 193.

6. Ibid.

7. Vaughan, 239–40.

8. Ibid., 182–86.

9. Kate Flint, *The Transatlantic Indian, 1776–1930* (Princeton: Princeton University Press, 2009), 60.

10. Samson Occom, "A Short Narrative of My Life," reprinted in *Native American Autobiography: An Anthology*, ed. Arnold Krupat (Madison: University of Wisconsin Press, 1994), 107.

11. Much of my discussion of Samson Occom is drawn from my book *That the People Might Live: Native American Literatures and Native American Community* (New York: Oxford University Press, 1997), 46–53.

12. Henry Warner Bowden, *American Indians and Christian Missions* (Chicago: University of Chicago Press, 1981), 139.

13. Qtd. in Vaughan, 195.

14. Qtd. in ibid., 195–96.

15. Qtd. in ibid., 196.

16. Weaver, *That the People*, 50; Vaughan, 191. The funds would form the seed of the endowment of Dartmouth College.

17. Qtd. in David Murray, *Forked Tongues: Speech, Writing and Representation in North American Indian Texts* (Bloomington: Indiana University Press, 191), 55 (emphasis mine). "Alma mater" is Latin for "nourishing mother," a term commonly used for colleges and universities. By using the "suckling" or nursing language, Occom is obviously playing off this. By substituting "alba mater" (i.e., "white mother"), he is highlighting that there will be no place for Indians at Dartmouth.

18. Qtd. in ibid., 54. The autobiography remained in the Dartmouth archives, unpublished, until Bernd C. Peyer, ed., *The Elders Wrote: An Anthology of Early American Prose by North American Indians, 1768–1931* (Berlin: Dietrich Reimer Verlag, 1982).

19. Qtd. in Murray, 53–54 (emphasis in original).

20. Qtd. in ibid.; Bernd Peyer, "Samson Occom: Mohegan Missionary and Writer of the 18th Century," *American Indian Quarterly* 6, nos. 3–4 (1982): 211.

21. Murray, 53.

22. Occom, "Short Narrative," 113 (emphasis in original).

23. Murray, 45.

24. Ibid., 46.

25. Qtd. in ibid.

26. Ibid., 46–47.

27. Bowden, 144.

28. As far as I know, the terms "white shamans" and "plastic medicine men" were coined by Cherokee literary critic Geary Hobson in the 1970s. See Geary Hobson, "The Rise of the White Shaman as a New Version of Cultural Imperialism," in *The Remembered Earth*, ed. Geary Hobson (Albuquerque: Red Earth Press, 1978), 100–108; see also Wendy Rose, "The Great Pretenders: Further Reflections on Whiteshamanism [*sic*]," in *The State of Native America: Genocide, Colonization, and Resistance*, ed. M. Annette Jaimes (Boston: South End Press, 1992), 403–21.

29. See Bernd C. Peyer, *American Indian Nonfiction: An Anthology of Writings, 1760s–1930s* (Norman: University of Oklahoma Press, 2007), 199.

30. George Catlin, *Catlin's Notes: Or, Eight Years' Travels and Residence in Europe, with His North American Indian Collection* (London: Published by the author, at his Indian Collection, 1848).

31. Ibid., 1:vi.

32. Ibid., vi–vii.

33. Flint, 57.

34. Ibid., 58.

35. See, e.g., Penny Petrone, ed., *First People, First Voices* (Toronto: University of Toronto Press, 1983), 94. Petrone also gives the English translation of his Indian name as Big Legging, instead of Great Hero or Courageous.

36. Qtd. in Donald B. Smith, *Sacred Feathers: The Reverend Peter Jones (Kahkewaquonaby) and the Mississauga Indians* (Lincoln: University of Nebraska Press, 1987), 187–88.

·37. Qtd. in ibid., 188.

38. Ibid., 200–201.

39. Peyer, *The Elders Wrote*, 206.

40. Maungwudaus [George Henry], *An Account of the Chippewa Indians, Who Have Been Travelling among the Whites, in the United States, England, Ireland, Scotland, France and Belgium* (Boston: Published by the author, 1848), 4.

41. Ibid., 3–6.

42. Ibid., 6.

43. Qtd. in Petrone, *First People*, 94.

44. Maungwudaus, 7.

45. Ibid.

46. Ibid., 8.

47. Ibid.

48. Ibid., 8–9.

49. Ibid., 1.

50. Ibid., 9.

51. Smith, 202.

52. Catlin, 2:301.

53. Smith, 202.

54. Catlin, 2:201.

55. Flint, 84.

56. Catlin, 2:309–10.

57. Ibid., 310.

58. Daniel Francis, *The Imaginary Indian: The Image of the Indian in Canadian Culture* (Vancouver: Arsenal Pulp Press, 1992), 113.

59. Flint, 279.

60. Betty Keller, *Pauline: A Biography of Pauline Johnson* (Toronto: Douglas and McIntyre, 1981), 7–9.

61. Penny Petrone, *Native Literature in Canada* (Toronto: Oxford University Press, 1990), 84.

62. Francis, 111–23.

63. Terry Goldie, *Fear and Temptation: The Image of the Indigene in Canadian, Australian, and New Zealand Literatures* (Kingston, Ontario: McGill-Queen's University Press, 1989), 61–62.

64. Beth Brant, *Writing as Witness* (Toronto: Women's Press, 1994), 7, 6.

65. Keller, 272, 267.

66. Francis, 115.

67. Keller, 75–76.

68. Ibid., 79.

69. Ibid., 80–81.

70. Ibid., 82–87.

71. Ibid., 207–9.

72. Ibid., 216; Flint, 284; Philip J. Deloria, *Playing Indian* (New Haven: Yale University Press, 1999), 189.

73. E. Pauline Johnson, *The Moccasin Maker* (Toronto: Ryerson, 1913), 139.

74. Francis, 120.

75. Qtd. in Petrone, *Native Literature*, 82.

76. Francis, 118–19.

77. Brant, 14.

78. Qtd. in Keller, 234–35.

79. Qtd. in Francis, 119.

80. Petrone, *Native Literature*, 84.

81. E. Pauline Johnson, *The Shaganappi* (Toronto: William Briggs, 1913), 5.

82. Francis, 118.

83. Qtd. in Flint, 285–86. I am indebted to Flint for this analysis. The Haude-nosaunee Confederacy has a diarchical political system in which both men and women share governance. Though men are the chiefs, women (the clan mothers) select them and can dismiss them. Though much debated and disputed, the most likely date for the founding of the confederacy is 1145 C.E. Bruce E. Johansen and Donald A. Grinde Jr., *The Encyclopedia of Native American Biography* (New York: Henry Holt, 1997), 101.

84. Brant, 7.

85. Flint, 279.

86. Qtd. in ibid., 279–81.

87. E. Pauline Johnson, *Flint and Feather* (Toronto: Musson, 1912) (emphasis in original).

88. Qtd. in Flint, 286.

89. Emphasis in original.

90. Petrone, *Native Literature*, 84.

91. Francis, 122.

92. Brant, 6.

93. Keller, 234 (emphasis mine).

CHAPTER 5

1. Carlos A. Jáuregui, *The Conquest on Trial: Carvajal's "Complaint of the Indians in the Court of Death"* (University Park: Pennsylvania State University Press, 2008), 4.

2. Felipe II married Queen Mary I of England. An act of England's Parliament provided that, as long as the marriage lasted, he and Mary would be co-monarchs. Felipe (or Philip) thus was king of both Spain and England.

3. Jáuregui, 9.

4. Ibid., 85; Carvajal, lines 171–80.

5. Jáuregui, 91–92; Carvajal, lines 221–30.

6. Jáuregui, 19, 81; Carvajal, lines 141–44.

7. Jáuregui, 20.

8. Ibid., 111; Carvajal, lines 411–18.

9. Jáuregui, 101; Carvajal, line 324.

10. Jáuregui, 105; Carvajal, lines 344–45.

11. Jáuregui, 20.

12. Bartolomé de Las Casas, *A Short Account of the Destruction of the Indies*, trans. Nigel Griffin (London: Penguin Books, 1992), 27–29.

13. Bartolomé de Las Casas, *The Tears of the Indians* (London: Nath. Brook,

1656), 1; Colin Steel, ed., *Tears of the Indians* (New York: Oriole Chapbooks, 1972), v–vi.

14. Gustavo Gutiérrez, *Las Casas: In Search of the Poor of Jesus Christ* (Maryknoll, N.Y.: Orbis Books, 1993), xix; George Sanderlin, ed., *Witness: Writings of Bartolomé de Las Casas* (Maryknoll, N.Y.: Orbis Books, 1971; 1992), 3; Francis Patrick Sullivan, ed., *Indian Freedom: The Cause of Bartolomé de Las Casas, 1484–1566* (Kansas City, Mo.: Sheed and Ward, 1995), 2–3.

15. Sanderlin, 4; Sullivan, 3–4; Daniel Castro, *Another Face of Empire: Bartolomé de Las Casas, Indigenous Rights, and Ecclesiastical Imperialism* (Durham, N.C.: Duke University Press, 2007), 65.

16. Gutiérrez, 46.

17. Ibid., xix–xx; see also, generally, Lewis Hanke, *All Mankind Is One: A Study of the Disputation between Bartolomé de Las Casas and Juan Ginés de Sepúlveda on the Religious and Intellectual Capacity of the American Indians* (DeKalb: Northern Illinois University Press, 1974); Stafford Poole, ed., *In Defense of the Indians* (DeKalb: Northern Illinois University Press, 1992); and Gael Guzmán-Medrano, "The 1550 Valladolid Debate: Las Casas v. Sepúlveda" (unpublished manuscript, 2012).

18. "Memorial al consejo de Indias," *Opúsculos*, 536a-b–538a-b; Castro, 144.

19. Ernest J. Burrus, ed., *The Writings of Alonso de la Vera Cruz* (Rome: Jesuit Historical Institute, 1972), 5:16–18.

20. Ibid., 2:13.

21. Ibid., 7.

22. Ibid., 191, 203, 199.

23. Ibid., 31.

24. Ibid., 337, 383.

25. Ibid., 383.

26. Ibid., 47 (emphasis in original).

27. The third of the five volumes in Burrus's edition for the Jesuit Historical Institute is a photographic reproduction of the original manuscript of *Defense of the Indians*.

28. Burrus, 3:4.

29. Castro, 182.

30. Juan Miguel Zarandona, "*The Biography of Vasco de Quiroga (1470–1565), Bishop of Utopia*, by Benjamín Jarnés (1888–1949)," *Spaces of Utopia: An Electronic Journal* 3 (Autumn/Winter 2006): 75, http://ler.letras.up.pt (Jan. 16, 2013).

31. Ibid., 76.

32. Guzmán-Medrano, 11; Zarandona, 75.

33. Voltaire, *Candide*, trans. Henry Morley (1922; New York: Barnes and Noble Classics, 2003), 71.

34. Ibid., 70–71.

35. Ibid., 74, 80.

36. Voltaire, *L'Ingenu*, in *Zadig and L'Ingenu*, trans. John Butt (London: Penguin Books, 1964), 106.

37. Ibid., 132–33.

38. Ibid., 136–37.

39. Ibid., 139–40.

40. Ibid., 143.

41. Ibid., 152, 160.

42. Ibid., 191.

43. Michelle Burnham, introduction to *The Female American*, ed. Michelle Burnham (Peterborough, Ontario: Broadview Press, 2001), 13.

44. Ibid., 24.

45. In reality, Wingfield had no offspring.

46. The reference is to her father's brother's family, with whom they had resided in England.

47. William Least Heat Moon [William Trogdon], *Blue Highways: A Journey into America* (Boston: Little, Brown, 1982), 388–89.

48. Burnham, 17.

49. Ibid., 27.

50. Ibid.

51. Richard Slotkin, *Regeneration through Violence: The Mythology of the American Frontier, 1600–1860* (Hanover, N.H.: Wesleyan University Press, 1973), 236.

52. Joseph F. Bartolomeo, introduction to *Reuben and Rachel*, by Susanna Rowson (Peterborough, Ontario: Broadview Press, 2009), 10–12.

53. Ibid., 12–13.

54. Carroll Smith-Rosenberg, "Subject Female: Authorizing American Identity," *American Literary History* 5 (1993): 500.

55. Bartolomeo, 32.

56. Jace Weaver, "Mr. Poe's Indians: *The Narrative of Arthur Gordon Pym of Nantucket* and Edgar Allan Poe as a Southern Writer," *Native South* 5 (2012): 39–60. This article is the starting point for my discussion herein and much is drawn from it.

57. Frederick S. Frank and Diane Long Hoeveler, introduction to *The Narrative of Arthur Gordon Pym of Nantucket*, by Edgar Allan Poe (Peterborough, Ontario: Broadview Press, 2010), 29.

58. Jace Weaver and Laura Adams Weaver, *Red Clay, 1835: Cherokee Removal and the Meaning of Sovereignty* (2010), 117, 160–61, http://www.barnard.edu/reacting/gamedev_redclay.html (forthcoming from W. W. Norton).

59. Frank and Hoeveler, 31.

60. I am reminded of early drawings of ferocious beavers created by Euro-

pean artists who had never seen the animal and relied on vague descriptions from travelers. Color aside, this reminds me of a platypus, which when the first specimen reached Britain in 1799 was thought to be a hoax. Frank and Hoeveler call the creature "one of the novel's best zoological grotesques and colorful hybrids." Frank and Hoeveler, 194.

61. John Carlos Rowe, "Poe, Slavery, and Modern Criticism," in *Poe's Pym: Critical Explorations*, ed. Richard Kopley (Durham, N.C.: Duke University Press, 1992), 132.

62. Ibid.

63. Christopher Frayling, *Spaghetti Westerns: Cowboys and Europeans from Karl May to Sergio Leone* (London: Routledge and Kegan Paul, 1981), 104, 106.

64. Unless otherwise noted or quoted from secondary sources, all quotations are taken from translations of May's works by Marlies Bugmann, privately published by the Australian Friends of Karl May. For example, Karl May, *Winnetou—Book 4*, trans. Marlies Bugmann (Copping, Tasmania, Australia: Australian Friends of Karl May, 2010).

65. Julian Crandall Hollick and Dean Capello, prods., "Winnetou and Old Shatterhand" (*Imagining America*, Littleton, Mass.: Independent Broadcasting Associates, 1992), produced for National Public Radio; Frederic Morton, "Tales of the Grand Teutons: Karl May among the Indians," *New York Times Book Review*, Jan. 4, 1987, 15; Frayling, 103–4.

66. Percy G. Adams, *Travelers and Travel Liars, 1660–1800* (New York: Dover, 1980), vii, 17.

67. Ibid., 4.

68. Morton, op. cit.

69. Christian F. Feest, "Europe's Indians," in *The Invented Indian: Cultural Fictions and Government Policies*, ed. James A. Clifton (New Brunswick, N.J.: Transaction Publishers, 1990), 316.

70. Ibid., 323–24.

71. Hollick and Cappello, op. cit.

72. Lisa Bartel-Winkler, "Das Drama des sterbenden Volkes," *Karl-May Jahrbuch 7* (Radebeul: Karl May Verlag, 1924), qtd. in Christian F. Feest, "Europe's Indians," in *Indians and Europe*, ed. Christian F. Feest (Aachen, Germany: Editions Herdot, 1987), 612.

73. Morton, op. cit.

74. Ibid.

75. Hollick and Cappello, op. cit.

76. Frayling, 112.

77. Peter Bolz, "Life among the 'Hunkpapas': A Case Study in German Indian Lore," in Feest, *Indians and Europe*, 486.

78. Feest, in Clifton, *Invented Indian*, 324.

79. Rudolf Conrad, "Mutual Fascination: Indians in Dresden and Leipzig," in Feest, *Indians and Europe*, 469–70.

80. Alfred Vagts, "The Germans and the Red Man," *American-German Review* 24 (1957): 17.

81. Jonathan Boyarin, "Europe's Indian, America's Jew," in *Indian Persistence and Resurgence*, ed. Karl Kroeber (Durham, N.C.: Duke University Press, 1994), 205.

82. Taggart also translated May's Kara-ben-Nemsi material as *Jack Hildreth on the Nile*. Taggart's editions have been reprinted by Dodo Press in Gloucester, England. They are also available on the web from arthursclassicnovels.com and karl-may-gesellschaft.de.

83. Qtd. in Hollick and Cappello, op. cit.

84. Frayling, 112.

85. Karl May, *Geographische Predigten*, qtd. in Conrad, 458.

86. Boyarin, 206.

CHAPTER 6

1. Hinrich Rink, *Tales and Traditions of the Eskimo* (Edinburgh: William Blackwood and Sons, 1875), 1.

2. Laura Adams Weaver, "Native American Creation Stories," in *Encyclopedia of Women and Religion in North America*, ed. Rosemary Skinner Keller and Rosemary Radford Reuther (Bloomington: Indiana University Press, 2006), 1:88–89; Knud Rasmussen, *Across Arctic America: A Narrative of the Fifth Thule Expedition* (Fairbanks: University of Alaska Press, 1999), 27–28.

3. L. Weaver, "Native American Creation Stories," 89. This is the most common version of the story and the one recorded by Rasmussen.

4. Forbes, *Africans and Native Americans*, 18–20; Jack D. Forbes, *Columbus and Other Cannibals* (Brooklyn: Autonomedia, 1992), 37.

5. Alden T. Vaughan, *Transatlantic Encounters: American Indians in Britain, 1500–1776* (Cambridge: Cambridge University Press, 2006), 1–3.

6. Robert Petersen, "Colonialism as Seen from a Formerly Colonized Area," plenary presentation, Eighth Inuit Studies Conference, Laval University, Montreal, Que., Oct. 25, 1992, 3, 14; Peter Høeg, *Smilla's Sense of Snow* (New York: Dell, 1997), 7; Jace Weaver, *Other Words: American Indian Literature, Law, and Culture* (Norman: University of Oklahoma Press, 2001), 119, 122. Petersen's paper was subsequently published in *Arctic Anthropology* 32, no. 2, 118–26. It should be noted that from 1380 to 1814, Norway was part of Denmark.

7. Jean Malaurie, *The Last Kings of Thule* (New York: E. P. Dutton, 1982), xviii.

8. Qtd. in Terrence Cole, introduction to *Across Arctic America: A Narrative*

of the Fifth Thule Expedition, by Knud Rasmussen (Fairbanks: University of Alaska Press, 1999), xii–xiii.

9. Malaurie, 194.

10. Nationalmuseet, Copenhagen, Denmark, July 2010. The National Museum of Denmark has a massive collection of artifacts and film from Rasmussen's expeditions.

11. Rasmussen, 64.

12. Peter Freuchen, *I Sailed with Rasmussen* (New York: Viking Press, 1958), 32.

13. Ibid., 32–35.

14. Ibid., 40.

15. Ibid., 48–49.

16. Ibid., 50–51.

17. Ibid., 52.

18. Malaurie, 228.

19. *Denmark v. Norway* (Sept. 5, 1933), http://www.worldcourts.com/pcij/english/decisions/1933.04.05_greenland.htm (Jan. 20, 2013); Freuchen, 58–59.

20. Freuchen, 63–65.

21. Rasmussen, 119.

22. Freuchen, 185.

23. Ibid.

24. Ibid., 195.

25. Ibid., 221–22.

26. Rasmussen, 118, 138.

27. Freuchen, 216.

28. Nationalmuseet, Copenhagen, Denmark, July 2010.

29. Freuchen, 222.

30. Judy M. Wilson, *Beavers in Connecticut: Their Natural History and Management* (Hartford: Connecticut Department of Environmental Protection, 2001), 2.

31. Ken Mitchell, "The Beaver Fur Trade," http://www.lib.umn.edu/bell/tradeproducts/beaver (2010; Jan. 23, 2013).

32. Jace Weaver, "Notes from a Miner's Canary," in *Defending Mother Earth: Native American Perspectives on Environmental Justice*, ed. Jace Weaver (Maryknoll, N.Y.: Orbis Books, 1996), 5–6.

33. Qtd. in Verner W. Crane, *The Southern Frontier, 1670–1732* (Durham, N.C.: Duke University Press, 1928), 111.

34. Ibid., 111–12; "Deerskin Trade Definition; Definitions for the Clothing & Fabric Industry," http://www.apparelsearch.com/definitions/miscellaneous/Deerskin_trade.htm (2011; Jan. 24, 2013). See also Richard B. Drake, *A History of Appalachia* (Lexington: University Press of Kentucky, 2001); and Donald

Edward Davis, *Where There Are Mountains: An Environmental History of the Southern Appalachians* (Athens: University of Georgia Press, 2000).

35. Crane, 112.

36. Ibid.

37. Alan Gallay, ed., *Indian Slavery in Colonial America* (Lincoln: University of Nebraska Press, 2009), 3.

38. Brett Rushforth, *Bonds of Alliance: Indigenous and Atlantic Slaveries in New France* (Chapel Hill: University of North Carolina Press, 2012), 1, 145.

39. Alan Gallay, *The Indian Slave Trade: The Rise of English Empire in the American South, 1670–1717* (New Haven: Yale University Press, 2003), 298–99.

40. Crane, 113.

41. Gallay, *Indian Slavery*, 15.

42. Daniel Richter, *Facing East from Indian Country: A Native History of Early America* (Cambridge, Mass.: Harvard University Press, 2001), 162–63.

43. Olaudah Equiano, *The Interesting Narrative of the Life of Olaudah Equiano, or Gustavus Vassa, the African, Written by Himself*, ed. Angelo Costanzo (Peterborough, Ontario: Broadview Press, 2001), 218–19.

44. Ibid., 218–21.

45. Ibid., 222.

46. It was always assumed that the elaborate symbols of the Maya were a form of hieroglyphics, that is to say, pictographic writing. It was not until 1992, with the publication of *Breaking the Maya Code* by anthropologist Michael Coe, that most found out that the glyphs represented sounds. The Mayan writing was actual written language. Michael Coe, *Breaking the Maya Code* (New York: Thames and Hudson, 1992).

47. See Miguel Leon-Portillo, *The Broken Spears: The Aztec Account of the Conquest of Mexico* (Boston: Beacon Press, 1962).

48. Kate Flint, *The Transatlantic Indian, 1776–1930* (Princeton: Princeton University Press, 2009), 17.

49. Ibid., 13 (emphasis in original).

50. J. Hector St. John de Crèvecoeur, *Letters from an American Farmer* (repr.; New York: Penguin, 1981), 66–70, 120–24.

51. Hislop Codman, *The Mohawk* (New York: Rinehart, 1948), 219–22.

52. Thomas Benjamin, *The Atlantic World: Europeans, Africans, Indians and Their Shared History, 1400–1900* (Cambridge: Cambridge University Press, 2009), 292–93.

53. Ibid., 293.

54. James Tully, *An Approach to Political Philosophy: Locke in Contexts* (Cambridge: Cambridge University Press, 1993), 143.

55. Dennis H. McPherson and J. Douglas Rabb, *Indian from the Inside: Native American Philosophy and Cultural Renewal*, 2nd ed. (Jefferson, N.C.: McFarland,

2011), 38. See also, generally, Dennis McPherson, "A Definition of Culture: Canada and First Nations," in *Native American Religious Identity: Unforgotten Gods*, ed. Jace Weaver (Maryknoll, N.Y.: Orbis Books, 1998), 77–98.

56. McPherson and Rabb, 38.

57. This quotation is from Franklin's 1783 *Remarks Concerning the Savages of North America*. Benjamin Franklin, *Bagatelles from Passy* (New York: Eakins Press, 1967), 3–4. See also Donald A. Grinde Jr. and Bruce E. Johansen, *Exemplar of Liberty: Native America and the Evolution of Democracy* (Los Angeles: UCLA American Indian Studies Center, 1991), 198–99.

58. Franklin Rosemont, "Karl Marx and the Iroquois," http://www.libcom .org/library/karl-marx-iroquois-franklin-rosemont (July 7, 2009; Jan. 26, 2013) (emphasis in original).

59. James Luna, "Phantasmagoria," Georgia College, Milledgeville, Ga., Jan. 24, 2013; James Luna, personal communication (Jan. 24, 2013).

60. Tac's writings were published in 2011. Lisbeth Haas, *Pablo Tac, Indigenous Scholar: Writings on Luiseño Language and Colonial History, c. 1840* (Berkeley: University of California Press, 2011). Haas identifies the Cheraw youth as Cherokee from South Carolina, presumably not understanding the distinction.

61. Frank Brennan, "Rethinking Indigineity in the Age of Globalisation" (un-published paper, Oct. 31, 2010), 16–24.

CABRINI COLLEGE LIBRARY
610 King of Prussia Road
Radnor, PA 19087-3699
(610) 902-8538